A MESSAGE FROM
THE PUBLISHER

PIANO BUYER
Acoustic & Digital

LARRY FINE

P9-CBA-072

Welcome to the Spring 2012 issue of *Acoustic & Digital Piano Buyer*, a semiannual publication devoted to the purchase of new, used, and restored acoustic pianos and digital pianos. *Piano Buyer* is the supplement and successor to the well-known reference *The Piano Book*, which, since 1987, has been the principal consumer guide to buying a piano in the U.S. and Canada. Partially supported by advertising, *Piano Buyer* is available free online at www.pianobuyer.com. It can also be purchased in print from the website and in bookstores.

Piano Buyer is a hybrid book/magazine. The "book" part consists of a collection of how-to articles on the many aspects of buying a piano. These basic articles are repeated in every issue to serve the many new buyers continually entering the piano market. The "magazine" part consists of features that change with each issue to cover topics of more temporary or niche interest, and to provide variety. Each issue contains several of these excellent features, many of which remain relevant for years. If you missed any of them, you'll find them under the website's Archive tab. The brand, model, and price reference material in the second half of the publication is updated, as needed, with each issue.

In this issue, we offer several new articles for your reading pleasure. From about 1880 to 1930, when piano manufacturing was one of the nation's most important industries, upright pianos were produced in a staggering array of cabinet styles, many of them embellished with highly intricate decoration. The cabinet styles were closely related to the social and economic climates of that period. If you're shopping for an older instrument, you're very likely to run across a number of these elegant relics of the past. Twenty-five years ago, piano rebuilder Martha Taylor discovered a warehouse full of them, and has been busy ever since restoring them. In this issue, she gives us a pictorial overview of the cabinet styles of that period, and of their historical context (p. 69).

Most adults move at least several times in their lives. For the piano owner, what to do about a beloved instrument is nearly always a big issue at moving time. Hiring a professional piano mover can be expensive, but, as Modern Piano Moving owner Russ Vitt shows, non-professional moving can be even more expensive—and dangerous (p. 102).

As new pianos from China become more mainstream, even the celebrated German piano makers are entering manufacturing alliances with the Chinese, sometimes openly, sometimes not. One of the more transparent of these relationships is between the German maker Feurich, established in 1851, and the Chinese maker Hailun, barely ten years old. Our resident reviewer, Owen Lovell, takes a look at a new line of pianos sold under the Feurich label, manufactured under contract by Hailun (p. 49).

Don't forget to explore the rest of our website. If you're shopping for a new piano, two searchable online databases of 3,000 acoustic and 250 digital models will help you quickly home in on the instruments that match your requirements for size, furniture style, budget, and features. If you're shopping for a used instrument, with this issue we debut Piano Buyer Classifieds, a feature jointly developed with the premier website for classified piano ads, PianoMart.com. Using PianoMart's powerful search engine, browse among thousands of used pianos for sale. And when you're ready to take a break from searching, treat yourself to some comic relief with our latest blog, Piano-Buying Stories.

Finally, if you're reading this online, consider buying a print copy of *Piano Buyer*. It's a handsome volume, printed in color on glossy paper, and will make a great reference, coffee-table book, or gift. You can purchase it through the website or in bookstores.

Piano Buyer exists to make shopping for a piano easier and more enjoyable. If you have a suggestion as to how we can do that better, please e-mail me at larry@pianobuyer.com.

Larry Fine, *Publisher*

Acoustic & Digital PIANO BUYER

The Definitive Guide to Buying New, Used, and Restored Pianos

PIANOBUYER.COM

THE PIANO BOOK

**SPRING 2012
Supplement to
THE PIANO BOOK**

Acoustic & Digital Piano Buyer is published semiannually, in March and September, by:

Brookside Press LLC   800.545.2022
P.O. Box 300168   617.522.7182
Jamaica Plain, MA 02130 USA 617.390.7764 (fax)
info@pianobuyer.com   www.pianobuyer.com

Acoustic & Digital Piano Buyer copyright © 2012 by Brookside Press LLC
All rights reserved

"The Piano Book" is a Registered Trademark of Lawrence Fine
"Piano Buyer" is a Registered Trademark of Brookside Press LLC

ISBN 978-192914533-1

Distributed to the book trade by Independent Publishers Group,
814 North Franklin St., Chicago, IL 60610
(800) 888-4741 or (312) 337-0747

Publisher and Editor
Larry Fine
larry@pianobuyer.com

**Contributing Editor
and Consultant**
Steve Cohen
steve@pianobuyer.com

Advertising Director
Barbara Fandrich
bjfandrich@pianobuyer.com

Design and Production
Julie Gallagher, Harry St. Ours

**Acoustic Piano
Technical Consultant**
Del Fandrich

**Digital Piano
Technical Consultant**
Alden Skinner

Copyeditor
Richard Lehnert

Research Associate
Barbara Fandrich

Contributors to this issue:
Ori Bukai, Brian Chung,
Mike Kemper, Lewis Lipnick,
George F. Litterst, Owen Lovell,
Alden Skinner, Chris Solliday,
Martha Taylor, Russ Vitt

See www.PianoBuyer.com
for more information.

Inside This Issue

DIGITAL PIANOS

HYBRID & PLAYER PIANOS

NEW-PIANO BUYERS' REFERENCE

ACOUSTIC PIANOS

DIGITAL PIANOS

KAWAI K-3 Professional Upright Piano
2011 Acoustic Piano of the Year

2010
KAWAI K-3 Professional Upright Piano
Acoustic Piano of the Year

2009
KAWAI K-3 Professional Upright Piano
Acoustic Piano of the Year

2008
KAWAI K-3 Professional Upright Piano
Acoustic Piano of the Year

2007
KAWAI CA91 Digital Piano
Digital Home Keyboard of the Year

2005
KAWAI RX Series Grand Pianos
Acoustic Piano Line of the Year

2004
KAWAI RX Series Grand Pianos
Acoustic Piano Line of the Year

2003
KAWAI RX Series Grand Pianos
Acoustic Piano Line of the Year

2002
KAWAI CN270 Digital Piano
Digital Home Keyboard of the Year

2001
KAWAI ES1 Digital Piano
Digital Keyboard of the Year

2000
KAWAI CP200 Digital Ensemble
Digital Keyboard of the Year

For the eleventh time in twelve years, KAWAI has received the coveted Dealer's Choice Award as selected by the readers of Musical Merchandise Review.

Thank heaven for
NUMBER ELEVEN

www.kawaius.com

THE PRODIGIOUS POWER OF PIANO PLAYING

BRIAN CHUNG

PRACTICE MAKES PERFECT. You've probably heard that saying a hundred times, especially if you've ever studied the piano. Mom said it, so it must be true, right?

Well, hold on a minute—nothing against Mom, but let's get real: "Practice makes perfect" is a terrible motto for piano players. First of all, it's incorrect—how can anything become "perfect" if, every time, you practice it *wrong*? And second, it can't even come close to capturing the prodigious power of playing the piano. So, with all due respect to that venerable axiom, trash it—and make way for a motto that proclaims the *real* benefits of piano playing: *Practice makes prosperous*.

People usually associate the word *prosperous* with wealth. While that's certainly part of its meaning, many dictionaries suggest a broader definition: to be *prosperous* is to *flourish*, to *thrive . . .* to *be successful*. Therefore, the phrase *practice makes prosperous* declares boldly that *those who play the piano are far more likely to flourish, thrive, and experience success in life than those who do not*. Quite a stretch, you say? Read on.

Thriving Children

Consider what happens when eight-year-old Bobby decides to embrace serious piano practice. Not only does he embark upon a wondrous musical adventure (possibly the greatest benefit of all) but, perhaps unconsciously, he acquires a diversity of skills far beyond the musical notes:

- **He learns to *work hard*.** Anyone who excels at the piano has made a commitment to practice with vigor and determination.

- **He learns to *focus*.** In a world where iPods, MySpace, Facebook, Twitter and mobile texting have made multi-tasking the de facto way of life, young people are at risk of losing the art of concentration. Piano practice reminds Bobby how to focus on *one thing*—and do it well.

- **He learns to be *responsible*.** Serious pianists learn that faithful, consistent practice—even when they don't *feel* like doing it—will bring great satisfaction over time.

- **He learns to *pay attention to details*.** As his skills mature, Bobby learns to observe the fine points and use the most subtle nuances to create art.

- **He learns to be *self-reliant*.** While practicing, Bobby can't always rely on Mom and Dad for help. To succeed, he must learn to work well on his own.

- **He learns to be *creative*.** Creativity is a musician's lifeblood. Pianists use it not only to express musical ideas, but also to conquer the physical and mental obstacles that arise when learning new music.

- **He learns to *persevere*.** There is little satisfaction in learning only *half* of a piece of music. The determined pianist finds joy in following through to the very end.

> **Those who play the piano are far more likely to flourish, thrive, and experience success in life than those who do not.**

These are only some of the skills Bobby will acquire as he devotes himself to diligent piano practice. So, how will such practice make him prosperous?

Ask employers what they look for when interviewing young job candidates for their top positions. Most are looking for a well-defined set of character traits. Specifically, they want people who know how to work hard, can focus well and avoid distractions, are responsible, will pay attention to details, are self-reliant and creative, and will persevere on a project from start to finish. Sound familiar?

You see my point. The skills Bobby learns by practicing the piano will be of immeasurable value to him not only in job interviews, but in every area of his life. People who have these skills are more likely to flourish in college, thrive in the work world, advance in their careers—and generally enjoy success in any field of endeavor.

Test scores support this contention. Studies show that students of music typically score higher on SATs than do non-music students—on average, 57 points higher on the verbal section and 41 points higher in math.[1] Further, a 1994 study showed that college undergraduate students who majored in music had the highest rate

---

[1] *Profile of SAT and Achievement Test Takers.* The College Board, compiled by Music Educators National Conference, 2001.

GROTRIAN
Because we love music.

these and many other classic hits for friends and family.

- **Her *mind and spirit are enlivened*.** The process of learning something completely new has been intellectually and emotionally stimulating for Nancy. She enjoys a sense of adventure when exploring new musical concepts and genres with her classmates. Playing the piano has made her feel more fully alive.

Studies have shown that recreational group music-making can significantly improve the quality of life and personal well-being among those who embrace it. So even when you're playing the piano just for fun, *practice makes prosperous* in meaningful ways that far exceed the balance in your 401(k).

of acceptance to medical school (66%).[2] *Practice makes prosperous.* Prepare your children for success in life: Introduce them to the piano.

Thriving Adults

But how about *you*? Are you among the 82% of adults who have always wanted to learn how to play an instrument?[3] Did you know that adults can gain as much as younger people from playing the piano?

Even if you've already achieved career success and significant wealth, there can be *so* much more to a prosperous life. Consider what happens when Nancy, a baby boomer and successful business owner, decides to join a recreational group piano class for adults:

- **She immediately feels *relief from stress*.** After hours of intense daily pressure at work, Nancy finds it easy to unwind at the piano. The class moves at a comfortable pace and no one is ever required to play solo—which means zero stress. In her personal practice and in class, Nancy can just relax and have fun.

- **She's *making new friends*.** Because recreational piano classes are taught in groups, Nancy enjoys getting to know others who share a common interest. Many of her classmates are professional people like her who, after raising a family, are finally getting to try the things they've always wanted to do. The warm camaraderie among class members is a wonderful surprise.

- **She enjoys *playing her favorite songs*.** Nancy always dreamed of learning her two favorite Beatles tunes. Now, she's thrilled to play

How about you?
Are you among the
82% of adults who
have always wanted to
learn how to play
an instrument?

To give the piano a whirl, contact a local music store or independent piano teacher to find out about recreational piano classes in your area. Whether you're young or old, striving for success or just playing for fun, the prodigious power of playing the piano can change your life. 🎹

Brian Chung is Senior Vice President of Kawai America Corporation and a leading proponent of the benefits of making music. He is also a pianist, and co-author (with Dennis Thurmond) of *Improvisation at the Piano: A Systematic Approach for the Classically Trained Pianist* (Alfred Publishing, 2007). Visit his website at **www.brianchung.net.**

---

[2] Peter H. Wood, "The Comparative Academic Abilities of Students in Education and in Other Areas of a Multi-focus University," ERIC Document ED327480 (1990).

[3] *U.S. Gallup Poll.* 2008 Music USA NAMM Global Report (August, 2008): 139.

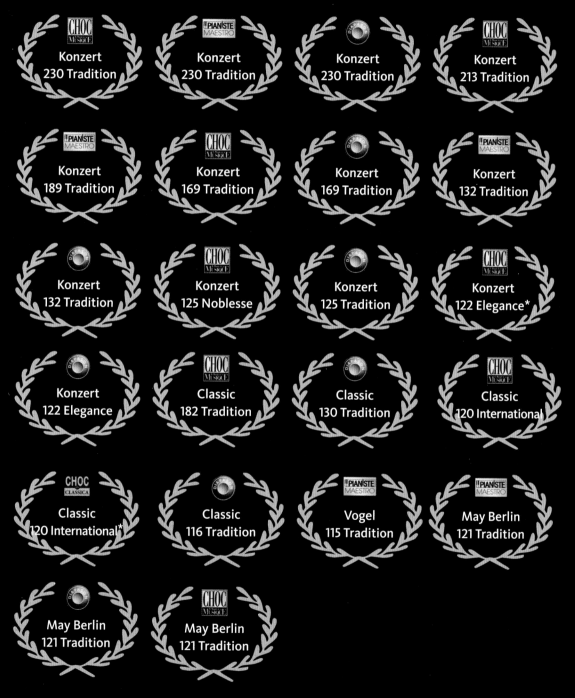

Franz Liszt

Johannes Brahms

Johann Strauss

Tori Amos

Oscar Peterson

BÖSENDORFER–FIRST CHOICE OF COMPOSERS, ARTISTS AND EMPERORS.

A long series of composers and artists have performed on Bösendorfer pianos since 1828, including Franz Liszt, Antonin Dvorák, Leonard Bernstein, the Beatles, Oscar Peterson, Tori Amos, and hundreds more. In addition, Napoleon III, the Emperor of Japan, Austria's imperial court and a Russian czar top the list of historical figures famously associated with Ignaz Bösendorfer's fine Viennese instruments. Today, the Bösendorfer line encompasses both traditional and custom-designed pianos, as well as the CEUS Reproducing system for recording and playing back performances. These hand made instruments, featuring premium materials, are meticulously crafted so modern performers can enjoy the same expressiveness and perfection that Liszt experienced 180 years ago.

Bösendorfer

Visit www.4wrd.it/bosadpb
Explore galleries of standard pianos, such as Model 290 shown here and unique, decorative special pianos – including the new Artist Series "Klimt" Model; the streamlined Porsche-designed model; the Liszt Anniversary model and more one-of-a-kind pianos.

ACOUSTIC OR DIGITAL:
What's Best for Me?

ALDEN SKINNER AND LARRY FINE

FOR MANY, there will be no easy answer to this question. Many factors play into this seemingly simple decision, some practical, some not. Ideally, perhaps, the answer should be "Both"—take advantage of the "organic" qualities and connection with tradition of the acoustic piano, as well as the extreme flexibility of the digital. But assuming that, for a variety of reasons, "Both" isn't an option, careful consideration of the advantages and disadvantages of each will probably quickly reveal which will be best for you.

The advantages of the acoustic piano start with the fact that it's the "real thing," inherently capable of nuances that are difficult for the digital piano to emulate. The experience of playing an acoustic piano—the harmonics, the vibrations, the touch, the visual appeal, the interaction with the room, the connection with tradition—is so complex that digitals cannot reproduce it all. And, provided that it's a decent instrument and properly maintained, the acoustic will continue to serve you or a subsequent owner for several generations, after which it might be rebuilt and continue to make music.

If you're a beginner, the tone and touch of a good-quality digital piano should not interfere with the elementary learning process for a while, but is likely to become less satisfactory as you advance. If your aspiration is to play classical piano literature, the choice is clear: A digital may serve as a temporary or quiet-time practice instrument (some well-known classical pianists request that a digital piano be placed in their hotel rooms for practice and warmup), but the first time you play an acoustic piano that stirs your soul, there will be no turning back. Although digitals continue to draw closer to the ideal, there is, as yet, nothing like the total experience of playing a fine acoustic instrument.

The downside of an acoustic piano? Initial cost is generally higher, they're harder to move, the best ones take up a lot of space, and tuning and maintaining them adds several hundred dollars a year to their cost. And—most important—*all they will ever be or sound like is a piano.*

So why do sales of digital pianos outnumber sales of acoustics by more than two to one? Because, in addition to making a piano sound, digitals can also sound like any other instrument imaginable. State-of-the-art digital pianos can allow a player with even the most basic keyboard skills to sound like an entire orchestra. Many models have features that will produce an entire band or orchestra accompanying you as the soloist. Digital pianos can also be used as player pianos. They can enhance learning with educational software. They can be attached to a computer, and you can have an entire recording studio at your fingertips, with the computer printing the sheet music for anything you play. Many fine players whose main piano is a quality acoustic also have a digital, providing the technology for band and/or orchestral compositions, transcriptions, and fun!

Add to all that the advantages of lower cost, convenience, lack of maintenance expense, the ability to play silently with headphones, meeting the needs of multiple family members, the obvious advantages for piano classes, and computer connectivity, and you have a powerful argument for the digital.

While digital pianos have a lot of advantages, it's important to also consider the disadvantages. In addition to those related to learning and playing classical music, mentioned above, the life expectancy of a good digital piano is limited, primarily by obsolescence (digitals haven't been around long enough to know how long they will physically last), while the life expectancy of a good acoustic piano is upward of 50 years. Acoustic pianos hold their value rather well, while digitals, like other electronics, quickly drop in value. Obviously, then, if you're buying a starter instrument and plan to upgrade later, from a financial perspective you would do better to start with an acoustic piano.

Both variations have places in our musical lives. Now, which is right for you?

(If you're still unsure, you might want to consider a hybrid piano—see our story on the subject in this issue.)

> **Both variations have places in our musical lives. Now, which is right for you?**

Introduction

An acoustic piano can be one of the most expensive—and difficult—purchases most households will ever make. The "difficult" aspect arises from several factors that are peculiar to pianos and the piano business. First, a "modern" piano is essentially a 19th-century creation about which few people—even those who have played piano all their lives—know very much, and about which much of what they *think* they know may not be accurate or current. Thus, a person who sets out to buy a piano is unlikely to have a social support network of family and friends to serve as advisors, as they might if buying a car, house, or kitchen appliance. Even music teachers and experienced players often know little about piano construction or the rapidly changing state of piano manufacturing. They often rely on their past experience with certain brands, most of which have changed significantly.

Second, acoustic pianos are marketed nationally in the United States under some 70 different brand names (plus dozens of additional names marketed locally) from a dozen countries, in thousands of furniture styles and finishes—and that's just new pianos! Many once-popular brands have long gone out of business, yet pianos still bearing their name are made overseas, often to much lower standards, and marketed here. Add in more than a century's worth of used pianos under thousands of brand names in an almost infinite variety of conditions of disrepair and restoration. Just thinking about it makes me dizzy.

Third, new pianos can vary in price from $2,000 to $200,000. But unlike most consumer items, whose differences can be measured by the number of functions performed, or buttons, bells, whistles, and conveniences contained, most pianos, regardless of price, look very similar

and do pretty much the same thing: they're shiny and black (or a wood color), play 88 notes, and have three pedals. The features advertised are often abstract, misleading, or difficult to see or understand. For this reason, it's often not clear just what you're getting for your money. This can lead to decision-making paralysis.

Last, while many piano salespeople do an honest and admirable job of guiding their customers through this maze, a significant minority—using lies, tricky pricing games, and false accusations against competing dealers and brands—make the proverbial used-car salesman look like a saint. And once you get through haggling over price—the norm in the piano business—you may be ready for a trip to a Middle East bazaar.

As you shop for a piano, you'll likely be bombarded with a great deal of technical jargon—after all, the piano is a complicated instrument. But don't allow yourself to be confused

or intimidated. Although some technical information can be useful and interesting, extensive familiarity with technical issues usually isn't essential to a successful piano-shopping experience, especially when buying a new piano. (A little greater familiarity may be advisable when buying a used or restored instrument.) Most technical information you'll come across relates to how the manufacturer designed the instrument. You should focus on how the instrument sounds, feels, and looks, not how it got that way. In addition, technical features are often taken out of context and manipulated by advertising and salespeople—the real differences in quality are often in subtleties of design and construction that don't make good ad copy.

For 20 years, *The Piano Book* has acted as a textbook on how to buy a piano, but over the years many people have asked for something a little simpler. *Acoustic & Digital Piano Buyer* is the answer, and this article is the beginning. For those readers who love reading about the finer technical details, *The Piano Book* is a must read. But in the interests of brevity and simplicity, we decided in this publication to keep technical details to a minimum.

The purpose of this article is modest: to provide an overview of the piano-buying process, with an emphasis on the decisions you'll have to make along the way, and on the factors that will affect any acoustic piano purchase. To do this succinctly, it will be necessary to make a number of generalizations, which you can discard in favor of more complete or nuanced explanations as you advance toward your goal. References are given to other articles in this publication, or to *The Piano Book*, for further information on selected topics. In addition, for answers to specific questions that arise while you shop, I recommend visiting the Piano Forum at Piano World (www.pianoworld.com), the premiere website for everything related to pianos and pianists.

Vertical or Grand?

Probably the most basic decision to make when buying a piano—and one you may have made already—is whether to buy a vertical or a grand. The following describes some of the advantages and disadvantages of each.

Vertical Advantages

- Takes up less space, can fit into corners
- Lower cost
- Easier to move

Vertical Disadvantages

- Sound tends to bounce back into player's face, making subtle control of musical expression more difficult.
- Action is not as advanced as grand; repetition of notes is slower and less reliable in most cases, and damping is sometimes less efficient.
- Keys are shorter than on grands, making subtle control of musical expression more difficult.
- Cabinetwork is usually less elegant and less impressive.

Vertical pianos are suitable for those with simpler musical needs, or where budget and space constraints preclude buying a grand. Despite the disadvantages noted above, some of the larger, more expensive verticals do musically rival smaller, less expensive grands. They may be a good choice where space is at a premium

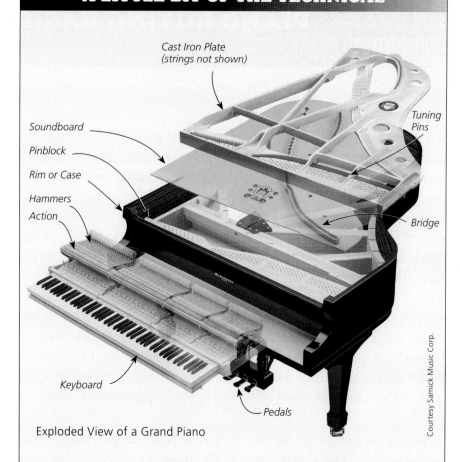

A LITTLE BIT OF THE TECHNICAL

Cast Iron Plate (strings not shown)
Soundboard
Pinblock
Rim or Case
Hammers
Action
Tuning Pins
Bridge
Keyboard
Pedals

Courtesy Samick Music Corp.

Exploded View of a Grand Piano

A little bit (but not too much) of technical information about the piano is useful to have while shopping for one. Important words are in **boldface**.

A piano can be thought of as comprising four elements: mechanical, acoustical, structural, and cabinetry.

Mechanical: When you press a piano **key** (usually 88 in number), the motion of your finger is transmitted through a series of levers and springs to a felt-covered wooden **hammer** that strikes the strings to set them vibrating. This complex system of keys, hammers, levers, and springs is known as the **action**. Also, when you press a key, a felt **damper** resting against each string lifts off, allowing the string to vibrate. When you let the key up, the damper returns to its resting place, stopping the string's vibration. **Pedals**, usually three in number, are connected to the action and dampers via **trapwork**

levers, and serve specialized functions such as sustaining and softening the sound. The right-foot pedal is called the **damper** or **sustain pedal**; it lifts all the dampers off all the strings, allowing the strings to ring sympathetically. The left-foot, **soft pedal** (on a grand piano, the **una corda pedal**) softens the sound. The function of the middle pedal varies depending on the type and price level of the piano (more on that later). As a **sostenuto pedal**, it selectively sustains notes or groups of notes, a function required only rarely in a small percentage of classical compositions. Other possible functions for the middle pedal include a damper pedal for the bass notes only, and a mute pedal that reduces the sound volume by about half.

Acoustical: Piano **strings** are made of steel wire for the higher-sounding notes (**treble**), and steel wire wrapped with copper for the lower-sounding

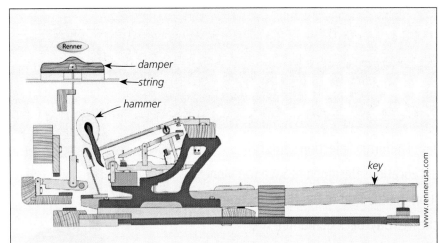

The key and action parts of a single note from a grand piano

[For online animation, click here.]

notes (**bass**). They are graduated in thickness, length, and tension, and strung tightly across the structural framework of the piano. Each note has one, two, or three strings associated with it. Each such set of strings is known as a **unison** because all the strings in a set vibrate at the same pitch. The strings lie across narrow hardwood **bridges** that transmit their vibrations to a wooden **soundboard**, usually made of spruce. The relatively large area of the soundboard amplifies what would otherwise be a rather weak sound and broadcasts the sound to the ears. The dimensions, arrangement, and positioning of all the acoustical elements in a piano is known as the piano's **scale design**. The scale design varies with the model and is a major determinant of the piano's tone.

Structural: The strings are strung across a gold- or bronze-colored **plate** (sometimes called a **frame** or **harp**) of cast iron, which is bolted to a substantial wooden framework. This heavy-duty structure is necessary to support the many tons of tension exerted by all the taut strings. A **vertical**, or upright, piano is one in which the structural element stands vertically, and is most commonly placed against a wall. A **grand** piano is one in which the structural

element lies horizontally. In a vertical piano, the wooden framework consists of vertical **back posts** and connecting cross beams. In a grand, wooden **beams** and the familiar curved **rim** comprise the framework. One end of each string is anchored to the plate toward the rear of a grand or the bottom of a vertical piano. The other end is coiled around a **tuning pin** embedded in a laminated hardwood **pinblock** hidden under the plate at the front (grand) or top (vertical). A piano is **tuned** by turning each tuning pin with a special tool to make very slight adjustments in the tension of its string, and thus to the string's frequency of vibration, or **pitch**.

Cabinetry: The piano's **cabinet** (vertical) or **case** (grand) provides aesthetic beauty and some additional structural support. A grand piano's rim is part of both the wooden structural framework and the case. Accessory parts, such as the music desk and lid, are both functional and aesthetic in purpose.

Although the acoustical and structural elements have been described separately, in fact the plate, wooden framework, soundboard, bridges, and strings form a single integrated unit called the **strung back**. A piano, then, consists of a strung back, an action, and a cabinet or case.

but a more subtle control of musical expression is desired.

Grand Advantages

- Sound develops in a more aesthetically pleasing manner by bouncing off nearby surfaces and blending before reaching player's ears, making it easier to control musical expression.
- More sophisticated action than in a vertical. Grand action has a repetition lever to aid in the speed and reliability of repetition of notes, and is gravity-assisted, rather than dependent on artificial contrivances (springs, straps) to return hammers to rest.
- Longer keys provide better leverage, allowing for significantly greater control of musical expression.
- Casework is usually more elegant and aesthetically pleasing.

Grand Disadvantages

- Takes up more space
- Higher cost
- Harder to move

What Size?

Both verticals and grands come in a wide variety of sizes. The important thing to know here is that size is directly related to musical quality. Although many other factors also contribute to tonal quality, all else being equal, the longer strings of larger pianos, especially in the bass and mid-range sections, give off a deeper, truer, more consonant tonal quality than the strings of smaller pianos. The treble and bass blend better and the result is more pleasing to the ear. Also, longer grands usually have longer keys that generally allow superior control of musical expression than shorter grands. Therefore, it's best to buy the largest piano you can afford and have

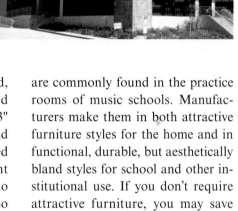
space for. Small differences in size between models are more significant in smaller pianos than in larger ones. However, a difference in size of only an inch or two is generally irrelevant, as it could be merely due to a larger cabinet or case.

Verticals

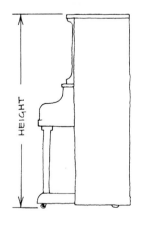

Vertical pianos are measured from the floor to the top of the piano. Verticals less than 40" tall are known as spinets. They were very popular in the post–World War II period, but in recent years have nearly died out. Verticals from 40" to about 43" or 44" are called consoles. Spinet and console actions must be compromised somewhat in size or placement within the piano to fit them into pianos of this size. The tone is also compromised by the shorter strings and smaller soundboard. For this reason, manufacturers concentrate on the furniture component of spinets and consoles and make them in a variety of decorator styles. They are suitable for buyers whose piano needs are casual, or for beginning students, and for those who simply want a nice-looking piece of furniture in the home. Once students progress to an intermediate or advanced stage, they are likely to need a larger instrument.

Studio pianos, from about 44" to 47", are more serious instruments. They are called studios because they are commonly found in the practice rooms of music schools. Manufacturers make them in both attractive furniture styles for the home and in functional, durable, but aesthetically bland styles for school and other institutional use. If you don't require attractive furniture, you may save money by buying the school style. In fact, many buyers prefer the simple lines of the institutional models.

Verticals about 48" and taller, called uprights, are the best musically. New ones top out at about 52", but in the early part of the 20th century they were made even taller. The tallest verticals take up no more floor space than the shortest ones, but some buyers may find the taller models too massive for their taste. Most uprights are made in an attractive, black, traditional or institutional style, but are also available with exotic veneers, inlays, and other touches of elegance.

The Piano Company

The width of a vertical piano is usually a little under five feet and the depth around two feet; however, these dimensions are not significantly related to musical quality.

Grands

Grand pianos are measured with the lid closed from the very front of the piano (keyboard end) to the very back (the tail). Lengths start at 4'6" and go to over 10' (even longer in some experimental models). Widths

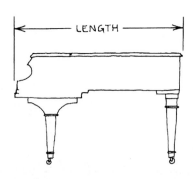

are usually around 5' and heights around 3', but only the length has a bearing on musical quality.

Grands less than 5' long are the musical equivalent of spinets and consoles; that is, they are musically compromised and are mainly sold as pieces of furniture. Grands between about 5' and 5½' are very popular. Although slightly compromised, they can reasonably serve both musical and furniture functions and are available in many furniture styles. (By the way, piano professionals prefer the term *small grand* to *baby grand*. Although there is no

ESTONIA GRAND PIANO — A Work of Art

Estonia Klaverivabrik
Kungla 41, Tallinn 10413, Estonia
Tel. (372) 508-4038
www.estoniapiano.com

1893
E S T O N I A

North American office:
7 Fillmore Drive
Stony Point, NY 10980 USA
Tel. (845) 947-7763

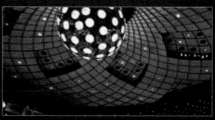

exact definition, a small grand is generally one less than about 5½' long.) Above 5½', pianos rapidly improve, becoming professional quality at about 6'. Pianos intended for the home or serious professional top out at about 7' or 7½'. These sizes may also satisfy the needs of smaller concert venues. Larger venues require concert grands, usually about 9' long.

When considering what size of piano is right for your home, don't forget to add two to three feet to the length of a grand or the depth of a vertical for the piano bench and pianist. Shoppers tend to underestimate what will fit and buy smaller pianos than necessary. Sometimes, the next-size-larger instrument can give you a great deal of tonal improvement at little additional cost. Dealers can usually lend you templates corresponding to different piano sizes to lay down on your floor so you can measure what will fit.

Budget

Your budget is probably the most important factor in your choice of piano, but it's hard to make a budget when you don't know how much pianos cost. Here is some rule-of-thumb information to get you started:

Most new vertical pianos sell in the range of $3,000 to $10,000, though some higher-end ones cost two or three times that, and a few cost less. Entry-level grand pianos generally go for $5,000 to $10,000, mid-range grands from $10,000 to $30,000, and high-end grands for $30,000 to $100,000 or more. Unrestored but playable used pianos cost from perhaps 20 to 80 percent of the cost of a comparable new instrument, depending on age and condition, with 15-year-old used pianos coming in at about 50 percent. The cost of restored instruments will be discussed later. More complete and accurate information can be found in the articles on **new** and **used** pianos, and in the

"Model & Pricing Guide" reference section, elsewhere in this issue.

Rent or Buy?

If the piano is being purchased for a beginner, there is a significant possibility that he or she will not stick with playing the piano. To handle this and other "high-risk" situations, most dealers offer a rental/purchase program. In the typical program, the dealer would rent you the piano you are considering purchasing for up to six months. You would pay round-trip moving expenses upfront, usually $300 to $400, plus a monthly rental fee, typically $50 to $100 for a vertical piano. (Rental/purchase programs do not usually apply to grand pianos.) Should you decide to buy the piano at any time before the end of the six-month term, all money paid up to that point would be applied to the purchase. Otherwise, you would return the piano and be under no further obligation.

Two pieces of advice here: First, make sure you rent the piano you ultimately wish to buy, or at least rent from the dealer who has that piano, and not simply the piano or dealer with the lowest rental rate—if you eventually decide to buy from a different dealer, you'll forfeit the rental payments already made to the first dealer. However, if you decide to buy a different piano from the same dealer from whom you rented, it's possible that dealer would agree to apply some or all of the rental payments to the new piano—but check on this in advance. Second, clarify issues of price before you decide whether to rent or buy. Specifically, find out whether you'll be allowed to apply the rental payments toward, for example, today's sale price, rather than toward the regular price six months from now—or conversely, if you'll be held to today's price should there be a sale six months from now. Keep in mind, however, that a "sale"

is generally a reduction in price designed to entice you to buy now.

Quality

Like just about everything else you can buy, pianos come in a range of quality levels. When we speak of *quality* in a piano, we are referring to how it sounds, plays, and looks, and how well it will hold up with time and use. These are functions of the care taken in the design of the instrument; the quality of the materials used and how they are assembled; and the amount of handwork put into the final musical and aesthetic finishing of the instrument. With a new piano, we are also concerned, to a lesser extent, with how much pre-sale service is required by the dealer to make the instrument ready—a dealer is less likely to perform a lot of "make-ready" on an inexpensive piano. Also important are the terms of the warranty and the manufacturer's (or other warrantor's) reputation for honoring warranties. The prestige value of the name and the history of the brand may also be perceived as a form of quality by some buyers. *The Piano Book* goes into great detail about what creates quality in a piano.

As you can imagine, any discussion of quality in pianos is likely to involve a lot of subjectivity and be somewhat controversial. However, a useful generalization for the purpose of discussing quality can be had

by dividing pianos into two types: performance-grade and consumer-grade. Performance-grade pianos are made to a single, high quality standard, usually in relatively small quantities, by companies that strongly favor quality considerations over cost. Consumer-grade pianos, on the other hand, are built to be sold at a particular price, and the design, materials, and level of workmanship are chosen to fit that price. Most consumer-grade pianos are mass-produced at a variety of price levels, with materials and designs chosen accordingly. Throughout much of the 20th century, the United States produced both types of piano in abundance. At the present time, however, most performance-grade pianos are made in Europe and the United States, while virtually all consumer-grade pianos are made in Asia. Due to globalization and other factors, the distinction between the two types of piano is beginning to blur. This is discussed at greater length in the article "**The New-Piano Market Today**," elsewhere in this issue.

The above explanation of quality in pianos is very general, and some aspects of quality may be more applicable to your situation than others. Therefore, it pays to take some time to consider exactly what you expect from your piano, both practically and in terms of lifestyle. Practical needs include, among others, the level of expressiveness you require in the piano's tone and touch, how long you want the instrument to last or intend to keep it, and what furniture it must match—as well as certain functional considerations, such as whether you use the middle pedal, desire a fallboard (key cover) that closes slowly, or need to be able to lock the piano. Lifestyle needs are those that involve the prestige or artistic value of the instrument, and how ownership of it makes you feel or makes you appear to others. Just as a casual driver may own a Mercedes, or one devoid of artistic abilities may own great works of art, many who don't play a note purchase expensive pianos for their artistic and prestige value.

A couple of the practical considerations require further discussion. Concerning expressiveness: What kind of music do you play or aspire to play? One can play any kind of music on any piano. However, some pianos seem better suited in tone and touch than other kinds to some kinds of music. Quality in piano tone is often defined in terms of the instrument's ability to excel at pleasing players of so-called "classical" music because this kind of music tends to make the greatest expressive demands on an instrument. So if you aspire to play classical music seriously, you may wish to one day own a fine instrument capable of the nuanced tone and touch the music demands. On the other hand, if classical music isn't your thing, you can probably get away with a much less expensive instrument.

A key factor concerns how long you want to keep the instrument: Is it for a beginner, especially a youngster, and you're not sure piano lessons will "stick"? Is it a stepping stone to a better piano later on? Then an inexpensive piano may do. Do you want this to be the last piano you'll ever buy? Then, even if your playing doesn't yet justify it, buy a piano you can grow into but never grow out of.

A note about how long a piano will last—a question I hear every day. The answer varies for pianos almost as much as it does for people. A piano played 16 hours a day in a school practice room might be "dead" in ten years or less, whereas one pampered in a living room in a mild climate might last nearly a century before requiring complete restoration to function again. A rule-of-thumb answer typically given is that an average piano under average conditions will last 40 to 50 years. If past experience is any guide, it would not be unreasonable to predict that the best-made pianos will last about twice as long as entry-level ones, given similar conditions of use and climate. However—and this is the important point—most pianos are discarded not because they no longer function—in fact, they may go on to long lives as used pianos for other people—but because they no longer meet the needs or expectations of their owners or players. A player may have musically advanced beyond what the instrument will deliver, or the owner may now be wealthier and have higher expectations for everything he or she buys—or perhaps no one in the house is playing anymore and the piano is just taking up space. Thus, the important consideration for most buyers, especially buyers of new or relatively young pianos, is how long the piano in question will meet their needs and expectations, rather than how long that piano will last.

INTRODUCING
STORY & CLARK
WITH PNOSCAN™

Choosing an acoustic piano used to be a confusing process. Not so anymore.

Now hidden in every Story & Clark piano is PNOscan, **a state-of-the art optical sensor strip that converts piano performances into digital information**. A discreetly placed USB/MIDI port then allows you to link your piano to your laptop, connecting you to the limitless opportunities of software for learning, recording, composing, scoring and more.

All without the worries of obsolescence that come with traditional digital and hybrid pianos.

CERTIFIED **USB**

Why settle for just a piano when you can have a Story & Clark with PNOscan — *for the same price?*

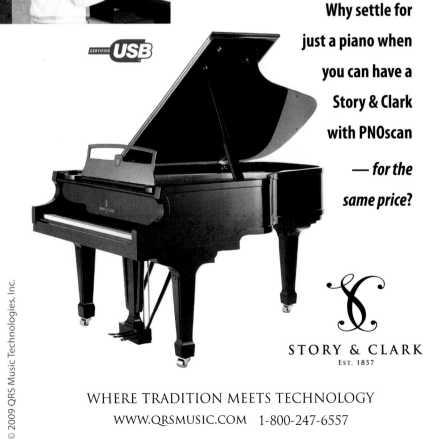

STORY & CLARK
EST. 1857

WHERE TRADITION MEETS TECHNOLOGY
WWW.QRSMUSIC.COM   1-800-247-6557

You'll get a better sense of what quality means in a piano if you play a wide variety of them, including ones that cost less than what you plan to spend, as well as ones you can't afford. Warning: The latter can prove dangerous to your bank account. It's not unusual for a buyer to begin shopping with the intention of buying a $3,000 vertical, only to emerge some time later with a $30,000 grand!

New or Used?

The next choice you'll have to make is whether to buy new or used. The market for used pianos is several times the size of the market for new ones. Let's look at the merits of each choice:

New Piano Advantages
- Manufacturer's warranty
- Little chance of hidden defects
- Lower maintenance costs
- Easier to shop for
- Usually more local choices
- Longer piano life expectancy
- Greater peace of mind after purchasing

New Piano Disadvantages
- Higher upfront cost
- Significant depreciation loss if resold within first few years
- Limited choice of attractive old styles and finishes

Used Piano Advantages
- Lower upfront cost
- Greater choice of attractive old styles and finishes
- Can be more fun and interesting to shop for (if you like shopping for old things)
- Restorer may detail instrument to an extent that rivals new piano
- Piano likely to be already significantly depreciated, resulting in little or no loss if resold

Used Piano Disadvantages
- No manufacturer's warranty (though there may be a dealer's or restorer's warranty)
- Greater chance of hidden defects (unless completely restored)
- Higher maintenance costs (unless completely restored)
- Shorter piano life expectancy (unless completely restored)
- Can be maddeningly difficult and confusing to shop for
- Need to pay technician to examine and appraise it
- Usually fewer local choices
- Possible need to size up restorer's ability to do a good job

Despite the longer list of disadvantages, most people buy used because of the lower upfront cost and because they feel they can manage the risks involved. The most important rule by far in managing risk is to have the piano professionally examined and appraised by a piano technician prior to purchase. This is especially important when buying from a private-party seller because there is no warranty, but it should also be done for peace of mind when buying from a professional seller, particularly if the piano is over ten years old. This will cost between $100 and $200 and is well worth the money. If you don't already have a piano technician you trust, hire a Registered Piano Technician (RPT) member of the Piano Technicians Guild (PTG). You can locate one near you on the PTG website, **www .ptg.org**. (To be designated an RPT, one must pass a series of tests. This provides the customer with some assurance of competence.)

A subset of used pianos consists of instruments that have been professionally restored. The complete restoration of a piano is known as *rebuilding*. There is no universally agreed-on definition of what is included in a rebuilding job, so you have to ask specifically what has been done. A minimal partial restoration is called *reconditioning*—often just

DUKE
ELLINGTON
GEORGE GERSHWIN
VLADIMIR HOROWITZ
COLE PORTER · SERGEI
RACHMANINOFF · RICHARD
RODGERS · IRVING BERLIN
FRANZ LISZT · ARTHUR
RUBINSTEIN · IGNACE
PADEREWSKI · LANG LANG
HARRY CONNICK, JR. · DIANA
KRALL · BILLY JOEL · BRUCE
HORNSBY · MICHAEL FEINSTEIN
MICHEL LEGRAND · PETER NERO
GEORGE WINSTON · RANDY NEWMAN
VLADIMIR ASHKENAZY · ROGER
WILLIAMS · AHMAD JAMAL · HELENE
GRIMAUD · YEFIM BRONFMAN · JOHN
BAYLESS · EMANUEL AX · DAVID
BENOIT · KEITH JARRETT · VAN
CLIBURN · MAURIZIO POLLINI
MORE THAN 1,500 OTHERS...

STEINWAY ARTISTS ARE NEVER PAID TO ENDORSE OUR PIANOS

We would like to thank all of our Steinway Artists—past and present—for their loyalty and for putting their music before all else. To view the entire roster of Steinway Artists, visit steinway.com.

STEINWAY & SONS

STEINWAY & SONS · ONE STEINWAY PLACE · LONG ISLAND CITY, NY 11105 · WWW.STEINWAY.COM

Reinstalling the cast-iron plate during the rebuilding of a grand piano

www.spaldingpiano.com

cleaning up the piano, replacing a few parts, and adjusting it. Vertical pianos are almost never completely rebuilt because the cost cannot be recouped in the sale price. However, verticals are frequently reconditioned. A complete rebuilding of a top-quality grand piano by a top-notch rebuilder generally costs from $20,000 to $40,000—and that's if you own the piano. If you're buying the piano too, figure a total cost of from 75 to more than 100 percent of the cost of a new piano of similar quality. A partial rebuilding of a lower-quality brand might cost half that, or even less.

Buying a used or restored piano is generally more difficult than buying a new one because, in addition to making judgments about the underlying quality of the instrument, you also must make judgments about its condition or about the skill and trustworthiness of the restorer—there's a greater concern about being burned if you make a mistake. Some find this too stressful or time-consuming. Others find the hunt fascinating, and end up discovering an entire world of piano buffs, and piano technical and historical trivia, in

their community or online. It helps to remember that a new piano becomes "used" the moment it is first sold. Although junk certainly exists, used pianos actually come in a bewildering variety of conditions and situations, many of which can be quite attractive, musically and financially. The subject is vast. *The Piano Book* has a chapter devoted to it, including how to do your own preliminary technical examination of a piano. A summary of the most important information, including a description of the most common types of used pianos, where to find them, and how much to pay, can be found in the article "**Buying a Used or Restored Piano**" elsewhere in this issue.

The Piano Dealer

The piano dealer is a very important part of the piano-buying experience, for several reasons. First, a knowledgeable and helpful salesperson can help you sort through the myriad possibilities and quickly home in on the piano that's right for you. Second, a dealership with a good selection of instruments can provide you with enough options to choose from that you don't end up settling for less than what you really want (although you can make up for this to some extent by shopping among a number of dealers). Third, all pianos arrive from the factory needing some kind of pre-sale adjustment to compensate for changes that occur during shipment, or for musical finishing work left uncompleted at the factory. Dealers vary a great deal in their willingness to perform this work. There's nothing worse than trying to shop for a piano, and finding them out of tune or with obvious defects. It's understandable that the dealer will put the most work into the more expensive pianos, but a good dealer will make sure that

even the lower-cost instruments are reasonably playable. Last, a good dealer will provide prompt, courteous, skilled service to correct any small problems that occur after the sale, and act as your intermediary with the factory in the rare event that warranty service is needed. Knowledge, experience, helpfulness, selection, and service—that's what you're looking for in a dealer.

Shopping Long-Distance via the Internet

The question often arises as to whether one should shop for a piano long-distance via the Internet. It turns out that this is really two different questions. The first is whether one should locate a dealer via the Internet, possibly far away, then visit that dealer to buy a piano. The second is whether one should buy a piano sight unseen over the Internet.

If you're shopping for a new piano, you'll probably have to visit a dealer. This is because dealers are generally prohibited by their agreements with manufacturers from quoting prices over the phone or via the Internet to customers outside their "market territory," the definition of which differs from brand to brand. But once you set foot in the dealer's place of business, regardless of where you came from, you're considered a legitimate customer and all restrictions are off, even after you return home. There are no such restrictions for advertising or selling used pianos.

Customers, of course, don't care about "market territories." They just want to get the best deal. Given the ease of comparison shopping via the Internet, and the frequency with which people travel for business or pleasure, dealers are increasingly testing the limits of their territorial restrictions, and more and more sales are taking place at dealerships outside the customer's area. This is a delicate subject in the industry, and the practice is officially discouraged by dealers and manufacturers alike. In private, however, dealers are often happy when the extra business walks in the door (though they hate like heck to lose a sale to a dealer outside their area), and some manufacturers are choosing to look the other way.

There are obvious advantages to shopping locally, and it would be foolish not to at least begin there. Shopping, delivery, and after-sale service are all much easier, and there can be pleasure in forging a relationship with a local merchant. That said, every person's lifestyle and priorities are different. A New Yorker who frequently does business in San Francisco may find it more "local" to visit a piano dealer in downtown San Francisco, near his or her business meeting, than to drive all over the New York metropolitan area with spouse and children on a Saturday morning. In the marketplace, the customer is king. As people become more and more at ease with doing business of all kinds long-distance with the aid of the Internet, it's inevitable that piano shopping will migrate in that direction as well. In recognition of this trend, several manufacturers now mandate that when a customer buys a piano from a dealer outside the customer's local area, the local authorized dealer of that brand will actually deliver the piano, and will receive a small percentage of the sale from the selling dealer in return for handling any warranty issues that may arise.

Buying a piano sight unseen (which, in view of the above discussion, must involve used pianos, not new) is something entirely different. Obviously, if you're at all musically sensitive, buying a piano without trying it out first is just plain nuts. But, as much as I hate to admit it, it may make sense for some people. In the piano business, we like to say (and I say it a lot) that a piano is not a commodity; that is, a product of which one example is more or less interchangeable with another. Each piano is unique, etc., etc., and must be individually chosen. But for someone who is buying a piano for a beginner, who has no preference in touch and tone, and just wants a piano that's reasonably priced, reliable, and looks nice, a piano may, in fact, actually be a "commodity." I might wish it were otherwise, just as an audiophile might wish that I wouldn't buy a stereo system off the shelf of a discount department store, but we're all aficionados of some things and indifferent about others, and that's our choice. Furthermore, just as people who buy electronic keyboards frequently graduate to acoustic pianos, the person who today buys a piano over the Internet may tomorrow be shopping at a local dealer for a better piano with a particular touch and tone. Although it isn't something I'd advise as a general rule, the fact is that many people have bought pianos over the Internet without first trying them out and are pleased with their purchase (and some people, probably, are not so pleased).

If you're thinking of making a long-distance purchase, however, please take some precautions (not all of these precautions will be applicable to every purchase). First, consider whether it's really worth it once you've taken into account the cost of long-distance shipping. Find out as much as you can about the dealer. Get references. Get pictures of the piano. Hire a piano technician in the dealer's area to inspect the piano (use the Piano Technicians Guild website, www.ptg.org, to find a technician) and ask the technician about the dealer's reputation. Make sure the dealer is experienced with arranging long-distance piano moves, and uses a mover that specializes in pianos. Find out who is responsible for tuning and adjusting the piano in your home, and for repairing any defects

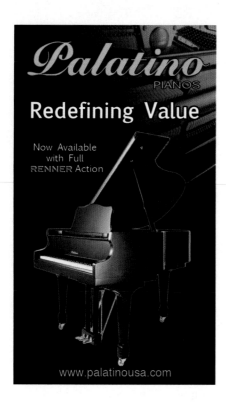
or dings in the finish. Get the details of the warranty, especially who is responsible for paying the return freight if the piano is defective. Find out how payment is to be made in a way that protects both parties. And if, after all this, you still want to buy long-distance, my best wishes for a successful purchase.

Negotiating Price and Trade-Ins

The prices of new pianos are nearly always negotiable. Only a handful of dealers have non-negotiable prices. If in doubt, just ask—you'll be able to tell. Some dealers carry this bargaining to extremes, whereas others start pretty close to the final price. Many dealers don't like to display a piano's price because not doing so gives them more latitude in deciding on a starting price for negotiation, depending on how they size up the customer. This makes shopping more difficult. Use the price information in the "**Model & Pricing Guide**" of the current issue of *Acoustic & Digital Piano Buyer* to determine the likely range within which a given model will sell. Don't give in too quickly. It's quite common for the salesperson to call a day or two later and offer a lower price. If there's an alternative piano at another dealership that will suit your needs just as well, it will help your negotiating position to let the salesperson know that.

Due to the high cost of advertising and conducting piano megasales (such as college sales, truckload sales, etc.), prices at these events are often actually *higher* than the price you could negotiate any day of the week, and the pressure to buy can be enormous. Shop at these sales only after you've shopped elsewhere, and look for the real bargains that occasionally exist.

If you're buying a new piano to replace one that's no longer satisfactory, you'll probably want to trade in the old one. Dealers will usually take a trade-in, no matter how bad it is, just to be able to facilitate the sale. In fact, in many cases the dealer will offer you what seems like a king's ransom for the old one. The downside is that when a generous trade-in allowance is given on the old piano, the dealer is then likely to offer you a less-generous price on the new one. To see if you're being offered a good deal, you'll have to carefully analyze the fair-market value of the old piano and what would be a likely price for the new one without a trade-in. Sometimes it will be to your advantage to sell the old piano privately, though in that case you'll need to take into account the hassle factor as well.

For more information about new-piano prices and negotiating, see the introduction to the "**Model & Pricing Guide**," elsewhere in this issue, as well as in *The Piano Book*.

Used-piano prices may or may not be negotiable. If the used piano is being sold by a dealer who primarily sells new pianos at negotiable prices, then the used-piano prices are probably also negotiable. Prices of restored pianos sold by the restorer are less likely to be negotiable, as technical people are usually less comfortable with bargaining. Prices of pianos for sale by private-party sellers are usually negotiable, in part because the seller often has little idea of what the piano should sell for and has just made up a price on the basis of wishful thinking. But even knowledgeable sellers will usually leave a little wiggle room in their price.

Electronic Player-Piano Systems

Prior to the Great Depression, most pianos were outfitted with player-piano mechanisms—the kind that ran on pneumatic pressure and

Typically, the control box for an electronic player-piano system is attached to the underside of the keybed.

paper rolls. Today's player pianos are all electronic; they run on CDs, iPods, floppy diskettes, or electronic downloads from the Internet, and are far more versatile and sophisticated than their pneumatic ancestors. Now you don't have to wait until Junior grows up to hear something interesting from the piano! A substantial percentage of new pianos, especially grands, are being outfitted with these systems. In fact, many pianos are being purchased as home-entertainment centers by buyers who have no intention of ever playing the piano themselves.

Several companies make these systems. Yamaha's Disklavier system is built into select Yamaha models at the Yamaha factory. PianoDisc and QRS Pianomation, the two major after-market systems, can be installed in any piano, new or used, typically by the dealer or at an intermediate distribution point. If installed properly by a trained and authorized installer, none of these systems will harm the piano or void its warranty. However, such installations are complicated and messy and must be done in a shop, not in your home.

The most basic system will play your piano and accompany it with synthesized orchestration or actual recorded accompaniment over speakers attached to the piano. These systems generally add about $4,000 to $7,000 to the price of the piano. Add another $1,500 to $2,000 to enable the piano to record your own playing for future playback. For a little bit more, you can mute the piano (stop the hammers from hitting the strings), turn on a digital piano sound, and listen through headphones. The range of prices reflects the variety of configurations and options available, including what music source you use (CD, iPod, MP3 player, etc.) and how much memory storage you purchase, among others. There are also higher-level systems at twice the price that provide touch screens with wireless connection for instant downloading of songs from the Internet. See the article "**Buying an Electronic Player-Piano System**" elsewhere in this issue for more information.

Furniture Style and Finish

Although for most buyers the qualities of performance and construction are of greatest importance in selecting a piano, a piano is also a large piece of furniture that tends to become the focal point of whatever room it is placed in. This is especially true of grands. Add to that the fact that you'll be looking at it for many years to come, and it becomes obvious that appearance can be an important consideration. For some buyers, it may be the most important consideration.

Vertical pianos without front legs are known as *Continental* style (also called *Contemporary*, *European Contemporary*, or *Eurostyle*). They are usually the smallest (42 to 43 inches high) and least expensive pianos in a manufacturer's product line.

Pianos with legs supported by *toe blocks* are sometimes known as *Institutional* or *Professional* style, particularly when the cabinet also has little in the way of decoration or embellishment.

School pianos are a subset of the institutional-style category. Generally 45 to 47 inches in height, these are institutional-style pianos made specifically for use in school practice rooms and classrooms. They usually come equipped with long music racks for holding multiple sheets of music, locks for both the lid and the fallboard, and heavy-duty casters for easier moving. They are generally available in ebony or satin wood finishes. Sturdy and sometimes plain-looking, they are also often purchased by non-institutional customers for less furniture-conscious locations. (If you're buying a piano for an institution, please read "Buying Pianos for an Institution," elsewhere in this issue.)

Vertical pianos with free-standing legs not reinforced by toe blocks are generally known as *Decorator* style. Common decorator styles are Queen Anne and French Provincial, generally in cherry (or Country French in oak), all with curved legs; Italian Provincial, typically in walnut with square legs; Mediterranean, usually in oak with hexagonal legs; and Traditional, most often in mahogany or walnut, with round or hexagonal legs. Matching music racks and cabinet decoration are common furniture embellishments. Furniture-style preference is an entirely personal matter. A practical consideration, however, is that front legs not supported by toe blocks have a tendency to break if the piano is moved frequently.

Hybrids styles, containing features of both institutional and

Institutional
Professional Style

Samick Music Corp.

School Style

Pramberger Piano Co.

Decorator Style:
French Provincial Cherry

Pramberger Piano Co.

Decorator Style:
Traditional Mahogany

Pramberger Piano Co.

Continental Style

Wyman/Orla

Decorator Style:
Mediterranean Oak

Samick Music Corp.

Hybrid Style

Wyman/Orla

decorator styles, are common, especially in Asian pianos.

Grand pianos come in far fewer styles than verticals. As you shop, it is likely you will see only a few different styles, in a number of woods and finishes.

The traditional grand piano case is likely familiar to everyone. It has rather straight or slightly tapered legs, often flaring slightly just above the floor (called a *spade* leg), and usually a rather plain, solid music rack.

Victorian style (sometimes called *Classic* style) is an imitation of a style in fashion in the late 1800s, with large, round, fluted legs and a fancy, carved music desk. Variations of the Victorian style have "ice-cream cone" or other types of round-ish legs.

As with verticals, grands also come in Queen Anne and French Provincial styles, with curved legs, and in other period styles. In addition to the leg style, these usually differ in the treatment of the music rack and cabinet embellishment as well.

Pianos come in a variety of woods, most commonly ebony (sometimes called ebonized), which is not actual ebony wood, but an inexpensive, sturdy veneer that has been painted black; as well as mahogany, cherry, walnut, and oak. Exotic woods include bubinga, rosewood, and many others, available on higher-priced uprights and grands. In pianos of lesser quality, sometimes a less expensive wood will be stained to look like a more expensive one. Pianos are also available in ivory or white, and it's often possible to special-order a piano in red, blue, or other colors.

In addition to the wood itself, the way the wood is finished also varies. Piano finishes come in either high polish (high gloss) or satin finishes. Satin reflects light but not images, whereas high polish is nearly mirror-like. Variations on satin include matte, which is completely flat (i.e., reflects no light), and open-pore finishes, common on European pianos, in which the grain is not filled in before finishing, leaving a slightly grainier texture. A few finishes are semigloss, which is partway between satin and high polish. As with furniture style, the finish is an entirely personal matter, though it should be noted that satin finishes tend to show fingerprints more than do high-polish finishes.

Most piano finishes are either lacquer or polyester. Lacquer was the finish on most pianos made in the first three-quarters of the 20th century, but it is gradually being supplanted by polyester. In my opinion, lacquer finishes—especially high-gloss lacquer—are more beautiful than polyester, but they scratch quite easily, whereas polyester is very durable. (Lacquer finishes can be repaired more easily.) Hand-rubbed satin lacquer is particularly elegant. Sometimes, when a customer desires a piano in a satin finish but the dealer has in stock only the high-polish polyester model, the dealer will offer to buff it down to a satin finish at a cost of $500 to $1,000. This is commonly done, and it works, but usually doesn't look as nice as the factory-made satin finish.

Touch and Tone

Touch, in its simplest form, refers to the effort required to press the piano keys. Unfortunately, the specifications provided by the manufacturers,

Straight Leg

Spade Leg

Victorian Style
with Ice-Cream Cone legs

Queen Anne Style

The Steinway *Europa III*

by Thomas Schrunk

Completed in January 2012, the Europa III features a stunning contrast of two rare burlwoods, Walnut and Carpathian Elm. The lid, sides and music desk feature a "fan" motif, with the Carpathian Elm elegantly framed with rich Walnut. The legs and lyre are solid walnut double-tapered pillars, accented with inlaid walnut burl to complete this refined and subtly complex design.

expressed in grams, don't do justice to this complicated subject. The apparent touch can be very different when the piano is played fast and loud than when it is played soft and slow, and this difference is not captured in the numbers. If you are other than a beginner, be sure to try it out both ways.

Advanced pianists tend to prefer a touch that is moderately firm because it provides better control than a very light touch and strengthens the muscles. Too light a touch, even for a beginner, can cause laziness, but too firm a touch can be physically harmful over time. The touch of most new pianos today is within a reasonable range for their intended audience, but the touch of older pianos can vary a lot depending on condition. A piano teacher may be able to assist in evaluating the touch of a piano for a beginner, particularly if considering an entry-level or used piano.

Piano *tone* is also very complex. The most basic aspect of tone, and the one most easily changed, is its brightness or mellowness. A *bright* tone, sometimes described by purchasers as *sharp* or *loud*, is one in which higher-pitched overtones pre-

dominate. A *mellow* tone, sometimes described as *warm*, *dull*, or *soft*, is one in which lower-pitched overtones are dominant. Most pianos are somewhere in between, and vary from one part of the keyboard to another, or depending on how hard one plays. The key to satisfaction is to make sure that the tone is right for the music you most often play or listen to. For example, jazz pianists will often prefer a brighter tone, whereas classical pianists will often prefer one that is mellower, or that can be varied easily from soft to loud; i.e., that has a broad dynamic range. However, there is no accounting for taste, and there are as many exceptions to these generalizations as there are followers. A piano technician can make adjustments to the brightness or mellowness of the tone through a process known as *voicing*.

Another aspect of tone to pay attention to is *sustain*, which is how long the sound of a note continues at an audible level, while its key is depressed, before disappearing. Practically speaking, this determines the ability of a melodic line to "sing" above an accompaniment, especially when played in the critical mid-treble section.

Most pianos will play loudly quite reliably, but providing good expression when played softly is considerably more challenging. When trying out a piano, be sure to play at a variety of dynamic levels. Test the action with your most technically demanding passages. Don't forget to test the pedals for sensitivity commensurate with your musical needs.

Room acoustics have a tremendous effect on piano tone, so you'll want to note the extent to which the acoustics of the dealer's showroom differ from those of your home, and make allowance for it. Hard surfaces, such as bare walls, tile, and glass will make the tone brighter. Absorbent surfaces—upholstered furniture, heavy drapes, plush carpeting—will make it mellower. Once the piano is in the home, a technician may be able to make adjustments to the tone, but to avoid unpleasant surprises, it's best to buy a piano whose tone is already close to what you want. Adjusting the room acoustics through the strategic use of wall hangings, scatter rugs, and furniture can also help. See the article **"How to Make Your Piano Room Sound Grand,"** elsewhere in this issue.

The Piano Warranty

The majority of pianos never generate a warranty claim. That said, few people would sleep well worrying about potential problems arising in such a major purchase. Key warranty issues are: what is covered, for how long, and who stands behind the warranty. The overwhelming majority of new-piano warranties cover the cost of parts and labor necessary to correct any defect in materials or workmanship. The warrantor (usually the manufacturer or distributor) also generally reserves the right to replace the piano should it choose to in lieu of repair. The warrantee (the customer) generally makes warranty claims to the dealer who, upon approval of the warrantor, makes the necessary repairs or replaces the instrument, as applicable. If the dealer is out of business, or if the customer has moved, warranty claims are made to the new local dealer of that brand, if any, or directly to the warrantor.

Warranties are in effect from the date of purchase and generally run between five and fifteen years, depending on the manufacturer. Note that there is little correlation between the length of warranty and the quality of the piano, as decisions on warranty terms are often made based on marketing factors. For example, a new manufacturer might well offer a longer warranty to help bolster sales. The Magnuson-Moss Warranty Act mandates that warranties be either *full* or *limited*. In the piano industry, the only significant difference is that full warranties remain in effect for the entire stated term, regardless of piano ownership, whereas limited warranties cover only the original purchaser. If you plan on possibly selling or trading up within a few years, a full warranty offers protection to the new owner, increasing the piano's value to them, and may justify a little higher selling price or trade-in value.

The final key issue about piano warranties concerns who stands behind the warranty. In most cases the warranty is backed by the actual manufacturer. This is advantageous, as the manufacturer has a major capital investment in its factory and has probably been in business for many years. The likelihood is that it will be around for the entire five- to fifteen-year period of your warranty. In today's piano market, however, many brands are manufactured under contract for a distributor, and the warranty is backed only by that distributor. Often, the distributor's only investment is a small rented office/warehouse and a few dozen pianos. Pianos are also often made to order for a particular dealership under a private brand name and are sold—and warranted—only by that dealership and/or its affiliates. In those cases, the warranty is further limited by the financial strength of the distributor or dealership, which can be difficult for the shopper to evaluate. In these situations, caution is called for.

When purchasing a used or restored piano, there is no warranty from a private, non-commercial seller, but a commercial seller will usually provide some kind of warranty, even if for only a few months. Pianos that have been completely restored typically come with a warranty with terms similar to that of a new piano, though of course it is backed by only the restorer.

Miscellaneous Practical Considerations

Bench

In all likelihood, your purchase of a new piano will include a matching bench. Benches for consumer-grade pianos are usually made by the piano manufacturer and come with the piano. Benches for performance-grade pianos are more often provided separately by the dealer.

Benches come in two basic types: fixed-height and adjustable. Consumer-grade pianos usually come with fixed-height benches that have either a solid top that matches the piano's finish, or a padded top with sides and legs finished to match the piano. The legs of most benches will be miniatures of the piano's legs, particularly for decorative models. Most piano benches have music storage compartments. School and institutional-type vertical pianos often come with so-called "stretcher" benches—the legs are connected with wooden reinforcing struts to better endure heavy use.

Adjustable benches are preferred by serious players, and by children and adults who are shorter or taller than average. The deeply-tufted tops

sostenuto, usually in favor of a bass sustain. (The obligatory nature of the sostenuto pedal—or any middle pedal—on a grand piano is a largely American phenomenon. Until fairly recently, many "serious" European pianos made for the European market had only two pedals.)

Fallboard (Keyboard Cover)

Vertical pianos use one of three basic fallboard designs: the Boston fallboard, a sliding fallboard (both of which disappear when open), or a one-piece "drop" fallboard with integrated music shelf.

The Boston fallboard is found on most furniture-style pianos and characteristically is a two-piece, double-hinged assembly. It is easily removed for service, and the rigidity provided by the hinges keeps the fallboard and the piano's side arms from being scratched when the fallboard is opened or closed.

The sliding fallboard, a one-piece cover that slides out from under the music desk to cover the keys, is considerably less expensive. However, if it is pulled unevenly and/or upwardly, it can scratch the fallboard or the inside of the piano's side arms.

The one-piece "drop" fallboard is commonly found on larger uprights. It is simply hinged at the back and lifts up to just past vertical, where it lies against the upper front panel of the piano. Attached to its underside is a small music shelf that is exposed when the fallboard is opened, then manually unfolded.

Grand pianos use a smaller one-piece "drop" fallboard that opens under the music desk. Fallboards on many newer grands are hydraulically damped so as to close slowly over the keys, eliminating the possibility of harming the player's or a young child's fingers. Aftermarket kits are available for pianos that lack this feature.

come in a heavy-duty vinyl and look like leather; tops of actual leather are available at additional cost. Adjustable benches vary considerably in quality. The best ones are expensive ($500 to $750) but are built to last a lifetime.

Finally, if the piano you want doesn't come with the bench you desire, talk to your dealer. It's common for dealers to swap benches or bench tops to accommodate your preference, or to offer an upgrade to a better bench in lieu of a discount on the piano.

For more information, see "**Benches, Lamps, Accessories, and Problem Solvers**," elsewhere in this issue.

Middle Pedal

As I mentioned near the beginning of this article, the function of the middle pedal varies. In some circumstances, you may need to consider whether the function of the middle pedal on a particular instrument will meet your musical needs.

On most new vertical pianos, the middle pedal operates a mute that reduces the sound volume by about 50 percent, a feature often appreciated by family members of beginning students. If your piano lacks this feature, after-market mute mechanisms are available for grands and verticals through piano technicians or dealers. On older verticals and a few new ones, the middle pedal, if not a mute, usually operates a bass sustain, although occasionally it's a "dummy" pedal that does nothing at all. I've never known anyone to actually use a bass-sustain pedal, so it might as well be a dummy.

On most grands and a few expensive uprights, the middle pedal operates a sostenuto mechanism that selectively sustains only those notes whose keys are down at the moment the pedal is pressed. This mechanism is called into action for only a relatively few pieces of classical music, yet it is generally considered obligatory for any "serious" instrument. Only inexpensive new and used grands omit the

WHEN I BEGAN servicing pianos during the 1970s, most pianos sold in the U.S. (with the important exception of the growing number of pianos from Japan) were made in the U.S. by about a dozen different makers, which together turned out hundreds of thousands of pianos annually. By current standards, many were not particularly well made. Today, only three companies make pianos in the U.S. in any real quantities, which combined amount to no more than a few thousand instruments per year. However, over 40,000 new acoustic pianos are sold here annually under some 70 different brand names, made by more than 30 companies in a dozen countries. The quality is the best it's ever been. Here are the highlights of what's happened:

- The Japanese "invasion" of the 1960s onward was followed by a wave of pianos from Korea in the 1980s and '90s. Together, these imports put most low- and mid-priced American makers out of business.
- Rising wages in Korea in the 1990s caused much of that country's piano production to move to Indonesia and China.
- The economic emergence of China during the 2000s resulted in a new wave of low-priced, low-quality pianos appearing in the U.S. and globally.
- Foreign firms and investors have combined low-cost Chinese and Indonesian labor with high-quality design and manufacturing expertise, parts, and materials from Western countries to greatly increase the quality of low-priced Chinese and Indonesian pianos.
- Cheaper equipment for computer-aided design and manufacturing has allowed for their more widespread use by small and large firms alike, with a consequent increase in precision of manufacturing at all price levels.
- Since the 1990s, a dozen or more European makers of high-quality pianos have been aggressively marketing their pianos in the U.S., challenging entrenched interests and creating more choice and higher quality in the high end of the piano market. They are currently hampered, however, by a disadvantageous exchange rate.
- To better survive in a global economy, high-end companies have diversified their product lines to include low- and mid-priced pianos, setting up factories or forming alliances with companies in parts of the world where labor is cheaper. At the same time, makers of low- and mid-priced pianos are creating higher-priced models using parts and expertise usually associated with the high-end companies, thus blurring the line between the high and low ends of the piano market.

Over 40,000 new acoustic pianos are sold here annually under some 70 different brand names, made by more than 30 companies in a dozen countries.

China

The first piano factory in China is said to have been established in 1895, in Shanghai (perhaps by the British?). During the 1950s, the Communists consolidated the country's piano manufacturing into four government-owned factories: Shanghai, Beijing, and Dongbei (means "northeast") in the northern part of the country, and Guangzhou Pearl River in the south. Piano making, though industrial, remained primitive well into the 1990s. In that decade, the government of China began to open the country's economy to foreign investment, first only to partnerships with the government, and later to completely private concerns.

As China's economy has opened up, the nation's rising middle and upper classes have created a sharp increase in demand for pianos. Tempted by the enormous potential of the Chinese domestic market, as well as by the lure of cheap goods manufactured for the West, foreign interests have built new piano factories in China, bought existing factories, or contracted with existing factories for the manufacture of pianos. The government has also poured money into its own factories to make them more competitive and to accommodate the growing demand.

Except for the government involvement, the piano-making scene in China today is reminiscent of that in the U.S. a century ago: Hundreds of small firms assemble pianos from parts or subassemblies obtained from dozens of suppliers and sell them on a mostly regional basis. The government factories and a few large foreign ones sell nationally. Most of the pianos sold in the Chinese domestic market are still primitive by Western standards. Primarily, the quality has markedly improved where foreign technical assistance or investment has been involved; only those pianos are good enough to be sold in the West.

Although in China the government factories have long had a monopoly on sales through piano dealers, that hold is gradually being eroded, and the government entities are experiencing great competitive pressure from all the smaller players. Combined with the inefficiencies and debt inherent in government operations, the current competitive situation is probably making the government think twice about continuing to subsidize the piano industry. Already, one of its factories, Dongbei, has been privatized through its sale to Gibson Guitar Corporation, parent of Baldwin Piano Company.

Besides the government-owned factories and Baldwin, the largest makers in China of pianos for the North American market are Yamaha (Japan), Young Chang (Korea), Sejung (Korea), and, for the Canadian market, Kawai (Japan)—all of whom own factories in China. Other foreign-owned companies that own factories in China or contract with Chinese manufacturers to make pianos for the U.S. market include Brodmann, Perzina, AXL (Palatino brand), Heintzman, Schimmel (May Berlin brand), Blüthner (Irmler Studio brand), and Bechstein (W. Hoffmann Vision brand). Many American distributors and dealers contract with Sejung, Pearl River, Dongbei, and Beijing, selling pianos in the U.S. under a multitude of names. Steinway & Sons markets the Essex brand, designed by Steinway and manufactured by Pearl River.

And one company, Hailun, is owned and operated by a Chinese entrepreneur, Chen Hailun.

For the first half of this decade, most sales of Chinese pianos in the U.S. were based on the idea of luring customers into the store to buy the least expensive piano possible. Dealers that staked their business on this approach often lost it. A growing trend now is to manufacture and sell somewhat higher-priced pianos that have added value in the form of better components, often imported to China from Europe and the U.S., but still taking advantage of the low cost of Chinese labor. The best ones are not just a collection of parts, however, but also have improved designs developed with foreign technical assistance, and sufficient oversight to make sure the designs are properly executed.

The oversight is especially important. Chinese piano manufacturers have been quite aggressive in acquiring piano-making knowledge, and are happy to use their alliances with Western distributors in furthering that end. There has been a tendency, however, for Chinese factory managers to ignore the advice and requests of Western distributors once their inspectors leave the factory, resulting in product that does not meet the standards or specifications contracted for. The distributors have gradually discovered that the only way to overcome this problem is to own the factory themselves, to maintain a constant presence at the factory, or to constitute such a large percentage of the Chinese company's business that they, the Westerners, can control production. Alternatively, a Western company can examine all the pianos in its home country before sending them on to dealers, but this is less satisfactory than stopping problems at the source. Western distributors of Korean pianos used to complain of a similar problem with Korean factory managers during the height of that country's piano industry in the 1980s and '90s. As in Korea, the situation in China is gradually improving as the Chinese become accustomed to Western ways of doing business and more focused on quality control.

Pianos made in China now dominate the North American market, constituting about a third of all new pianos sold in the U.S. At the beginning of this decade, most were just barely acceptable technically, and not musically desirable. Over the years, however, both the technical and musical qualities have taken big leaps forward. While some remain at the entry level, others rival the performance of more expensive pianos from other parts of the world. The jury is still out as to whether some of these pianos will hold up over the long term and in demanding climates and situations. Reports often suggest less consistency than with pianos from other countries, and a continuing need for thorough pre-sale preparation by the dealer

A growing trend [in Chinese pianos] is to sell somewhat higher-priced pianos that have added value in the form of better components.

(who sometimes must weed out the bad ones and return them to the factory), but otherwise few major problems. Prices on the better ones are increasing, but for many entry-level buyers, and even for some mid-level buyers, many brands are still good value despite their short track records. Certainly, as short-term investments, and in milder climates and less demanding situations, they should be fine.

Indonesia

Indonesia is China's closest competitor in terms of price and quality. But unlike China, in which many small and large companies, domestic and foreign, are involved in piano manufacturing, virtually all pianos made in Indonesia are the products of three large, foreign players: Yamaha, Kawai, and Samick. For the U.S. market, Yamaha makes only one model, an entry-level grand, in Indonesia; Kawai makes all its small and medium-sized verticals there, and one entry-level grand; and Samick makes all its pianos for sale in North America there, both grand and vertical.

Overall, the manufacturing quality is similar to China's, but Indonesia got to this level of quality more rapidly and is perhaps more consistent. This may have been due to the smaller number and, on average, larger size of Indonesia's piano manufacturers, as well as to cultural and political differences between the countries. Development of manufacturing in Indonesia was aided by the fact that the country was already a democratic (more or less), capitalist nation with strong ties to the West, and accustomed to Western ways of working and doing business, with English widely spoken. The government does not own or manage the factories.

One of the big challenges in Indonesia, as in the rest of tropical Asia (which includes southern China), is climate control inside the factories, and the proper handling of wood to avoid problems later on when the instruments are shipped to drier countries and the wood dries out. All three companies, as well as Pearl River in southern China, have done a good job of meeting this challenge (though some only recently), but caution and proper climate control by the consumer are especially advised when these pianos are to be used in very difficult, dry indoor climates.

Korea

The Korean piano industry has had a tumultuous history, from its beginnings in the war-torn 1950s through its meteoric global rise in the 1980s; through labor unrest, the Asian economic crisis, and the abrupt collapse of the country's piano industry in the 1990s; and most recently through bankruptcies, reorganizations, aborted takeovers, and more bankruptcies. Today, both Samick and Young Chang seem to be on relatively stable financial footing, the latter having just emerged from bankruptcy after being purchased by Hyundai Development Company. As mentioned earlier, due to high labor costs in Korea, both companies have moved most of their manufacturing elsewhere, limiting production at home to the more expensive models.

Quality control in the Korean models is now nearly as good as in pianos from Japan, but getting there has taken 30 years of two steps forward, one step back. The reasons for the slow development are probably numerous, but undoubtedly some are cultural in nature: Western piano-company personnel have often reported that their Korean counterparts can be proud people, reluctant to take advice from Americans (not that they necessarily should—unless they're trying to sell products to Americans).

Musically, the two companies' pianos have never really gained clear, aesthetic identities of their own, other than as very acceptable musical products. Periodic redesigns by German engineers, or American engineers with Germanic names (always sought by piano makers), have brought some progress, but never as much as was hoped for. Part of the reason for the lack of identity may be that there have been such a multitude of product lines made in different factories to constantly changing specifications that nothing has settled down long enough to stick. Internal politics and dealing with quality-control problems have also taken up much energy over the years.

Things are settling down now for both companies. Samick, in its upper- and mid-level lines, is producing some of its nicest pianos ever. Young Chang is playing catch-up, but also has some good designs, with new ones in the pipeline. Both companies' top-level products have much to offer at good prices.

Japan

Japan's two major piano manufacturers, Yamaha and Kawai, began making pianos around 1900 and 1927, respectively, with export to the United States beginning in earnest in the early 1960s. The first few years of export were spent learning to season the wood to the demands

> **Quality control in the Korean models is now nearly as good as in pianos from Japan, but getting there has taken 30 years of two steps forward, one step back.**

of the North American climate, but since then the quality control has been impressive, to say the least, and the standard to which other piano manufacturers aspire. Both companies also have outstanding warranty service, so customers are never left hanging with unsatisfactory instruments. As in Korea, labor costs in Japan have risen to the point where both companies have been forced to move much of their manufacturing elsewhere, making only their more expensive models in Japan. With some exceptions, their grands and tallest uprights are made in Japan, small and mid-sized verticals in other Asian countries.

The tone of Japanese pianos tends to be a little on the bright and percussive side (Yamaha more than Kawai), though less so than in previous years, and pleasing in their own way. In addition to their regular lines, both companies make high-end lines with more "classical" qualities, as well as entry-level lines that reflect a compromise between price and quality. The pianos are very popular with institutions and are real workhorses. Although more expensive than most other Asian pianos, a Japanese-made Yamaha or Kawai piano is hard to beat for reliability. Kawai also manufactures the Boston brand, designed by Steinway and sold through Steinway dealers.

United States

Only three companies manufacture pianos here in any numbers: Steinway & Sons, Mason & Hamlin, and Charles R. Walter. A couple of other makers are in very limited production: Astin-Weight in Salt Lake City, whose factory was shut down several years ago by storm damage, says it still makes a few pianos; and pianos are once again being assembled in Chicago under the Kimball name

using parts sourced from around the world. A few boutique makers, such as Ravenscroft, build high-end pianos to order. Baldwin, for a century one of the largest American producers, finally ceased most production at its American factory in 2009, having moved nearly all piano production to its two plants in China.

Steinway & Sons has been making high-quality pianos in New York City since its founding in 1853 by German immigrants. For most of the past century, the company has had little competition in the U.S.: when one desired to buy a piano of the highest quality, it was simply understood that one meant a Steinway. The last decade or two has seen a gradual erosion of that status by more than a dozen European firms and our own Mason & Hamlin. Although each by itself is too small to make a dent in Steinway's business, their combined effect has been to claim a substantial share of the market for high-end pianos in the home. (Steinway still dominates the concert-grand market and, to some extent, the institutional market.) This has been made easier by the fact that in certain respects these European-made pianos are visibly and audibly of higher quality than American-made Steinways (to be distinguished from Steinways made at the company's branch factory in Hamburg, Germany, which are of the highest quaity). Steinways have classic designs and use proven materials and methods of construction, but the musical and aesthetic finishing of the American-made pianos has too often been left uncompleted at the factory in the expectation,

The rush to sell to Americans has caused some European companies to reconsider the tonal designs of their instruments.

frequently unmet, that the dealers would finish it off. Fortunately, the past few years have seen a reversal of this trend in the form of many small improvements at the factory, as well as perhaps better performance by dealers. Though there is room for further improvement, the ratio of compliments to complaints, in my experience, has become more favorable. The recent replacement of American Steinway management by personnel from Steinway's European branches may also be having a salutary effect.

Mason & Hamlin, Steinway's principal competitor in the early part of the 20th century, went into a long period of decline after the Great Depression. After a series of bankruptcies and reorganizations in the 1980s and '90s, Mason & Hamlin was purchased in 1996 by the Burgett brothers, owners of PianoDisc, a leading manufacturer of player-piano systems. Over the past 14 years, from an old brick factory building in Haverhill, Massachusetts, the Burgetts have completely restored the company to its former excellence, and then some. They and their staff have designed or redesigned a complete line of grand pianos and modernized century-old equipment. Rather than compete with Steinway on Steinway's terms, Mason & Hamlin has repositioned itself as an innovator, seeking out or developing high-quality but lower-cost parts and materials from around the world, and combining them with traditional craftsmanship to produce a great piano at a somewhat lower price.

Charles R. Walter, a piano design engineer by profession, has

been making high-quality vertical pianos in Elkhart, Indiana, since the 1970s, and grands for over ten years. The factory is staffed in large part by members of his extended family. The instruments are built using the best traditional materials and construction practices. Right now, times are tough for small companies such as this, which produce an excellent product but are neither the high-priced celebrated names nor the low-cost mass producers. If you're looking to "buy American," you can't get any more American than Charles R. Walter.

Europe

European makers that regularly sell in the U.S. include: Bechstein, Blüthner, Feurich, August Förster, Grotrian, Sauter, Schimmel, Seiler, Steingraeber, and Wilh. Steinberg (Germany); Bösendorfer (Austria); Fazioli and Schulze Pollmann (Italy); Estonia (Estonia); and Petrof (Czech Republic). Most are of extremely high quality; even the least of them is very good. Until two decades ago, most of these brands were virtually unknown or unavailable in the U.S., but as the European demand for pianos contracted, many of the companies found that Americans, with their large homes and incomes, would buy all the grand pianos they could produce. The liberation of Eastern Europe resulted in an increase in the quality of such venerable brands as Estonia and Petrof, which had suffered under Communist rule, and these brands, too, became available and accepted here.

The rush to sell to Americans has caused some European companies to reconsider the tonal designs of their instruments and to redesign them for better sound projection, tonal color, and sustain—that is, to sound more like American Steinways. Considering that some of these companies are five or six generations old and have redesigned their pianos about that many times in 150 years, this degree of activity is unusual. Some of the redesigns have been great musical

> **The worldwide changes in the piano industry are making it more difficult to advise piano shoppers.**

successes; nevertheless, the loss of diversity in piano sound is to be mourned.

Several German companies have started or acquired second-tier lines to diversify their product lines, and have gradually shifted much of their production to former Soviet-bloc countries with lower labor costs, producing brands such as Bohemia and W. Hoffmann (by Bechstein) in the Czech Republic, and Vogel (by Schimmel) in Poland. Today, there is enough commonality in business practices, laws, and attitudes toward quality among the countries of Europe that the distinction between Eastern and Western Europe carries little meaning—except for labor costs, where the savings can be great.

Globalization, Quality, and Value

The worldwide changes in the piano industry are making it more difficult to advise piano shoppers. For many years, the paradigm for piano quality has been an international pecking order: pianos from Russia, China, and Indonesia at the bottom; followed by Korea, Japan, and Eastern Europe; and, finally, Western Europe at the top, with pianos from the U.S. scattered here and there, depending on the brand. This pecking order has never been foolproof, but it has served a generation of piano buyers well enough as a rule of thumb.

Now this order is being disturbed by globalization. High-end and low-end makers are, to some extent, adopting each other's methods and narrowing the differences between them. On the one hand, some Western European and American makers of high-end pianos are partially computerizing the manufacture of their "hand-built" pianos, quietly sourcing parts and subassemblies from China, and developing less expensive product lines in Eastern Europe and Asia. On the other hand, some Korean and Chinese makers are importing parts and technology from Germany, Japan, and the U.S., producing pianos that sometimes rival the performance of more expensive pianos from the West. Global alliances are bringing new products to market that are more hybridized than anything we've seen before. Although the old pecking order still has some validity, the number of exceptions is increasing, causing temporary confusion in the marketplace until a new order emerges.

At the same time that the range of quality differences is narrowing, the range of prices is widening, bringing into greater prominence issues of "value." Eastern European brands have emerged as "value" alternatives to Western European brands, the latter becoming frightfully expensive due to high labor costs and the rapid appreciation of the euro against the dollar. Some of the better pianos from China, Korea, and Indonesia have become value alternatives to Japanese pianos. Brands that don't scream "value" are being squeezed out of the market.

As mentioned above, one of the consequences of globalization is that parts and materials formerly available

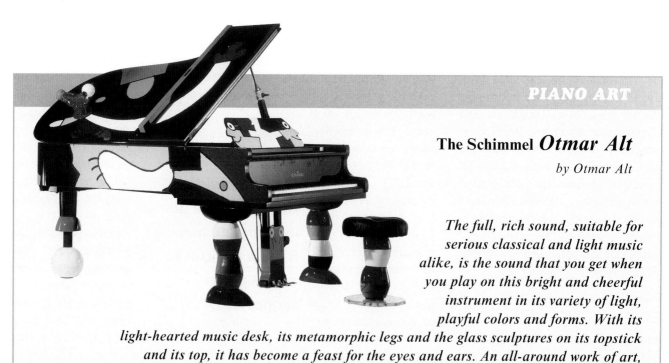

only to high-end makers are now for sale to any company, anywhere, that's willing to pay for them. Thus, you'll see a number of Asian firms marketing their pianos with a list of well-regarded brand-name components from Germany and North America, such as Renner, Röslau, Mapes, and Bolduc. The question then naturally arises: Given that high-end pianos are so expensive, and that today one can buy for so little a Chinese-made piano with German design, German parts, and perhaps even a German name, is it still worth buying a performance-grade piano made in the West? Are there any differences worth paying for?

There's no question that high-end components, such as Renner hammers and Bolduc soundboards, add to the quality and value of consumer-grade pianos in which they're used. But in terms of quality, components such as these are only the tip of the iceberg. Although the difference between performance- and consumer-grade pianos has narrowed, in many ways the two types of manufacturers still live in different worlds. Differences are manifested in such things as the selection, drying, and use of wood; final regulation and voicing; and attention to technical and cosmetic details.

Makers of performance-grade pianos use higher grades of wood, selected for finer grain, more even color, or greater hardness, strength, and/or acoustical properties, as the use requires. Wood is seasoned more carefully and for longer periods of time, resulting in greater dimensional stability and a longer-lasting product. Veneers are more carefully matched, and finishes polished to a greater smoothness. Action assemblies purchased from suppliers may be taken apart and put back together to more exacting tolerances than originally supplied. The workspace

is set up to allow workers more time to complete their tasks and a greater opportunity to catch and correct errors. Much more time is spent on final regulation and voicing, with an instrument not leaving the factory, in some cases, until a musician has had an opportunity to play it and be satisfied. Of course, the degree to which these manifestations of quality, and many others not mentioned, are present will vary by brand and circumstance, but underlying them all is this philosophical difference: with performance-grade pianos, the driving force behind decision-making tends to be the quality of the product; with consumer-grade pianos, cost is a greater factor.

A MAP OF THE MARKET FOR NEW PIANOS

The chart and commentary that follow are intended to provide the

newcomer to the piano market with a simple summary of how the brands compare with one another in overall quality and recommendability, taking into account each brand's features, performance, and track record.

Any such rating system is obviously not scientific but subjective, the product of my contacts with dozens of piano technicians, dealers, and other industry personnel, as well

PERFORMANCE-GRADE PIANOS

Highest Quality	High Quality	Good Quality
Verticals: $17,000–$42,000	Verticals: $13,000–$34,000	Verticals: $9,300–$21,000
Grands 5' to 7': $52,000–$105,000	Grands 5' to 7': $29,000–$85,000	Grands 5' to 7': $31,000–$61,000
C. Bechstein	Bechstein (Academy)	Petrof
Blüthner	Estonia	Schimmel (Classic)
Bösendorfer	Feurich (Germany)*	Schulze Pollmann
Fazioli	August Förster	Wilh. Steinberg (IQ)
Grotrian	Haessler*	Charles R. Walter
Sauter	Shigeru Kawai	
Steingraeber & Söhne	Mason & Hamlin	
Steinway & Sons (Hamburg)	Schimmel (Konzert)	
	Seiler (Germany)	
	Steinway & Sons (New York)	
	Yamaha (CF)	

*Tentative, based on very limited information

PROFESSIONAL-GRADE PIANOS

Verticals: $8,000–$15,000
Grands 5' to 7': $18,000–$40,000
Bohemia
W. Hoffmann (Tradition)
Vogel
Boston (Japan)
Kawai (RX) grands
Kawai verticals (Japan)
Yamaha (C) grands
Yamaha verticals (Japan)

CONSUMER-GRADE PIANOS

	Chinese	Samick	Young Chang	Yamaha/Kawai
Upper Level Verticals: $3,600–$9,300 Grands 5' to 7': $9,900–$30,000	Perzina verticals	Wm. Knabe (Concert Artist) J.P. Pramberger (Platinum)	Albert Weber	
	Brodmann (PE) grands Hailun Ritmüller			Kawai (GE) grands Kawai verticals (Indonesia) Yamaha (GC) grands Yamaha verticals (China)
Mid-Range Verticals: $2,900–$8,400 Grands 5' to 7': $7,500–$24,000	Brodmann (PE) verticals Heintzman May Berlin Palatino Perzina grands*	Wm. Knabe (Academy) Kohler & Campbell (Millennium) Pramberger (Signature) Story & Clark (Signature)		Kawai (GM) grands Yamaha (GB) grands
	Baldwin (China)* Essex Everett grands Hallet, Davis & Co. (HD) grands Pearl River			Cable-Nelson (Yamaha)
Entry Level Verticals: $2,800–$5,500 Grands 5' to 7': $6,900–$17,000	Cristofori Henry F. Miller	Wm. Knabe (Baltimore) Kohler & Campbell (New Yorker) Pramberger (Legacy) Samick Story & Clark (Heritage)	Weber (W) Young Chang (Y)	
	Altenburg Hobart M. Cable Everett verticals Falcone Hardman, Peck & Co. Geo. Steck Wyman	*To better understand this chart, please read the accompanying commentary.*		

*Tentative, based on very limited information

as my more than thirty years of involvement with the piano industry. My sense is that most knowledgeable people in the industry would agree in broad terms with this comparison, though many will disagree with me—and with each other—about the details. (See my blog at **www.pianobuyer.com** for additional comments on the subject of piano ratings.)

The key to proper use of this chart is not to cling to it too tightly but to understand that, given its subjectivity and simplicity, it should be used only as a learning tool. In addition, use common sense when comparing one brand with another. Compare verticals with verticals and grands with grands, and compare only similar sizes, or models whose selling prices fall within the same range.

Note that, for the sake of simplicity, there may be quality differences within a single product line that are not shown here; also, a few brands were omitted due solely to lack of sufficient information about them.

A generalization useful to understanding the piano market is that pianos can be divided into two types, Performance and Consumer, both of which are necessary to meet the needs

of the wide variety of piano buyers. Performance-grade pianos generally have one or more of the following attributes: They are built to a single high standard, almost without regard to cost, and the price charged is whatever it takes to build such a piano and bring it to market. A greater proportion of the labor required to build them is in the handwork involved in making custom refinements to individual instruments. Most are made in relatively small quantities by firms that have been in business for generations, often under the same family ownership. As a result, many have achieved almost legendary status, and are often purchased as much for their prestige value as for their performance. Finally, these are the instruments most likely to be called into service when the highest performance level is required, particularly for classical music. Most performance-grade pianos are made in Europe or the United States.

Consumer-grade pianos, on the other hand, are built to be sold at a particular price, and adjustments to (i.e., compromises in) materials, workmanship, and method and location of manufacture are made to meet that price. Most are mass-produced, usually in Asia, with less in the way of custom refinement of individual instruments.

As discussed elsewhere in this publication, globalization and the computerization of manufacturing have, to some extent, blurred the distinction between performance- and consumer-grade pianos. Increasingly, makers of performance-grade instruments have been creating lower-cost brands by manufacturing instruments and components in countries with cheaper labor, while makers of consumer-grade pianos have been bringing to market higher-quality models by perfecting automation and sourcing parts worldwide. This has created difficulties in classifying brands by means of a two-grade system, both because some brands defy such classification, and because of the bottleneck that results from the attempt to rate too many brands relative to one another in a restricted space.

To alleviate this problem, I have spun off a third type of piano, called Professional Grade, intermediate between Performance and Consumer, consisting of some of the lower-level performance-grade brands and some of the upper-level consumer-grade ones. The pianos on the performance-grade side are lesser product lines from companies principally known for their higher-grade brands. They inherit some of the quality of their superior cousins, but otherwise are quite different. The instruments on the consumer-grade side are brands that in recent years have become so advanced in their designs, materials, and manufacturing technologies that they now rival some performance-grade pianos in musicality and quality control, and are sometimes recommended as a substitute for them, often at a lower price. Truthfully, a number of the consumer-grade brands could fit this description, but I've labeled here as professional grade only those that have received the greatest market acceptance as instruments suitable for professional use. I'm sure, in time, others will follow.

The chart for each grade is divided into two or more levels of quality; for consumer-grade pianos, each of these levels is further broken down into two subgroups. **Within each group or subgroup, the brands are listed in alphabetical order. No**

judgment of these brands' relative quality should be inferred from this order.

Within each grade of piano, the distinctions between one group or subgroup and the next can be quite subtle, so don't get hung up on small differences. Furthermore, the preparation of the piano by the dealer can be far more important to the quality of the product you receive than some of the distinctions listed in the chart.

Prices shown for each group are the approximate lowest and highest typical selling prices of new pianos in the least expensive style and finish.

Performance-Grade Pianos

Highest Quality

Most of the pianos in this group, and in the next, "High Quality," are for those buyers who want the best and can afford it. The companies that make them use the very best materials, and their manufacturing processes emphasize much hand labor and refinement of details. These companies' painstaking execution of advanced designs puts considerations of quality far ahead of cost

and volume of production. These instruments are suitable for the most advanced and demanding professional and artistic uses.

It was easier to arrive at a consensus about the brands in this group than about any other group in this rating system. So celebrated are the brands in this group that dealers eagerly nominated even their competitors for the list. These pianos have everything, and the attention to detail paid in their manufacture can only be called fanatical. (Note that pianos made by Steinway & Sons/ Hamburg are not routinely available in North America; I include the brand here for informational purposes only.)

High Quality

The pianos in this group are also fabulous, but are in second place here either because their workmanship is not quite as refined as the first group, or because their musical designs are considered slightly less desirable, or perhaps because their names have not yet earned as much prestige value as those in the first group. However, preferences among performance-grade pianos are greatly dependent on musical

taste, and most of the brands in this group have their devoted followings.

Most knowledgeable observers of the piano business would consider the brands in this group to span quite a range of quality within the rarefied air of high-end pianos, and would insist that it be divided into two or more subgroups. The problem is that I found an utter lack of agreement among my many contacts as to which brands each subgroup should contain. Furthermore, the relative ranking of these brands is one of the most hotly debated topics among piano aficionados. Rather than arbitrarily impose my own preferences, I have chosen to leave the group undivided. Since this chart is primarily intended for newcomers to the piano market, any further division of this group would be academic.

Good Quality

The brands in this group, though very good, are considered to have less finesse than those in the first two groups. However, most of these models are also considerably less expensive than the ones above, and may be a better value where the highest quality or prestige is not needed.

Consumer-Grade Pianos

The chart for consumer-grade pianos is organized differently from that for performance-grade pianos. The Korean-based companies Samick and Young Chang each has its own column listing all the brand names each makes for the U.S. market, including brands made under contract for other distributors; the Japanese-based companies Yamaha and Kawai share a column for their brands (other than those listed under Professional Grade); and there is a column for all brands made in China not already included in the other columns.

Within the Samick, Young Chang, and Yamaha/Kawai columns, the various brand names or model groupings are organized approximately as the respective companies themselves position them in the marketplace by price and features. Some small adjustments have been made for subjective reasons. The brands within the Chinese column are organized by approximate overall recommendability, which also tends to fall along lines of price and features, though not uniformly so.

The tricky part of organizing this chart was figuring out how to align each column with the others to indicate the relative recommendability of the brands. As you can see, the brands and models in the Yamaha/Kawai column are concentrated toward the top of the chart, whereas those in the Chinese column are skewed slightly downward. This reflects, in large part, the differences in these brands' track records for durability, reliability, and warranty service. It must be noted that many dealers and others compare pianos only on the basis of their musical performance qualities when new, but a true comparison must also include their track records for these other factors. How *much* each factor is to be valued is a highly subjective matter, thus reasonable people will disagree as to how these columns should be aligned.

As can be expected, the upper-level consumer-grade pianos generally have premium components and better performance and quality control than the lower-level instruments. In fact, as mentioned earlier, some may even compare favorably to professional-grade instruments, and may be less expensive, too. The entry-level models are basic, no-frills pianos suitable for beginners and casual users, but which a conscientious student may outgrow in a few years. The mid-range pianos usually have better design, performance, quality control, track record, and/or components than the entry-level ones, but not as good as the upper-level ones. As piano quality in general improves, the distinction between levels becomes more subtle and difficult to discern.

FEURICH (NINGBO) PIANOS are a new range of models resulting from the merger of Wendl & Lung, of Vienna, Austria, and Feurich, a very-small-production German company. These less-expensive instruments (three grand and three upright sizes are currently offered), formerly marketed under the Wendl & Lung brand, are built at the Hailun factory in Ningbo, China, and supplement the traditional series of Feurich pianos, which continue to be produced exclusively in Gunzenhausen, Germany.

Although the sizes and place of manufacture of the new Feurich (Ningbo) pianos match specific Hailun-branded models, their parts specifications and acoustic design elements are unique. Also of note is a European approach to prep work that is unusual for a lower-priced piano: Prior to being shipped to dealers, assembled instruments are sent to an authorized distribution center for extensive prep that includes tuning, regulation, and, particularly, voicing.

From a distance, the 48" Feurich F 122 looked like a typical tall upright finished in polished ebony—until I slid back the bench and opened the fallboard: the hinges, pedals, and nameplate were all finished in chrome. The effect was special, and elegant to my eye, though the U.S. distributor noted that these parts can also be ordered in traditional brass finish. The tone quality was warm and pleasant through the bass and tenor, while the treble range was intimate—this instrument was voiced not to overpower a smaller room. The bass/tenor transition (a problem area for many pianos) was satisfactory, whereas the lowest few bass notes lacked the sonic authority of larger and/or more expensive uprights. I felt that the projection and sustain

of the treble register of this particular instrument were in need of refinement. The F 122's action was light, easy to play, and fairly deep under my fingers—characteristics matched by the instrument's pedal mechanism.

The theme of aesthetic enhancements is carried over to the polished

ebony 5' 10" Feurich F 178 grand, whose opened lid revealed a beautiful inner rim of bird's-eye maple. Most impressive was the simple, open-design music desk—a sort of contemporary Craftsman furniture style carried over from the German Feurich pianos. A fringe benefit of this distinctive music desk was its sonic transparency; from the player's perspective, most solid music desks reflect a good deal of the sound back into the piano.

The well-prepped F 178 I auditioned had a beautifully regulated action that was quite even, and controllable down to the softest dynamics. The touchweight was moderate, while the key dip—the distance the key travels downward when depressed—was slightly shallow. Its tone was focused and clear, but not bright and strident unless I pushed it past *forte*. Considering the Feurich's modest size, its pitch clarity throughout the bass register was good, though the bass/tenor transition was more noticeable than I would have liked.

Priced near the higher-rated Chinese brands and less than Japanese-made Yamaha, Kawai, and Boston pianos of the same size, these new Feurich models are solid entries with real visual appeal in a growing segment of the market: pianos made in China with upgraded features and design elements. Dealer and additional model information can be found online at **www.feurichusa.com**.

Dr. Owen Lovell is an Assistant Professor of Piano at the University of Wisconsin–Eau Claire. He concertizes frequently as a soloist, chamber musician, and advocate of new music. For more information, visit his website at www .owenlovell.com.

Portland's Own *Piano Shop on the Left Bank:*
www.classicportland.com

Visitors to *Classic Pianos* of Portland, Oregon are surprised to discover the ambiance of an old-world *Restoration Shop* and three distinctive *Piano Salons* within a museum-like atmosphere of used brick walls, waxed concrete and rough plank floors, original wall art created from antique piano parts, and hanging re-bronzed piano harps.

Adjacent to the piano shop is a circa 1912 craftsman mission chapel that once served as offices for the Episcopal Diocese of Oregon. Now restored and enlarged to include a condominium for out of town guests, this quaint structure for auditioning pianos has been renamed *The Schimmel House (Das Schimmel Haus)*.

Classic Pianos, located at the East End of the Ross Island Bridge, crossing over the Willamette River into Portland's historic southeast *"Brooklyn Neighborhood,"* has reached national and international recognition. Guests often comment that it's a chapter right out of Thad Carhart's national bestseller, *THE PIANO SHOP ON THE LEFT BANK:* "Discovering a Forgotten Passion in a Paris Atelier."

Classic Pianos is owned by Maurice Unis and his three sons, Brian, Aaron, and Taylor. Winner of every *Top Dealer Award* from European, Asian, and American, piano manufacturers, *Classic Pianos* represents *Bösendorfer, Schimmel, Yamaha, Mason & Hamlin,* and also showcases a *CLASSIC COLLECTION* of vintage-restored *Steinway & Sons* and *Mason & Hamlin* grands.

CLASSIC COLLECTION — Fully restored 1928 *Steinway & Sons* Model B Louis XV. Sold and shipped to Dr. and Mrs. J. Berg of San Luis Obispo, California.

Classic Collection sales and shipments coast-to-coast in U.S. and Canada

CUSTOMER COMMENTS: **"In the course of a nation-wide search, we finally discovered Classic Pianos.... We could not have made a better choice. Classic Pianos is home to an amazing group of professionals. "**
— Julie Berg, San Luis Obispo, California
Pianist, Teacher, and College Educator

VISITOR COMMENTS: **"I was overwhelmed: I had never, previously, encountered such a galaxy of new pianos... among the finest obtainable in the United States, in Europe, and in the Orient."**
— Lucien Needham , Alberta, Canada
Associate, Graduate, and Fellow, *Guildhall School of Music*

COMMENTS BY CONCERT PIANISTS: **"I have known Maurice Unis, and some of his associates, for over 25 years. His understanding of technical rebuilding and piano restoration is, in a word, 'unparalleled.' "**
— Mark Westcott, Portland, Oregon
Master of Music, Eastman School of Music
Winner of Five International Competitions, including Third Prize
Van Cliburn International Piano Competition, 1969.

"Your masterful approach to tuning, voicing, regulating, and restoring heirloom Mason & Hamlin and Steinway grands recalls another bygone era of the Golden Age of Pianos. Bravo!"
— Eric Himy, Washington, DC
Master of Music, *The Juilliard School*, New York.
Winner of numerous piano competitions, including the
Gold Medal at the 1988 *World Piano Competition*

CLASSIC 𝄞 PIANOS

A PASSION FOR PIANOS
3003 SE Milwaukie Avenue   Portland, Oregon 97202   Telephone: (503) 239-9969
www.classicportland.com

(This article is adapted from Chapter 5, "Buying a Used Piano," of The Piano Book, Fourth Edition, *by Larry Fine. Steve Brady updated the depreciation schedule and used-piano pricing information. Before reading this article, be sure to read "Piano Buying Basics"—especially the section "New or Used?"—elsewhere in this publication.)*

WHAT TO BUY:
A Historical Overview

1700–1880

The piano was invented about 1700 by Bartolomeo Cristofori, a harpsichord maker in Padua, Italy. Cristofori replaced the plucking-quill action of the harpsichord, which can pluck only with unvarying force and hence unvarying volume of sound, with a newly designed striking-hammer action, whose force could be precisely controlled by the player. Thus was born the *gravicembalo col piano e forte* (keyboard instrument with soft and loud). This name was later shortened to *pianoforte*, then *fortepiano*, and finally just *piano*. In the 1700s the new instrument, made mostly by craftsmen in their shops, spread quietly through upper-class Europe. A number of different forms of piano action and structure were invented, such as the Viennese action, the English action, the square piano, and so on. Replicas of early

fortepianos are popular among certain musicians who prefer to play the music of that period on the original instruments for which that music was written.

In the 1800s the piano spread more quickly through the middle classes, and across the ocean to North America. Riding along with the Industrial Revolution, piano-making evolved from a craft into an industry. Many important changes took place during the 19th century: The upright piano was invented; the modern grand piano action was invented, incorporating the best aspects of the previous rival actions; the cast-iron plate was invented, vastly strengthening the structure and allowing the strings to be stretched at a higher tension, thus increasing the power and volume of sound; the range of the instrument was extended from about five octaves to the present seven-plus octaves; and, toward the end of the century, the square piano died out, leaving just grands of various sizes and the full-size upright. By 1880, most of these changes were in place; the pianos made today are not very different from those of a hundred or more years ago.

In your search for a piano, you're unlikely to run across instruments made before 1880, with two exceptions. The square piano, or square grand, as it is sometimes called, looks like a rectangular box on legs (see illustration), and was very

popular as a home piano during the 19th century. Its ornate Victorian case makes very pretty furniture—but it also makes a terrible musical instrument for 21st-century playing and practicing. Tuning, servicing, and repair are difficult and expensive, very few piano technicians know how to do it, and parts are hard to come by. Even at their best, these instruments are unsuitable to practice on, even for beginners.

Another piano to avoid is a type of upright made primarily in Europe from the middle to the end of the 19th century. The dampers on these piano are positioned *above* the hammers and actuated by wires in *front* of the action—the reverse of a modern-day upright. This overdamper system has been nicknamed the "birdcage action" because the damper wires form an enclosure that resembles a bird cage. Besides being very difficult to tune and service through the "bird cage," these pianos are usually so worn out that they won't hold a tuning longer than about ten seconds, and their actions work erratically at best. Many of these pianos were cheaply made to begin with, but they often have ornate cabinets and fancy features,

Cristofori Piano, circa 1720

Square Grand, 19th Century

<table>
<tr><td colspan="2">Some of the well-regarded piano brand names of the 1900–1930 period, in alphabetical order.</td></tr>
</table>

Apollo	Jewett
Baldwin	Kimball
Bechstein	Wm. Knabe
Blüthner	Krakauer
Bösendorfer	Lester
A.B. Chase	Mason & Hamlin
Chickering	McPhail
Emerson	Henry F. Miller
Everett	Packard
Haines Bros.	Sohmer
Hallet & Davis	Steinert
Hamilton	Steinway & Sons
Heintzman	Chas. Stieff
Hume	Vose & Sons
Ibach	Weber
Ivers & Pond	Wing

such as candlestick holders, that make them attractive to antique collectors.

Although most pianos you'll come across made prior to 1880 will have little practical or financial value, the few that have historical value are best left to specialists and collectors who can properly conserve them.

1880–1900

The years from 1880 to about 1900 were a transition period, as some old styles were slow to fade. But some pianos from this period may be suitable for you. A piano with only 85 instead of 88 notes may be perfectly satisfactory if you don't anticipate ever needing the highest three notes. The resale value of such a piano may be slightly lower than its modern equivalent, but so should be the price you pay for it. A piano with an old-style cast-iron plate that, while extending the full length of the piano, leaves the pinblock exposed to view is, for all practical purposes, just as structurally sound as one in which the plate covers the pinblock.

Avoid, however, the so-called "three-quarter-plate" piano, in which the plate ends just short of the pinblock. These pianos have a high rate of structural failure. Pianos with actions that are only very slight variations on modern actions are fine as long as the parts are not obsolete and absolutely unobtainable.

Most pianos this old will need a considerable amount of repair and restoration to be fully usable, so the best candidates from this period will be those instruments that justify the expense involved, such as Steinway, Mason & Hamlin, Bechstein, and Blüthner grands, or, in rare instances, a more ordinary brand that has been exceptionally well preserved. With occasional exceptions, the vast majority of uprights and cheaper grands that survive from this period are not worth repairing, unless for historical or sentimental reasons.

1900–1930

The period from about 1900 to 1930 was the heyday of piano manufacturing in America. The piano held an important place in the national economy and as a symbol of culture and social status. Hundreds of small firms turned out millions of pianos during this time; in fact, far more pianos were made annually then than are made today. If you're shopping for a used full-size upright or a grand, some of the pianos you'll see will probably be from this period. Smaller pianos weren't introduced until later. Although some well-preserved instruments from this period may be usable as is, most will need rebuilding, or at least reconditioning.

Those in the market for a used piano often ask for recommendations of specific brands from this period. This is a problem, because the present condition of the piano, the kind of use you'll be giving it, and the cost of the piano and repairs are far more important factors than the brand when considering the purchase of an old piano. Even a piano of the best brand, if poorly maintained or badly repaired, can be an unwise purchase. Time and wear are great levelers, and a piano of only average quality that has not been used much may be a much better buy. Nevertheless, since that answer never satisfies anyone, I offer a list (see box) of some of the brand names of the period that were most highly regarded. Please note that this list, which is by no means complete—or universally agreed on—applies only to pianos made before about 1930, since in many cases the same names were later applied to entirely different, usually lower, quality standards.

During this period, a large percentage of the pianos made were outfitted with pneumatically driven player-piano systems. When these mechanisms eventually fell into disrepair, they were often removed. Although there is still a small group of technicians and hobbyists dedicated to restoring these fascinating relics of the past, in most cases it is not economically practical to do so except for historical or sentimental reasons.

GRAY-MARKET PIANOS

If you're looking for a piano made within the last few decades, there is usually a plentiful supply of used Yamaha and Kawai pianos originally made for the Japanese market. However, there has been some controversy about them. Sometimes called "gray-market" pianos, these instruments were originally sold to families and schools in Japan, and some years later were discarded in favor of new pianos. There being little market for these used pianos in Japan—the Japanese are said to have a cultural bias against buying any used goods—enterprising businesspeople buy them up, restore them to varying degrees, and export them to the U.S. and other countries, where they are sold by dealers of used pianos at a fraction of the price of a new Yamaha or Kawai. Used Korean pianos are available under similar circumstances. (Note: The term "gray market" is used somewhat erroneously to describe these pianos. They are used instruments, not new, and there is nothing illegal about buying and selling them.)

Yamaha has taken a public stand warning against the purchase of a used Yamaha piano made for the Japanese market. When Yamaha first began exporting pianos to the United States, the company found that some pianos sent to areas of the U.S. with very dry indoor climates, such as parts of the desert Southwest and places that were bitterly cold in the winter, would develop problems in a short period of time: tuning pins would become loose, soundboards and bridges would crack, and glue joints would come apart. To protect against this happening, Yamaha began to season the wood for destination: a low moisture content for pianos bound for the U.S., which has the greatest extremes of dryness; a higher moisture content for Europe; and the highest moisture content for Japan, which is relatively humid. The gray-market pianos, Yamaha says, having been seasoned for the relatively humid Japanese climate, will not stand up to our dryness. The company claims to have received many calls from dissatisfied owners of these pianos, but cannot help them because the warranty, in addition to having expired, is effective only in the country in which the piano was originally sold when new.

My own research has led me to believe that while there is some basis for Yamaha's concerns, their warnings are exaggerated. There probably is a little greater chance, statistically, that these pianos will develop problems in conditions of extreme dryness than will Yamahas seasoned for and sold in the U.S. However, thousands of gray-market pianos have been sold by hundreds of dealers throughout the country, in all types of climates, for many years, and I haven't found evidence of anything close to an epidemic of problems with them. In mild and moderate climates, reported problems are rare. There are, however, some precautions that should be taken.

These pianos are available to dealers in a wide variety of ages and conditions. The better dealers will sell only those in good condition made since about the mid-1980s. In some cases, the dealers or their suppliers will recondition or partially rebuild the pianos before offering them for sale. Make sure to get a warranty that runs for at least five years, as any problems will usually show up within that period if they are going to show up at all. Finally, be sure to use some kind of humidity-control system in situations of unusual dryness. Remember that air-conditioning, as well as heating, can cause indoor dryness.

It's not always possible to determine visually whether a particular instrument was made for the U.S. or the Japanese market, as some original differences may have been altered by the supplier. The dealer may know, and Yamaha has a utility on its website (**www.yamaha.com/pianoserials/index.asp**) that will look up the origin of a particular Yamaha piano by serial number.

1930–1960

The rise of radio and talking pictures in the 1920s competed with pianos for the public's attention and weakened the piano industry, and the Great Depression decimated it. During the Depression, many piano makers, both good and bad, went bankrupt, and their names were bought up by the surviving companies. Sometimes the defunct company's designs continued to be used, but often only the name lived on. Still, piano making in the 1930s, though reduced in quantity from earlier years, was in most cases of a similar quality.

To revive the depressed piano market in the mid-1930s, piano makers came up with a new idea: the small piano. Despite the fact that small pianos, both vertical and grand, are musically inferior to larger ones, the public decided that spinets, consoles, and small grands were preferable because they looked better in the smaller homes and apartments of the day. There has always been a furniture aspect to the piano, but the degree to which piano makers catered to that aspect from the mid-'30s onward marked a revolution in piano marketing.

During World War II, many piano factories were commandeered to make airplane wings and other wartime products, and what piano making there was fell somewhat in quality because of a lack of good raw materials and skilled labor. Things changed for the better in the postwar period, and you'll sometimes find used pianos from this period, still in reasonably good condition or needing some reconditioning, from such brands as Steinway, Baldwin, Mason & Hamlin, Sohmer, Everett, Knabe, and Wurlitzer.

1960–Present

In the 1960s, the Japanese began exporting pianos to the U.S. in large numbers. Although at first they had

some difficulty building pianos to the demands of our climate, by the mid- to late-'60s their quality was so high and their prices so low that they threatened to put all U.S. makers out of business. In response, most of the mid-priced American makers cheapened their product to compete. As a result, the 20 years from about 1965 to 1985 are considered, from a quality standpoint, to be a low point in U.S. piano manufacturing. In any case, the Americans were unable to compete. The international takeover of the U.S. piano market accelerated in the 1980s as the Koreans began to export here, and by 1985 all but a few U.S. piano makers had gone out of business. As in an earlier period, some of their brand names were purchased and later used by others.

Please see the article "The New-Piano Market Today" for more information on the post-1960 period.

A used piano made within the past few decades can often be a very good deal, as these instruments may still show very few signs of age and wear, but with a price far below that of a new piano. The most recently made used pianos may even come with a warranty that is still in effect. Also, the influx of new, low-priced, Chinese- and Indonesian-made pianos has driven down the price of used pianos, in some cases rather substantially, as the imports offer the opportunity to buy a new piano for a price only a little higher than a decent used one previously commanded. If you're considering a piano from this period, you may wish to read applicable articles in this publication about new pianos, as well as current and past editions of *The Piano Book*. See also the accompanying article about so-called gray-market pianos.

Though in each decade both good and bad pianos have been produced, and each piano must be judged on its own merits, this brief historical

overview may give you some idea of what to expect to see as you shop for a used piano. You can determine the age of a piano by finding its serial number (*The Piano Book* tells how) and looking it up in the *Pierce Piano Atlas* (www.piercepianoatlas.com), or perhaps by asking a piano dealer or technician to look it up for you.

How to Find a Used Piano

Finding a used piano essentially involves networking, a concept very much in vogue these days. Some networking can be done by computer, and some with old-fashioned phone calls and shoe leather. Here are some of your options—you may be able to think of others.

- ■ *Contact piano technicians, rebuilders, and used-piano dealers*

People who service pianos often have customers who want to sell their instruments. Some technicians also restore pianos for sale in their shops. Contacting these technicians or visiting their shops is a good way to acquaint yourself with local market conditions, to better understand what's involved in piano restoration, and to see an interesting slice of life in your community you might not otherwise encounter. If you decide to buy from a technician, you may pay more than you would a private party, but you'll have the peace of mind of knowing that the piano has been checked over, repaired, and comes with a warranty. Even though you trust the seller, it's a good idea to hire an independent technician to inspect the piano before purchase, just as you would if the piano were being sold by a private party, because even the best technicians can differ in their professional abilities and opinions.

■ *Visit dealers of new pianos*

New-piano dealers take used pianos in trade for new ones all the time, and need to dispose of them to recoup the trade-in allowance they gave on the new piano. Although many of the trade-ins will be older pianos, it's quite common for a customer to trade in a piano purchased only a few years earlier for a bigger or better model, leaving a nearly new piano for you to buy at a substantial discount on its price when new. Again, you may pay more than you would from a private party—usually 20 to 30 percent more—but it may be difficult to find something like this from a private party, and the dealer will likely also give some sort of warranty. Some of the best deals I've seen have been acquired this way. If you're also considering the option of buying a new piano, then you'll be able to explore both options with a single visit. On the other hand, sometimes dealers advertise used pianos just to get customers into the store, where they can be sold on a new piano. The used piano advertised may be overpriced, or may no longer be available. When you have a used piano inspected, make sure the technician you hire owes no favors to the dealer who's selling it.

■ *Shopping via the Internet*

The best way to use the Internet to shop for a used piano is to look for sellers, both commercial and non-commercial, within driving distance of your home. That way, you can more easily try out the piano, develop a face-to-face relationship with the seller, and get a better sense of whether or not you want to do business with them. Craigslist (www.craigslist.org), though not a piano-specific site, seems to have become the preferred classified-ad site for this purpose, as it's both free and is organized by city. If you travel frequently, you should check out sellers in other cities, too—easy to do on Craigslist. Other popular piano classified-ad sites include **www .pianoworld.com** (which also has extensive forums for exchanging information and getting answers to your questions), **www.pianomart.com** (smartly organized for easy searching), and **www.pianobroker.com**. These sites either charge a monthly fee to list or a small commission upon sale, but are free to buyers.

You'll also find pianos for sale on the Internet auction site **eBay**. Search on a variety of keywords, as each keyword will bring up a different group of pianos for sale. This can be frustrating, as either too broad or too specific a search term may yield unsatisfactory results. The bidding process generally provides a window of time during which you can contact the seller for more information, see the piano, and have it inspected before placing a bid. This is definitely not a good way to buy a piano unless you have the opportunity to first try out the piano and have it inspected. On both eBay and the classified-ad sites mentioned above, many listings that appear to be non-commercial will actually turn out to have been placed by commercial sellers, who may have many more pianos for sale than the one in the ad you answered.

The website of the Piano Technicians Guild (www.ptg.org) has a listing of dealer websites and other resources that may be useful in locating used or restored pianos. If your situation is such that finding a local source of used pianos is unlikely, one reliable source that ships nationwide is Rick Jones Pianos in Beltsville, Maryland (www .rickjonespianos.com).

If you're thinking of making a long-distance purchase, the precautions mentioned in the section "**Shopping Long-Distance via the Internet**," in the article "Piano Buying Basics," bear repeating: First, take into account the cost of long-distance shipping and consider whether it's really worth it. If buying from a commercial source, find out as much as you can about the dealer. Get references. If you haven't actually seen the piano, get pictures of it. Hire a technician in the seller's area to inspect the piano and ask the technician about a commercial seller's reputation. Make sure the dealer has experience in arranging long-distance moves, and uses a mover that specializes in pianos. Find out who will be responsible for tuning and adjusting the piano in your home, and for repairing any defects or dings in the finish. Get the details of any warranty, especially who is responsible for paying the return freight if the piano is defective. Find out how payment is to be made in a way that protects both parties.

■ *Non-Internet Techniques*

In this age of the Internet, it's important not to forget older, more conventional methods of networking that still work, such as placing and answering classified print ads in local newspapers and want-ad booklets; and posting and answering notices on bulletin boards anywhere people congregate, such as houses of worship, community centers, laundromats, etc. Other, more aggressive, techniques include contacting movers and storage warehouses to see if they have any pianos abandoned by their owners; attending auctions; contacting attorneys and others who handle the disposition of estates; and just plain old asking around among coworkers, friends, and acquaintances.

■ *Obtaining a Piano from a Friend or Relative*

It's nice when pianos remain in the family. I got my piano that way. But pianos purchased from friends and relatives or received as gifts are as likely as any others to have expensive problems you should know about. It's very hard to refuse a gift, and perhaps embarrassing to hire a piano technician to inspect it before you accept it, but for your own protection you should insist on doing so. Otherwise you may spend a lot of money to move a "gift" you could have done without.

Which of these routes to finding a used piano you end up following will depend on your situation and what you're looking for. If you have a lot of time and transportation is no problem, you may get the best deal by shopping around among private owners or in out-of-the-way places. If you're busy or without a car but have money to spend, it may be more convenient to shop among piano technicians, rebuilders, or dealers, who may be able to show you several pianos at the same time and spare you from worrying about future repair costs and problems. If you travel a lot to other cities or have few piano resources in your local area, the Internet can be a big help in locating an appropriate commercial or non-commercial source far away. (See the ads in this publication for movers that specialize in long-distance piano moving.) The best route also depends on where you live, as some communities may have a brisk trade in used pianos among private owners but few rebuilding shops, or vice versa, or have an abundance of old uprights but few grands.

Buying a Restored Piano

Three terms are often used in discussions of piano restoration work: *repair*, *reconditioning*, and *rebuilding*. There are no precise definitions of these terms, and any particular job may contain elements of more than one of them. It's therefore very important, when having restoration

work done on your piano or when buying a piano on which such work has been done, to find out exactly what jobs have been, or will be, carried out. "This piano has been reconditioned" or "I'll rebuild this piano" are not sufficient answers. One technician's rebuilding may be another's reconditioning.

Repair jobs generally involve fixing isolated broken parts, such as a broken hammer, a missing string, or an improperly working pedal. That is, a repair does not necessarily involve upgrading the condition of the instrument as a whole, but addresses only specific broken or improperly adjusted parts.

Reconditioning always involves a general upgrading of the entire piano, but with as little actual replacement of parts as possible. For instance, reconditioning an old upright might include resurfacing the hammer felt (instead of replacing the hammers) and twisting (instead of replacing) the bass strings to improve their tone. However, definitions of *reconditioning* can vary widely: Many technicians would consider the replacement of hammers, tuning pins, and strings to be part of a reconditioning job in which more extensive work is either not needed or not cost-effective; others would call such work a partial rebuild.

Rebuilding is the most complete of the three levels of restoration. Ideally, *rebuilding* means putting the piano into "like new" condition. In practice, however, it may involve much less, depending on the needs and value of the particular instrument, the amount of money available, and the scrupulousness of the rebuilder. Restringing the piano and replacing the pinblock in a grand, as well as repairing or replacing the soundboard, would typically be parts of a rebuilding job. In the action, rebuilding would include replacing

Restoring the piano case to like-new condition

the hammer heads, damper felts, and key bushings, and replacing or completely overhauling other sets of parts as well. Refinishing the piano case is also generally part of the rebuilding process. Because of the confusion over the definitions of these terms, sometimes the term *remanufacturing* is used to distinguish the most complete rebuilding job possible—including replacement of

the soundboard—from a lesser "rebuilding." However, there is no substitute for requesting from the technician an itemization of the work performed.

When considering buying a rebuilt piano, or having a piano rebuilt, particularly an expensive one, the rebuilder's experience level should count heavily in your decision. The complete rebuilding of a piano requires many dissimilar skills. The skills required for installing a soundboard, for example, are very different from those required for installing a new set of hammers or for regulating the action. Mastering all of these skills can take a very long time. In a sense, you should be shopping for the rebuilder as much as for the piano.

Many rebuilders contract out portions of the job, particularly the refinishing of the piano's case, to others who have special expertise. Although this has always been so, more

recently groups of technicians, each with his or her own business and shop, have been openly advertising their close, long-term collaboration with one another on rebuilding jobs. In a typical collaboration of this type, one person might rebuild the strung back or soundbox (soundboard, bridges, pinblock, strings, tuning pins, cast-iron plate); another would

Gluing a new soundboard into the rim of a grand piano

A rebuilt grand piano action with new hammers is ready for regulating and voicing.

rebuild the action and do the final musical finishing, such as regulating and voicing; and the third would refinish the case. Collaboration of this kind is a positive development, as it means that each technician does only what he or she does best, resulting in a better job for the customer. But make sure you know with whom you are contracting or from whom you are buying, and which technician is responsible for making things right if problems arise.

It may occur to you that you could save a lot of money by buying an unrestored piano and having a technician completely restore it, rather than buying the completely restored piano from the technician. This is often true. But the results of a rebuilding job tend to be musically uncertain. That is, if you are particular in your taste for tone and touch, you may or may not care for how the instrument ultimately turns out. For that reason, especially if a lot of money is involved, you might be better off letting the technician make the extra profit in return for taking the risk.

"Vintage" . . . or New?

"Vintage" pianos are those made during the golden years of piano-making in the United States—roughly, from 1880 to World War II. More specifically, the term usually refers to the Steinway and Mason & Hamlin pianos made during that period, though it's occasionally applied to other great American makes as well. In the last few decades the demand for these pianos, and consequently their prices, has mushroomed due to a (until recently) strong economy, increased entrepreneurial activity on the part of rebuilders and piano brokers, allegations by rebuilders and others that today's new pianos are not as well made as the older ones were, and the purchase of many older

---

The following is a list of the tasks that might comprise a fairly complete rebuilding of a grand piano. Any particular job may be either more or less extensive than shown here, depending on the needs and value of the instrument and other factors, but this list can serve as a guide. See also *The Piano Book* for information about specific rebuilding issues pertaining to Steinway and Mason & Hamlin pianos.

Notice that the restoration can be divided into three main parts: the soundbox or resonating unit, the action, and the cabinet. The *soundbox* (also known as the *strung back* or *belly*) includes the soundboard, ribs, bridges, strings, pinblock, tuning pins, plate, and the structural parts of the case; the *action* includes the keyframe and action frame, keys and keytops, hammers, dampers, trapwork, and all other moving action parts; the *cabinet* includes cosmetic repair and refinishing of the case and of the nonstructural cabinet parts and hardware. Note that the damper parts that contact the strings are restored with the soundbox, whereas the damper underlever action is treated with the rest of the action.

There is very little overlap among the three types of work; each of the three parts could be performed alone or at different times, as technical conditions permit and/or financial considerations require. In a typical complete rebuilding job, restoration of the soundbox might comprise 45 percent of the cost, the action 30 percent, and the cabinet 25 percent, though these percentages will vary according to the particulars of the job.

Soundbox or resonating unit

- Replace or repair soundboard, refinish, install new soundboard decal (if not replacing soundboard: shim soundboard cracks, reglue ribs as necessary, refinish, install new soundboard decal)
- Replace pinblock
- Replace bridges or bridge caps
- Replace or ream agraffes, restore capo-bar bearing surface
- Refinish plate, paint lettering, replace understring felts
- Replace strings and tuning pins, tune to pitch
- Replace damper felts, refinish damper heads, regulate dampers

Action

- Replace hammers, shanks, and flanges
- Replace or overhaul wippen/repetition assemblies
- Replace backchecks
- Replace front-rail key bushings
- Replace balance-rail key bushings or key buttons
- Replace or clean keytops
- Replace key-end felts
- Clean keys
- Clean and refelt keyframe
- Replace let-off felts or buttons
- Clean and, if necessary, repair action frame
- Regulate action, voice
- Overhaul or replace damper underlever action and damper guide rail
- Overhaul pedal lyre and trapwork, regulate

Cabinet

- Repair music desk, legs, other cabinet parts, as needed
- Repair loose or missing veneer
- Strip and refinish exterior; refinish bench to match piano
- Buff and lacquer solid-brass hardware, replate plated hardware

---

Steinways by Steinway & Sons itself for rebuilding in its factory.

What makes these vintage pianos so alluring? Many musicians and technicians believe that these instruments, when rebuilt, sound and play better than new pianos. However, no one knows for sure why this

---

should be so, since most of the components in the piano are replaced during rebuilding. Some point to the fact that Steinway operated its own plate foundry until about World War II, afterward using a commercial plate foundry (which it now owns). Because this radical change in the manufacture of such an important component roughly corresponds with the end of the vintage era, and because the plate is one of the few original parts to survive the rebuilding process, some speculate that it holds the key to the difference. Others say it has to do with changes in the quality of the wood available to Steinway and other companies. Still others say it wasn't any single thing, but rather a combination of many fortuitous factors, including extremely skilled and talented craftsmen, that enabled these companies to make such special pianos during that period, but allegedly not afterward (though that doesn't explain why the rebuilt ones from that period should be better).

Steinway & Sons, for its part, disputes the entire idea that older Steinways are better, dismissing it as a romantic notion spread by purveyors of those pianos in their own financial interest. The company says it has done extensive testing of both plates and woods, and the idea that the older plates and woods were better has no scientific basis. It says it has also carefully inspected hundreds of older Steinways at its factory rebuilding facility, which is the largest Steinway rebuilding facility in the world, and finds no evidence that the older pianos were built better than today's—in fact, it believes that just the opposite is true. Steinway acknowledges that some pianists may prefer the sound of specific older pianos for subjective artistic reasons, but says that those considering the purchase of a restored, older instrument should do so to save money, not to seek better quality.

For more discussion of this topic, and of specific technical issues applicable to the rebuilding of a Steinway or Mason & Hamlin, please see *The Piano Book*.

How Much Is It Worth?

Three methods are typically used by professional appraisers to appraise pianos and many other goods: fair market value, depreciation, and idealized value minus the cost of restoration.

Fair market value is determined by comparing the piano being appraised to recent actual selling prices of other pianos of like brand, model, age, and condition. In the chart "Prices of Used Pianos," I and my staff have attempted to approximate the fair market value of pianos of various types, ages, and conditions, though I stress that we do not have enough data to do more than make rough estimates.

Note that insurance appraisals are often for "replacement cost." This is the cost of a *new* piano of the same or comparable make and model, not the fair market value of the used one.

A *depreciation* schedule, an example of which is provided here, shows how much a used piano is worth as a percentage of the actual selling price of a new piano of comparable quality (or of the same brand and model, if still in production and of the same quality).

Idealized value minus the cost of restoration is the difference between the cost of a rebuilt piano and the cost to restore the unrebuilt one to like-new condition. As an example, if a rebuilt piano of the same or comparable model costs $15,000, and it would cost $10,000 to restore your piano to like-new condition, then according to this method your unrebuilt piano is currently worth $5,000.

These three methods of appraising will typically yield three very different values. Which you choose to use will depend to some extent on your reason for having the piano appraised (buying, selling, insuring, etc.). Professional appraisers will sometimes use all three methods, then average them to obtain a final value. (See my blog at **www.pianobuyer.com** for additional comments on the subject of determining a piano's value.)

When considering a used piano being sold by a private, non-commercial seller, keep in mind that many such sellers really have no firm idea of how much their piano is worth, and have made up something based on little more than a wish. Therefore, don't let a high asking price keep you from making a more reasonable offer. Ask the seller how they arrived at their asking price. If you can back up your offer with your own technician's appraisal (including a list of the things that need to be fixed), credible listings of similar pianos, or other evidence of the piano's true value, you stand a good chance of getting the piano at or close to your price.

Depreciation Schedule for Pianos

There is no universally agreed-on depreciation schedule for pianos, but one such schedule is provided above. The percentages given represent what the unrestored, used piano is worth relative to the actual selling price today of a new piano comparable in quality to the used one in question. The values computed are meant to reflect what the piano would sell for between *private, non-commercial parties*. We suggest adding 20 to 30 percent to the computed value when the piano is being sold by a dealer unrestored, but with a warranty. These figures are intended only as guidelines, reflecting our general observations of the market. "Worse," "Average," and "Better" refer to the condition of the used piano for its age. A separate chart is given for Steinway pianos. Other fine pianos, such as Mason & Hamlin, may command prices in between the regular and Steinway figures.

Prices of Used Pianos

The valuation of used pianos is difficult. Prices of used pianos vary wildly,

APPRECIATE OR DEPRECIATE?

Some piano manufacturers market their instruments as "investments" and tout their potential for appreciation in value. If that's the case, then why a *depreciation* schedule? Do pianos appreciate or depreciate?

It depends on how you look at it. Imagine parking a sum of money in a savings account earning 2 percent interest at a time when inflation is at 3 percent. Each year, the balance in the account grows . . . and *loses* purchasing power. This is something like the situation with pianos. After a large initial drop in value during the first five to ten years (because, unless given an incentive to buy used, most people would prefer a new piano), used pianos lose value in comparison with similar new ones at about 1.5 to 2 percent per year. However, because the price of *everything* (including pianos) is rising in price at 3 or 3.5 percent per year (the rate of inflation), the value of your used piano will appear to *rise* by 1 to 2 percent per year (the difference between the depreciation and the inflation).

Why do we figure depreciation from a comparable new piano instead of figuring appreciation from the original price of the used one? Theoretically, it could be done either way. But the price of a comparable new piano is easier to look up—one might have to do a lot of research to find out what grandma paid for her piano. And the price of the new piano embodies all the inflation that has occurred between the original purchase of the used piano and the present, avoiding the trouble of having to look up the change in the cost of living during that time. The case is even stronger for using this method with foreign-made pianos: Tying the value of a used piano to the cost of a comparable new one makes it unnecessary to calculate the changes in the currency exchange rate—and sometimes changes in the currency itself!—that have occurred since the used piano was new.

Figuring depreciation from a comparable new piano is not without its own problems, however. With so many piano brands of the past now defunct or made to entirely different standards (usually in China), the task of figuring out what constitutes a "comparable" new piano can sometimes be formidable, if not impossible.

depending on local economies, supply and demand, and the cosmetics and playing condition of the instrument at hand, including the amount and quality of any restoration work done. As if this weren't enough, it's almost a certainty that no two piano technicians or piano salespeople would return exactly the same verdict on any given piano's value. Art being what it is, beauty is in the eye and ear of the potential purchaser, and values are very much subjective.

These disclaimers aside, we've tried to assemble some used-piano values as general guidelines for shoppers. We asked a number of knowledgeable piano industry professionals to give their opinions of prices for used pianos in each of our categories, then reconciled their varied responses to produce a price range for each category. We also consulted the online service Pianomart.com, though the prices listed there are asking prices, not selling prices. The chart is organized by categories of vertical and grand piano broken down by age (pre-1950 and 1950–1980), quality (Average, Better, Best), and condition (Worse, Average, Better, Reconditioned, and Rebuilt). For prices of pianos made since 1980, we suggest you use the depreciation schedule accompanying this article.

The price ranges given reflect the wide possibilities a buyer faces in the used-piano market. At the low end of each range is a price one might find in a poor economy or a

"buyer's market," where supply exceeds demand. At the high end, the prices are consistent with both a better economy and a higher demand for the type of instrument indicated. In some categories, the prices we received from our sources varied all over the map, and we had to use a considerable amount of editorial discretion to produce price ranges that were not so broad as to be useless as guidelines, and to retain at least a modicum of internal consistency in the chart. For that reason, you should expect to find some markets or situations in which prices higher or lower than those given here are normal or appropriate.

The prices given here for pianos that are not reconditioned or rebuilt (those labeled Worse, Average, Better) are the price ranges you might expect to find when buying pianos *from private owners.* The Reconditioned and Rebuilt categories represent prices you might encounter when shopping for such pianos *at piano stores or from piano technicians,* with a warranty given. In some cases we have omitted the Rebuilt price because we would not expect rebuilding to be cost-effective for pianos of that general age and type. In every case, prices assume the least expensive style and finish; prices for pianos with fancier cabinets, exotic veneers, inlays, and so forth, could be much higher.

Quality

"Best brands" include Steinway, Mason & Hamlin, and the very best European makes, such as Bechstein, Blüthner, and Bösendorfer. "Better brands" include the well-regarded older names mentioned in the accompanying article for the pre-1930 period, such as Knabe and Chickering; and names such as Baldwin, Everett, Kawai, Sohmer, Yamaha, and others of similar quality for the 1950–1980 period. "Average brands" are pretty much everything else.

DEPRECIATION SCHEDULE			
Age in Years	Percent of New Value		
	Worse	*Average*	*Better*
1	75	80	83
2	72	77	80
3	69	74	77
5	63	68	71
10	52	57	60
15	43	48	51
20	36	41	44
25	29	34	37
Verticals only			
30	22	27	30
35–70	15	20	23
Grands only			
30–70	25	30	33
Steinways			
1	75	80	83
2	72	77	80
3	70	75	78
5	66	71	74
10	58	63	66
15	50	55	58
20	42	47	50
25	34	39	42
Verticals only			
30	28	33	36
35–70	25	30	33
Grands only			
30	31	36	39
50	30	35	38
70	28	33	36

Condition

Worse, Average, and Better refer to the condition of the piano in comparison to the amount of wear and tear one would expect from the piano's age. However, even Worse pianos should be playable and serviceable. Note that because many buyers are quite conscious of a piano's appearance, pianos that are in good shape musically but in poor shape cosmetically will often sell at a price more consistent with the Worse range than with a higher one. This offers an opportunity for the less furniture-conscious buyer to obtain a bargain.

PRICES OF USED PIANOS (US$)				
	Private Seller			Dealer	
	Worse	Average	Better	Reconditioned	Rebuilt
Vertical, pre-1950, average brand	0–300	300–750	600–1,000	1,000–1,500	N/A
Vertical, pre-1950, better brand	150–500	400–1,000	700–1,500	1,200–2,000	N/A
Vertical, pre-1950, best brand	500–1,000	1,000–3,000	2,000–5,000	3,000–6,000	10,000–16,000
Vertical, 1950–1980, average brand	200–600	400–1,000	1,000–1,500	1,200–2,500	N/A
Vertical, 1950–1980, better brand	400–800	700–1,500	1,000–2,500	2,000–4,500	N/A
Vertical, 1950–1980, best brand	700–2,000	1,500–2,500	3,000–5,000	4,000–7,000	7,000–10,000
Vertical, 1980–	Use Depreciation Schedule				
Grand, pre-1950, average brand, 5'	0–500	700–1,500	1,000–2,500	1,500–3,500	N/A
Grand, pre-1950, average brand, 6'	500–1,200	1,500–2,000	2,000–3,000	3,500–4,500	N/A
Grand, pre-1950, average brand, 7'	800–1,500	1,500–3,500	3,000–5,000	4,000–7,000	8,000–10,000
Grand, pre-1950, better brand, 5'	500–1,000	2,000–3,000	2,500–4,000	5,000–8,000	N/A
Grand, pre-1950, better brand, 6'	1,000–2,500	2,500–4,000	4,000–7,000	7,000–10,000	12,000–18,000
Grand, pre-1950, better brand, 7'	1,800–3,500	3,500–7,000	6,000–10,000	8,000–15,000	18,000–30,000
Grand, pre-1950, best brand, 5'	3,000–6,000	6,000–9,000	8,000–15,000	15,000–20,000	15,000–25,000
Grand, pre-1950, best brand, 6'	5,000–8,000	7,000–15,000	12,000–20,000	15,000–28,000	28,000–50,000
Grand, pre-1950, best brand, 7'	7,000–10,000	12,000–18,000	20,000–35,000	20,000–40,000	35,000–65,000
Grand, 1950–1980, average brand, 5'	500–1,200	1,500–2,500	2,000–4,000	3,000–5,000	N/A
Grand, 1950–1980, average brand, 6'	800–2,000	2,000–3,000	3,000–5,000	3,500–7,000	N/A
Grand, 1950–1980, average brand, 7'	1,500–2,500	2,500–4,000	4,000–7,000	4,000–8,000	8,000–12,000
Grand, 1950–1980, better brand, 5'	800–2,000	2,000–4,000	2,500–5,000	5,000–9,000	N/A
Grand, 1950–1980, better brand, 6'	1,500–3,000	2,500–5,000	4,000–9,000	8,000–12,000	12,000–22,000
Grand, 1950–1980, better brand, 7'	3,000–6,000	5,000–10,000	8,000–15,000	10,000–20,000	15,000–30,000
Grand, 1950–1980, best brand, 5'	4,000–7,000	7,000–10,000	9,000–18,000	16,000–21,000	17,000–25,000
Grand, 1950–1980, best brand, 6'	6,000–10,000	8,000–15,000	12,000–20,000	20,000–28,000	28,000–50,000
Grand, 1950–1980, best brand, 7'	8,000–12,000	14,000–20,000	18,000–30,000	20,000–40,000	35,000–65,000
Grand, 1980–	Use Depreciation Schedule				

For a discussion of the definitions of *reconditioned* and *rebuilt*, please see the section "Buying a Restored Piano" in this article. **For the purposes of this chart, however, we have adopted the requirement that a piano has not been *rebuilt* unless its pinblock has been replaced, and that a piano that has been restrung, but without a new pinblock, is considered to have been *reconditioned*.** Note that these definitions are not precise, and that both the quality and the quantity of the work can vary greatly, depending on the needs of the instrument and the capabilities of the restorer. These variations should be taken into account when determining the piano's value.

Inspect, Inspect, Inspect

In closing, I'd like to remind you that your best protection against buyer's remorse is having the piano inspected by a piano technician prior to purchasing it, particularly if the piano is more than ten years old. Sometimes it will be sufficient to speak to the seller's technician about the piano, if he or she has serviced it regularly and has reason to believe that he or she will continue servicing it under your ownership. However, in most situations, you'll be better off hiring your own technician. You can find a list of Registered Piano Technicians in your area on the website of the Piano Technicians Guild, www.ptg.org.

More Information

If you're serious about buying a used piano, additional information in *The Piano Book* may be useful to you, including:

- How to remove the outer cabinet parts to look inside the piano

- How to do a preliminary inspection of a piano to rule out those that are not worth hiring a technician to inspect, including an extensive checklist of potential problem areas

- A discussion of issues that frequently come up in regard to the rebuilding of Steinway pianos

- A complete list of older Steinway models, from 1853 to the present

- How to locate the serial number of a piano

- A list of manufacturing dates and serial numbers for Steinway pianos.

The American Heritage of

The craftsmanship that makes the Knabe one of the world's best pianos is not the acquisition of one generation but a pedigree of skills that have run through more than three hundred years.

Making a great grand piano starts with the determination not to compromise in any aspect of the design, materials, or craftsmanship.

Experience the 174-year heritage of this historic American brand and become a part of a storied tradition. Visit knabepianos.com to find your local Knabe dealer.

Wm. Knabe & Co. - Exceptional. Elegant. Extraordinary.

WKG90 shown

From about 1880 to 1930, when piano manufacturing was one of the nation's most important industries, pianos were produced in a staggering array of cabinet styles, many of them highly intricate, embellished, and decorated, others dull and pedestrian. The cabinet styles were closely related to the social and economic climates of that period—to changes in values in an emerging consumer culture, and to economic cycles that affected the quantity, styles, and quality of the pianos made during that time. This article is an overview of those styles, and their historical context, as they pertain to upright pianos.

This **1892 Henry F. Miller** is an example of the supreme achievement of the cabinet maker's art.

Online viewers: Click any of the photos in this article to enlarge.

1884 Decker Bros.
An 1880s piano is immediately identifiable by the three-paneled jigsaw scrollwork of its front board. This open filigree scrollwork always has repeated patterns, and is backed with rich, brilliantly colored silk. The elaborate legs feature a large top and large base. Victorian pianos have minuscule fold-down music desks, and the cheeks and fallboard are always curved.

The Piano's Various Forms

The original harpsichord shape of the piano gradually evolved into today's grand piano shape in order to meet the acoustical needs of concert halls and the musical demands of professionals and dedicated amateur players. In the process, the piano became a status symbol for the upper classes. With the rise of a middle class during the Industrial Revolution, the opportunity to learn to play the piano, and to appreciate and own the finer things in life, became available to large numbers of people for the first time.

In the mid-19th century, the square piano, also known as the square grand, constituted the largest share of the American piano market. Although often a beautiful piece of furniture, the square's oblong, rectangular shape was a manufacturing and design nightmare due to its limited ability to withstand the tension of the strings. This and other faults, including its large size, contributed

to the beginning of its demise, in favor of the upright, soon after the Civil War. Uprights were cheaper to manufacture, which made them more affordable; and, being smaller, they fit better in the narrower dwellings of the middle class, who constituted the new generation of piano owners. By 1890, square pianos had all but disappeared from piano showrooms.

Although not a piano, the reed organ, also known as the pump organ, reigned as the most popular keyboard instrument for the home from 1850 to 1894. It was inexpensive, easy to manufacture, and durable. However, as improved manufacturing methods led to lower piano prices, the public turned away from the reed organ in favor of the piano. Many notable piano manufacturers, including Mason & Hamlin, Baldwin, and Kimball, got their start making reed organs.

Since 1880, the most historically significant form of the piano has been the upright. Eminently affordable, uprights were made by the millions, and countless specimens made between 1880 and 1930 still exist to be admired and studied. The upright, like the grand, reached its current technical design around 1880. Because of this, although the furniture of an 1880s upright may be considered antique, such a piano is considered mechanically modern.

The Industrial Revolution in America

The Industrial Revolution took root in America in the late 1860s, following the Civil War. The biggest technological advancement was the displacement of water power by steam power, which allowed industry to move away from the banks of fast-moving rivers in the Northeast and spread across the nation. Coal was increasingly used to fuel the new steam engines and to heat the factories. These factories were generally located in cities, which were crowded with foreign immigrants and rural Americans seeking the jobs made possible by the Industrial Revolution, and which thus had an abundant supply of cheap labor.

Early in this period, most piano manufacturers were located in Eastern cities such as New York, Boston, and Baltimore. As railroads opened up the West, Chicago retailers supplied the emerging frontier towns with pianos from the East. Eventually, these towns grew large enough to bypass the Chicago merchants and deal directly with Eastern manufacturers. In response, a number of Chicago retail firms, such as Lyon & Healy and W.W. Kimball, began to make their own pianos and thus challenge the dominance of the Eastern makers. Because labor unions had yet to organize there, pianos made in Chicago were cheaper, though many were also of mediocre quality.

By the 1880s, the adoption of mass production and assembly-line techniques led to extraordinary price reductions in goods of all kinds, including pianos. To expand the market, retailers adopted installment sales, a practice pioneered by the Singer Sewing Machine Company; by the 1890s, the vast majority of pianos were sold on installment credit.

During this later period, some piano makers made most of their own parts and kept their quality standards high. Some of the better-known names included Steinway, Chickering, Henry F. Miller, Vose, and Weber. But most of the several hundred piano manufacturers active in this period merely assembled parts supplied by other firms that specialized in making soundboards, plates, actions, hardware, and cabinet components. Some of these assembly shops produced nice pianos, and proudly had their names cast into the plates. Others sold their pianos on a "stencil basis"; that is, the pianos bore no brand name or manufacturer identification. Typically, the dealer would place on the instrument a decal with the name of his store. Sometimes, however, an unscrupulous dealer would use a name nearly identical to that of a high-end piano, in order to dupe customers into believing that, say, a "Stienway" was actually a Steinway. Stenciled pianos were generally of low quality, and were a constant source of aggravation for the makers of high-quality instruments.

The Victorian Period

The term *Victorian* generally describes British society from 1837 to 1901, the years of the reign of Queen Victoria; or, in America, the late 19th century. However, the term defines a collection of interrelated attitudes more than an actual time span, and conjures up images of prudery, domesticity, sentimentality, social conservatism, romanticism, fussy and overfurnished parlors, middle-class stuffiness, and the opulence of an upper class of super-rich industrialists.

Recall the world that had come before. In America, many had lived on the frontier, with only the objects necessary for daily subsistence. The new, urban-based industrial age created an abundance of work for the newly

1881 B. Shoninger. The kneeboards of many Victorian pianos mirror the top front-panel design.

Victorian Legs. Elaborately turned legs dripping with ornamentation are a dominant design feature of the 1880s pianos. The details of this leg are derived from nature: The sun casts its rays on the acanthus leaf. The column, on closer examination, is actually a flower: petals curl around the top of the leg, and the column is a stem sprouting from a cluster of leaves.

have its daughters play the instrument (whether or not they wanted to or had any musical talent), became an emblem of prosperity. It was a fashionable and convenient way to introduce a young lady to society and, if she was lucky, attract a wealthy husband. This glorification of the piano was no mere fad; the instrument became a moral institution. By 1886, seven out of ten pupils in the U.S. public schools were being taught to read music, and it is estimated that there were a half million piano students in the country.

Although Queen Victoria had little to do with the American furniture style named for her, the association persists, and conveys a meaning. Victorian furniture designers drew inspiration for their work from a variety of other eras; most noteworthy among these were the gothic (12th to early 16th centuries) and the rococo (18th century). The style was eclectic, ornate in design, and, some would say, cluttered. Homes were filled to the brim with big furniture and excessive amounts of ornamentation. Victorian pianos are instantly recognizable: they had lots of curves, glossy finishes with rounded corners, and flamboyant ornamentation—the more the better. American Victorian-era piano design was split into two main phases: the styles of the 1880s and those of the 1890s.*

Styles of the 1880s

An 1880s piano is immediately identifiable by the three-paneled jigsaw scrollwork of its front board. This open filigree scrollwork always has repeated patterns, and is backed with rich, brilliantly colored silk. The fabric's purpose is twofold: it displays the design of the scrollwork, and permits the music to radiate out from the piano's interior toward the player, for a much more present sound.

The elaborately turned legs feature a large top and large base dripping with ostentatious ornamentation. Also, Victorian pianos had minuscule fold-down music desks, either attached to the curved fallboard, or located on the bottom edge of the front board's center panel.

The woods were highly figured veneers, predominately of mahogany and rosewood. Repeating patterns of rococo involute carving extend from the pilaster onto the cheek, appearing as if squeezed from a tube of cake frosting. The sides of these early pianos were also often curved or paneled.

arrived immigrants. There was a significant increase in wages for laborers and clerical workers alike, which in turn led to the formation of a growing class of individuals who were comfortable but not rich. The industrial age produced a new materialistic view of the world that encouraged people to consume as much as they could, and people began to collect things.

One of the most coveted objects was a piano, which symbolized the middle-class values of the Victorian age—not only the virtues attributed to music, but also of home and family life, respectability, and a woman's place and duty. Music making and music appreciation became feminized. For a family to own a piano, and to

*Although it's often possible to estimate a piano's date of manufacture within a few years by its cabinet style, the years in which different styles were introduced to or withdrawn from the market varied both regionally and among manufacturers. The dates cited here are approximate, and provided only to highlight general trends in cabinet styling.

1892 Geo. Steck. 1890s pianos can be identified by the stenciled designs carved or pressed into their varnish. These etchings are found in the recessed alcoves of a three-paneled front board. The border of this Geo. Steck piano's etching has a repeating geometrical design of regularly placed points joined by mixed lines. The oblong pressed design in the alcove interiors is one of vines and stylized leaves. These 1890s pianos were characterized by an infinite complexity of form that pulled together design features from many different places and eras. In this instrument's pilaster, a "strung coin" motif is topped by an acanthus leaf.

1893 Mehlin. Besides geometrical elements, the ornamental art of the 1890s is composed of groupings of flowers, leaves, and musical instruments. The instruments symbolize the various arts. Singing, for example, is represented by a lyre, with or without sheets of music; dancing, by the tambourine; and music, by violins, horns, pan's pipes, etc. This Mehlin shows these designs very distinctly because of the unusual treatment of gold rubbed into these etchings.

1892 Henry F. Miller. The more expensive instruments from the 1890s continue the elaborate ornamentation of the 1880s. The surface enrichments on this instrument are borrowed from many fields of classical design. The olive branch, a symbol of peace, is entwined with ribbons and foliage around a lyre, the symbol for singing. The pilaster is terminated in an Ionic capital. The curved side, a standard element of Victorian pianos, is painstakingly veneered with a grain pattern that flows onto the adjacent flat surfaces.

Styles of the 1890s

The decade of the 1890s was, economically, a generally depressed period that included two monetary panics; growth did not resume until about 1898. The 1893 panic, a global collapse of the value of U.S. currency caused by a partial abandonment of the gold standard, was short-lived, but in some ways hit the nation harder than did the Great Depression of the 1930s. Manufacturing came to a near standstill—in 1894, in response to a precipitous drop in demand for pianos, piano production plummeted by more than 50 percent, and manufacturers slashed salaries. The panic also fostered protectionist and anti-immigrant sentiment.

To reduce costs, some of the more labor-intensive furniture designs were simplified. Intricate jigsawn front panels were replaced by stenciled etchings, usually of other musical instruments, carved into the varnish. The decorative motifs ranged widely, from classical designs to floral patterns to repetitive geometric forms. The ebonized finish first appears in this decade, as it was less expensive to finish a piano in black than in a wood finish. However, legs were still heavily ornamented, though not as lavishly as in the 1880s, with a large base and top (long, columnar legs didn't appear until the 1900s). The music desk is still tiny, the fallboard and cheeks are curved, and the cheeks are sometimes carved. Higher-end models of the 1890s still have the lavish carvings and highly figured veneers of the 1880s.

Changing Mores

The Chicago Columbian Exposition of 1893, dedicated to displays of technological advancement and a precursor of the World's Fairs of the 20th century, was visited by 12.5 million people, or about 20 percent of the U.S. population at that time. The piano manufacturers' displays there stimulated piano sales and amateur musicianship, and hastened the demise of the reed organ.

The Columbian Exposition came at a time of strict social mores and sexual restraint. The new music introduced there consisted of gayer, more vulgar tunes than any previously played in American parlors. These syncopated melodies soon became ragtime, a forerunner of jazz. With advances in the printing of sheet music, formerly oriented mostly toward professional musicians, the family piano became the center of an enormous business in sheet music, eventually known as Tin Pan Alley, that sold these peppy tunes. The popularity of ragtime, and its greater availability through sheet music, contributed to the breakdown of Victorian attitudes and the ushering in of a new social era as the 19th century came to a close.

Player Pianos

Beginning in 1889, scores of inventions for an automated piano began appearing. Sales of player pianos really took off in 1905, when a standardized piano song roll was designed that could be used in instruments made by different companies. Player pianos were amazing machines that altered the nation's musical and social landscapes. For one thing, through rolls of punched paper, ragtime music, originally composed and played only by black musicians, could now be played in the homes of white middle-class Americans. For another, unprecedented numbers of nonmusicians were now being exposed to music. The player-piano industry was big business. It is estimated that, by 1918, 800,000 player pianos were in operation east of the Mississippi River.

Most player pianos were "standard" models—that is, they played at a single volume and a single speed. One would sit at the piano, pumping the foot-operated bellows. To add expression to the music, one could manipulate the loud/soft and fast/slow levers. There was also a phenomenal device called a reproducing piano, which could reproduce an artist's full range of virtuosity—the nuances, the phrasing, the dynamics. For 30 years, practically all of the great artists recorded rolls for these pianos, including Johann Strauss, Béla Bartók, Gustav Mahler, and Ignace Paderewski. Reproducing-piano mechanisms were placed in high-end pianos, such as grand and upright models from Steinway and Mason & Hamlin, and were considered the advanced recording technology of their day.

Upright player pianos are easily identified by a sliding two-door panel in the front board. The hinged keyslip pivots open to expose the control levers. Standard players have a door above the pedals. The case designs follow the characteristics of the era in which they were made, though usually with less ornamentation than their nonplayer counterparts.

1915 Kurtzmann. Player pianos were usually made with less ornamentation than their nonplayer counterparts. Player models are distinguished by two sliding doors in the middle of the top front panel that open to reveal the roll box. Standard players have a sliding door in the knee board where the pumping pedals fold out. The player mechanisms of most player pianos still in existence have been removed because they no longer function.

Elements of the Victorian era are still prevalent in this transitional piano from 1901: curved and paneled sides, and legs with a very large cap. The new 20th-century style, however, is seen in the legs, which are now freestanding, cylindrical, full-length columns. Applied moldings are the norm in pianos of this era; the incorporation of hand carving alongside easily reproduced faux carving gives this piano the feel of an expensive, one-of-a-kind, instrument.

A New Century

At the dawn of the 20th century, the piano was found at all levels of American society. It had become a significant piece of middle-class furniture—a necessary accessory to domesticity, and as familiar as the armchair. Before the bathroom became the shrine of the American home, there were more pianos and organs in this country than bathtubs.

Molds

A major change affecting case styles of the early 1900s came with the application to piano manufacturing of the composition mold. These molds allowed what looked like painstakingly intricate hand carvings to be inexpensively and easily reproduced. A design pattern was carved in wood just once, and a mold was then formed over the carving to create a negative of the original. A paste of animal glue, linseed oil, resin, and sawdust was then poured into this mold to make a precise replica of the original carving. Apply a faux finish, and voilà—it looks like a hand carving.

Two types of raised-design moldings are found on pianos of the early 20th century. One type consists of a panel that has been molded in its entirety, with all of its raised designs already part of the mold. The entire panel then needed to be faux finished. More commonly, individual design elements were cast from molds, then applied with nails or glue to the piano's front board and/or its columns and legs. The most convincing applied moldings are those that are interspersed with genuine carvings.

Styles of 1900–1909

There were several major design changes in the pianos of the early 20th century. Instruments made in this decade are easily identifiable by the applied moldings on the front board.

Gone are the top-heavy legs; the pianos now had full-length columns for legs. Turn-of-the-century legs could be round, tapered, reeded, and/or fluted. Early turn-of-the-century pianos usually have turned columns with more elaborate capitals. There is still a rounded quality to the overall appearance of these early-20th-century models, most notably in the cheeks and fallboard, but the side panels were nearly always straight. The revolving, claw-foot piano stool was phased out, and a bench with legs that matched those of the piano was now provided for each instrument.

Sheet music, now in plentiful supply, has made the little fold-out music desk obsolete. A wide music-desk shelf now runs the length of the piano, and the front board pivots out at an angle to support the music, which can be spread out across the entire front board.

The fallboards of this era are in two pieces, joined by a hinge, and are usually rounded to correspond to the rounded cheeks. When opened, the fallboard tucks all the way under the music desk.

Rosewood has all but disappeared. The predominant woods are now mahogany and walnut, with a smattering of oak pianos being produced.

There is a great difference in the look of applied moldings from 1900 to 1909. At the beginning of this period, the imitation wood carvings were usually very small and delicate. As time went by, they grew larger and more crude-looking until, about 1909, they were about the size of cow patties. By 1912, virtually all piano cases lacked such ornamentation.

1902 A. B. Chase, The new leg style is one of full-length, cylindrical columns. The applied molding on the front board is delicate and skillfully executed.

1908 Bush and Lane.
The recurring influence of the Greek Corinthian order is ever present in pianos of the turn of the last century. The acanthus leaf became a consistent design motif.

1903 Haddorff.
Wreaths are a common molded design applied to the front board. The exceptionally small music desk of the Victorian era has been replaced by one that runs the length of the front board.

Styles of 1909–1929

With the expansion of the middle class, the demand for pianos skyrocketed, which caused piano manufacturers to modernize and simplify the time-consuming detailing of the piano cases. Removing the ornate carvings allowed them to produce fine instruments at a faster rate and more profitably. Although many fantastic pianos were made during this time, these two decades saw a steady progress toward less expensive, lower-quality instruments.

Pianos of the 1910s and 1920s generally have straight-sided cases with square legs. The early models from this era of change have a front-board design of three inset panels, with architectural molding around the edges. Later, the three-panel design was discarded in favor

Marshall & Wendell. By 1909, most applied moldings have evolved into larger, clumsier designs.

1908 Bush and Lane. Bush and Lane pianos are known for their immensity and strength. This Pompeian model's front board is adorned with a highly recognizable design patented by the manufacturer, and used on its pianos over a period of a decade or more. A poor refinishing job has stripped the faux finish from the acanthus leaves, revealing a perfect example of what appears to be carving, but is actually a molded form comprising hide glue and sawdust.

1909 Bush and Lane. Around 1909, raised applied moldings give way to recessed panels, and here is a beautiful specimen of veneering applied to that style. The continuity of the oak grain from surface to surface illustrates the high level of precision craftsmanship still being employed in the first decade of the 20th century, but which diminished in the teens.

of a single flat panel. The columns on the sides of the front boards are straight; the cheeks and fallboards are squared.

As choice woods became more scarce, there was a subtle but notable change in the veneers of the teen years: Mahogany became less figured, mostly ribbon striped, without the intense flame pattern. Oak, better suited to middle-class homes due to its less-formal look, became more popular. Lower-end pianos were now finished with cheaper varnishes that didn't hold up well over time.

Heading into the 1920s, the quality of ivory used for keytops significantly declined, becoming more translucent, and apt to have a straight grain that looks like milk running down a glass rather than one resembling fingerprints, as in earlier pianos. The presence of celluloid keytops, distinguishable by squiggly lines in imitation of ivory grain running down the key, indicates a lower-priced piano of the late teens and twenties.

This **1909 Cable** has handsome bee's-wing mahogany veneer whose grain pattern is artfully installed in the three recessed panels.

1924 Ludwig. By the mid-1910s, front boards comprising three recessed panels have given way to a single, flat, unadorned board. By the 1920s, round legs have become square. As choice woods become scarcer, there is a subtle but notable change in the veneers of the late teens and beyond: grain patterns are less figured and rather boring. With the popularity of the radio, piano sales plummet in the mid-1920s; to stay in business, piano manufacturers begin to offer shorter, less-expensive models. This instrument's relatively small size is a clue that it was made in the mid- to late 1920s.

The Arts and Crafts Movement

In England in the late 19th century, and in America from about 1910 to 1920, the Arts and Crafts movement arose in reaction to the Industrial Revolution, mass production, shoddy consumer goods, and the poor treatment of workers. This movement emphasized pride in craftsmanship, and the idea that it was possible to provide both well-made consumer goods for the public and decent employment for workers, without the craftsman becoming a mere cog in the wheel of massive factory production. In England, the movement tended to result in high-priced goods that only the wealthy could afford. But in America, prices were kept affordable by combining the use of factory methods for basic components with handcraftsmanship for assembly and finishing.

There were a number of furniture styles associated with the American Arts and Crafts movement. The one most often used with pianos, known as the Mission style, incorporated elements of the traditional furnishings of the Spanish and Native Americans of the American Southwest, as exemplified by the basic, solid furniture of the Spanish missions of California. Piano cabinets, usually of oak, were produced with exposed mortise-and-tenon joinery, and included hardware of hand-hammered brass.

World War I and the Roaring '20s

The growth of the piano industry was interrupted briefly by World War I, due to severe material shortages and a tax on luxury goods, but rebounded quickly after war's end, and reached its peak in the early 1920s. The market was glutted with old non-player upright pianos, and dealers took this opportunity to sell into every home a new player piano that anyone and everyone could play, without tedious lessons, time-consuming practice, or even having to pump the pedals—the pumping systems of many models were now electrified.

The world was changing at a fast pace, especially the role of women in society. They no longer stayed home being good little girls, doing needlepoint and spending hundreds of tortuous hours in front of the piano. They now had bicycles and automobiles in which to fly about town. There were motion pictures, the "talking machine" (phonograph), and—due to Prohibition—speakeasies. It was an exciting new time in which the piano played an important role, though now less as a symbol of femininity and family values, and more as a passive home-entertainment device.

But the dominance of the piano was about to end. By 1925, the newly developed radio had begun to replace the player piano as a source of home entertainment. A

The starkly elegant Arts and Crafts ideal of native materials worked with honest handcraftsmanship is portrayed in this **1910 E. Gabler & Bro.** piano. The workmanship must be precise and the wood of the best quality, as any imperfections will be obvious in furniture of such simple lines. The metalwork is hammered brass.

One branch of Arts and Crafts furniture was a successful composite of many different antique architectural motifs. Heavy and substantial, this **1909 Price & Teeple** piano has a medieval flair: Gothic ornamentation marked by latticework and pagoda-like pediments.

radio was far less expensive than a piano, smaller, and more versatile in the sounds it could reproduce. The decline of the player piano accelerated when, in 1927, the radio was adapted for use with alternating electrical current (AC). Sales of player pianos peaked in 1923, at 200,000 units, but only six years later had fallen to little more than 2,000. As most player pianos had been sold on installment plans, there were massive defaults and repossessions, and warehouses were soon stuffed with unpaid-for, unsellable instruments. In an attempt to stay afloat, from the mid-1920s on, manufacturers began building smaller, less-expensive, studio-size upright pianos.

After 1930

The few piano manufacturers to survive the Great Depression rescued themselves by introducing smaller, less expensive pianos, especially spinets, and consoles in various period-revival decorator styles, to which the public responded enthusiastically. This trend toward smaller instruments lasted for a generation, but was reversed when, beginning in the 1960s and continuing through the 1980s, Japanese and Korean manufacturers offered larger verticals with simple, unadorned lines. The success of these Asian pianos over smaller, fancier American models reflected, in part, a gradual turn toward simplicity, even starkness, in furniture design after World War II, a change to which most American makers did not adapt—and therefore went out of business.

Today's vertical pianos are made in a potpourri of styles: consoles (but no longer spinets) in period styles; bland but functional, studio-size verticals for school use; taller uprights with sleek, straight lines; and hybrid styles. The highly ornamented styles of the past are no longer common, in part because today's mass-production processes make them too costly, and in part because tastes in furniture design continue to trend toward simpler lines; still, some high-end brands offer them in custom-made cabinets. And for those who seek original examples of piano styles past, a few specialist rebuilders continue to restore and make available older instruments. 🎹

25 years ago, **Martha Taylor** came across an abandoned warehouse of 500 upright pianos. She has been very busy ever since. Her company, the Immortal Piano Company, in Portland, Oregon, specializes in the reconditioning and rebuilding of upright pianos. See her work at www.immortalpiano.com.

Selected Bibliography

Ehrlich, Cyril. *The Piano: A History.* King's Lynn, Norfolk, UK: Biddles Ltd., 1979.

Good, Edwin M. *Giraffes, Black Dragons, and other Pianos: A Technological History from Cristofori to the Modern Concert Grand.* Palo Alto, CA: Stanford University Press, 2001.

Loesser, Arthur. *Men, Women, & Pianos: A Social History.* New York: Simon and Schuster, 1954.

Majeski, Brian T., editor. *The Music Trades 100th Anniversary Issue: A History of the U.S. Music Industry.* 1990.

Roell, Craig H. *The Piano in America, 1890–1940.* Chapel Hill: The University of North Carolina Press, 1989.

American Heritage Dictionary, Vol. 17, No 1. New York: American Heritage Publishing Co., 1965.

Correspondence

Dr. William E. Hettrick, Professor of Music, Coordinator of Music History, Hofstra University, Hempstead, NY.

Since the piano's invention by Bartolomeo Cristofori in 1700, its evolution has been driven by the desire to meet the changing musical needs of the times, by advances in technology, and by the business and marketing requirements of the piano manufacturers. High-end pianos exemplify this evolutionary process.

Early pianos were limited by the technology of the day to a lightweight structure, and a design that produced a tone—bright and intimate, but with short sustain and low volume—that evolved from the sound of the harpsichord. This complemented both the musical styles favored by the Classical period, especially chamber music, and the smaller, more intimate venues in which music was then customarily performed. As technology advanced, it became possible—using cast-iron plates, stronger strings, and higher-tension scale designs—to produce more robust instruments capable of filling a large hall with sound. This suited the composer-virtuosos of the Romantic period, such as Liszt and Brahms, whose works for the piano demanded from the instrument greater power, and the ability to be heard above the larger orchestras of the day. However, this louder, more overtone-filled sound could also conflict with and overpower other chamber instruments and their performance settings.

The great American pianos, having come of age during the Romantic era, tend toward the Romantic tonal tradition. The great European piano makers, however, embedded in a culture steeped in centuries of musical tradition, have long had to satisfy the conflicting tonal styles of different ages, and this has resulted in a wide variety of instruments with different musical qualities. As the American market for European pianos grows, the European companies are further having to reconcile remaining true to their own traditions with evolving to please the American ear. While all brands make full use of technological advances and are capable of satisfying diverse musical needs, some tend toward a more pristine tone, with plush but low-volume harmonics, perfect for chamber music or solo performances in small rooms; others are bright and powerful enough to hold their own above the largest symphony orchestras; and many are in between.

The good news is that the best way to find the right piano for you is to play as many as you can—a simply wonderful experience!

What follows is a story with a valuable perspective from a well-respected dealer of performance-quality instruments.

—*Editor*

THE BEST PIANO: A STORY
by ORI BUKAI

"I'm tone deaf," declared the husband. "I can't tell the difference between one piano and another."

His wife nodded in agreement. "He *is* tone deaf. And while I can hear some differences, it's all so confusing. All we want is a piano that our kids can learn to play on. We don't need a *great* piano."

A short conversation ensued in which I learned, among other things, that this couple had three children, ranging in age from seven years to six months.

"Our daughter just turned seven," the wife said. "She's interested in piano lessons, but we're not sure how committed she'll be."

"You know kids," the husband shrugged. "She may want piano lessons now, but in a few months' time . . .?"

"You're right," I said. "Kids change their minds all the time. I started piano lessons at the age of six, and stopped only a few months later. But the piano stayed in our home, and at the age of 12 I was drawn back to it. I played a few tunes by ear, and after a while I started lessons again. But . . . would you like your youngest child to play the piano as well?"

They looked at each other. It seemed that the possibility of their six-month-old baby taking lessons sometime in the future was something they hadn't considered.

"This means that whatever instrument we choose, it will probably stay in our home for a very long time," the woman said to her husband. "Perhaps we should look at a greater range of instruments than just the few we had in mind . . .?"

"But still," he said, turning to me, "is there enough difference in the tone of the pianos to justify a greater investment, and a possible increase in our budget?"

Such conversations are not rare. Some people feel they won't be able to hear the differences between pianos, or that a high-end piano will be wasted on them. Others try to accommodate only what they perceive their needs to be at the time of purchase, rather than over the many years they may end up owning a piano.

Often, piano buyers form an idea of what they want and how much to spend, and consider only a few brands, without ever sufficiently researching the differences in manufacturers' philosophies and how these might affect the tone, touch, musicality, and price of the instrument. However, such information can help the consumer clarify his or her true needs and preferences. Many shopping for a piano all but ignore higher-end models, considering them beyond their needs or means. But for more than a few of these buyers, a better-quality piano may prove the better fit and value.

There are significant differences in manufacturing methods between performance-oriented instruments, which are often referred to as "hand-made," and mass-produced instruments, in which some musical qualities are sacrificed to meet a lower retail price.

Performance-oriented manufacturers, especially at the highest level, are looking to capture a wide range of tonal characteristics. Some of these qualities, such as sustain, tonal variation, and dynamic range, are universally accepted as helping the playing of pianists of all levels sound more musical. All makers of high-end pianos strive to make pianos that excel in these areas. Other tonal characteristics, however, such as tonal color—the specific harmonic structure of the tone—can reflect a particular manufacturer's philosophy of what the best piano should sound like, and are the elements that separate one high-end make from another. A piano maker's decision to emphasize certain musical qualities over others is manifested through differences in the instrument's design, in the instrument's resulting tone and touch, and in its appeal to a particular player or listener.

"Would you like to hear some higher-end instruments as well, just to compare?" I asked the couple.

"Yes, please," replied the woman

And so we went on a tour of Piano Land, playing, listening to, and assessing the tone of a variety of instruments. "Ooohhh," said the wife in response to one particular make. "Aaahhh," sighed her husband, as the realization struck him: He actually *could* hear the differences between these pianos; not only that, he had some rather clear preferences.

"But which is the *best* piano?" he asked. There are quite a few instruments here, all so beautiful, but so different from each other. Which *is* the best?

This is a question customers ask me again and again when visiting our showroom—we represent most of the high-end makers, and side-by-side comparisons are always possible. And while, time after time, our customers do find the absolute "best," for each of those customers the "best" is represented by a different make, according to his or her preferences. The combination of musical qualities

The tone of a Blüthner piano combines
effortless power with the smoothest pianissimo.
Perfection of design created by piano masters.
Hand crafted in Germany since 1853.

Bluthner USA, LLC
5660 West Grand River Avenue
Lansing, Michigan 48906, USA
Tel: 800 954 - 3200
Fax: 517 886 - 1574
info@bluthnerusa.com
www.bluthnerusa.com

Blüthner
THE GOLDEN TONE PIANOS

emphasized by one piano maker may speak to one customer while leaving another indifferent—who, in turn responds enthusiastically to an instrument made by another manufacturer that has left the first customer cold. Some people prefer a bold, outgoing, and powerful sound; others want a more delicate, clear, and melodic tone. Some like focused, defined, and pure tonal characteristics, while others look for instruments whose sound is more robust, deep, and dark.

At the top end of piano manufacturing, each instrument should have a high level of design, parts, materials, execution, workmanship, and attention to detail. However, it is personal preference—the buyer's response to the various manufacturers' interpretations of the "perfect sound"—that determines the answer to the question of "But which is the *best* piano?" The answer is different for every customer.

But which piano is the "best" is also a matter of other factors. Some high-end instruments might be considered the "best" in one setting, but not quite the best in another. A piano that sounds its best in a large concert hall with hundreds of people may not necessarily be the right fit for the typical living room.

"The best instrument," I replied to the couple, "is the one that you'll most enjoy listening to as your children—and perhaps, before you know it, your grandchildren—play and develop their musical skills. The 'best' piano is the one you'll be happy with over the many years it will live in your home, and that one day, when you have the time, perhaps may tempt you to take lessons yourself. The best piano is the one that will deliver to you and your family the joy of music, now and over the long run."

Ori Bukai owns and operates Allegro Pianos in Stamford, Connecticut, which specializes in the sale of new and restored high-end pianos. Visit his website at **www.allegropianos.com**.

BUYING PIANOS FOR AN INSTITUTION

GEORGE F. LITTERST

[*This article assumes you are already familiar with the basics of piano-shopping (see "Piano Buying Basics" and other appropriate articles in this publication), and treats only those aspects of the subject that are specific to the institutional setting.—Ed.*]

Institutional Basics

Institutions vary so widely in size, makeup, and needs that it is impossible to cover in a single article all the variables that might apply. For example, the studio of a graduate-school piano professor might be 12 feet square, carpeted, and cluttered with bookshelves, desk, and chairs, but still needs a performance-grade instrument. A church sanctuary—often a carpeted, irregularly shaped room with a raised dais and filled with pews, glass windows, and lots of sound-absorbing people—needs a piano that can accompany the choir, be heard throughout a huge room, and also be used as a solo instrument for visiting artists. A school may need dozens of pianos for everything from tiny practice cubicles to a concert hall.

However, regardless of whether you're purchasing a piano for a church, school, performance space, or another institutional location, you need to start with some basic questions that will help identify the piano (or pianos) that are appropriate for your situation.

For example:

- Who will use the piano—beginners, advanced players, or concert artists?
- How often will the piano be played—in the occasional concert, or for 18 hours per day of intense student practice?
- How will the piano be used—lessons for graduate students? church services? recordings?
- Will the piano's location be fixed, or will it be moved often?
- In what size room will it primarily be used?

After answering these questions, this article will help you establish some basic parameters, including:

- Grand vs. Vertical
- Size
- New vs. Used
- Digital vs. Acoustic
- Traditional Acoustic vs. Acoustic with Record/Playback/Computer Features

Budget

Once you've narrowed down the parameters of your ideal instrument or group of instruments, you need to consider your budget. In doing so, it's best to remember that quality instruments properly maintained will last a long time. Accordingly, it's best to view the cost of each instrument not as a one-time expense, but as a total expense amortized over the life of the instrument.

When figuring out the true annual cost of an instrument:

- Spread out the instrument's purchase price over the span of its working life
- Factor in the cost of money, that is, the interest you would pay if you were to finance the purchase (even if you don't actually plan to finance it)
- Include costs of tuning (typically three to four times a year, but far more often for performance instruments), regulation, and repairs

When you figure the cost of an instrument this way, you may even discover that certain more expensive instruments are more affordable than you thought.

Once you've determined your budget, and the size and other features of the instruments you desire, you can use the **online searchable database** accessible through the electronic version of this publication to assist you in finding the specific brands and models that will fulfill your needs.

Grand vs. Vertical

Many situations are adequately served by vertical pianos, including:

- Practice rooms where the piano is used primarily by, or to accompany, non-pianist musicians
- Places where there is no room for a grand
- Instruments that are not used for intense playing or difficult literature

A number of features of vertical pianos are commonly sought by institutional buyers:

- Locks on fallboard and tops
- A music desk long enough to hold multiple sheets of music or a score
- Toe-block leg construction with double-wheel casters—particularly important if the piano will be moved often

Both digital and acoustic pianos are available with a variety of modern technologies. Do you need:

- A piano that can be connected to another piano over the Internet for the purpose of long-distance lessons, concerts, and master classes?
- An instrument that, for study purposes, can record and play back a student's performance, or play selections from a library of pre-recorded performances?
- An instrument that can accompany a vocalist, or string player or wind player, when they practice—even if a pianist isn't available?
- A piano that connects to a computer and can function as an interactive composition tool?
- A piano that can be used with score-following software so that the player can enjoy automatic page-turning, or rehearse a concerto with an electronic orchestra that follows the soloist?

The piano has a history of more than 300 years of technological change and innovation. New technologies are ever more rapidly becoming integral parts of our musical landscape. You want the piano that you purchase today to last for a long time. In making your selection, therefore, be sure to consider your current and future technological needs.

- Heavy-duty back-post and plate assembly for better tuning stability
- Climate-control systems
- Protective covers

Grand pianos, however, have keys, actions, and tonal qualities that are more appropriate for practicing and performing advanced literature, and are therefore preferred in situations where they are largely used by piano majors or performing pianists.

Grands are preferred by piano majors even for small practice rooms, because the students use these instruments primarily to develop advanced technical facility, something that's almost impossible to do on vertical pianos. Commonly sought features of grands are:

- Mounting on a piano *truck* (a specialized platform on wheels) for moving the piano easily and safely
- Protective covers to avoid damage to the finish
- Climate-control systems
- Lid and fallboard locks

Size

Carefully consider the size of your space. You can easily spend too much on a piano if it's larger than the space requires, and you can easily waste your money if you purchase an undersized instrument. For more information about how room acoustics might affect the size of instrument you should purchase, see "**How to Make Your Piano Room Sound Grand**," elsewhere in this issue.

Of course, the tonal quality and touch of the instrument are related, in large part, to its size. If you're purchasing pianos for teaching studios in which artist faculty are instructing graduate piano majors, or for practice rooms used primarily by piano majors, there may be musical reasons for choosing larger grands despite the fact that the spaces are small. You'll be able to capture most of the advantages of a larger grand's longer keys with an instrument six to six-and-a-half feet long. Any longer will be overkill for a small teaching studio or practice room. A larger teaching studio may be able to accommodate and make good use of a seven-foot grand. The size of the piano is much less important in the training of beginning pianists or non-pianist musicians. There, other

The Yamaha model P22 has typical school-piano features, such as locks, a long music desk, toe-block leg construction, and double-wheel casters.

factors, such as the size of the room, will be the dominant considerations.

Vertical pianos made for institutions are almost always at least 45 inches tall. Smaller verticals may have inferior actions and tone, and cabinetry that is more prone to breakage. Verticals taller than about 48 inches are probably unnecessary for most small studio and practice rooms, but may be appropriate in larger spaces where a larger sound is needed but a grand is out of the question.

A special problem often occurs when a house of worship or small recital venue with limited funds tries to make do with a grand piano that's too small for the space. The pianist will tend to play much harder than normal, and overuse the sustain pedal, in an effort to make the piano heard at the back of the sanctuary or hall, causing strings and hammers to break and pedal systems to wear out prematurely. Generally, a small- to medium-size sanctuary will require a grand six to seven feet long to adequately fill the hall with sound, but this can vary greatly depending on the size of the hall, its acoustics, how large an audience is typically present, whether the piano is being used as a solo instrument or to accompany others, and whether the sound is amplified. A piano dealer can help sort out these issues and recommend an appropriate instrument.

New vs. Used

Excellent acoustic pianos that are well maintained should last for decades. Given this fact, should your institution consider purchasing used instruments and thus save some money? If this is something you're considering, read "**Buying a Used or Restored Piano**" in this issue before continuing. When comparing a used piano to a new one, consult a trusted piano technician to get a sense of the used instrument's condition and remaining useful life. Then amortize the cost of the pianos, including expected repair costs, over their expected lifetimes to determine which is the better value.

If considering a used acoustic piano with embedded electronics, such as an electronic player piano, be careful to avoid purchasing an instrument whose technology is so obsolete that you can't use it productively. On the other hand, if your intention is to use a player piano's MIDI features mostly in conjunction with a computer, you do have one protection against obsolescence on your side: Although MIDI has been around since 1982, it's still an industry standard that works well and shows no sign of disappearing in the near future. Accordingly, you can continue to upgrade the features of an older MIDI piano merely by upgrading the software you use on your computer.

Acoustic vs. Digital

Digital pianos continue to improve every year, and the benefits realized for every dollar spent on a digital piano continue to grow with advances in technology.

Here are some examples of institutional situations in which a digital piano is generally the preferred instrument:

Yamaha

- Class piano, where students and teachers wear headsets and the teacher controls the flow of sound in the room with a lab controller
- Multipurpose computer/keyboard labs where students need to work independently on theory, composition, and performance projects without disturbing others in the room
- A church that features a so-called "contemporary service" in which the keyboard player needs an instrument with lots of on-board sounds, registrations, and automatic accompaniments

In other situations, the preferred choice may not be so obvious. For example, if a school has a practice room largely used by singers and instrumentalists (not pianists), should you supply a digital piano or a vertical?

When weighing these and similar questions, keep in mind:

- In an institutional setting, a typical, well-maintained acoustic piano has a life expectancy of 20 to 40 years; a higher-quality instrument might last 30 to 50 years. Because the digital piano is a relatively recent invention, we can't be as certain how long they will last in an institutional setting. A reasonable estimate for a good-quality digital instrument might be 10 to 20 years. However, digital instruments are subject to

a rapid rate of technological advance that may eventually limit the instrument's usefulness, even though it still functions. On the other hand, the digital piano won't need tuning, and may go for years before it needs any other maintenance.
- Some digital pianos are simply a substitute for the acoustic equivalent. Others have additional features that may be highly desirable, such as connectivity to a computer, orchestral voices, and record and playback features.
- Some acoustic pianos are also available with digital-piano–like features, such as record and playback, and Internet and computer connectivity. If your choice comes down to an acoustic piano (for its traditional piano features of touch and tone) and a digital piano (for its embedded technologies), you may need to consider a hybrid digital/acoustic instrument. (See the article on **hybrid pianos** in this issue of *Piano Buyer*.)

Assessing Pianos Before Purchase

Assessing digital pianos is a relatively straightforward matter. You simply play and compare the features of various makes and models and make your selection. If you choose Model X, it doesn't matter if you take possession of the actual floor model that you tried: All Model X digital pianos will be the same.

Acoustic pianos are a different animal. There is more variation among pianos of the same model from a given manufacturer. However, it is important to note that some manufacturers have a reputation for producing uniformly similar instruments, while others have a reputation for producing more individually distinctive instruments.

If you're purchasing a single acoustic piano or a small number of acoustic pianos, you can and should take the opportunity to audition each one of them and make your selection carefully. If you're purchasing a concert or other very large grand, you may need to travel to the manufacturer's national showroom in order to make your selection. If so, factor the cost of the trip into your budget. In some situations it may be possible to audition a large grand in the space in which you intend to use it. This will give you an opportunity to know for sure that you're making the right decision. On the other hand, if you're purchasing a dozen practice room upright pianos, or are completely replacing your inventory of instruments, it's more practical to audition just a sample of each model and make your purchase decision on that basis.

Keep in mind that any fine acoustic piano can be adjusted within certain parameters by a concert-quality technician. If a piano sounds too bright when it is uncrated, skilled needling of the hammers can result in a noticeable mellowing of the sound. Similarly, a new action may require some additional adjustment (called *regulation*) to provide you with a keyboard that is optimally responsive.

Preparation, Tuning, and Maintenance

All pianos require maintenance, and acoustic pianos more than digitals. New acoustic pianos need to be properly prepared before they're deployed. All acoustic pianos should be tuned regularly, and regulated as needed. Acoustic pianos with record and playback systems also may need periodic calibration of their embedded systems. See the **accompanying article** for more information on the maintenance of acoustic pianos in institutions.

Who Should Make the Purchase Decision?

As the foregoing discussion suggests, there are many intersecting practical, artistic, and financial factors to be considered when making an institutional purchase of a piano or group of pianos. This raises the question: Who should make the purchase decision?

No single answer fits all situations. By tradition, a church's decision-making process may be handled by the music director, the pastor or priest, or perhaps by a lay committee. In a school of music, decisions may be delegated to the chair of the piano department, the chair of the music department, the dean of fine arts, or some other individual or faculty committee.

In many instances, well-intentioned individuals with no knowledge of pianos find themselves having to make a final decision. It is important that those involved in the process commit themselves to understanding the intersecting issues, and bring into the decision-making process appropriate people from the artistic, technical, and/or financial sides. At a minimum, that means the piano technician, and the most advanced, or most frequent, professional users. If a digital-technology–based instrument is being considered, someone should be involved who can speak to those technical issues as well. A department chair who has not actually used the technology in question may or may not be in a position to evaluate it.

Negotiating a Purchase

Before negotiating a price or sending a proposal out to bid, it's usually a good idea to do some price research. This can be tricky, however.

For example, if you or someone you know simply calls up a dealer and asks for a price, you're unlikely to be told the lower "institutional price" that you might ultimately get. Some dealers are reluctant to quote prices over the phone, or are prohibited by their suppliers from doing so. Others will refuse to quote a price if they know that the purchase will ultimately go out to bid.

Your institutional purchase may benefit the dealer or manufacturer in

LOAN PROGRAMS: AN ALTERNATIVE TO PURCHASING

Often, institutions find themselves needing to acquire a number of pianos at one time. Perhaps the institution needs to replace a large number of aging instruments or to furnish a newly expanded facility or program—or a school may want to acquire a number of new instruments each year to demonstrate to prospective students that it has a music program of high quality. Such situations can pose a budgetary dilemma—the simultaneous purchase of even a few pianos can cause fiscal stress. Fortunately, relief is sometimes available in the form of a school loan program.

On the surface, a school loan program may seem too good to be true: free pianos, loaned for an academic year. At the end of the year, the pianos are sold. More free pianos the next year.

In truth, a school loan program can work only when it makes sense for both the school and the local dealer. (Although the manufacturer may be a participant in the program, the contract is normally with the local dealer.) Both sides of the agreement have obligations to the other.

For example, a school *may* receive any of the following, depending on the structure of the program:

- Free or very-low-cost use of a significant number of pianos
- Free delivery
- Free tuning and maintenance
- Name association with a prestigious manufacturer

A school may also have any of these obligations:

- Liability for damage
- Delivery charges
- Tuning and maintenance costs
- Requirement to purchase a certain percentage of the instruments
- Requirement to supply an alumni mailing list to the dealer for advertising purposes
- Requirement to provide space for an end-of-year piano sale

When evaluating a loan program, it's generally a good idea to consider:

- The quality of the dealership that stands behind the program
- The appropriateness of the mix of pianos offered
- The school's vulnerability if the program were to be discontinued by the dealership after the current year

That last point is a key issue. What happens if you replace your inventory of old pianos with loaned instruments and the loan program becomes unavailable the next year? Suddenly and unexpectedly, you are faced with having to buy replacement instruments.

Generally speaking, it is a good idea to include with your loan program a purchase component so that you are building your inventory of quality instruments over the course of the loan.

---

ways other than the profit from the sale. Therefore, when discussing your possible purchase, don't hesitate to mention:

- How prominently positioned the instruments will be in your institution or in the community
- How many students or audience members will come in contact with the instruments on a regular basis
- How often you or your institution is asked for purchase recommendations

- How musically influential your institution is in the surrounding community

The bottom line is this: You won't know what the final price will be until an official representative of your institution actually sits down with the dealer principal or until bids are awarded. Before you reach that point, however, and for planning purposes, you can make discreet inquiries and put together some estimates. As a rule of thumb, and only

for the purposes of budgeting, if you subtract 10% to 15% from the dealer's "sale" price, you will likely come close to the institutional price.

If you represent a school that's required to send purchase requests out to bid, you may not have much of a role to play in negotiating a price. However, the way in which you word your bid will have a lot to do with the bids that you receive and the instruments that the bidding rules will compel you to purchase.

For example, if you really want Brand X with features A, B, and C, be sure to write your bid description so that it describes—within acceptable guidelines—the instrument that you wish to purchase, and rules out instruments that don't fit your needs. If your bid description is loosely written, you may receive low bids for instruments that don't meet your requirements.

Because pianos can last a very long time, any piano-buying decisions you make today for your institution can have consequences for a generation or more. Therefore, it pays to take the time to think carefully about your institution's present and future needs, to budget sufficient funds for purchase and maintenance, and to consult with individuals both within and outside your institution who may have special expertise or be affected by your decision. If you take the time to do this properly, then your constituents—be they students, faculty, worshippers, or concert-goers—will enjoy the fruits of your work for years to come. ▥

George Litterst (www.georgelitterst .com) is a nationally known music educator, clinician, author, performer, and developer of music software. In the last role, Mr. Litterst is co-author of the intelligent accompaniment program *Home Concert Xtreme*, the electronic music-blackboard program *Classroom Maestro*, and the long-distance teaching program *Internet MIDI*, all from TimeWarp Technologies (www.timewarptech.com).

PIANO MAINTENANCE IN INSTITUTIONS

CHRIS SOLLIDAY, RPT

THE ADEQUATE AND EFFECTIVE MAINTENANCE of pianos in institutional settings differs from the typical service needs of the home environment in two major ways. Pianos in schools, churches, and colleges are, first of all, usually subjected to heavy use, and second, are very often situated in difficult climatic environments. These pianos will require more frequent service by technicians with special skills, and greater attention to climate control.

In college and university settings, pianos are frequently used eight to twelve hours a day by many different players. Some students have practice habits that involve a great deal of repetition, which causes greater wear to the actions and keys of the instrument in a way that reflects the patterns of their practice. This can easily be ten times more patterned repetition than a piano normally receives in your home. The parts of piano keys and actions that will show the greatest wear are made of felt, leather, and wood, and there are thousands of them in each piano. These materials are chosen, designed, and treated by manufacturers to maximize their working life, and considering the repetitive nature of their use, it's a wonder they last as long as they do.

No matter how well made, however, the nature of these materials dictates that when the piano is used for many hours, day after day, week after week, the wear and deterioration can be extensive. To maximize their longevity, it is very important to keep these pianos in good regulation so that the wear proceeds more evenly. Along with tuning, regular regulation of the action, pedals, and tone should be basic parts of any effective plan of piano maintenance. Without this, neglected instruments in such environments will quickly become impossible to regulate without extensive overhaul or replacement of parts.

At some point, of course, parts *will* have to be replaced, worthy instruments rebuilt, and unworthy ones replaced. But there is no need to

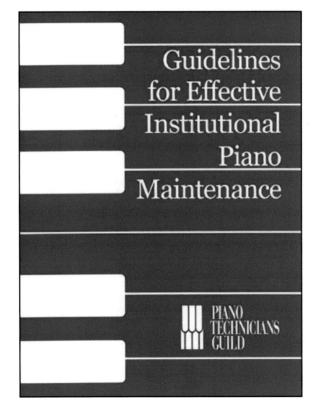

Guidelines for Effective Institutional Piano Maintenance

PIANO TECHNICIANS GUILD

hasten the inevitable by subjecting pianos to the worst form of abuse: neglect. Frequent and regular servicing of pianos is a requirement for any institution that hopes to maintain an adequate performance or learning situation that will not only meet the needs of its members, but serve as a vehicle for the recruitment of new students.

Depending on the security and rules established for using the pianos, abuse can also come in the form of vandalism or simple carelessness. Rules should be established that keep food and liquids away from pianos. Procedures for the safe moving of pianos should be established and strictly enforced to protect the instruments as well as those who do the moving. Untrained personnel should never move a piano anywhere.

The single largest factor affecting the need for piano maintenance, however, is a fluctuating climate. While an environment that is always too hot or too cold, or too wet or too dry, can cause deterioration, pianos can usually (within reason) be regulated to reliably perform in such an environment. However, many institutions provide interior climates of constant change. It's not unusual to find a school or church whose HVAC system produces 80°F and 8% relative humidity during the winter heating season, but 76°F and 80% relative humidity in the summer. These systems' air-exchange devices

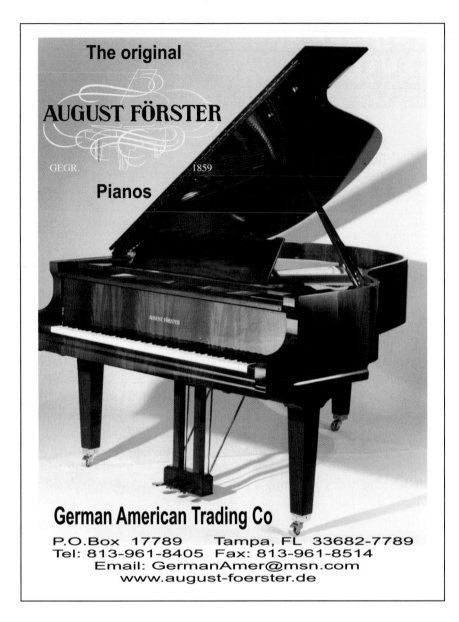
technician can contribute to an accelerated rate of deterioration and shorten the lives of the instruments under his or her care. Some fully qualified technicians, mostly manufacturer-trained, have no formal credentials. However, hiring a Registered Piano Technician (RPT) member of the Piano Technicians Guild (PTG) ensures that at least a minimum standard of expertise has been tested for and achieved. A good way to begin planning any institution's piano-maintenance program is to read PTG's *Guidelines for Effective Institutional Piano Maintenance*, available in printed form or as a free download from www.ptg.org.

Chris Solliday, RPT, services the pianos at several institutions, including Lafayette College, Lehigh University, and East Stroudsburg University. He lives in Easton, Pennsylvania, and can be reached through his website at www.csollidaypiano.com.

can also create drafts that blow directly on the piano, further varying the temperature and relative humidity by a great deal. Often, the temperature settings on these systems are changed during vacation periods. A good target for any piano's environment is 68° F and 42% relative humidity. Installation of inconspicuously-located climate-control systems for the pianos is almost always necessary in institutional environments. A plan for the daily monitoring of these systems should also be considered. [*See the article,* "Caring For Your Piano," *for more* *information on climate-control systems for pianos.—Ed.*]

The most important factor in maintaining the utility and longevity of any institution's pianos is the choice of piano technician. An institutional technician should possess the advanced skills and experience required to prepare pianos for public concerts, organize and manage a large inventory of instruments, deal daily with high-level pianists and educators, and be familiar with the techniques necessary for the time-efficient maintenance of practice-room pianos. An underqualified

HOW TO MAKE A PIANO ROOM SOUND GRAND

LEWIS LIPNICK

SINCE I JOINED the National Symphony Orchestra in 1970, I have performed in large, small, and medium-size rooms. Some have sounded wonderful, some not so wonderful. One night we play at the Kennedy Center, and the next in a high school gymnasium. Same music, same conductor, same musicians, but the two performances sound like two different orchestras. Why? The *room*. Change the room, and you change the musical result. Taking this one step further, we can even say that the room is an integral part of the performance. But where does the sound of the performer end and the sound of the room begin?

Our music rooms, whether large concert halls or smaller spaces in the home, can help or hinder our performance. Too large a room can strip our sound of energy and resonance, while too small a space can cause sonic overload, making the sound muddy, harsh, and overbearing. To enable an instrument built to fill a great concert hall to also work in much smaller domestic spaces and studios requires proper planning. Do you want to practice in an environment in which clarity of sound is more important than volume and resonance, or do you want to be able to play solo and chamber-music concerts in your home, in emulation of a small concert venue? These will require different approaches to room design, and possibly the choice of instrument.

The art of acoustical design for live music is part science, part empirical knowledge, part musical intuition, and part common sense. I call it an "art" mainly because one has to be creative when working in a space that needs to be both sonically and aesthetically pleasing. After all, few piano owners want to see their living rooms turned into sound laboratories simply to achieve their desired musical goals.

Based on my twenty-five years of experience as an acoustical consultant, as well as a professional musician, in this article I will tell you about the things you can do yourself to improve the acoustical qualities of your piano room. However, if you plan to buy a larger, higher-quality grand piano, I suggest that you consider allocating some additional funds to have your room tuned by an acoustical professional or by a contractor experienced in the acoustical treatment of small music rooms. Acoustical treatment techniques have come a long way in recent years, and there are many products that can be integrated into just about any domestic environment without making the room look like a recording studio. I have done this many times, without sacrificing musical *or* visual aesthetics.

Room Size

Vertical pianos are designed to work optimally in smaller rooms. They are usually placed up against a wall, and present relatively few problems in the typical domestic environment. The same is true of small grands. But the amount of

---

---

sonic energy produced by anything larger than about a 6-foot grand can present some big problems in smaller rooms. While concert halls and piano showrooms are big enough to allow the sound of a larger grand to properly resonate, small rooms can't absorb so much sound, and will easily overload when the instrument is played full out. Like other fine musical instruments built to be played in large spaces, a large grand sounds best from some distance away. For instance, stand next to me when I play my contrabassoon's lowest B-flat (half a step above the lowest A on a piano), and while you can physically feel the power of that note, you won't be able to decipher its actual pitch until you walk several feet away from the instrument. The same thing occurs with a double bass, tuba, or pipe organ. At the opposite end of the scale, a really fine violin won't sound its best until the listener is several feet away, when the sound becomes more resonant, with more clearly defined pitch. This is the situation

we face when placing a large piano in a room smaller than it was designed for. While we can do many things to just about any room to make it more friendly to a large piano, there *are* limits, dictated by the laws of physics, that we can't break without paying a price in quality of sound.

How large a piano room needs to be depends on the size of the instrument. Empirical data indicate that the combined length of a room's walls (assuming that the room's ceiling is 8 feet high) should be *at least 10 times* the length of a grand or the height of a vertical piano. For example, a 15 by 20-foot room (15+15+20+20=70 feet) should accommodate a 7-foot grand. This formula doesn't take into account openings into other rooms, irregular room shapes, etc., but it's a good starting point.

Low frequencies have the longest wavelengths and cause the most problems in smaller rooms because the length of the wave exceeds the largest dimension of the room. The lowest A on a piano has a frequency of 27.5

Hz (cycles per second), which translates into a wavelength of about 41 feet! For this reason, the lower two octaves of a 7-foot grand, having less sonic power, will probably sound clearer in a small room than those of a 9-foot instrument in the same space, even though the larger instrument has the potential for greater low-bass clarity. This is the same principle that applies when designing audio systems and home theaters. In a smaller room, a smaller loudspeaker that *pressurizes* less air to reproduce a given frequency will actually *sound* clearer and deeper than a far bigger speaker in that room, even if the larger speaker's bass can go a bit lower in pitch. Therefore, common sense tells us that putting a full-size 9-foot concert grand into a 12 by 15-foot room with an 8-foot ceiling will probably not yield the best results without a huge amount of dedicated acoustical treatment, and probably not even then.

If your piano room is L-shaped, or opens into another large space, this can help your piano's low-octave bass response—the much-longer low-frequency soundwaves can travel *through* large open spaces. This is one reason why, in a small room, opening the doors to adjacent rooms can often make your piano's low octaves sound a bit clearer. (Because the shorter, high-frequency waves tend to bounce off any flat surface closest to the piano, the extra space won't improve their clarity.)

Try to avoid square rooms, or rooms with wall lengths and ceiling heights having a relationship of 1:1, 1:2, or multiples thereof (for example, 16 feet long by 8 feet wide by 8 feet high). Such rooms exacerbate the buildup of low-frequency *coincident modes* (resonant frequencies caused by standing waves), which can make the lowest octave of your piano sound uneven, overemphasizing some notes while making others virtually disappear.

Ceiling Height

Greater ceiling height is always desirable for resonance, but be careful with this. As mentioned above, it's best that the ceiling height not be the same as the length of one of the walls, or that length divided or multiplied by 2 or a multiple of 2. For example, if one wall is 16 feet long, the ceiling should not be 8, 12, or 16 feet high. If your ceiling is more than one-and-one-third times the length of the shortest wall, you may have a problem of reflected soundwaves that will require some dedicated acoustical treatments, though not necessarily. I've worked in some rooms with very high ceilings that sounded fabulous, mainly because the extra headroom helped the low notes sound more full and deep. It all depends on how "live" (resonant) the space is, and exactly which room surfaces are reflecting the sounds of the piano. If you have a sloped ceiling, the best results will likely be achieved by placing a vertical piano against the wall where the ceiling is lowest, or a grand piano facing *out* from the same wall and into the area where the ceiling is highest.

Where to Place the Piano in the Room

[Note: Moving a piano can be dangerous. Have professional movers present to avoid injury to persons or damage to the piano and floors.]

Try not to push the tail of a grand, or the end of a vertical, all the way into a corner of the room. While doing so might give the lowest octave more power (low frequencies are boosted by adjacent wall and floor surfaces), pitch clarity and tonal evenness will suffer. The hard sound reflections coming off both corner walls can also kick back into the player's ears a lot of high-frequency "hash." Vertical pianos are best placed against a room's short wall,

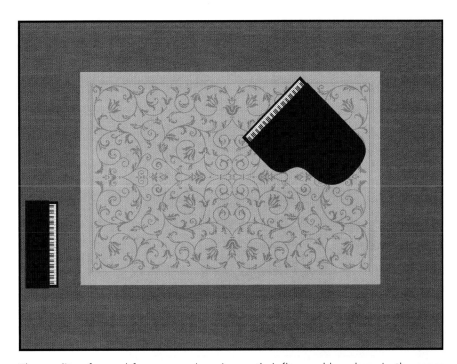

The quality of sound from your piano is greatly influenced by where in the room you place it. In general, pianos should not be positioned too close to corners. A grand is best placed at a diagonal to the walls, one-fifth or one-third of the way between diagonally opposite corners. A vertical is best placed along the shorter wall, one-fifth or one-third of the way between adjacent corners. Grands in particular will usually sound better with a carpet or rug under the instrument. See text for details.

with the center of the piano one-fifth or one-third of that wall's length from the nearest corner. Try the instrument in both locations, listening for evenness of tone across the scale. Then slowly move it, a few inches at a time, in either direction to fine-tune the sound for clarity.

Finding the right spot in the room for a grand piano involves some effort but is not difficult. Begin with the piano near a corner of the room; if possible, position it with the long side across the corner at a 45° angle to the walls, with the open lid facing out into the room toward the diagonally opposite corner. This will keep both ends of the piano equidistant to the walls and corner behind the instrument, enhancing evenness of tone throughout the piano's frequency range.

Now, measure the distance between the corner behind the piano

and the diagonally opposite corner. Then, keeping the piano at a 45° angle, move the piano one-fifth of that distance out from the corner, in the same direction you just measured. Open the lid and play scales through the instrument's entire range, listening for even tonal quality and clarity of pitch. Then move the piano farther in the same direction, until it's now one-third of the way out from the corner. Play it again. Then, placing the piano in the best-sounding location of the two, slide it, in very small increments, back toward the wall closest to the keyboard end of the piano, maintaining the 45° angle, and playing the same scales after every change in position. Then, once you find the "sweet spot," begin slowly rotating the piano by moving the keyboard end very slightly, a few inches at a time, in either direction, playing the same scales every

The Steinway *Pianissimo*

by James Schriber

The soft-edged look of this lovingly crafted piano gives the instrument an alluring appeal. Created in Pearwood solids and veneer with curly maple accents, the flowing lines of the piano draw not only the eyes, but the soul as well.

time. This procedure can take some time, but it's well worth the effort, and not as difficult as it sounds. You'll probably be amazed at how big a difference very small changes in position can make in the way your piano interacts with the room boundaries. While this may not solve all of your room problems, I have yet to find a situation where it didn't significantly help.

Reflection, Diffusion, Absorption

Sound behaves in much the same way as light. Shine a flashlight at a mirror in a dark room, and a hard glare will be reflected right back into your eyes. Shine the same flashlight onto a frosted piece of glass, and you'll notice that the light is evenly distributed in a pleasing circle on the surface of the glass, which will also reflect more light *around* the dark room than the mirror did. Apply this to music in an enclosed space, and you can understand why diffusion—the random scattering of sound—is far better than hard reflection. The latter makes the music itself sound hard and brittle, while diffusion provides clarity, warmth, and an evenness of sound throughout the

room. And because diffusion more evenly distributes high- and mid-frequency sound throughout a room, it adds greatly to musical clarity.

Absorption is useful in reducing the amount of sonic energy in a room. Many people make the mistake of cutting down reflections by deadening their music rooms with heavy draperies, thick carpets, and overstuffed furniture. However, this will not absorb all frequencies evenly, and can make a room sound dull in the upper octaves and too heavy in the bass—or the other way around. While in "live" rooms some absorption is desirable, even necessary, I suggest a combination of absorption and diffusion. This can be done by placing books, bookcases, artworks, chairs, and other randomly shaped objects along the walls to break up reflections, as well as scattering around the room *some* soft surfaces, such as upholstered furniture. Some of the best music rooms have mostly hard surfaces with little absorption, but they all have *many* diffusive surfaces that break up the reflections, which keeps the sound live, warm, and resonant. Partially closed wooden blinds or other irregularly shaped treatments for windows and glass doors will help diffuse reflections coming off of those glass surfaces. Note that flat artworks, even when not covered with glass, can cause degrading reflections unless they have a very irregular diffusive surface. Fabric wall hangings, especially quilts and other thick, soft, irregular surfaces, can absorb a lot of high-frequency reflections, when used in moderation—but not heavy drapes, unless the room is especially "live" and reverberant.

Floor Coverings

What you put *under* your grand piano can make a huge difference in its sound. In designing a music room, whether or not it will contain a piano, I normally specify hard floor surfaces, whether of hardwood, ceramic tile, or marble. The center of the floor should be covered with an acoustically absorbent surface, such as a carpet or rug. The idea here is to have sound absorption in the central part of the floor to cut down on reflections, while keeping the edges of the room more "live" for resonance. If the best-sounding location for your piano is not far enough out into the room for the instrument to be placed on the carpet or rug, place under the piano a separate area rug large enough to cover the piano's entire footprint. The bottom of a grand piano's soundboard produces a great deal of sound that a hard floor will reflect, thus making the sound harsh and brittle—unless something is there to help absorb that energy. If you don't mind how it looks, you can store piles or boxes of music or recordings on the floor directly under the piano, which will provide absorption *and* diffusion. In very "live" rooms, a thick fabric cover (similar to a full piano cover) can be suspended *under* the instrument's soundboard. This is especially useful in practice rooms, where clarity is more important than generating a big sound.

Vertical pianos, normally placed against or near walls, don't interact with hard floor surfaces as intimately as do grands. However, if your vertical is in the middle of a very "live" space, such as a dance studio or theater rehearsal room, it can benefit from some sort of floor covering under it that extends a few feet out from the piano on all sides. If a vertical's sound is still too resonant or bright, whether the piano is up against a wall or out in the middle of the room, you can eliminate some of this by hanging a heavy fabric cover or blanket over the back of the instrument. Not very stylish, but it works.

BUILDING A DEDICATED MUSIC ROOM

When building a music room, it's best to use multiples and divisions of 3 or 5 for interior dimensions (rather than 1, 2, or multiples of 2). For example, let's say you plan to buy a Steinway model B grand, which is 6 feet 10½ inches long (I'll round that off to 7 feet for purposes of discussion). Applying the principle that the total wall length should be at least 10 times the length of the piano, this gives us a minimum total wall length needed of 70 feet (10 × 7). If we take one-fifth of 70 feet (=14 feet) for each of the two short walls, that would leave 42 feet, or 21 feet each, for the two long walls. The ceiling height would be calculated as one-fifth of 21 feet (the long wall), × 2 = 8.4 feet. Therefore if your room is approximately 14 feet by 21 feet by 8.4 feet high, the piano should sound good, particularly for practice purposes. However, if you want a room in which you can perform for others on the same piano, or play chamber music with your colleagues, I suggest that your minimum total wall length be 15 times the length of the instrument. This could give you room dimensions of 21 feet by 31.5 feet by 12.6 feet high.

These specific proportions are offered only as examples. Unless you're building your room from the ground up as a dedicated piano studio, you may not be able to strictly adhere to this formula. If your chosen piano room doesn't come close to any optimal proportions (using the 3 and 5 multiply/division formula, you can come up with quite a few), all is not lost. It might take a little more time to get the sound right, with the possible addition of some acoustical treatments to absorb coincident low-frequency room modes. But the larger the room, the less critical of an issue this becomes.

If you're building your piano room from scratch, I suggest you consider making all of the interior walls non-parallel, in order to avoid the typical *flutter echo* often produced in small and medium-size rooms with parallel walls. Splaying the walls (sort of like a trapezoid) at angles of 5° to 10° can do a lot to prevent flutter. You'll hardly notice that the room isn't a perfect rectangle, and it will sound a lot better.

Something else to consider when building a dedicated piano studio: Don't make the inside walls of the room too stiff by using several layers of gypsum drywall or similar material. The interior walls of your music room should be able to flex a little bit to allow them to resonate—like the skins of a huge drum—and absorb the low frequencies produced by a larger piano in a smaller room. The more the walls can flex, the more excess sound energy they can absorb. For walls, use one or two layers of drywall set on 16-inch centered wood studs (or metal studs, in most high-rise and commercial construction). If you need to acoustically isolate your piano room from the rest of the house, build an additional, heavier, outer wall separated from the inner wall by at least 6 inches of air space. Suspend your music-room ceiling from the ceiling joists using "Z-channels" or a similar system, so that it, too, can flex a bit.

Some high-end piano dealers will give you time to audition an instrument in your home or studio before you make a final commitment to purchase. I strongly recommend taking advantage of any such offer—the room in which you place your piano is as important as the instrument itself in determining the ultimate sound. ▥

Lewis Lipnick is the principal contrabassoonist of the National Symphony Orchestra in Washington, DC, and an internationally-acclaimed soloist and teacher. His consulting firm, Lipnick-Design, specializes in designing high-resolution audio and video systems, recording studios, and home theaters; in environmental sound control; and in the acoustical design of commercial and residential spaces. Visit his website at www.lipnickdesign.com.

MOST OF US HAVE SEEN OR HEARD a humorous story of ordinary people attempting to move the heaviest thing ever made: a piano. Just thinking about it can give otherwise macho adults lower-back pain. A typical vertical piano weighs 300 to 500 pounds; some larger uprights can weigh over 800. Grand pianos typically weigh about 100 pounds per foot of length, but some concert grands weigh as much as 1,400 pounds. While pianos are abnormally heavy, with thousands of moving parts, they are also fragile. Additionally, many pianos have fine finishes that are sensitive to extremes of temperature and humidity. Then, to make things even more interesting, there are obstacles to maneuver, such as steps, turns, overhangs, hills, culs-de-sac, wet grass, and long gravel driveways. So, as someone who needs a piano moved, what are your options?

As the owner of a professional piano-moving company, I can't recommend moving a piano yourself. Risk of personal injury and damage to the instrument outweigh the advantage of saving a few dollars. Here are just a few of the many mistakes people make, and the dangers that await you if you try to do it yourself:

Letting the piano get away from you: Gravity can be a powerful tool when used properly, but it's dangerous if not respected. If someone slips or loses their grip, the piano will start moving by itself. In *The Piano Book*, Larry Fine tells the story of some friends who tried to move an upright piano. As they tipped the piano back, the bottom scooted away from them, causing the instrument to fall. The top edge gouged the wall and severed an electric cable, which started a fire that burned down the house. If something like this can happen in the home, imagine what gravity will do on steps or a steep outside grade. I'm sure you've seen those commercials in which a piano is being hoisted by crane and falls from a great height, breaking into smithereens. The truth, though, is that for many moves, particularly those above the second floor, hoisting by crane is much safer than moving a piano by hand. In some kinds of geography, additional equipment and creativity may be needed. One move we did in hilly San Francisco, on a street too steep for a truck to maneuver, required three professionals, two tow straps, an all-terrain vehicle, and an SUV! Don't think you can do this yourself.

Moving a piano without securing it to the vehicle: A piano sitting on a truck may seem just fine in the driveway, but a piano is not like a refrigerator, which is heavy mostly at its base. An upright piano's weight is evenly distributed from top to bottom, and some may even be top-heavy. Even a slight turn or grade can encourage a piano to jump ship.

A moving crew takes a baby grand piano out of a second story window because the steps were not an option. A forklift was used to secure the piano and lower it down.

A steep hillside poses a problem for moving a piano.

One story has the proud piano owner playing his instrument in the back of a pickup as they ride down the road. When the truck turned at a traffic light, the piano, motivated by inertia to keep going straight, did a back flip out of the truck, whereupon it ceased being in one piece.

Moving a grand piano without removing the legs and lyre: We delivered a grand to a customer who thought he was being helpful when he removed the entire sliding-door assembly from the family room. He didn't realize that a grand piano is moved only after it's been laid on its side and its legs and pedal lyre have been removed. The caster wheels attached to the legs are designed for minor adjustments of location in-room, not for the driveway or the yard. Stories abound of grand pianos being dragged over cement, gravel, grass, deep carpeting, or in-floor heating ducts, only to have the legs snap off and the instrument collapse. In addition, a grand must be protected by the proper special equipment before it can be moved. The piano is placed on its side on a special moving board, and secured

with straps and blankets. The lid is either removed or positioned to protect it from damage.

Almost as scary as moving a piano yourself—or scarier, depending on the outcome—but without the cost savings, is finding a non-professional mover. Typically, this category includes anyone who will move anything anywhere for one low price. They can be found online at what seems like a cheap price, and some of them demand payment before pickup. To make matters worse, sometimes these folks are merely brokers and have no truck or workers. They take your money, then find someone to do the job. There's a well-known saying: "The bitterness of poor service remains long after the sweetness of low price is forgotten." This is very true of piano moving.

Professional furniture movers are a step better, but you run the risk of being assigned to a driver who has little training or experience in moving a piano. Many drivers hate to see a piano in a shipment because they know pianos require special care. When the largest household mover in the U.S. bought another large mover in the 1990s, the wife of one of their top managers hired my company to move her piano. She knew the system, and wanted the comfort of knowing that the crew moving her cherished instrument moved several pianos every day, not several a year.

The best way to avoid unprofessional service is to look for a professional piano mover. You can find good companies online. (Yellow Pages ads are old-school; some professional movers, particularly those who provide interstate service, don't advertise in local books.) Just check a few important issues: The name of a company that specializes in moving pianos will most often include the word "piano" or "keyboard." An interstate mover's website should offer its Department of Transportation

(DOT) number, which indicates that it is regulated and has the required insurance and authorization. Some states also regulate intrastate movers, and require them to publish their state registration number in advertisements. Regulated or not, a company should be able, on request, to show you proof of insurance. The company's actual street address should accompany a local phone number. Check the company's Better Business Bureau rating at **www.BBB .org**. Check for its membership status in the National Association of Music Merchants (NAMM), the American Moving and Storage Association (AMSA), or that the owner is a member of the Piano Technicians Guild (PTG). How long a company has been in business will suggest whether it has been able to weather economic storms while continuing to satisfy its customers. A positive reference from one or more friends, family, or a professional such as a piano dealer or technician is always helpful. I suggest you

A blizzard in Colorado made truck and parking access almost impossible. The truck ramps allowed the use of a shuttle truck (an ATV) to bring the piano up the steep and icy hill.

Hefting a heavy organ safely takes planning, coordination, and a few muscles.

exercise a reasonable amount of due diligence, and try to use a company for which you have been given two or three referrals.

Long-distance moving presents its own set of options. Basic service involves a local piano mover picking up the piano and holding it in storage. Then the long-distance trucking company picks it up and takes it to the destination piano mover, who delivers it to the home. If you're moving your own household goods in a rental truck, you should have the local piano mover at the point of origin move the piano from the house into the truck and properly secure it, then have the local mover at the destination remove it from the truck and move it into the house. This method is usually the cheapest, the downside being that there are two or three different companies to deal with.

Better still is working with one company from start to finish. The office folks, the logo on the truck, and the uniforms on the moving personnel remain the same throughout your piano's travels. This way, you don't have to worry about complex scheduling problems or liability issues. For example, what happens if your rental truck or moving van is delayed? Will the local movers at the points of origin and destination still be available when you need them? If damage is discovered after your piano is moved into your new home, which of the three parties is responsible?

The best companies offer custom trucks and trailers specifically designed to transport pianos. Air-ride suspension, which keeps road vibrations and pot holes from shaking your piano apart, has proven to give the best ride. Proper load control, lift gates, and ramps further ensure that your piano is getting special care. Climate control is critical during especially warm or cold seasons; some finishes can be ruined if allowed to freeze. A professional piano mover handles all these variables for you.

When calling a long-distance moving company, be as specific as possible about any known difficulties associated with the move, such as difficult truck access in a rural or urban area, a very steep driveway, or no cell-phone service. Verify that the price is all-inclusive (includes moving the piano between house and truck), and not just for curbside delivery. Ask about any additional charges that might apply if, for example, you later decide to have the piano delivered to the second floor instead of the first.

Check your budget and schedule to determine the level of service you need. For long-distance moves, typically allow 30 days for pickup and another 30 days for delivery. If the move needs to be done more quickly, it will likely cost more; if you can give the mover more time, it will cost less. Most companies accept credit cards, which can allow you to spread the cost over several payments if necessary. Then sit back and enjoy a professional experience. Although a little more expensive than the nonprofessional kind, it will be less stressful for both you and your piano. 🎹

Russ Vitt is owner of Modern Piano Moving, the country's first door-to-door nationwide piano mover. The company has warehouse locations throughout the U.S., with headquarters in Sullivan, Missouri. For additional information, see its website at **www.modernpiano.com.**

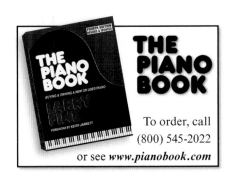

CARING FOR YOUR PIANO

LARRY FINE

A PIANO MAY LOOK large and imposing, but there is a great deal inside it that is delicate, and sensitive to both use and environmental changes. You have made a considerable investment in the instrument and now should protect that investment, as well as maximize your enjoyment of it, by properly caring for it. For most pianos in good condition receiving moderate use in the home, a budget of $300 to $500 per year should suffice for normal service.

If you bought the piano from a commercial seller, your first service will probably be a few weeks after delivery, by a technician associated with the seller. If you bought a used piano from a private seller and do not have a trustworthy recommendation to a technician, you can find the names of Registered Piano Technicians (RPT) in your area from the website of the Piano Technicians Guild (PTG), www.ptg.org. To become an RPT, one must pass a series of exams, assuring at least a minimum level of competence in piano servicing.

The following are the major types of service a piano needs on a regular or semi-regular basis. More information can be found in *The Piano Book*.

Tuning

Pianos go out of tune mostly because of seasonal changes in humidity that cause the soundboard and other parts to alternately swell and shrink. This happens regardless of whether or not the piano is played. Pianos vary in their responsiveness to fluctuations in humidity, but the variance is not always related to the quality of the instrument. People also differ in their sensitivity to tuning changes. New or newly restored pianos should be tuned three or four times the first year, until the strings are fully stretched out. After that, most pianos should be tuned between one and three times per year, depending on seasonal humidity changes, the player's sensitivity, and the amount of use. Pianos that receive professional levels of use (teaching, performance) are typically tuned more often, and major concert instruments are tuned before each performance. A regular home piano tuning typically costs between $100 and $200. However, if the piano has not been tuned regularly, or if it has undergone a large change in pitch, additional tuning work may be required at additional cost.

Regulation

Pianos also need other kinds of service. Due to settling and compacting of numerous cloth and felt parts, as well as seasonal changes in humidity, the piano's action (key and hammer mechanism) requires periodic adjustments to bring it back to the manufacturer's specifications. This process is called *regulation*. This should especially be done during the first six months to two years of a piano's life, depending on use. If it is not done, the piano may wear poorly for the rest of its life. After that, small amounts of regulating every few years will probably suffice for most pianos in home situations. Professional instruments need more complete service at more frequent intervals.

The thousands of parts in a piano action need periodic adjustment, or **regulation**, to compensate for wear and environmental changes.

A piano has over 200 strings, each of which must be individually tuned.

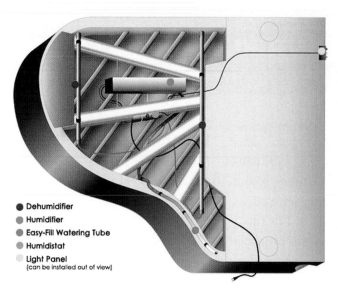

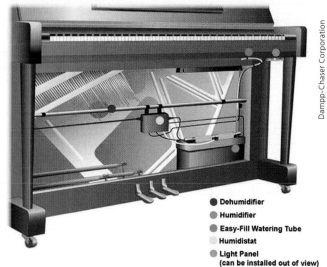

- ● Dehumidifier
- ● Humidifier
- ● Easy-Fill Watering Tube
- ● Humidistat
- ● Light Panel
  (can be installed out of view)

- ● Dehumidifier
- ● Humidifier
- ● Easy-Fill Watering Tube
- ● Humidistat
- ● Light Panel
  (can be installed out of view)

Dampp-Chaser Corporation

Voicing

Within limited parameters, the tone of a piano can be adjusted by hardening or softening the hammers, a process called *voicing*. Voicing is performed to compensate for the compacting and wear of hammer felt (which causes the tone to become too bright and harsh), or to accommodate the musical tastes of the player. Voicing should be done whenever the piano's tone is no longer to your liking. However, most piano owners will find that simply tuning the piano will greatly improve the tone,

and that voicing may not be needed very often.

Cleaning and Polishing

The best way to clean dust and finger marks off the piano is with a soft, clean, lintless cloth, such as cheesecloth, slightly dampened with water and wrung out. Fold the cloth into a pad and rub lightly in the direction of the grain, or in the direction in which the wood was originally polished (obvious in the case of handrubbed finishes). Where this direction is not obvious, as might be

the case with high-polish polyester finishes, rub in any one direction only, using long, straight strokes. Do not rub in a circular motion, as this will eventually make the finish lose its luster. Most piano manufacturers recommend against the use of commercially available furniture polish or wax. Polish specially made for pianos is available from some manufacturers, dealers, and technicians.

To clean the keys, use the same kind of soft, clean cloth as for the finish. Dampen the cloth slightly with water or a mild white soap solution, but don't let water run down the sides of the keys. If the keytops are made of ivory, be sure to dry them off right after cleaning—because ivory absorbs water, the keytops will curl up and fall off if water is allowed to stand on them. If the black keys are made of wood, use a separate cloth to clean them, in case any black stain comes off (not necessary for plastic keys).

Dust inevitably collects inside a piano no matter how good a housekeeper one is. A piano technician can safely vacuum up the dust or otherwise clean the interior of the piano when he or she comes to tune it.

Custom voicing of a piano for optimal tonal quality is considered by piano technicians to be an art form.

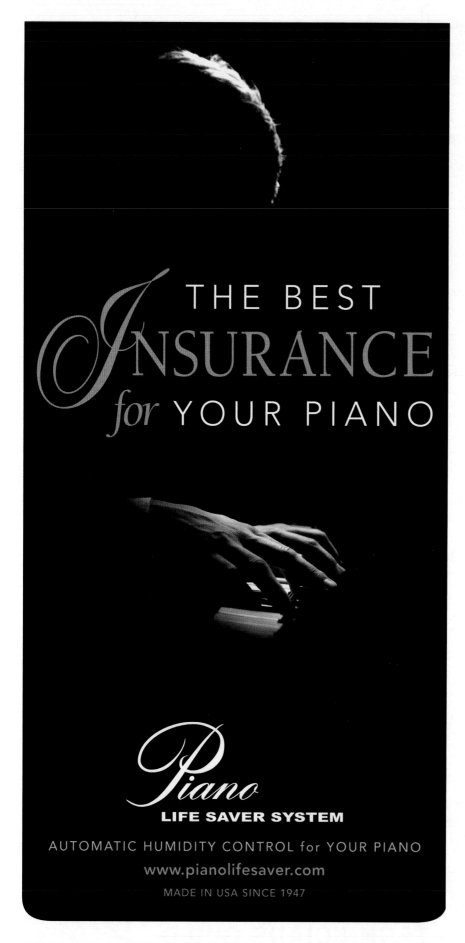
Humidity Control

Because pianos are made primarily of wood, proper control of humidity will greatly increase both the life span of the piano and your enjoyment of it. A relative humidity of 42% is sometimes cited as ideal for a piano, but any humidity level that is relatively constant and moderate will suffice. Here are some common steps to take to protect your piano from fluctuations and extremes of humidity:

- Don't place the piano too near radiators, heating and cooling ducts, fireplaces, direct sunlight, and open windows.

- Avoid overheating the house during cold weather.

- Use air-conditioning during hot, humid weather.

- Add humidity to the air during dry weather with either a whole-house humidifier attached to a central air system or with a room humidifier. Room humidifiers, however, have to be cleaned and refilled frequently, and some make a lot of noise. If you use a room humidifier, don't place it too near the piano.

Instead of the above, or in addition to it, have a climate-control system installed in the piano. They make no noise, require very little maintenance, and cost $350 to $500 for a vertical piano or $400 to $600 for a grand, ordered and installed through your piano technician or piano dealer. The illustrations on the previous page of the Dampp-Chaser climate-control system show how the system's components are discreetly hidden inside the piano. For more information about these systems, see www.pianolifesaver.com.

When to tune your piano depends on your local climate. You should avoid times of rapid humidity change and seek times when the humidity will be stable for a reasonable length of time. Turning the heat on in the house in the fall, and then off again in the spring, causes major indoor humidity changes, and in each case it may take several months before the piano's soundboard fully restabilizes at the new humidity level.

In Boston, for example, the tuning cycle goes something like that shown in the graph. A piano tuned in April or May, when the heat is turned off, will probably be out of tune by late June. If it is tuned in late June or July, it may well hold its tune until October or later, depending on when the heat is turned on for the winter. If the piano is tuned *right* after the heat is turned on, however, say in October or November, it will almost certainly be out of tune by Christmas. But if you wait until after the holidays (and, of course, everyone wants it tuned *for* the holidays), it will probably hold pretty well until April or even May. In my experience, most problems with pianos in good condition that "don't hold their tune" are caused by poor timing of the tuning with the seasonal changes.

Note that those who live in a climate like Boston's and have their piano tuned twice a year will probably also notice two times during the year when the piano sounds out of tune but when, for the above reason, it should probably *not* be tuned. The only remedies for this dilemma are to have the piano tuned more frequently, or to more closely control the humidity.

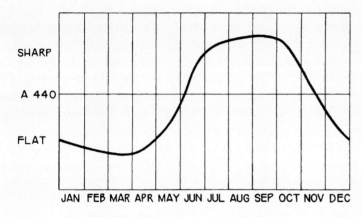

The pitch of the piano in the tenor and low treble ranges closely follows the annual cycle of indoor humidity. The graph shows how a typical piano in Boston might behave. Most areas of the country that have cold winters will show a similar pattern.

Another solution to the humidity-control problem is **Music Sorb**, a non-toxic silica gel that naturally absorbs excess moisture from the air during humid times and releases it during times of dryness. It comes in packets or pouches sold through piano technicians. Enough for a single piano costs $65 to $70 and must be replaced once a year. Music Sorb probably won't control humidity changes in the piano quite as well as a Dampp-Chaser system, but may suffice in less severe climates, or in situations where plugging in and maintaining such a system is out of the question—or until the piano owner can afford the larger initial outlay of funds required for the system.

Benches

In all likelihood, your purchase of a new piano will include a matching bench. Benches for consumer-grade pianos are usually made by the piano manufacturer and come with the piano. Benches for performance-grade pianos are often provided separately by the dealer.

Benches come in two basic types: *fixed-height* or *adjustable*. Consumer-grade pianos usually come with fixed-height benches that have either a solid top that matches the piano's finish, or a padded top with sides and legs finished to match the piano. The legs on most benches will be miniatures of the piano's legs, particularly for decorative models. Most piano benches have music storage compartments. School and institutional-type vertical pianos often come with so-called "stretcher" benches—the legs are connected with wooden reinforcing struts to better endure heavy use.

Both solid-top and padded benches work well. The padded benches tend to be a little more comfortable, especially for those who have little natural padding of their own. They tend to wear more quickly, however, and are subject to tearing. Solid-top benches wear longer but are more easily scratched.

Adjustable benches are preferred by serious players who spend hours at the piano, and by children and adults who are shorter or taller than average. The standard height of a piano bench is 19" or 20". Adjustable benches typically can be set at anywhere from about 18" to 21". By adjusting the bench height and moving it slightly forward or backward, one can maintain the proper posture and wrist angle to the keyboard.

High-quality adjustable benches have a very heavy steel mechanism—so strong you could almost use it as a car jack! The duet-size bench (seats two) weighs well over 60 pounds. These benches are made of hard rock maple and come in most leg styles and finishes. The deeply tufted tops come in a heavy-duty vinyl and look like leather; tops of actual leather are available at additional cost. Both look great and wear well. The best ones, such as those made by Jansen, are expensive ($500 to $750) but are built to last a lifetime. Over the past few years, lesser-quality adjustable benches have come on the market. While these benches are adjustable within a similar range, the mechanisms aren't as hardy. They may be fine for light use, but most will not last nearly as long as the piano.

Legs for both fixed-height and adjustable benches are attached by a single bolt at the top of each leg. These bolts should be tightened anytime there is wobble in the bench. Don't over-tighten, however, as that might pull the bolt out of the leg.

Finally, if the piano you want doesn't come with the bench you desire, talk to your dealer. It's common for dealers to swap benches or bench tops to accommodate your preference, or to offer an upgrade to

Padded Bench

Wood Top Bench

Stretcher Bench

Adjustable Artist Bench

www.pljansen.com

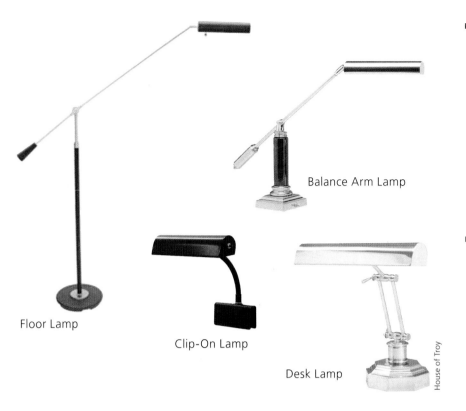

Floor Lamp

Balance Arm Lamp

Clip-On Lamp

Desk Lamp

House of Troy

- **Caster Cups**. Caster cups are small cups that go under the wheels of vertical and grand pianos to protect the floor or carpet. They come in plastic or a variety of woods, and in clear acrylic that allows the carpet or hardwood floor to show through. If the caster cups have felt on the bottom, however, be careful, as the dye from the felt can bleed into carpeting, especially if it gets damp.

- **Piano Covers**. Used mostly in churches and schools (and homes with cats), piano covers are designed to protect the piano's finish from accidental damage, and are available to fit any size of piano. They come in vinyl or mackintosh (a very tight-weave fabric that is very water-resistant), brown or black on the outside, and a fleece-like material on the side that touches the piano. A thicker, quilted, cotton cover is available for use in locations where the piano is moved frequently or may get bumped.

- **Bench Cushions**. Bench cushions are made in a variety of sizes, thicknesses (1" to 3"), fabrics, and colors. They are also available in tapestry designs, most with a musical motif, tufted or box-edged, and all have straps to secure them to the bench.

a better bench in lieu of a discount on the piano.

Lamps

Having adequate lighting for the piano music is critical. It's hard enough to learn how to read music without having to deal with a lack of illumination, or with shadows on the sheet music. The ideal solution is track lighting in the ceiling just above the player. In many homes and institutions, however, this is not feasible. In those instances, a piano lamp may well be the answer.

Piano lamps fall into two major groups: floor lamps and desk lamps. Floor lamps arch over the piano and hover over the music rack, while desk lamps sit directly on the piano or are attached to the music rack itself. Desk lamps are subdivided into three groups: a standard desk lamp that sits atop a vertical piano directly over the music rack; a "balance-arm" lamp that sits off to the side on a grand piano's music desk and has a long arm that hovers over the music rack; and a clip-on lamp that attaches directly to the music rack itself (see illustrations).

Piano lamps come in a variety of qualities, sizes, styles, finishes, and bulb types. The better ones are usually made of high-quality brass, while the least expensive are often made of very thin brass or are simply brass-plated. The light from incandescent-bulb lamps tends to be a tad harsh, but the bulbs are less expensive than those for fluorescent lamps, which, though pricier, emit a softer light.

Piano lamps are available through most piano dealerships as well as at lighting stores. A limited selection can also be found at The Home Depot and Lowe's.

Accessories and Problem Solvers

Only a few accessories are used with pianos, and most are available at your local piano dealership. You might consider:

Wood

Caster Cups

Lucite

www.perfectlygrand.com

Piano Covers

Bench Cushions

- **Pedal Extenders**. These extension devices are available for those whose feet do not comfortably reach the pedals. Some are nothing more than a brass pedal that bolts on to the existing pedal, while others are a box, finished to match the piano, that sits over the existing pedals and has pedals with rods to operate the piano's pedals.

- **Metronomes**. Many music teachers recommend using a metronome to improve students' timing. Any piano or musical-instrument dealership will generally have a wide selection, from the solid walnut, wind-up, oscillating metronome like the one your grandmother had on her piano, to a new, beeping digital model.

- **Grand Piano String Covers**. Wool string covers are available in a variety of colors that complement the piano's finish. When in place, they provide a reduction in sound volume, and protection against dust (and cats). Thicker sound-reduction covers and baffles are also available.

- **Lid and Fallboard Slow-Close Systems.** Raising and lowering the lid of a grand piano is frequently difficult, and can be downright dangerous. This is due to the combination of its weight, which can exceed 50 pounds, and its position, which makes it hard to reach. Enter a new product that solves at least the weight problem: Safety-Ease Lid Assist. Safety-Ease consists of pneumatic cylinders that effectively counterbalance the weight of the lid and damp its movement so that it can be easily raised or lowered, even by a child. It mounts under the lid, between the lid hinges on the piano's rim, is finished in polished ebony to match most pianos, and requires no drilling or permanent installation. This unique system is sold and installed only by piano dealers or technicians. The installed price for small and mid-size grands is $500 to $600. More information is available at **www.safety-ease.com**.

  The fallboard (keyboard cover) can also be a danger, not so much for its weight or position, but for the swiftness of its fall and because, when it falls, little fingers are likely to be in its path. Many new pianos today come with a pneumatically or hydraulically damped, slow-close fallboard. For those that don't, aftermarket devices are available from piano dealers or technicians.

- **Touch-Weight Adjustment Systems.** *Touch* or *touch weight* refers to the pressure required to press a piano key. Too little touch weight, or touch weight that is uneven from note to note, makes a piano action difficult to control;

Pedal Extenders

Metronomes

too much touch weight makes a piano tiring to play, and can cause physical problems for the player over time. Touch-weight problems can be caused by poor action design, worn parts in older pianos, or incorrectly dimensioned replacement parts in restored pianos.

Historically, discussions, measurements, and adjustments in this area of piano technology have been about *static* touch weight—the force needed to make a piano key just begin to move slowly downward. Less well understood, and usually ignored, has been *dynamic* touch weight—the force required to press a key in actual normal, rapid playing. Here, the rapid movement of the key creates *inertia* (i.e., the tendency of a moving mass to keep moving in the same direction and at the same speed, and the tendency of a stationary mass to remain stationary.) Unlike static touch weight, which depends on the *relative* amount and positioning of mass on either side of the key's balance point, as well as on

friction, dynamic touch weight depends on the *total* amount of mass in the system. Attempts to fix problems in static touch weight by adding mass to the front or rear of the key can cause problems with dynamic touch weight by creating excessive inertia.

Until fairly recently, technicians resorted to a patchwork quilt of homemade, trial-by-error remedies for problems with static touch weight; dynamic touch weight wasn't even on their radar. More recently, a greater understanding of touch weight has emerged, and more sophisticated techniques for solving touch-weight problems are being developed. The gold standard among these techniques is that of David Stanwood, who developed the first system for mathematically describing, measuring, and solving problems related to dynamic touch weight. His system is applied by a network of specially trained technicians who, because of the comprehensive nature of the system and the remedies it suggests, tend to use it on higher-end instruments and those

undergoing complete restoration. More information can be found at **www.stanwoodpiano.com**.

A simpler remedy, but only for heavy or uneven static touch weight on a grand piano, is a product called TouchRail, available through piano technicians. TouchRail is a rail with 88 individually adjustable springs that replaces a grand piano's key-stop rail. The springs press gently on the keys to the front of the balance point, enabling the technician to effectively "dial in" a desired touch weight and make it perfectly even from note to note. Because it's spring-based rather than mass-based, TouchRail won't add inertia to the action system, though of course it won't cure any pre-existing problems with excessive inertia, either. Installation requires no drilling, cutting, or other permanent modification of the piano, and the rail can be removed and replaced in seconds during routine piano service, just like a traditional key-stop rail. The installed price is around $500. See **www.pitchlock.com** for more information.

Express through touch.
Impress through sound.

30th
Anniversary

AP-620   AP-420   AP-220

The Celviano line of pianos has been refined for those who demand an authentic grand piano experience. Its elegant design houses new grand piano sounds and an enhanced keyboard touch. Utilizing a new tri-sensor spring less 88-note graded hammer action, every nuance and detail of your performance is captured. A new 4 layer stereo grand piano sound delivers a natural, expressive and dynamic piano experience. Featuring 128 notes of polyphony, USB MIDI, Duet Mode and more, Celviano's advanced technology and sound deliver a powerful piano performance.

CELVIANO

CASIO.

www.casiousa.com

BUYING A DIGITAL PIANO
ALDEN SKINNER

IF, AFTER HAVING READ "Acoustic or Digital: What's Best for Me?," you've decided on a digital piano, the next step is shopping for and selecting the right model for your needs. There are currently over 200 models of digital piano on the market. Narrowing the field requires exploring some basic issues. This article covers the needs of both entry-level shoppers and those interested in more sophisticated, feature-laden models. If you're looking for an entry-level instrument and are just interested in learning the basics, you can read "The Starter Digital Piano" below, then skip to "Shopping Options," toward the end of this article.

The Starter Digital Piano

If nothing else, a digital piano should be able to emulate an acoustic piano in basic ways. Fulfilling this function requires features found on most digital pianos today. Some first-time buyers, however, opt for an instrument with more than just the basics, and buy a model with additional sounds and "easy-play" features.

Matching the Player's Needs. Unless you expect to buy another piano in a year or so, you need to consider your long-term requirements. Who will be the primary player today? If it's for the family, how long will it be until the youngest child has the opportunity to learn? Does Mom or Dad harbor any musical interests? If so, it's likely that one family member or another will use the instrument for many years to come. This argues for getting a higher-quality instrument, whose advantages of better tone, touch, and features will be appreciated over time.

If multiple players will use the instrument, it needs to meet the expectations of the most advanced player. At the same time, a beginner in the family will benefit from educational features that are of no interest to the advanced player, and still another family member may just want to fool around with the instrument once in a while. Easy-play features and software will keep these players happy—and you might be surprised how many people are enticed into learning to play as a result of these easy first steps. So, obviously, an individual player may search among a very narrow range of instruments, while a family may have to balance the needs of several people. Fortunately, the wealth of available choices can easily accommodate any combination of individual and/or family needs.

Is a keyboard with fewer than 88 notes a viable alternative? In a word, no.

Voices and Expanded Capabilities. Most entry-level digitals have a few different piano voices, as well as a dozen or so other instrumental voices, such as harpsichord, church and jazz organ, vibes, and strings. These models, designed mainly to emulate the piano, are referred to as "standard" digital pianos. Many other,

slightly more expensive models, called "ensemble" digital pianos, come with expanded capabilities: all the instruments of the orchestra (and more), easy-play background accompaniments, rhythms, special effects, and much more. You might not think you need the additional capabilities of an ensemble digital, but having them can enable the beginner, as well as family members who don't take lessons, to have a lot more fun and sound like pros with minimal practice. For an advancing player, the opportunities for musical creativity are significantly enhanced.

If at all possible, you should try at least two or three instruments in your price and style range to determine which sounds best to *you*. If you plan to use headphones in your home (yes, parents—your children can practice silently using headphones), be sure to try out the pianos through headphones, as this can make a tremendous difference in sound. (For consistency of comparison, bring your own headphones.) Sometimes the instrument's weakest link is its built-in speaker system.

88-note Weighted Keyboard. Even entry-level digitals should feel much like an acoustic piano. If you have some playing experience, you'll want to try two or three competing models to see what feels best to *you*. None of the available models has an overly heavy touch. So-called semi-weighted keyboards, which depend on springs for their weight,

Slab type

Console type

Digital grand

should be avoided, as they don't feel enough like an acoustic piano. Is a keyboard with fewer than 88 notes a viable alternative? In a word, no. None have a decently weighted keyboard. In addition, students who use instruments with short keyboards tend to outgrow them quickly, and suffer some degree of disorientation when taking lessons on an 88-note keyboard.

Ease of Use. Make sure you understand how the instrument's controls work—additional features are of little use if you can't figure out how to use them. Ask to see the owner's manual (or download it from the manufacturer's website) and make sure that it's understandable.

Cabinet Type. Another factor that may shape your options is where the instrument will live. Is space at a premium? Are there limited placement options? If home is a dorm room or a small studio apartment and you need to make the most efficient use of every square inch, you may opt for a portable model (not a furniture-style cabinet) that can be placed on a stand for practice and stuck in a closet when not in use. Bear in mind that this type of design, typically called a slab, doesn't necessarily limit the quality of instruments available to you—professional stage pianos also fit into this category. Slabs generally come with a single pedal, but many have optional stands that, like an acoustic piano, have three pedals. If you do go with a stand, don't get the cheapest one you can find. These are fine for 61-note portable keyboards, but tend to wobble when supporting the greater weight of a digital piano, and may not be able to be adjusted low enough to put the keyboard at the proper height from the floor (about 29 inches to the tops of the white keys). It should be noted that *portability* is a relative term: instruments in this category can range in weight from 25 to over 70 pounds, without stand.

Another option in the entry-level category is what is variously referred to as the vertical, upright, or console digital piano. The cabinetry of these models ranges from two flat side supports with a cross member for stability, to elegant designs that would look at home in the most posh surroundings. It's common for individual models in this category to be available in multiple finish options, including synthetic wood grain, real-wood veneers, and, on some of the better models, the lustrous polished ebony often found on acoustic pianos. Most of these models have three pedals.

If space is no problem and you love the look of a grand piano, several digital pianos are available in "baby grand" cases. Remember that, most of the time, you pay a significant premium for this look, and that few of the digital grand models actually use the additional internal space to enhance the instrument beyond the non-grand model it's based on. There are two size classes of digital grands, one about five feet long and the other closer to three feet—just long enough for the tail to curve in a quasi-grand shape.

Additional Features. Virtually all models of digital piano include headphone connections for private practice, and MIDI and/or USB connections that allow you to connect the instrument to a Mac or PC for use with a variety of music software. Other features included in many entry-level instruments are a built-in metronome, the ability to play more than one instrumental voice at a time (called *layering* or *splitting*; see "Digital Piano Basics"), and the ability to record and play back anything you play. While you may not be ready for a recording contract, the ability to listen to what you're practicing is a great learning tool.

Pricing. Slab models start at $500, console models at around $1,000. Digital grands begin at about $1,500, but the better-quality models start at around $5,000. In each category

there are many options; spending more will usually get you some combination of better sound, features, touch, and appearance.

Those who are shopping for an entry-level digital and want to keep it simple can skip the next section and go directly to "Shopping Options."

Further Considerations for More Serious Shoppers

Before reading further about shopping, I suggest that you read the two "Digital Piano Basics" articles, and explore the **brand profiles** and the **charts of features and specifications**, all elsewhere in this issue. There you'll find detailed information about the features and benefits of both standard and ensemble digitals. Once you have a grasp of what these instruments can do and how they differ from one another, you'll be able to shop with a better idea of which features and level of quality you desire, which in turn will make your shopping efforts more efficiently focused and enjoyable.

Serious Listening

You've decided what type of instrument you're looking for and how much you're going to spend (unless, of course you hear something that just knocks your socks off, and your budget along with them). There are still a couple of last steps in preparation for the hunt.

If you don't already have a good set of headphones, this is the time to get them. Headphones are probably the most widely used accessory for digital pianos, and it's a sure bet that you, or another player in the house, will need them or wish the other player were using them—and they're an invaluable tool for auditioning digital pianos. Part of what you hear when you compare instruments is the speaker system, and this is a critical element; but headphones can also isolate you from noise in the store and give you a common baseline as you go from place to place trying different instruments. Most stores have headphones available, but they're typically low-end models, and never the same as the ones you listened to in the last store. I've

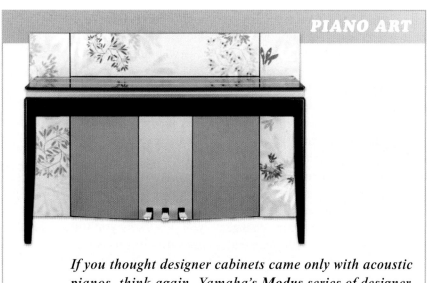

PIANO ART

If you thought designer cabinets came only with acoustic pianos, think again. Yamaha's Modus series of designer digital pianos features a colorful contemporary look.

always found it odd that people will agonize over the choice of a digital piano, spend hundreds—frequently thousands—of dollars on their choice, and then listen to it through $19.95 headphones. (See "**Digital Piano Basics, Part 2**" for a discussion of headphones.)

The final step is to "calibrate" your ears. Listen to recordings of solo piano. Listen to what you enjoy, be it jazz, classical, or ragtime—just listen a lot. For part of this listening, use the headphones you bought for your digital piano. This will embed in your head, as a benchmark, the sound of high-quality acoustic pianos. One of the great things about digital pianos is that if you love, say, honky-tonk piano, all you have to do is make sure the instruments you're considering have a Honky-Tonk setting. Then you can "change pianos" at will. But for the moment, listen to the best piano recordings you can get your ears on.

When you start to audition instruments, you'll become aware that some of what you're hearing isn't the instrument, or at least not what the instrument is supposed to do. Part of what you'll be hearing is the result of room acoustics and the instrument's placement in the showroom. If there are a lot of hard surfaces nearby—uncarpeted floors and large windows—the results will be different from what you'll hear in a "softer" environment, such as a carpeted living room with drapes, bookshelves, and upholstered furniture. Placement in the room will also affect the sound. If you're serious about buying a particular instrument, asking the dealer to move it to another part of the showroom isn't an unreasonable request. Another thing to be aware of is that the voice settings of most digital pianos include some degree of reverberation. This isn't a bad thing, but it's worthwhile to listen to the piano voice, and any other voices that are important to you, with the reverb and all other effects turned off. This will allow you to judge those voices without any coloration or masking from the effects.

Evaluating Tonal Quality

Almost by definition, evaluating an instrument's tone is very subjective, and judging the tone of instruments that have a lot of voices can be overwhelming. Your best bet is to select the five or six instruments you think you'll use most and make them the standard for comparison as you shop. If you choose the piano on which those voices sound best to you, it's likely you'll find the others satisfying as well.

Digital pianos are really computers disguised as pianos, and the engineers who design them strive to develop a set of sounds and features unique to their brand. Like some features of a PC, many of the capabilities of digitals are hidden from view, accessible by pressing a sequence of buttons or through multi-screen menus. While the owner's manual will explain how to access these features or sounds, it's impractical for you to study the manuals of every instrument under consideration. Enter the salesperson! This is one of those instances where a well-trained salesperson can be invaluable.

Most manufacturers arrange trainings for their retailers' sales staffs, to enable them to demonstrate the relative advantages of that brand's features. Even if you're a proficient player, having a salesperson demonstrate and play while you listen can be a valuable part of the evaluation process. But remember that the salesperson is not going home with you! Don't be swayed by his or her talent—a really good player can make even a poor-sounding piano "sing." Focus your attention on the instrument itself.

You should make sure that you get the answers to a few key questions, either through the salesperson's demonstration or your own experimentation:

Generally, one of the instrument voices used most frequently is the piano. There is a great deal of variation in "good" piano tone. Many players like a bright, crisp sound, while others prefer a mellower tone. Some like a great deal of harmonic content, others a bell-like clarity with fewer harmonics. Whatever your preference, will you be satisfied with the piano sound of the model you're considering?

Many instruments sound slightly different as a note begins to play.

> **There is a great deal of variation in "good" piano tone. Many players like a bright, crisp sound, while others prefer a mellower tone.**

For example, a flute takes a quarter of a second or so to build up enough air pressure to reach the pitch of the note, resulting in a "breathiness" to the sound. The same is true of many other wind instruments. Guitarists and other players of stringed instruments "bend" notes by varying their touch. Jazz organs often have a percussive "pop" at the beginning of the note. How well do the digital voices of the model you're evaluating emulate the actual instruments?

Even entry-level standard digitals include such effects as Reverb and Chorus. More sophisticated models have many other effects, as described in the "Digital Piano Basics" articles. Having heard them demonstrated, do you think these effects will be useful to you?

Take your time. Following the salesperson's demonstration, most dealers will let you spend time experimenting—although some may prefer that you use headphones.

Evaluating Touch

Aside from sound, the most important element in the selection of an instrument is likely to be the feel of the action. Unless you're considering only digital pianos that employ an actual acoustic action (see "Hybrid Pianos," elsewhere in this issue), you'll be selecting from a variety of actions that all try to emulate the feel of an acoustic action. The aspect of action feel that seems to generate the most discussion is whether the touch weight is light or heavy, and which is better. This is covered in more detail in "Digital Piano Basics, Part 1," but here's the bottom line: Just as there is no single correct piano sound, there is no single correct touch weight; rather, there is a range of acceptable touch weights. If you spend the majority of your playing time with a heavy action, when you encounter an instrument with a lighter action,

be it acoustic or digital, you'll play too heavily—and vice versa. The only cure is to play as many instruments as possible, as often as possible. Listen to how each piano responds and adjust your touch accordingly. You've probably driven cars with light steering and cars with heavy steering, and generally managed to avoid hitting any trees with either of them. With varied experience, you learn to adapt.

Common to acoustic and digital actions is mechanical noise. Digitals are frequently accused of having noisier actions because their sound can be reduced to a whisper or played through headphones, leaving the action noise audible, whereas the sound of an acoustic piano tends to always mask its action noise. This is not to say that some digital actions aren't unusually noisy, but to honestly compare them, you have to play them with the volume turned off. In addition to letting you compare action noise, this prevents your mind from judging the *feel* of an action based on the *tone* of the instrument.

New or Used?

Because digital technology advances at a blistering pace relative to acoustic-piano technology, there is much less interest in used digitals than in used acoustics. Many of today's digital pianos eclipse the capabilities of the models of even five years ago. Combine this technological advancement with the fact that support of older instruments may be limited—after production of a particular model ceases, electronics manufacturers are required to maintain replacement parts for only seven years—and investing in older models becomes worthy of serious second thoughts.

> Aside from sound, the most important element in the selection of an instrument is likely to be the feel of the action.

Owner's manuals no longer accompany many used instruments. If you find an interesting used instrument, make sure that the manual is either still with it, or is readily available from the manufacturer or on the Internet. The manual is your best tool for ensuring that everything on the instrument still works correctly. It's not simply a matter of pressing every key, button, and pedal to see that they work; to thoroughly check the instrument, you also need to know what some of the less obvious controls are supposed to do. None of this is to say that used instruments should be avoided—I've played ten-year-old digital pianos that worked perfectly. But when considering an older digital piano, extra care should be exercised.

Shopping Options

Your shopping options depend on the type of digital piano you've decided to buy and the region you live in. In North America, different categories of instruments are available through different types of outlets. Furniture-style models, particularly the higher-end models manufactured by the largest suppliers, are available only through traditional bricks-and-mortar piano or full-line music retailers. The lower-priced furniture-style, slab, or stage models, and some of the less widely distributed brands, are available from a cross section of traditional bricks-and-mortar music retailers, club and warehouse chains such as Costco, consumer-electronics chains such as Best Buy, and online retailers.

Perhaps the biggest difference between shopping for digital and acoustic pianos is that you usually

The Steinway
Roger Williams Gold
by James Schriber

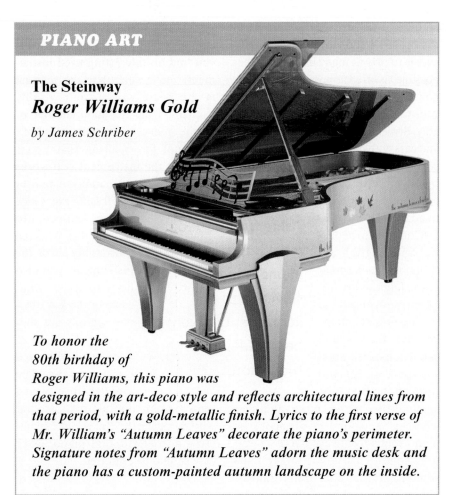

To honor the 80th birthday of Roger Williams, this piano was designed in the art-deco style and reflects architectural lines from that period, with a gold-metallic finish. Lyrics to the first verse of Mr. William's "Autumn Leaves" decorate the piano's perimeter. Signature notes from "Autumn Leaves" adorn the music desk and the piano has a custom-painted autumn landscape on the inside.

want to make sure you get the specific acoustic piano you played on the showroom floor. But once you've decided on a model of digital piano, it doesn't matter if you get the one you actually tried or not. Every unit made of the same model will be identical to all other units.

Negotiating the price of a digital piano at a bricks-and-mortar retailer is no different from negotiating the price of an acoustic piano, which is discussed in "**Piano Buying Basics,**" elsewhere in this issue. However, many of the simpler furniture-style digitals and nearly all portable or stage-piano models that are sold through a variety of local and online stores are virtually always sold at the same price, wherever you shop. This is due to a pricing model

called minimum advertised price, or MAP, used for many categories of products. A manufacturer's or distributor's MAP is the lowest price at which a dealer is allowed to *advertise* an item. Since prices are easily compared and all retailers want an even chance to win your business, everyone advertises at the MAP. And since the MAP is typically lower than the price at which the dealer might have preferred to sell the item, the price almost never drops below the MAP. Therefore, MAP has become the standard pricing for all non-piano-dealer models of digital piano.

You should find out how warranty service is handled for the instrument you've selected—not only the terms related to coverage for parts and labor, but where the

service is performed. Like acoustic pianos, most digital models available only through piano dealers have a warranty specifying in-home service; that is, the technician comes to you. Models sold outside of traditional piano stores must be brought to the technician's shop for warranty service. Ask your salesperson where the closest authorized service technician is located, or check the manufacturer's website.

You can see from the chart of digital piano specifications that it's not unusual for different models from the same manufacturer to have different warranty terms. It would be tempting to attribute this to differences in quality, but most often it's based on differences in anticipated use (home vs. commercial), and on marketing decisions for a given product segment. Unlike some warranties for acoustic pianos, I'm aware of no digital piano warranty that is transferable to a subsequent owner.

There are many decisions to be made when selecting a piano, digital or acoustic. But in the end, there is no substitute for playing and listening for yourself. The best anyone else can do is tell you what he or she would buy. But unless that person's requirements exactly match your own, all you'll end up with is a piano that's perfect for someone else.

Go out and try everything you can get your hands on— and enjoy the process! ▥

For more information

If, after reading the articles in *Piano Buyer*, you still have questions about buying a digital piano, I recommend visiting the Digital Pianos—Synths & Keyboards Forum on Piano World (**www.pianoworld.com**), the premiere website for everything related to pianos and pianists. The helpful folks there have a wealth of knowledge and advice they are happy to share.

IN PART 1 OF THIS ARTICLE, we describe how a digital piano performs its most basic function—imitating the acoustic piano. We begin with tone production, then move on to controls—the keyboard and pedals—and conclude with the instrument's audio system. In Part 2, we explore all the ways that digital pianos can go beyond simply duplicating the functions of the acoustic piano.

Tone Production

Sample Rate and Bit Rate

The technology now used in most digital pianos to emulate the complex tonal behavior of the acoustic piano is called *sampling*. Sampling, in its simplest form, is the process of making a digital recording of a sound for later playback. A collection of samples, such as those needed to reproduce the tone of a piano, is called a *sample set*. There are many decisions to be made in compiling a sample set for an instrument as sonically complex as a piano, perhaps the most important being the *sample rate* and *bit rate*.

The *sample rate* determines how many times per second the sound will be measured. The sound must be sampled often enough to avoid missing changes that occur between sample times. This rate, in turn, depends on the frequency of the sound being sampled. The fundamental frequency of the highest note on the keyboard is 4,186 cycles per second, or hertz (Hz). But the overtones that accompany these fundamentals vibrate at multiples of the fundamental's

frequency, and must be properly recorded in order to accurately reproduce the tone. Fortunately, the inventors of the Compact Disc were well aware of this requirement, and long ago adopted the sampling rate of 44,100Hz for audio CD recordings.

The other decision is how finely to measure at each of those 44,100 times per second. Just as we don't want to miss changes in the sound that occur between the times we measured it, we also can't afford to miss the details of those changes. In digital recording, this is called the *bit rate*, or, as recording pros call it, the *bit depth*. The higher the bit rate, the

finer the detail that can be recorded. In computers, an 8-bit number represents up to 256 levels of detail, a 16-bit number can represent 65,536 levels, and a 24-bit number tops out at 16,777,216 levels. Once again, we will bow to the decision of the developers of the Compact Disc and go with the choice of a 16-bit number as our standard.

What all of this means is that, under the audio-CD standard, every second of sound sampled is measured 44,100 times at a degree of detail that can represent up to 65,536 individual levels. This one second of sample information takes up just over 86 kilobytes (KB) of memory space. Because digital piano manufacturers do not release information about their sampling standards, there's no basis for comparison with the audio-CD standard. However, the rates stated by developers of software pianos tend to be higher than this standard, so it's reasonable to assume that some digital piano manufacturers may exceed these rates as well.

Looping

One interesting characteristic of a piano note is that it can sustain for several seconds, but after the first couple of seconds much of the initial complexity of the sound is gone; the remaining seconds of sustained sound go through very little change other than gradually decreasing in volume. This opens up the

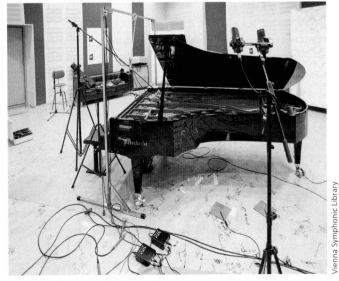
Bösendorfer mic'd for sampling

Vienna Symphonic Library

possibility to save some memory space, and thus some money, by introducing a process called *looping*. Looping involves selecting a short duration of the sound that remains essentially unchanged over a period of time, and repeating it over and over at gradually reduced volume levels. Done with care, the result is barely detectable when listening intently to the sustain of one note, and becomes completely lost in the commotion when playing normally.

Spatial Relations

The notes produced by an acoustic piano have a physical point of origin in the instrument's strings, and can be heard moving from left to right as you play a scale from the left (bass) end of the keyboard to the right (treble) end. To preserve this spatial relationship, the samples in a digital piano are recorded in two-channel stereo. This feature, often called "panning," adds to the realism by physically positioning the sounds in ways similar to what is heard from an acoustic piano.

Number of Notes Sampled

Now we must decide how many notes to sample. The obvious answer would seem to be "all of them," and some manufacturers take this route. But in the interest of keeping the cost of the digital piano under control, many manufacturers seek alternatives to sampling all 88 notes.

In an acoustic piano, the tonal behavior of the longer, bass strings is different from that of the shorter, treble strings. In fact, this tonal variation goes through several changes as you play up the keyboard from the bottom. Some of these changes are due to the differences in string length, others to differences in the types and numbers of strings associated with different ranges of notes. In the lowest bass, the hammers strike a single string per note. This

string is wrapped with heavy copper wire to slow its rate of vibration to produce the proper pitch. Depending on the piano's scale design, a couple of octaves up from the bottom of the keyboard it switches to two strings per note, each wound with a lighter copper wire. Finally, by mid-keyboard, three plain-wire strings are used for each note. (Each set of one, two, or three strings per note is known as a *unison* because all the strings in a given set are tuned at the same pitch to sound a single note.) The subtle changes brought about by these different string arrangements also figure in the tonal variations we hear as we move up and down the keyboard.

But the tonal changes from one note to the next are not always noticeable; sometimes, all that changes is the pitch. It turns out that it's a fairly simple matter for the digital piano to play back a sample at a different pitch. This makes it possible to save memory space by using one sample as the basis for two or three consecutive notes. Taken too far, this would result in obvious tonal problems. But if at least a third of the notes are sampled, with careful attention to areas of the keyboard where there are more noticeable changes, these shared samples can produce a convincing, if basic, tonal progression.

Sampling Dynamics

One more source of tonal variation—the effect of dynamics (variation in volume or loudness)—must be dealt with before we move on from our basic sample set. Striking a string harder results in a larger number and greater prominence of higher overtones, which, in addition to making the sound louder, give the tone more

"edge." Currently, in all but the least expensive instruments, digital pianos use from three to five dynamic samples. As you play with varying degrees of force, the digital piano selects the closest appropriate dynamic sample for playback. Entry-level pianos that use a single sample level for dynamics also use variable filtering of a note's overtones to simulate these tonal differences, sometimes with remarkable success.

Sampling Other Effects

Many digital pianos incorporate additional types of samples aimed at capturing more of the nuance of an acoustic piano. At this time, the two most common such samples are *string resonance* and *damper effect*. As with so many features, different manufacturers seldom use the same terms for the same effects. String resonance is related to the strings' overtones. Each of the overtones generated by a vibrating string are at, or close to, the fundamental frequencies of higher notes whose frequencies bear a mathematical relationship to the one played. This results in a weak sympathetic or resonant vibration of the strings of the related notes, and adds another dimension to the sound. (To hear this effect, slowly press the keys of a chord—for this discussion, let's make it a C chord—without actually sounding them. While holding these keys down, quickly strike and release the C an octave below the held chord and you'll hear, faintly, the sympathetic resonance of the C chord above.)

In an acoustic piano, a note's felt damper moves away from the string(s) when its key is depressed, and returns to stop their vibration when the key is released. The effect on the

Many digital pianos incorporate additional types of samples, capturing more of the nuance of an acoustic piano.

sound is not instantaneous; it takes a fraction of a second for the strings' vibration to stop. During this time the tone is altered as its overtones rapidly decay. Damper-effect samples are triggered by releasing a key, and add another subtle dimension to the digital piano's sound.

Polyphony

Finally, we have to consider how many notes the instrument can play at once, which is expressed as its *polyphony*. A quick glance at your hands may suggest that 10 ought to be plenty. But consider what happens when you play a series of chords, or an arpeggio, while holding down the sustain pedal. Each note that continues to sustain takes up one note of polyphony. If you press the sustain pedal and play a three-note chord with both hands, then repeat those chords three more times in successively higher octaves, you will now be sustaining 24 notes. Played with layered voices (a combination of two different voices, such as piano and strings), that example would require 48 notes of polyphony. Some models of digital piano have 32 notes of polyphony, but most current models have 64 or more.

A cautionary note: As you delve into the specifications of digital pianos, the temptation to rank instruments based on numbers—how many notes were sampled, how much memory the sample set takes up, and so on—will be high. And the results would be highly unreliable. Designing a digital piano involves choices driven by economics (e.g., how much a model will sell for), by the intended customer's needs (beginner or professional), and, in no small part, by the engineering talent at the manufacturer's disposal. Engineering creativity, or lack of it, can turn the numerical specifications on their head, resulting in an instrument that sounds better—or worse—than its numbers would suggest.

Controlling Tone— The Keyboard

Just as in an acoustic piano, the role of the keyboard is to provide the player with intimate, reliable control of the instrument's tonal resources. But just as there is no single correct tone, there is no single correct feel; rather, there is an acceptable range of touch characteristics.

Touch Weight

As in an acoustic piano, the action of most digital pianos is primarily an arrangement of levers, but the digital action is far less complex and doesn't require regular adjustment. Players use a few definable criteria to judge an action. Some are easily measured, others are largely subjective. Among the most frequently debated by digital piano buyers is *touch weight*.

Touch weight is the amount of force, typically measured in grams, required to depress a key. A touch weight in the range of 50 to 55 grams is generally considered normal for an acoustic piano. The resistance offered by the key is a combination of friction and the mass of the parts being moved. Both of these factors behave slightly differently in acoustic pianos than in digital pianos. Measuring the touch weight of an acoustic piano is typically done with the sustain pedal fully depressed, which removes the weight of the dampers and reduces the force required to depress the key. The problem is, digitals don't *have* dampers, so the digital manufacturer has to decide between the higher weight the pianist will feel when the dampers are being lifted by the key, and the lighter weight when the dampers have been lifted by the sustain pedal. There is no single right answer—just design choices.

Friction is also a bigger factor in the action of an acoustic than in a digital piano. Most of the friction in an acoustic action is due to various hinge points and bearing surfaces, many of which have cloth or felt bushings. Over time, these bushings wear away or become compacted, reducing friction and the amount of force required to depress a key. Another factor is humidity. Felt and wood parts readily absorb and release moisture, effectively increasing or decreasing friction with changes in the amount of moisture in the air. Because digital actions contain far fewer felt parts and—with the exception of a few upper-end actions sporting wooden keys—no wooden parts at all, changes in friction due to wear and fluctuations in humidity are substantially reduced.

Yet another aspect of touch weight is that it varies from one end of the keyboard to the other. In an acoustic piano, the hammers are significantly heavier at the bass end of the keyboard than at the treble end, which results in heavier touch weight in the bass and lighter touch weight in the treble. Enter the *graded hammer action*: To replicate the touch weight of the acoustic piano keyboard, most digital piano actions employ in their designs the equivalent of graduated hammer weights. Rather than using 88 different weights across the span of the keyboard, which would be cost-prohibitive and of questionable value, it's common to use four different touch-weight values, each one used uniformly throughout one touch-weight zone.

Key Design

Some high-end digital pianos employ wooden keys to subtly move you closer to the feel of an acoustic action. The physical properties you may detect would be a slight flexing of the key, a difference in the mass of the key, and possibly a very slight difference in the shock absorption of wood vs. plastic when the key is depressed and bottoms out (although this is mostly masked by the felt pad under the key).

Another aspect of key design is the tactile property of the keytop material. Ivory is so prized (and missed) by acoustic piano players not for its appearance, but for the fact that it's porous, and thus offers a degree of "grip" that slick-surfaced plastic keytops don't. This grip is particularly valued when the playing gets serious and the pianist's fingers become sweaty, which typically occurs during demanding passages, when the pianist's accuracy and control are pushed to their limits. Ivory substitutes, such as Kawai's Neotex, Roland's Ivory Feel, and Yamaha's Ivorite, provide the positive properties of ivory without the discoloring, cracking, and chipping for which ivory is equally famous. Other manufacturers have since added this feature, and it's one worth considering when comparing instruments.

Dynamic (Velocity) Sensors

The final aspect of the digital piano action we'll explore is how it measures the force the player's fingers apply to the keys. This is typically done using two electrical contact switches that are closed in rapid succession as the key is depressed. Alternatively, some high-end digital hybrids use optical sensors to sense the key's motion—a small flag attached to the key breaks a beam of light as it descends. However, what these sensors actually measure is not force—that is, how hard the

key is depressed—but the speed or *velocity* with which it is depressed. This is why you'll sometimes see the term *velocity sensing* in the keyboard specifications. As the key moves to the bottom of its travel, the instrument measures how much time has elapsed between the signals received from the first and second sensors. A longer time indicates that the key was traveling slowly and tells the instrument to produce a softer tone; a shorter time means a faster, harder keystroke, and thus a louder tone—it's that straightforward. Some actions employ additional switches to trigger other sample types, such as the damper effect mentioned earlier.

The Pedals

Modern acoustic pianos have three pedals. Let's take a look at how they work, and how their functions translate to the digital piano.

In the common three-pedal arrangement of an acoustic piano, the pedal on the right is the *sustain pedal*. In the case of digital instruments having only one pedal, it is the sustain pedal. Some refer to this as the *damper pedal*, because its mechanical function on an acoustic piano is to lift the dampers away from the strings. On a digital piano, the sustain pedal is an electronic switch. When depressed, it tells the instrument to allow played notes to gradually decay as they would on an acoustic piano.

The most frequent question about a digital piano's sustain pedal is whether it can perform a function called *half pedaling*. The acoustic piano's sustain-pedal mechanism can move the dampers from a position of rest on the strings to a position completely clear of the strings—or anywhere in between. Between these two positions is the highly useful half-pedal position, which allows the player more control of tone and

> To replicate the touch weight of the acoustic piano keyboard, most digital piano actions use a graded hammer action.

sustain. While half-pedal capability is now commonly found on upper-end digitals, it is not always present on lower-priced instruments, where the sustain pedal is more likely to be a simple on/off switch that allows full sustain or no sustain, but nothing in between. Some lower-priced digitals come with a separate square plastic or metal foot switch rather than something that looks like a piano pedal. However, even if the piano itself is capable of half-pedal control, the foot switch may provide only on/off sustain. The same may be true even with some pedals that have the appearance and movement of a piano pedal. It's always worth checking the specifications to be sure that both instrument *and* pedal are capable of half-pedal control.

At the left end of the three-pedal group is the *soft pedal*. The proper term for this in an acoustic grand piano—*una corda*, or "one string"—relates to its function. In an acoustic grand, this pedal, when depressed, laterally shifts the entire action—from keys to hammers—slightly to the right. Recall (from **"Tone Production,"** above) that, on an acoustic piano, most notes have two or three strings associated with them. When the action is shifted to the right by the soft pedal, the hammer strikes only two of the three strings in each three-string unison. This has two effects: it reduces the volume of the sound, and it slightly alters the tonal quality.

As with the sustain pedal, the digital version of this pedal is simply an electronic switch that activates an equivalent effect. Since the digital piano action can play at much lower volumes than the acoustic piano, the practical importance of this pedal for reducing sound volume is considerably lessened. However, its ability to alter tonal quality remains relevant—assuming it actually does so. Most do not.

The mysterious center pedal is the *sostenuto*. The easiest way to think of the sostenuto's function is as a selective sustain pedal. Play one or more keys anywhere on the keyboard and, while holding these keys down, press and hold the sostenuto pedal. The sostenuto mechanism will hold the dampers for these keys away from the strings, sustaining them even after you release the keys, but any subsequent keys played will not sustain when released (unless you also use the sustain pedal). Clear? The bottom line is that all three-pedal digital pianos incorporate this feature exactly as it works on an acoustic piano. In written music, the sostenuto pedal is called for in only a few pieces of classical music. If you need it, it's there, but chances are you never will. In digital pianos, the middle pedal is often assigned another function, **discussed in Part 2 of this article.**

The Audio System

The final component of most digital pianos is the audio system—its amplifiers and speakers—which perform the same job as an acoustic piano's soundboard: making the piano's sound audible at useful volume levels. I say *most* digital pianos because some instruments designed specifically for stage use lack an onboard audio system, as they will always be connected to a sound-reinforcement, or public address (PA), system.

The digital pianos currently on the market offer anywhere from 12 to 360 watts (W) of output power, channeled through from two to twelve speakers. To understand why there is such a wide range of options, we need to look at how the system's power-output capability (and the type, number, and placement of speakers) relates to what we hear.

The smallest change in volume that most people can detect is 3 deci-

dB	WATTS	DYNAMICS
64	0.015	ppp
67	0.03	
70	0.06	pp
73	0.12	
76	0.24	p
79	0.48	
82	0.96	mp/mf
85	1.92	
88	3.84	f
91	7.68	
94	15.36	ff
97	30.72	
100	61.44	fff
103	122.88	

bels (dB), and to achieve a 3dB increase in volume requires a doubling of the output power in watts. With these relationships in mind, let's look at some numbers.

Based on measurements of three of the most frequently encountered concert grand pianos—Bösendorfer model 290, Steinway & Sons model D, and Yamaha model CFIIIS—I arrived at a model dynamic range. This range extends from the softest note possible, at 64dB, to the loudest chord I could produce, at 103dB. Assigning a modest 0.015W—we're assuming a *very* efficient audio system—to produce the softest (64dB) note, the chart below traces the progression of amplifier power required to keep up with the increasing volume to the top of the piano's dynamic range. Different audio systems will have different starting points, depending on the size and number of speakers being powered, the efficiency of those speakers' use of power, and the notes played (bass requires more power to match the treble volume). Dynamic markings have been added to bring some musical perspective to the numbers.

If you've not seen this sort of table before, the results are startling. It's the last three or four steps of volume that really demand power from the amplifiers.

When the audio system attempts to reproduce a sound louder than it can accommodate, it goes into "clipping" and produces a distorted version of the sound. One thing to remember is that even the most powerful instruments can be driven into clipping if played loudly with the volume turned all the way up. Aside from distorting the sound, overdriving the system can damage the speakers and amplifiers. The key is to set the volume no higher than 75 to 80% of its maximum level.

If you've already peeked at the specification charts toward the end of this book, you know that only a few digital pianos produce 100-plus watts of output power per channel (left and right). Many of the models that do have that much power also separate the low-demand treble frequencies from the power-hog bass frequencies by providing each frequency range with its own amplifier and speaker(s). A very few go so far as to divide the audio system into three separate subsystems, for the bass, midrange, and highs. These designs, called "bi-amped" or "tri-amped," can make a noticeable difference in sound and power efficiency by using amplifiers and speakers optimized for specific frequency ranges rather than sending the entire frequency spectrum to a single full-range audio system.

Speakers

Because all of the digital pianos we'll consider in this publication have stereo audio systems, all discussions of speakers will assume matching left and right channels.

The least expensive digital pianos employ a single full-range speaker per side. While these speakers are typically described by the manufacturer as "full-range," they are in fact a compromise dictated by cost and, in the case of the most compact designs, space. While a full-range speaker may reproduce much of the 20Hz–20kHz frequency range required by the piano samples, those frequencies will not be treated equally. The frequency response of a speaker is judged not only by its range, but also by its "flatness," or accuracy. If we send to a speaker multiple signals at different frequencies but at the same volume level, then measure the speaker's output volume when producing those sounds, we will see the speaker's "frequency-response curve." The full-range speaker will usually be acceptably flat through the middle of the frequency range, but will fall off in volume at the upper and lower reaches of the spectrum. In other words, the speaker will not accurately reproduce the full range of the signal sent to it. This is not the result of poor speaker design. As a matter of fact, I'm frequently amazed at what the engineers can coax out of these speakers. But the fact remains that they are inaccurate, and in ways that color our perception of the instrument's sound. Even the best sample set is rendered unimpressive if the sparkling highs and thunderous lows are weak or missing.

For this reason, most upper-end models use three speakers, one of each optimized for the bass, midrange, or treble frequencies. Accurate reproduction of bass frequencies requires the movement of a great deal of air. This is accomplished by combining a relatively large surface area with a high degree of in-and-out movement. These bass speakers, or *woofers*, are largely responsible for our impression of an instrument's "guts."

At the opposite end of the frequency spectrum is the high-frequency speaker, or *tweeter*. The tweeter, which is physically quite small, is responsible for reproducing the nuances of the upper range of the instrument. Besides the obvious frequency difference between the outputs of the woofer and tweeter, they also differ in their placement requirements. Whereas low frequencies tend to radiate in all directions, the higher the frequency of the sound, the more directional it is, which means that the precise placement of the tweeter is much more important. Most of the low- and mid-frequency speakers on digital pianos are located below the keyboard because there's plenty of room there. The more directional nature of the high frequencies requires pointing the tweeters directly at the player's head, usually from somewhere on the instrument's control panel.

The newest twist in speaker systems—one that appears to be unique to digital pianos—is the *soundboard speaker*. This technology will be discussed in the article "**Hybrid Pianos**," elsewhere in this issue.

So we now have all the makings of a digital piano: a sound source, and the means to control and hear it. But none of the current crop of digital pianos stops there; all of them have additional capabilities. These extras range from a handful of additional voices to direct Internet access. Even if your current needs don't extend past the basics, you should understand the other features present on your instrument, and how they might surprise and lure you into musical adventures you've never contemplated. To continue, please read "**Digital Piano Basics, Part 2: Beyond the Acoustic Piano**." ▥

> **Even the best sample set is unimpressive if sparkling highs and thunderous lows are weak or missing.**

Simply Beautiful...Inside and Out

Play / Record

Acoustic style pedals

Easy operation

Silent practice

THE FIRST INSTRUMENTS we now call digital pianos were specialized versions of the synthesizers of the day (early 1980s). These synthesizers were capable of producing a staggering array of sounds, and allowed the player to exercise control over many details of those sounds. A standard feature of many synthesizers was the ability to produce the sounds of pianos and other conventional instruments, which led to the spin-off we now call the digital piano.

The first digital pianos retained some of the other capabilities of their parent instruments by including a few preset voices besides that of the acoustic piano. It wasn't long before subsequent models appeared with expanded voice capabilities, reverberation effects, background accompaniments, the ability to connect to other digital instruments and computers, and much more. In this article we'll look at each of these categories of "extras," what they do, and how they might enhance your musical experience.

Instrumental Voices

The designers of the first digital pianos correctly assumed that someone who needed the sound of an acoustic piano would probably benefit from a handful of related voices, such as the harpsichord, an organ sound or two, the very different but highly useful sounds of such electric pianos as the Fender Rhodes, and so on. To this day, even the most basic digital pianos feature voice lists very similar to those of the original models. What's changed over the years is the quality or authenticity of those voices, and the cost of producing them.

So far, in Part 1 of this article, I have discussed only samples of acoustic pianos. For most models of digital piano, the same sampling technology is used to reproduce the sound of other acoustic instruments. Typically, an expanded selection of high-quality instrumental samples is found in only the more expensive models. Remember that, depending on the sample rate used, samples may be more or less accurate representations of the original voice. Because manufacturers almost never reveal these sample rates, our ears must judge the relative quality of the voices of the digital piano models we're comparing.

Note that many manufacturers have trademarked their names for a particular sampling technology or other aspect of an instrument. The important thing to remember about trademarks is that while the trademarked name is unique, the underlying technology may be essentially the same as everyone else's. For instance, the generic term for digital sampling, discussed in Part 1, is Pulse Code Modulation, or PCM. But a manufacturer may call their PCM samples *UltraHyperDynoMorphic II Sampling*, and rightly claim to make the only product on the market using it. However, that makes it only a unique *name*, not necessarily a unique technology.

Layering and Splitting

Layering—the ability to have one key play two or more voices at the same time—is available on virtually all digital pianos. Some combinations, such as Piano and Strings, are commonly preset as a single voice selection. On many instruments, it's possible to select the voices you'd like to combine. This is frequently as simple as pressing the selection buttons for the two voices you want to layer. Once these are selected, many instruments then allow you to control the two voices' relative volumes. Using the popular Piano and Strings combination as an example, you may want the two voices to play with equal volume, or you may want the Piano voice to be the dominant sound, with just a hint of Strings. Other possible settings include the ability to set the apparent positions of the individual voices in the left-right stereo field—with Strings, say, predominantly on the left. The most advanced instruments make it possible to have only one voice's dynamics respond to your touch on the keyboard, while the other voice responds to a separate volume pedal (this is described in greater detail under "Other Controls").

The other commonly available voice option is *splitting*. Whereas layering provides the ability to play two voices with one key, splitting lets you play one voice on the right side of the keyboard, and a different voice on the left side—for instance, piano on the right and string bass on the left. This essentially lets the instrument behave as though it had two keyboards playing two different voices. The *split point* is the point in the keyboard where the right and left voices meet. While this split point has a default setting, it can also be moved to provide more playing room for one voice or the other. As with layered voices, there may be preset combinations, but you can also set up your own voice pairings; typically, additional options are available to vary relative volume levels and other settings between the two voices.

Effects

Digital *effects* electronically change a sound in ways the originally sampled source instrument typically could not. Effects can be loosely divided into those that mimic the acoustic properties of a performing space and those that modify the sound in non-acoustic and, in some cases, downright unnatural ways.

The most popular effect—in fact, the one most people never turn off— is Reverberation, or *Reverb*. The easiest way to understand reverb is to think of it as an echo. When reflective surfaces are close to the sound source and to you, the individual reflections of the original sound arrive at your ears from so many directions, and so closely spaced in time, that they merge into a single sound. But when the reflective surface is far away, there is a time lag between the original and reflected sounds that the ear recognizes as an echo, also known as "reverberant sound." The strength and duration of the echo depends on a number of factors, among them the volume and frequency of the original sound, and the hardness and distance of the reflective surfaces. Different amounts of Reverb lend themselves better to different types of music. Although you can just leave Reverb on the default setting, you also can broaden the instrument's tonal palette by exploring alternate settings.

The other common effect is *Chorus*. When a group of instruments play the same notes, the result is not simply a louder version of those notes. Even the best performers will be very slightly out of synchronization and out of tune with each other. This contributes to what's variously referred to as a "full," "fat," or "lush" sound. The Chorus effect is frequently built into ensemble voices like Strings and Brass and, of course, Choir.

Before we leave the subject of effects, there is one other application to be covered here: dedicated effects speakers. Some upper-end digital pianos now come with speakers whose role is not to produce the primary sound, but to add to the apparent ambience of the instrument and the room. These speakers and their associated effects can significantly alter the sound of instrument and room. When done well, these effects are not noticed until they're turned off, when the sound seems to "collapse" down to a smaller-sounding source.

Alternate (Historical) Tuning

One of the advantages offered by the digital piano is the fact that it never requires tuning. This does not, however, mean that it *cannot* be tuned. Just as we tend to think of the piano as something that has always sounded as it does today, we similarly tend to think that tuning is tuning, and has always been as it is now. In fact, our current practice of setting the A above Middle C at 440Hz, and the division of the octave into intervals of equal size for the purpose of tuning, are relatively recent developments.

Evidence suggests that international standard pitch, while a bit of a moving target depending on where, when, and for whom you were tuning, had pretty well settled down to A = 440 Hz by the mid-19th century. And by the late 19th century, following a few centuries of variation, we had arrived at the tuning system of equal temperament.

Now that all that has been settled, why bother with alternate tunings? You may never use this capability, but for many it is a profound experience to hear firsthand how the music of J.S. Bach sounded to Bach himself, and thus to realize why he wrote the way he did. Instruments that include alternate tunings list in a menu the most common historical temperaments (tuning systems). Select an appropriate temperament, adjust the pitch control, and you have a time machine with keys. It's a simple and invaluable tool for those interested in music history, and some instruments allow you to create your own unique temperaments for the composition of experimental or modern music.

MIDI

Electronic musical instruments had been around for decades, but were unable to "talk" to each other until 1982 and the introduction of the Musical Instrument Digital Interface (MIDI) specification. Many musicians used two, three, or more synthesizers in their setups, each with a distinctive palette of sounds, to provide the widest possible range of voices. The problem was that the musicians couldn't combine sounds from different synths and control them from a single keyboard, because of differences in the electronic commands to which each synth responded. This ultimately led to a proposal for a common set of commands to which all digital musical instruments could respond.

In short, MIDI is not a sound source, but a set of digital commands—or, in the language of MIDI, *messages*—that can control a sound source. MIDI doesn't even refer to notes by their proper names; for example, middle C is note number 60. When you use the recording feature included in most digital pianos, what you're actually recording is a sequence of digital messages; hence the term *sequencer* for a MIDI recorder (some upper-end models now allow both MIDI and audio recording). These messages form a datastream that represents the musical actions you took. Some of the most common messages are listed in the table below.

There are *many* more message types, but this should give you an idea of how MIDI "thinks." Nothing is a sound—everything is a number. When recording or playing back a sequence of MIDI messages, timing—just as in a piece of music—is obviously a critical element, so MIDI uses a "synchronization clock" to control the timing of each message. MIDI can also direct different streams of messages to different channels. Each channel can be assigned to communicate with different devices; for instance, your computer and another keyboard.

While the MIDI specification of 1982 standardized commands for events such as note on, note off, control change, and program change, it didn't include a message type for instrumental voice. It was still necessary to manually set the voice that would play on each synth because there was no consistency between instruments from different manufacturers, or sometimes even within a single manufacturer's product line, as to which command would produce which voice. This changed with the adoption in 1991 of the General MIDI (GM) standard, updated in 1999 to General MIDI 2 (GM2).

Product specifications now frequently state that an instrument is General MIDI, or GM, compatible. Like MIDI, General MIDI specifies not a sound source but a standardized numbering scheme. Any digital instrument "thinks" of the different voices it produces not as Piano or Violin or Harpsichord, but as

BASIC MIDI MESSAGES	
Message	Action
Note On Event	The number of the note played and the key velocity (i.e., how fast the key went down)
Note Off Event	The number of the note released and the key's release velocity
Control Change	When the position of a control such as a pedal is changed, a message indicates the number assigned to that control and a value representing its new position
Program Change	When a new voice is selected, a message indicates the "patch" number of the new voice (the term patch goes back to the early days of the synthesizer, when different electronic elements were literally wired to each other with "patch cords")

Program Change numbers. General MIDI established a fixed list of Program Change Numbers for 128 "melodic instruments" and 1 "drum kit." GM2 later expanded this to 256 melodic voices and 9 drum kits. So all GM-compatible instruments use the same numbers to represent a given voice: Acoustic Grand Piano is always Program Change Number 1, Violin is always 41, and Harpsichord is always 7. A standardized numbering scheme of 256 melodic instrumental voices seems big enough to cover everything under the sun with room to spare, until you notice that some MIDI voices are actually combinations of instruments. For instance, Program Change Numbers 49 and 50 are String Ensemble 1 and 2, representing different combinations of string instruments playing in ensemble. Also, there are many Ethnic instruments (voices 105 through 112), and several Sound Effects, from chirping

birds to gunshots. If this has you feeling that perhaps 256 wasn't an unreasonably high number of voices after all, consider that many higher-end digital pianos have more than 500 voices, and some more than a thousand. This means that when you record using voices from the far end of the list on one manufacturer's "flagship" model, then play the recording back on someone else's top-of-the-line model, voice consistency once again flies out the window. Perhaps the most important thing to remember is that the GM standard doesn't specify the technology used to create the listed voices. One hint of the degree of variation possible under this system is the fact that your current cell phone is probably GM compatible.

In the 1990s, two proprietary extensions to the General MIDI standard were made, by Roland and Yamaha. Roland's GS extension was largely incorporated into the GM2 standard. Yamaha's XG extension defines far more voices than the other schemes, but hasn't been as widely adopted as General MIDI.

Connecting to a Computer

MIDI is now standard on all digital pianos. While it does allow your instrument to control or be controlled by other instruments, today it's most often used to connect the instrument to a computer. Connecting your instrument to a computer allows you to venture beyond the capacity of even the most capable and feature-packed digital piano.

MIDI-standard DIN connector

Connecting two instruments to each other requires two MIDI cables—one for each direction of data transmission between the two devices. Standard MIDI cables use a

5-pin DIN connector, shown here. Since personal computers don't use 5-pin DIN connectors, connecting a keyboard to a computer requires an adapter that has the MIDI-standard DIN connector on one end, and a computer-friendly connector on the other.

USB Connectors:
To Device (Type A),
To Host [Computer] (Type B)

In 1995, the USB standard was introduced to reduce the number of different connectors on personal computers. Subsequently, MIDI over USB has emerged as an alternative that replaces two MIDI cables with a single USB link. In addition to being a common connector on personal computers, USB's higher transmission speed increases MIDI's flexibility by allowing MIDI to control 32 channels instead of the 16 specified in the original MIDI standard. USB connectivity is now finding its way into the digital piano. All current digital instruments still have 5-pin DIN connectors for traditional MIDI, but many now sport USB connectors as well. One thing to be aware of is that there are two types of USB connections that can appear on instruments. One, "USB to Device," allows direct connection to a variety of external memory-storage devices. The other, "USB to Host," allows connection to computers. If you plan to use these connections, you need to check the type of USB connections available on the instruments you're considering. Simply stating "USB" in the specifications doesn't tell you the *type* of USB connectivity provided.

External Memory
External memory consists of any storage device that's connected to

the instrument rather than being built in. As instruments become more advanced, they can require larger amounts of memory to store MIDI recordings, audio recordings, additional rhythm patterns and styles, even additional voices. Since different users will put different demands on memory resources, it's becoming increasingly common for manufacturers to allow the user to attach external disk drives and USB flash memory to augment onboard memory.

Floppy-disk drives have long been popular on digital pianos. While the floppy disk is rapidly disappearing from the computer world, it has remained a staple of the digital piano due to the volume of MIDI files that have traditionally been distributed on floppies. These files run the gamut, from complete song arrangements to files that use the special learning features of a particular instrument model to guide you through the process of learning a new piece of music. It's now possible to download these files from the Internet, but getting them from the computer to the instrument hasn't always been a straightforward process. As this transfer process becomes more user-friendly, the floppy will become less important. However, many teachers still use instructional books that come with a floppy disk that contains files to be used in conjunction with the book, so we can count on the humble floppy disk to stick around for a while.

If the instrument you select has the capability to record audio to external memory via USB, you'll want to add an external, or desktop, USB hard drive. These audio recordings are saved as uncompressed .WAV files, typically at the same sampling rates (though not the same file format) used for commercial audio CDs: one five-minute song can consume up to 50MB of memory space.

Not long ago, I might have suggested getting at least an 80-Gigabyte hard drive for this purpose, but it's becoming increasingly difficult to find external hard drives much smaller than 320GB, and Terabyte drives are now becoming increasingly common. Obviously, there's little need to worry about storage space.

The final external storage option—and my favorite—is the USB flash drive. These are the ultimate in handy storage and now range up to 64GB. Not only are they unobtrusive when attached to the instrument, but if your digital piano and computer aren't in the same room, they make file transfers quick and painless.

Computer Software
As mentioned briefly in the discussion of MIDI, perhaps the most powerful option that accompanies the digital piano is the ability to connect your instrument to your personal computer and enhance your musical experience by using different types of music software. Software can expand capabilities your instrument may already have, such as recording and education, or it could add elements like music notation and additional voices. While it's beyond the scope of this article to describe music-software offerings in detail, we'll take a quick look here at the different categories: Recording and Sequencing, Virtual Instruments, Notation, and Educational.

Recording can take two forms on the digital piano: data and sound. All models that offer onboard recording (i.e., nearly all of them) record MIDI data. This means that all of the actions you take when you play a piece—both key presses and control actions—can be recorded by a MIDI sequencer. But remember that a MIDI sequence, or recording, is data, not sound. Recording the actual *sound* of your music is a different issue, and few digital pianos can do this.

Enter **recording software**. Recording software ranges from basic packages—even the most modest of which will exceed the recording capabilities of most digital pianos—to applications that can handle complete movie scores, including film synchronization. The higher-end applications are called Digital Audio Workstations (DAWs). These software applications cost more than many of the lower-priced digital pianos, and can be used to record, edit, and mix combinations of MIDI and audio tracks, limited only by the processing power and storage capacity of the computer. If you have an opportunity to look inside a modern recording studio, you'll find that computers running DAW software have replaced multi-track tape recorders.

Virtual instrument software can be controlled, or "played," by your digital piano via MIDI, and can also be played by recording software that resides on the computer. Virtual instruments can take the form of standalone software or plug-ins. Standalone instrumental software doesn't rely on other software, but plug-ins require a host application such as the DAW software described above, or other software developed specifically as a plug-in host. Virtual instruments can be sample sets for strings, horns, or even pianos, or they can accurately emulate the sonic textures and controls of popular electronic instruments that are no longer produced, such as certain legacy synthesizers. (A number of piano-specific virtual instruments are explored in the article "My Other Piano is a Computer," elsewhere in this issue.) While virtual instruments allow you to expand your sound palette beyond the onboard voices of your digital piano, they can place heavy demands on your computer's

processor and memory. A mismatch of software demand and hardware capability can result in *latency*—audible delay between the time the key is played and the time the sound is heard. If both the digital piano's onboard voices and the virtual instrument's sounds are played simultaneously, there could be a time gap between the two outputs that would make the result unusable. Virtual instruments can be an exciting addition, but be prepared for the technical implications.

Notation applications are the word processors of music. If you have a tune in your head and want to share it, simply recording it will allow others to hear it. But in order for most people to *play* your music, it must be written out in standard notation. In the early days of notation software, it was necessary to place each note on the staff individually using the computer's keyboard and mouse. The advent of MIDI created the ability to play a note on a musical keyboard and have it appear on the computer screen. Today's notation programs virtually take musical dictation: you play it, and it appears on the screen.

But there's a slight hitch that must be addressed. The computer's capacity to accurately capture the timing of your playing, down to tiny fractions of a second, allows it to reproduce subtle nuances with great precision. In a recording, this is a great asset; in notation, it can be a complete disaster. If—in the computer's cold calculations—you've just played a passage involving dotted 128th-note triplets, the software will happily display them. Unless notation applications are told otherwise, they are perfectly capable of creating notation that is absolutely

accurate *and* absolutely unreadable. This is where *quantization* comes in. Quantization—also applicable to the recording capabilities of higher-end digital pianos—allows you to specify, as a note value, the level of timing detail you desire. If the software is told to quantize at the eighth-note level, the printed music will contain no 16th notes—nothing shorter than an eighth note will be scored. If quantization is set at 16th notes, there will be more detail; if set to quarter notes, the music will be devoid of any timing detail beyond that value. This must be used judiciously; too much quantization and musical detail is lost, too little and the notation becomes an indecipherable pile of notes (for a good laugh, Google "Prelude and The Last Hope in C and C# Minor"). As with recording applications, there is a wide range of capabilities available, from programs that will let you capture simple melodies, to applications that will easily ingest the most complex symphonic works, transpose and separate the individual instrumental parts, and print them out.

The final category we'll discuss is **educational software**. Just as there are educational programs and games to assist in learning math or reading, there are applications that use the MIDI connection between your instrument and computer to help you learn different aspects of music. A music-reading program may display a note, chord, or passage on the screen; you play the displayed notes on the digital piano and the software keeps track of your accuracy and helps you improve. An ear-training application may play for you an interval that you then try to play yourself on the keyboard. The

> **Software can expand your instrument's capabilities or add elements like music notation and additional voices.**

application will tell you what you did right or wrong and help you improve your ear. Other types teach music history and music theory. While many of these applications are geared to specific levels or ages, some can be set to multiple levels as you progress, or for use by multiple players.

Onboard Recording

Recording has been discussed above, in the "Computer Software" section. However, because nearly all digital pianos come with at least basic recording capability, it deserves a bit more attention. You may say that you have no intention of recording your music for others to hear, but in ignoring the instrument's ability to record what you've played, you may be overlooking one of the simplest ways of improving your playing. Whether you're just starting to play or are beginning to learn a new piece, being able to hear what you've just played is a learning accelerator.

I know what you're thinking: "I heard it while I was playing it." While most professional musicians have reached a level where they can effectively split their attention between the physical act of playing the instrument and the mental act of critically listening to what they're playing, few of the rest of us can do this. Recording and listening to yourself will reveal elements of your playing that you never noticed *while* you were playing, and will allow you to see where to make changes in your performance. This is even more useful when working with a teacher. Imagine listening with your teacher, music score in hand, and pausing the playback to discuss what you did in a particular measure. This is one of many reasons piano teachers are adding digital pianos to their studios; they're great learning tools.

One final thought on recording on the digital piano: Most manufacturers list recording capacity as a certain number of notes—typically in the thousands of notes. But not everyone is counting on the same number of fingers. Recall that MIDI records data "events," including note on, note velocity, note off, program change, control change, and a variety of others, many or all of which could have happened in conjunction with the playing of a single note. Each of these events consumes a certain amount of internal memory. Because this memory capacity is fixed, unless we know which events each manufacturer is counting as "notes," it's pointless to try to decide, based on these specifications, who offers more recording capacity. On the one hand, most instruments have more recording capacity than most owners will use. On the other hand, if recording capacity is important to you, this is another of the many areas in which simply buying the biggest numbers, or the most numbers for the dollar, is not a good strategy for selecting an instrument.

Automated Accompaniments, Chords, and Harmony— the Ensemble Piano

Some people, even some professional musicians, will tell you that using automated accompaniments—those rhythmic combinations of drums, bass lines, and chords—constitutes "cheating." This has never made sense to me. If I use a tool to do something that I couldn't possibly have done with my bare hands, am I cheating?

Whether or not a digital piano has these automatic features, frequently referred to as *styles*, is the primary factor that separates standard digital pianos from *ensemble* pianos. If your musical interest is focused solely on the classical piano repertoire, then this capability will probably be of no interest to you.

If, however, you or someone in your household plays or plans to play a wide variety of musical styles, the ability to have backup instrumentalists at your beck and call is just entirely too much fun. No matter how good a player you may be, you can't be four people at once— or eight, or twelve, or an entire orchestra. These accompaniments are typically divided into groups by musical genre: Swing, Latin, Rock, World, and so on. The best of these styles are of a caliber that the best record producers would be proud of.

One thing to watch out for is the impact of automatic accompaniments on polyphony (see Part 1). Every bass line, drum beat, string sound, and guitar strum takes a toll on the number of simultaneous notes the instrument can produce. Thirty-two notes of polyphony can get used up in a big hurry when a complex style is playing in the background. If styles are important to you, look for higher polyphony numbers. Also, see if the instrument you're considering is capable of downloading additional styles, and how many styles are available for that model.

How do these styles "know" which key to use when playing all those chords and bass lines? In the simplest "single finger" settings, if the player needs an accompaniment style played in C, for example, she plays a C with the left hand. As chords change in the music, the player makes the appropriate change in the left hand to indicate what the accompaniment should play. Once the harmonies have been determined, the instrument can also apply them to the right hand by filling in the notes of the appropriate chord under the melody note. More sophisticated systems can decipher complex chords by evaluating all of the notes played on the keyboard, so that even advanced players can use the accompaniment styles without being held back from their normal style of playing.

All of this technology can make raw beginners sound as if they've been playing for years. While many players will progress beyond the simplest settings, other members of the family may continue using these playing aids for their own enjoyment.

Memory Presets

With the huge variety of voices, splits, layers, effects, and styles, it's handy to have a way to store favorite combinations. Many digital pianos come with a number of preprogrammed presets, and almost all of the more advanced models have programmable presets as well. These presets should be able to capture every possible setting on the instrument, from the obvious to the most obscure. Aside from the number of presets available, the placement of the preset buttons themselves can make a huge difference in their usefulness. Small, closely spaced, inconveniently placed presets might as well not be there—part of the pleasure of presets is not simply to instantly recall a setting that you've worked out in excruciating detail, but also to access that setting quickly and easily while playing. Even better is being able to assign preset changes to a seldom-used pedal (anything other than the sustain), so that each time you press the pedal, the instrument advances to the next preset. This can enable the creative player to step through sonic and rhythmic changes with ease while keeping his hands on the keyboard and distractions to a minimum.

Song Settings, Music Libraries, and Educational Tools

Many digital pianos are equipped with a list of *song presets*, a feature that goes by a variety of names depending on the brand of instrument.

Educational feature: A light indicates to the student which key should be pressed next.

A less expensive alternative is to use a keyboard display.

Like the memory presets described above, song presets incorporate all of the capabilities of that particular digital piano, but they work with particular songs. When you're new to the vast choices offered by some of the more advanced digital pianos, and unsure what sounds and styles to use for a song, these presets will set everything for you in a way suited to that song. Of course, this depends on the song you want to play being included in that instrument's song list in the first place. These lists range from a hundred or so built-in songs to downloadable databases containing thousands of songs, and the best of them accurately reflect the instrumentation, rhythms, and tempo (which you can slow down or speed up if necessary) of the original recordings. It's important to note that these song presets don't play the music for you; they just set up the

instrument so that it will sound right when *you* play the music.

A related feature, but with a different purpose, is the *song library*. Once again, this feature goes by different names depending on the instrument's brand. Unlike the song presets, the song libraries *do* contain the actual music. In most cases these are from the classical piano repertoire and are recorded with the left- and right-hand parts on separate MIDI channels. They can be played with both hands turned on for listening or studying, or with only one hand turned on so the player can practice one hand's part while the instrument supplies the part for the other hand. In this way each part can be worked on separately, while both parts are heard. Although the tempo can be adjusted (for most of us, slowed way down), playing along with the other part keeps your

---

134

tempo steady and your meter honest. Even without built-in libraries, an enormous amount of music has been recorded in this manner and can be purchased—frequently with the printed notation—or downloaded free from the Internet.

Combinations of song libraries and computer-based educational software can be found on both entry-level and top-end instruments. These range from simple separation of left-hand/right-hand practice to complete lessons, tests, and tips on fingering. Some of the greatest aids to beginners are systems that combine the display of notation with visual cues as to which keys to play. Upper-end models use either lights aligned with each key, or movement of the key itself, to give the beginner a hand in correctly associating the note on the printed music with its key on the instrument. However, seeing which key to play, and actually playing it before the music has moved on, are two different things, and trying to do so can be a frustrating experience. Some instruments make it easier to follow the light or key movements by waiting until the correct key is played before moving on to the next key. As a less expensive alternative, some lower-priced instruments show a small keyboard on the display with the required key indicated. While this still provides some guidance for the beginner, it's not nearly as easy to associate movements between the tiny keys in the display with the correct keys on the keyboard.

Other Controls

The ability to connect an accessory volume pedal is fairly common on upper-end and professional digital pianos. While the thought of a volume pedal attached to a piano may at first seem odd, it can actually add some interesting possibilities. Although it can be used to control the volume of the entire instrument, some models will allow you to select which aspects of the instrument are controlled by the pedal. One of my favorite ways to use the volume pedal is to layer an orchestral string voice with the piano voice and have the volume pedal control only the strings. This allows me to fade the strings in and out while the piano remains within its normal dynamic range.

While we're on the subject of pedals, it's worth noting that many instruments allow you to assign different functions to the standard piano pedals. As with the addition of the volume pedal above, this may initially strike you as a strange thing to do, but the presence of the non-piano voices can make sense of the situation. Some of the most common and handiest examples of alternate functions for the less-used sostenuto and soft pedals are pitch bend, rotary-speaker speed control, and triggering rhythm breaks.

Pitch bend, as the name suggests, allows you to temporarily raise or lower the pitch of a note, then allow the note to slide back to its normal pitch. The most common setting is to have a pedal set to lower the pitch of a note by a half step (the very next note below), then allow the pitch to slide back up to normal when the pedal is released. Think of the opening clarinet line in Gershwin's *Rhapsody in Blue*—the trill leads to an ascending scale, and the player slides to the last note at the top of the scale. This effect is duplicated by depressing the pedal (set for pitch bend) and playing the upper note of the slide at the time you would have played the lower note. The pitch bend will cause the key for the upper note to instead play the lower note; then lift the pedal and you'll slide from the lower note to the upper one. It requires some practice, but isn't as difficult as it sounds.

Setting a pedal for *rotary-speaker speed control* allows the digital piano player to duplicate the effect produced by the rotating baffle and horns of the classic Leslie speaker, typically used with "drawbar" or "jazz" organ sounds. One of the techniques used by players of this type of organ is switching between the slow Chorus rotation of the speaker and the fast Tremolo rotation. As this is done while playing, being able to tap a pedal to switch speeds makes the effect much easier to use.

One of the easiest and most useful pedal assignments is to trigger a *rhythm break*. The break is a brief variation in the rhythm or style in use at the time. Once again, the ability to activate a feature without taking your hands off the keyboard makes use of that feature much more spontaneous.

Many instruments allow you to assign different functions to the standard piano pedals.

Special controls usually found only on professional stage pianos are the *pitch bend* and *modulation wheels*. The pitch-bend wheel acts in the same way as the pitch bend described above, but with a dedicated control instead of a pedal. A number of different effects can be assigned to a modulation wheel, depending on the voice in use or the player's choice. The most common default setting is *vibrato*, a repeating pattern of up-and-down pitch variation around a note, such as the wavering sound in a singer's voice. The modulation wheel allows the player to control the amount of vibrato in real time while playing. This is particularly useful in creating additional realism with solo instrumental voices such as Saxophone, Violin, and Guitar.

Vocals

Many who love to play also love to sing, and the digital piano has something for vocalists as well. Many instruments now feature a microphone connection. In its most elementary form, this simply uses the digital piano's audio system as a PA for vocals. But some models throw the full weight of their considerable processing power behind the vocalist. Many vocal recordings and performances take advantage of effects processing to enhance the performer's voice. This can range from adding reverberation to effects that completely alter the performer's voice, making it sound like anything from Barry White to Betty Boop. Top-of-the-line digital pianos can even go beyond what some recording studios can do. Perhaps even more amazing is the ability of some instruments to combine the vocal input with their ability to harmonize, resulting in your voice coming out in four-part harmony. Display of karaoke lyrics is also common; the presence of a video output on some instruments allows the lyrics to be displayed on a TV or other monitor.

Moving Keys

When an acoustic player piano plays, the keys must move in order for the hammers to strike the strings and produce sound. The digital piano does not share this mechanical necessity, yet we now have digital pianos whose keys move when playing a recording. You'll recall from the section on recording that the digital piano can record and reproduce your playing, or can reproduce a MIDI file from another source. The sounds are produced by sending the playback data directly to the tone-production portion of the instrument, bypassing the keyboard. But since there is no dependency on moving keys, why go to the extra expense of making them move? Two reasons: First, it's one way for the instrument to direct beginners to the next melody note in the educational modes of some models, as described earlier under "Educational Tools." Second, it's just fun to watch. However, you should measure the value of this feature against the additional cost, and be mindful of the increased possibility of mechanical failure due to the additional moving parts of the key-drive mechanism.

Human Interface Design

The Man-Machine Interface, or MMI, as designers and engineers typically refer to it, defines how the player interacts with the instrument's controls. All of the amazing capabilities of the modern digital piano are of little value if the player can't figure out how to use them, or can't access them quickly while playing. The considerations here are the location, spacing, grouping, size, shape, colors, and labeling of the controls. Take the example of the rhythm break discussed earlier. Its purpose is to alter the rhythm during playing. If the button that activates this feature is inconveniently located, small, and surrounded by closely spaced buttons of a similar size, shape, and/or color, its usefulness is severely limited. If, however, it's within easy reach of the keyboard, of decent size, and somewhat distinctive in appearance or markings, it becomes a useful tool.

In the case of instruments with displays, considerations include the size, resolution, and color capabilities of the screen and—more important—the logic behind its operation. Two types of screen interfaces are currently used on digital pianos: *touchscreens* and *softkeys*. Most readers are already familiar with touchscreens from ATMs and other modern institutional uses. The term *softkeys* doesn't refer to the feel of the keys, but to the fact that their functions are displayed on the adjacent screen, and change depending on the operation being displayed by the screen. This is as opposed to *hardkeys*, which have a single dedicated function. Each method has its proponents, but the interface type is less important than the MMI design. A smaller monochrome display that you can intuitively understand is better than a large color display that makes no sense to you.

Also worth considering is the placement of connections you'll use often. If you frequently switch back and forth between speakers and headphones, you'll want to make sure the headphone jack is easy to locate by sight or feel, and that the cord will be out of your way when plugged in. If you'll be using a USB memory device to transfer files between instruments or between the instrument and a computer, make sure the USB port is easy to get to. In newer designs, a USB port is placed above the keyboard level for easy access, as opposed to earlier models in which the port was below the keyboard or on the instrument's rear panel.

We can't leave the subject of user interfaces without discussing the owner's manual. As with the MMI itself, a well-written manual can make it a pleasure to learn a new instrument, and a bad manual can be worse than useless. This is particularly important for higher-end instruments. Fortunately, many manufacturers allow you to download the manuals for their instruments. This lets you compare this critical aspect of the instruments you're considering. The manual should be thoroughly indexed, and clearly written and illustrated.

Third-party tutorials are available for some instruments, especially the more complex models. These tutorials step you through the model's functions with audio or video instructions, and provide an alternative to sitting down with the manual.

Firmware Upgrades

The digital piano is, at heart, a highly specialized computer, and like all computers, its functions are dependent on its software. When we speak of the software that runs on the digital piano, we are typically talking about what is properly classified as *firmware*. Firmware is software that is embedded in a hardware device such as a microprocessor or associated memory chip. This can be done in two ways: the firmware can either be permanently burned into the chip, or it can be written in the chip's memory, which also means it can be rewritten if necessary. Just as computers occasionally need a software upgrade to fix a previously undetected problem—a "bug patch"—the more complex digital pianos can benefit from the ability to accept firmware upgrades. This may never be necessary for a given model, or it may fix an obscure feature interaction or update the instrument's compatibility with external devices. In addition to checking on this capability, it's worth finding out how you would be notified of an update and what the actual update procedure involves. In most cases today, it's an easy, do-it-yourself procedure.

Headphones

Headphones are by far the most popular and frequently used digital-piano accessories. One of the advantages of digital pianos is the option to practice without disturbing others—or them disturbing you. Whether you're an occasional head-

Sennheiser around-the-ear (circumaural) headphones

Shure in-ear, earbud-style headphones

Grado on-the-ear headphones

phone user, or your instrument or situation dictates constant headphone use, selecting the right headphones will make a big difference in your playing comfort and enjoyment.

When I select headphones, I evaluate them using four criteria: fit, sound, isolation, and budget. Although it may seem that starting with sound is the obvious choice, my first priority is fit—it doesn't matter how great they sound if you can't stand to wear them for more than a few minutes. There are three basic styles of headphones: those that fit *around* the ear (circumaural) with the cushions resting on your head, those that rest directly *on* the ear, and those that fit *in* the ear. The style of headphone you choose will also determine the level of isolation. If isolation is critical for your situation, it should dictate the style of headphones.

There are a couple of variations on the circumaural and in-ear styles. Circumaural headphones can be open or sealed. Open designs don't cut you off from the outside world, and their output can be heard—very

softly—by anyone nearby. Sealed designs offer more isolation but introduce some acoustic design problems that are difficult to get around until you get into the higher price ranges. In-ear headphones are available in the earbud style that sits in the outer ear, and the ear-canal type that fits inside the ear canal itself. The latter offers, by far, the best isolation in both directions, even when compared to headphones with active noise canceling.

Sound is very much a matter of personal preference and perception. One thing that can make the selection process easier is to bring a familiar CD with you when you audition headphones. While you may initially favor headphones that color the sound in some attractive way, this can become sonically tiring with extended listening. If you aim for a neutral sound, you'll end up with headphones that won't tire your ears over extended periods, and that will most accurately represent the sound produced by your digital piano or by the models you're considering.

IF THE DIGITAL PIANO is thought of as a complete instrument that's ready to play right out of the box, piano software can be thought of as part of a "piano kit." The standard digital piano is completely self-contained in that it's made up of the memory and processing electronics required to produce the sound, the firmware (software residing on a chip) that is the source of the sound, a keyboard to control the sound, and, more often than not, the audio system needed to hear the sound. If viewed as separate components of a piano kit, however, a personal computer can take on the role of memory and processing, piano software becomes the sound source, a keyboard (very possibly your digital piano) provides control, and powered monitor speakers and/or headphones let you hear your new invention. If you have a digital piano (or an acoustic piano with hybrid features) and a personal computer (Mac or Windows), you already have most of the ingredients of a software-based piano.

The obvious question: If you already have a digital piano, why would you want to add a software piano? Most digital pianos are capable of producing more than one piano sound, but typically, all of these sounds are based on a single piano as a sample source. Think of it this way: If you could add a Bösendorfer, Blüthner, Fazioli, or Steinway to your palette of piano samples for only the cost of the software, would you do it? (I hear the sounds of pianos and computers being pushed together even now.) How about being able to virtually design your own instrument with piano software based on physical modeling? (See "**Digital Piano Basics, Part 1**" for more information on *physical modeling*.)

Adding a software piano to your existing piano, or building your own piano from a "piano kit," is a bit more involved than putting your computer and your piano in the same room—but not by much. Let's take a look at the requirements on both the computer and piano sides. Since the requirements for the piano are pretty simple, we'll start there.

Digital and Hybrid Piano Considerations

If your existing piano is going to serve as the basis for your extended piano family, the minimum requirement is that it have MIDI-out capability—USB MIDI makes it slightly easier, but regular MIDI connections will do as well. The good news here is that all currently available digital pianos and most acoustic hybrid pianos already have, or can add, this capability. The next step is to be able to get your existing "host" piano to stop producing its own sound. For digital pianos, this consists of a brief trip to the owner's manual to learn how to set it up as a

"controller" or "master" keyboard. Acoustic pianos must either be capable of "silent" mode or must be converted to enable it (see "**Hybrid Pianos**" in this issue).

Computer Considerations

Requirements for the computer vary considerably, depending on the piano software used and the choices you make in software settings. Just as with digital pianos, sample-based software is highly dependent on the size of the computer's memory, while physical modeling software—which creates the sound in real time rather than retrieving an existing sound sample—primarily depends on the speed of the computer's processor. At a minimum, hardware requirements will involve processor type and speed, and the amount of random-access memory (RAM) and hard-disk space. These requirements range from packages that can run on most recent-vintage mid-range computers, to those requiring higher-speed processors, 4 Gigabytes (GB) of RAM, over 250 GB of free hard-disk space (preferably on a 7200rpm drive), and a dedicated sound card. Either way, you need to check the hardware requirements of the individual software package you'd like to run to make sure it will work properly on your computer—or use it as an excuse to get a new computer.

Aside from making sure that you have enough memory to store and run these packages, processor and sound-card choices will also keep *latency* in check. Latency is how long it takes the computer to produce a

sound from the time you press a key. When latency becomes noticeable, your brain doesn't know whether to slow your playing so that the sound can catch up, or to speed up to make the sound happen faster. Neither of these works. (Anyone who plays the pipe organ knows what latency is, and will adapt to it without a second thought.)

Software

This is where the real fun starts. There are currently over two dozen software-piano packages available, at prices ranging from $79 to $895. These include both sample-based packages and packages based on physical modeling. Several host acoustic pianos (i.e., the sources of the samples) are available via software, including instruments made by Bechstein, Bösendorfer, Blüthner, Fazioli, Kawai, Steingraeber, Steinway, and Yamaha. If you'd like to add some period instruments to your palette, there are also packages with samples from historical fortepianos.

If you're not particularly into computers, software pianos may not be for you. But if you enjoy even a mild bit of tinkering, and have dreamed of owning a collection of the world's finest pianos or even of "designing" your own piano, you may find software pianos an irresistible temptation. If you're interested in following the world of piano software, it's discussed in Piano World's "**Digital Pianos—Synths & Keyboards**" forum.

Don't Just Take *Our* Word For It. Listen to What the Pros are Saying.

Dealers Award It

MMR Dealers' Choice Awards crowned the AvantGrand as 2011 "Product of the Year." "Since the introduction of these innovative pianos a few years ago, we've watched the AvantGrand steadily gain ground in the "Product of the Year" category. Yamaha's innovative Spatial Acoustic [...] System allows for playback that is virtually identical to that of an actual acoustic grand piano." MMR (Music Merchandise Review)

Performers Applaud It

"It blew me away! The feel is exactly like a grand piano [...] it's very smooth. Once I started getting in the flow, I could lose myself in the music, as I like to do." Chick Corea: Legendary Jazz Pianist

"The AvantGrand N2 is an absolute wonder. Its grand piano action and sampled sound are so lifelike that [...] the tactile and aural playing experience clearly equals that of a fine acoustic grand piano." Jackson Berkey: Mannheim Steamroller

Educators Embrace It

"How do you get the technique and feel of a Yamaha concert grand piano action and the sound of a 9' premium grand into a small office/studio space? You take advantage of Yamaha hybrid technology with the AvantGrand N3. It's hard to believe how well this instrument works... Bravo Yamaha!" David Brian Williams: President of the College Music Society, Emeritus Professor of Music at Illinois State University

"I love my Yamaha AvantGrand! My friends, colleagues and students are blown away by its sound!" Kathleen Theisen, NCTM: Pianist, Conductor

Reviewers Praise It

TIME Techland's Matt Peckham purchased a Yamaha AvantGrand N2 to prep for a product review and fell in love with it. His pre-review write-up (Dec. 12, 2011) declared: "I've only had a few hours with the N2 [...] but I'm startled by how honest both the sound and feel are." The N3 was also well-received by Techland, which selected it as one of "Our Favorite Things" Last Minute Gift Ideas for 2011. To read the complete N2 pre-review, please visit http://4wrd.it/N2ADPB and for the N3 story, go to http://4wrd.it/N3ADPB.

◈YAMAHA AVANTGRAND

MENTION THE WORD *hybrid* today and most people think of cars that combine a traditional internal-combustion engine with an electric motor to improve gas mileage and reduce emissions. By definition, a hybrid—whether a rose, a breed of dog, or a car—results from the combination of two different backgrounds or technologies. Now the piano has joined the ranks of the hybrids.

A hybrid piano combines electronic, mechanical, and/or acoustical aspects of both acoustic and digital pianos, in order to improve or expand the capabilities of the instrument. While applying the term *hybrid* to piano designs is a recent development, the practice of combining elements from acoustic and digital pianos is more than 25 years old.

Acoustic-based Hybrids: the MIDI Controller

On the acoustic side, the original hybrid instruments were not new pianos, but modifications of already existing pianos. In 1982, with the advent of Musical Instrument Digital Interface (MIDI), a computer language for musical instruments, instruments from different makers could "speak" to one another. Soon after, various kinds of mechanical contacts were invented for placement under the keys to sense keystroke information such as note, key velocity, and duration, and convert it into MIDI data. This MIDI information was then routed to synthesizers, which turned the information into whatever instrumental sounds the attached synthesizer was programmed to produce. When one instrument is used to control another in this manner through the transmission of MIDI information, the first instrument is called a MIDI controller. At the beginning, however, the sound of the acoustic piano could not be turned off, though it could be muffled in vertical pianos.

Early mechanical key contacts were subject to breakdown, or infiltration by dust, and their presence could sometimes be felt by sensitive players and interfere with their playing. The more advanced key contacts or sensors used today involve touch films or optical sensors that are more reliable and accurate, and add no significant weight to the touch. In time, also, mechanisms were invented for shutting off the acoustic piano sound entirely, either by blocking the hammers from hitting the strings, or by tripping (escaping) the action train of force earlier than normal, so that the hammers lacked the velocity needed to reach the strings. Headphones would block out any remaining mechanical noise, leaving only the sounds of the electronic instrument.

Not surprisingly, most makers of these MIDI controller/acoustic hybrid systems have been manufacturers of electronic player-piano systems. The same MIDI sensor strip used under the keys of these systems for their Record feature (which allows players to record their own playing for later playback) can also transmit the MIDI information to a digital sound source: either an internal source that comes with the piano (a *sound card*) or an external one, such as a synthesizer or a computer with appropriate software installed. All player-piano systems today allow, through MIDI control, for the accompaniment of the acoustic piano sound by digitally produced sound, be they other piano-like sounds, other instrumental sounds, or even entire orchestras.

In addition to the accompaniment function, it turns out that these hybrid systems in which the acoustic piano can be silenced potentially have another very practical function. If your playing is likely to meet

A hybrid piano can be created from either an acoustic or a digital piano, but we need to be clear about our definitions of *acoustic* and *digital*. The essential difference between acoustic and digital pianos is in how the sound is produced. In an acoustic piano, a sound is produced by the mechanical act of a hammer hitting strings, causing the strings to vibrate. In a digital piano, the sound is produced electronically, either from previously sampled acoustic pianos, or by physical modeling that employs a mathematical algorithm to produce sounds like those of an acoustic piano. (Here we're speaking only of that aspect of a digital piano that is designed to produce a piano-like sound. Digitals typically also can produce many other instrumental and non-instrumental sounds.)

with objections from neighbors or family, being able to silence the piano and then play as loudly as you want, while listening through headphones, can be very handy. Realizing this, the major player-piano manufacturers make the MIDI controller feature available—without the player piano—relatively inexpensively. These MIDI controllers include a MIDI sensor strip under the keys, or optical sensors for keys and hammers, but no hardware and electronics that would make the piano keys move on their own. Usually, these systems come with a "stop rail" or other mechanical device to prevent the hammers from hitting the strings, an internal digital sound source, and headphones. When you move a lever to stop the acoustic piano sound, you turn on the digital sound source, which is heard through the headphones. Yamaha calls this instrument Silent Piano (formerly MIDIPiano). Piano-Disc calls their add-on system QuietTime; QRS's version is called SilentPNO. More information about these systems is included in the article "**Buying an Electronic Player-Piano System.**"

But the accompaniment and "silent" functions of a hybrid MIDI controller/acoustic piano are only the beginning of what it can do. Just as the MIDI signal can be sent to a synthesizer or sound card, it can also be sent to a personal computer or transmitted over the Internet. Regardless of whether a MIDI controller originates in an acoustic or a digital piano, it enables the instrument to interact with music software to record, produce notation, control instrumental voices on a personal computer, or interact with other pianos in the same room or on different continents. The potential for hybrids in creating and teaching music is limited only by the imagination of the user. Notation

softwares—from MakeMusic's Finale, Avid's Sibelius, GenieSoft's Overture, and others—allow the hybrid piano's key input (playing) to be converted to music notation. This notation can be edited, transposed, split into parts for different instruments, played back, and printed out. The possibilities for teaching are perhaps even more powerful. Taking a lesson from a teacher in a different state or a master class from a performer in a different country becomes possible with hybrid technology, particularly when combined with the player-piano features. Exacting copies of performances can be sent to similarly equipped instruments for playback, and critiques—with musical examples—can be sent back to the student. Some systems enable this interaction in real time over broadband connections, complete with synchronized video.

As we've said, most of the activity in the field of acoustic hybrids has been among player-piano makers, whose offerings have been either specialized (Silent Piano) or add-ons (QuietTime, SilentPNO). However, MIDI capabilities are now standard in all acoustic pianos, vertical and grand, made by Story & Clark, a subsidiary of QRS, the only piano maker so far to have done this. If you add a stop rail to silence the piano (available from QRS) and a sound source, you could turn one of these instruments into a "silent"

All Story & Clark pianos come with a factory-installed PNOscan MIDI strip beneath the keys.

type of hybrid like those described above. But even without those additions, a Story & Clark piano can be used with a personal computer and music software for recording, notation, controlling computer-produced instrumental voices, or any of the myriad other uses possible with a MIDI controller.

Digital-based Hybrids: Replicating the Acoustic Experience

Now, you may wonder: If you're just going to use a piano to interact with a computer, play piano sounds silently, or make other instrumental sounds, why bother with an acoustic piano at all? Why not just use a digital piano or keyboard of some kind? The reason is: the *experience*. Digital pianos are long on functionality but short on, shall we say, atmosphere. For those used to the looks, touch, tone, or other, less tangible aspects of acoustic pianos, digital pianos, in their "pure" form, just don't cut it—so digital piano makers have spent a great deal of time, energy, and money trying to mimic one or more of these aspects of acoustic pianos. The closer they get to duplicating the experience of playing an acoustic piano, the more they earn the right to the *hybrid* designation—because, when you get down to it, the function of an acoustic piano *is* the experience.

The first aspect of an acoustic piano that digital piano makers mimicked was, of course, the looks, and a large segment of the digital piano market consists of acoustic piano look-alikes. But that alone isn't enough to earn the title *hybrid*. Next, the mechanism of the acoustic piano found its way into the digital piano. Much engineering has gone into the numerous action designs in digitals, always in the attempt to make their feel and response as close as possible to that of a "real" piano. For example, Yamaha's GranTouch line of digital pianos uses a slightly modified acoustic piano action to trigger the piano's sensors (the hammers are small and don't actually strike strings). With such an action, there's no need to simulate certain action processes, such as escapement, because it actually occurs mechanically. Many digital piano actions these days have weighted and/or wooden keys, and other enhancements that do a reasonable job of emulating an acoustic piano action; still, advanced pianists, especially classical ones, are unlikely to be satisfied by most of them.

Of course, digital piano makers have put more effort into copying the tone of the acoustic piano than any other aspect. How they've done this is beyond the scope of this article (see "**Digital Piano Basics**" for this information), but one interesting attempt is that of adding a soundboard to the digital. The Kawai CA-91, introduced in 2006, with its Soundboard Speaker System; and the Yamaha CGP-1000 Clavinova in 2007, with its Hybrid Active Soundboard System, both use an actual piano soundboard, set in motion by transducers, to augment the conventional speakers and impart a more natural tone to the instrument.

The latest entry in the hybrid arena is also the first instrument to formally appropriate the title of Hybrid Piano. Yamaha unveiled its AvantGrand N3 at the 2009 music industry (NAMM) trade show in January, and its vertical cousin, the N2, a few months later. The Avant-Grand elevates the digital piano to a new level with a number of hybrid technologies. First among them is the use of a grand piano action. As mentioned above, this eliminates any discussion of whether or not it *feels* like an acoustic piano action—it *is*

one. (However, whether the action feels *right* is still a legitimate topic of discussion.) This action controls the digital voices through the use of optical sensors, which measure the velocity of the keys and hammers without actually contacting any part of the action. It's important to note that this same grand piano action is employed in the vertical model N2, eliminating the second-class citizenship of the vertical piano.

(This brings up the interesting observation that, with digital pianos, there is absolutely no meaningful distinction between "grand" and "vertical" pianos. In an acoustic piano, the principal difference between grands and verticals is that in a grand, the cast-iron plate, strings, and supporting wooden structure lie horizontally, whereas in a vertical they stand vertically. The actions are arranged differently to

accommodate the different structures. But because there are no such structural parts in a digital piano, and the actions are the same, any perceived differences are in name and furniture styling only.)

One element of the traditional acoustic vs. digital argument that changes with the presence of a real action is the digital's advantage of rarely needing maintenance. While the AvantGrand will never need to be tuned, eventually its action will require some degree of adjustment or regulation. (We'll bet the piano technician will be in for a surprise when, on arriving to regulate the action, he or she finds the "piano" is a digital.)

But there's more to the feel of an acoustic piano than its action, and this brings us to the last of the acoustic piano attributes that digital piano makers attempt to copy: the intangibles. In this case, the "intangible"

is actually tangible—the vibration generated by the strings and transmitted throughout the instrument. Yamaha has added this ingredient by connecting transducers to the action to send the appropriate frequency and degree of vibration to the player's fingers when playing. This is where the experience of playing the AvantGrand becomes a bit . . . spooky. Not unlike the experience of amusement-park rides that convince your brain that you're dodging asteroids while hurtling through space when you are, in fact, fairly stationary, the AvantGrand's Tactile Response System quickly convinces you that you're feeling the vibrations of strings that aren't actually there.

The illusions don't stop there. When you depress a digital piano's sustain pedal, you're pressing a spring with a constant tension. This is not how the sustain pedal feels on most acoustic pianos, in which the initial movement meets little resistance as the pedal takes up a bit of slack in the mechanism that lifts the dampers. Once the mechanism begins to lift the dampers, the resistance increases noticeably. Here again, the AvantGrand does a convincing job of conveying the feel and—perhaps more important—the pedal control available on an acoustic piano, including half-pedaling and incremental control. A four-channel sample set and a 12-speaker audio system are also convincing, easily tricking your ear into thinking that there are considerably more than four feet of piano in front of you.

Which Side Are You On?

One area in which digital pianos are not intended to emulate acoustics is that of price. The AvantGrand model N3, with the sound, and perhaps the feel and experience, of a Yamaha concert grand, has

Yamaha AvantGrand model N3

Yamaha

an MSRP of $19,999 and a street price of around $15,000. This is roughly comparable to the price of a 5'3" Yamaha model GC1M, one of Yamaha's lower-level consumer-grade acoustic grands. This could create something of a dilemma for a potential buyer: acoustic or digital? Actually, the comparison would be more valid if the GC1M were fitted with an aftermarket "silent" mechanism, sound card, and MIDI sensor strip at a cost of about $2,500, or if the comparison were with, say, a Yamaha 5'3" model C1S Silent Piano, with a street price of about $22,000. Then, the AvantGrand would be from 15% to more than 30% less costly than the acoustic-based hybrid, and with features the acoustic did not have, such as onboard recording, USB memory, transposition, and alternate tunings. (Of course, if you compared the price of the AvantGrand with an actual Yamaha concert grand, which the AvantGrand is intended

to emulate, the savings would be around 90%.)

As the market for hybrid pianos heats up, buyers will increasingly have to choose between acoustic pianos with digital enhancements and digital pianos that try to create the acoustic experience. Decisions will be made by weighing the relative quality, and importance to the buyer, of action, tone, looks, price, and features. More advanced classical pianists whose digital needs are modest, and buyers who, among other things, are looking to fill up a living room with a large, impressive piece of furniture, will probably tend to stick with the acoustic-based hybrid for now. Those whose musical needs are more general, or who have a strong interest in digital features, may find digital-based hybrids more cost-effective.

Another factor that may come into play is that of life expectancy. A good acoustic piano will typically function well for 40 or 50 years, if not longer. Few digital pianos made 15 to 20 years ago are still in use, due either to technological obsolescence or to wear. True, the relevant technologies have evolved, as has the design of digital pianos and the quality of their construction. Realistically, however, if past experience is any guide, pianos that are largely acoustic with digital enhancement may well last for many decades, while those that are digitals enhanced with acoustic-like features are unlikely to last as long.

The piano has evolved a great deal since Bartolomeo Cristofori invented it in 1700, and that evolution continues. Today it is possible to buy a piano with an ABS-Carbon action (Kawai), a carbon-fiber soundboard (Steingraeber Phoenix), or one that looks as if it was made for the Starship *Enterprise*! The hybrid piano's blending of acoustic and digital technologies is just another step—or branch—in that evolution. ▥

SOME OF YOU may have fond memories of gathering around Grandma's old upright player piano and pumping those huge pedals to make it play—until you could hardly walk! As with so many other devices, technology has revolutionized the player piano, replacing the pneumatic pressure and rolls of punched paper with electronics, CDs, and iPods. Today, nearly one out of every three new grand pianos is sold with an electronic player-piano system installed. The capabilities of these systems range from those that simply play the piano (often all that's desired for home use) all the way to those that allow composers to create, play, and print entire orchestral scores without ever leaving the piano bench. You can even watch a video of Billy Joel in concert on a screen built into your piano's music rack while, simultaneously, his "live" performance is faithfully reproduced on your piano! The features and technological capabilities are vast and still evolving.

Before you begin to wade through the possibilities, you should carefully consider your long-term needs. Since many of the features of the more sophisticated systems are related to recording one's performance, you should first decide whether or not you want the ability to record what you or others play on your piano. In many typical family situations, the piano, just like Grandma's, is primarily used for the children's lessons and for entertainment. If that's the case, one of the more basic systems, without recording capabilities, will likely be satisfactory. Most systems can be upgraded to add recording and other more advanced features, should you later find them desirable. However, as technologies advance, it may become increasingly difficult to upgrade your older system.

Some player systems can be added (retrofitted) to any new or used piano, while others are available only on a specific make of piano. When installed in a new piano, some must be installed by the piano manufacturer, while others can be installed by the dealer or at an intermediate distribution point. A factory-certified local installer of a retrofit can usually match the quality of a factory installation. Installation is messy and must be done in a shop, not in your home; but when done correctly, it won't harm the piano or void its warranty.

The player systems currently on the market can be described as falling into two categories: those intended primarily as home-entertainment systems or for lighter professional use (including commercial use in restaurants, hotels, etc.), and those whose playback and recording functions are of "audiophile" quality and are intended for the most discriminating or high-level professional users. Generally speaking, the first category includes systems by PianoDisc, Pianoforce, QRS, and most Yamaha Disklaviers; the second category includes the Bösendorfer CEUS, Live Performance, and Disklavier Pro models. However, this classification scheme doesn't entirely do justice to "home entertainment" systems, which can be more sophisticated in other respects, such as versatility and functionality, than some "audiophile" systems.

The quality of a piano performance, either by a sophisticated electro-mechanical reproducing system or by a human being, greatly depends on the overall quality and condition of the instrument being played. Thus, an out-of-tune and/or ill-voiced

The underside of a grand piano with solenoid rail (uncovered), power supply, and speaker installed.

QRS Music Technologies, Inc.

ELECTRONIC PLAYER SYSTEMS

HOW DO THESE THINGS MAKE THE PIANO PLAY?

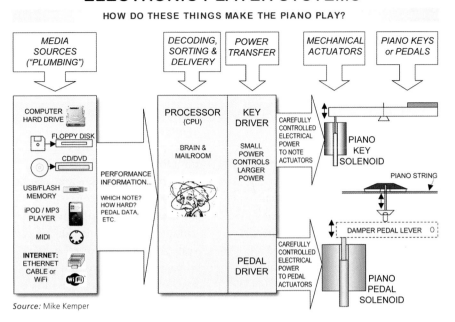

Source: Mike Kemper

piano with a poorly regulated action would result in an unpleasant listening experience, whether played by human or machine. This, of course, emphasizes the importance of regular and proper maintenance of the instrument. With new pianos, the performance quality of the player-piano system is limited, to a large extent, by the performance quality of the piano itself. Don't scrimp on a piano to afford a player system.

How a Typical Electronic Player-Piano System Works

Basic player systems consist of:

- a solenoid (electromechanical actuator) rail installed in a slot cut in the piano keybed (the structural part of the piano that supports the keys and action)
- a processor unit and other electronics mounted under the piano
- a control box that plays floppy disks and/or CDs (depending on the model), and is either mounted under the keybed at the front of the piano, or sits on or near the piano. In some models, the con-

trol box contains no disk drives and is hidden away under the piano, depending instead on your own CD player, MP3 player, or other device for the musical input.
- a remote-control device for operating the control box from a distance
- one or more amplified speakers, unless you choose a system configuration that uses your own speakers

On the solenoid rail, there is one solenoid for each key. There is also a solenoid for the damper pedal and, sometimes, one for the una corda (soft) pedal. Each solenoid contains a mechanical plunger that, when activated by an electronic signal, pushes against a key or against the pedal trapwork. When playing compatible specialized software, one track contains the MIDI signal that drives the piano solenoids; the other tracks provide an instrumental and/or vocal accompaniment that plays through a stereo system or through amplified speakers that come with the player system. The accompaniment may be in the form of

synthesized or sampled sounds, or actual recordings of live musicians.

For recording, keystroke and pedaling information are recorded in MIDI format by a sensor strip installed beneath the keys and sensors attached to the pedals. Some systems also record hammer motion. This information can be stored for later playback on the same piano, stored on other media, or sent to other MIDI-compatible devices.

The same sensors used for recording can turn the piano into a MIDI controller. Add headphones, a device for mechanically silencing the acoustic piano, and a sound card or other tone generator, and you essentially have a hybrid acoustic/digital piano you can play late at night without disturbing anyone. Because this feature can be used independently of the player piano, most manufacturers of these systems make it available separately under such names as Silent Piano (Yamaha), Quiet-Time (PianoDisc), and SilentPNO (QRS). Of course, the MIDI controller can also be used with or without a tone generator to send a MIDI datastream to a computer for use with composing and editing software, among other applications. (See the article **"Hybrid Pianos"** in this issue for more information.)

Common Features

Basic player-piano systems share a number of features:

- playback of piano music with a good reproduction of the artist's performance
- playback of piano music with a full band, orchestral, and/or vocal accompaniment (yes, it will sing!)
- a repertoire of thousands of songs and the ability to download music from the Internet
- connectivity to home sound or home-theater systems
- remote control

Other capabilities, in a variety of applications, are considered valuable tools for composers, educators, and students, as well as performers. They include:

- a system of sensing key and pedal motions that can capture and record the nuances of a live performance for later playback or editing
- playing every instrument of the orchestra (and then some!), using the piano keyboard coupled with an onboard and/or outboard sound module
- the ability to import and export performances through a variety of wired/wireless connections, including MP3s, iPods, the Internet, etc.
- synchronizing a solo-piano performance on your piano with a commercially available CD or DVD of a famous performing artist
- Internet radio that streams data specifically formatted for the player system, for a virtually unlimited supply of musical input
- connectivity to a computer, facilitating music editing, enhancing, and printing
- connecting to teachers and other players anywhere in the world via the Internet

In addition to bundling some amount of music software with the purchase of their systems, most manufacturers record and separately sell software for their systems on floppies, CDs, or DVDs, or as downloads from a website. A significant caveat is that one manufacturer's software may—by design—not work unconditionally with another player's hardware.

Questions to Consider

To list and compare the wide variety of features and capabilities offered by each of the player systems would be beyond the scope of this article.

However, the most significant concerns, aside from price, are the following. Ask your dealer or installer about the ones that interest or concern you.

- **Installation:** Can the system be installed in any piano (retrofit), or is it exclusive to a particular brand of piano? If exclusive, this will limit your options as to what brand of piano to buy.
- **Music Source:** Do you have a preference of source of music for the system: CDs, floppies, Internet downloads, iPod, MP3 player, etc.? This will influence your choice of system brand and configuration.
- **Recording:** Do you need recording capability, or the ability to use the system as a MIDI controller? This will also allow you to play silently with headphones, or to connect to a computer to edit and transcribe music, among other benefits.
- **Wireless:** Do you need to operate the system from a distance? Most systems have a wireless remote control available. Some can also be adapted for wireless transmission of music from the control box to the piano—for example, in a commercial establishment, where a CD player must be located some distance from the piano.
- **Visibility:** Is it important to you that the control unit not be visible or be very unobtrusive? Some models may be more suitable in this regard than others.
- **Equipment:** Do you need a system with a CD player, floppy disk drive, and/or iPod included, or will you be supplying your own? Do you need speakers or a video monitor, or will you be connecting the system to your own stereo system or home theater?
- **Memory:** Do you need internal memory for data storage, or will

you be using external data storage? Can external memory be connected?

- **Software Compatibility:** Can it play the music libraries of other manufacturers' systems? It's important to note, however, that because competitors sometimes change their formats and encryption, the ability to play the data format of a particular competitor's software may not be guaranteed.
- **Dynamic Resolution:** How many gradations of volume can the system record and play back? Most systems record and play back in 127 increments, which is more than sufficient for most uses. Some pre-recorded CDs play back with as little as 16 levels of expression—still probably enough for casual use, but you should test out the type of music you expect to listen to to see if it meets your musical expectations of dynamic range (gradations of loud and soft). A few systems can handle 1,000 or more increments. This may be desirable for high-level professional or recording applications, or for the most authentic playback of complex classical compositions. Likewise, some have higher processor speeds that scan the system a greater number of times per second for greater resolution. Some record by sensing only key movements, while others, for greater accuracy, also sense hammershank movements.
- **How many notes play back?** Some systems provide playback support for all 88 notes, while others come standard with as few as 80 solenoids (the highest and lowest four notes are not supported), with 88 as an option. The reason for providing only 80 is that installing more than that number sometimes requires removing

some wood from the top of the piano legs to accommodate the extra solenoids. This is not visible and doesn't harm the piano, but may not be desired by some customers. Most available music software will play just fine on 80 notes. But if you're planning to record yourself and use the notes at the extremes of the keyboard, or if you know you'll be playing back music recorded elsewhere that uses all 88 notes, you'll want the system to be able to play them. If that's the case, be sure to let the dealer or installer know.

- **Pedals:** Which pedals are played by hardware (solenoids) and which, if any, are mimicked by software? Hardware provides a more authentic piano performance, but duplication of pedal functions by software is simpler. Most important is hardware support for the sustain (damper) pedal, and all systems currently provide that. Only a few also provide hardware for the soft pedal (less important), and fewer still for the sostenuto (middle) pedal (unimportant).

- **Damper Pedal Performance:** Does it record multiple damper-pedal positions, allowing for pedaling techniques such as "half-pedaling," or does it simply record an "on" or "off" position? As with dynamic resolution, the recording and playback of multiple pedal positions is desirable for an authentic performance experience. The on/off mode is sufficient for very casual or simple uses.

- **Pedal Functionality:** Some add-on (retrofit) systems, when installed, may alter the functionality or feel of the pedals, especially the middle pedal. If possible, try playing a piano on which a similar player system is installed to see if the pedal operation is

okay for you. If only the middle pedal is affected, it might not matter to you, because this pedal is rarely used.

- **Playing Softly:** How well does the system play softly without skipping notes and without excessive mechanical noise? This is especially important if you plan to use the player piano for soft background music. If so, be sure to try out the system at a low volume level to be sure it meets your expectations.

- **Music Software:** How well does the available music software satisfy your needs?

- **Options:** What special features, advantages, and benefits are included or are optionally available? Examples include the ability to synchronize the piano with commercially available CDs and DVDs, features used for teaching purposes, built-in video monitor, subscriptions to Internet music libraries or streaming radio that make available virtually unlimited input to your piano, bundled music software, and so forth.

- **Upgradability:** To what extent is the system upgradable? Most systems are highly upgradable, but the upgradability of some entry-level systems may be limited.

How Much Player-Piano Systems Cost

The cost of electronic player-piano systems varies enormously, not only from one system to the next, but even for the same system, depending on where it is installed and other factors.

A dealer has several ways of acquiring an add-on (retrofit) player system, which can affect the price at which the system is sold. Factory-installed systems—installed while the piano itself is being manufactured—

are the least expensive for the dealer to acquire. Several large piano manufacturers are authorized to do this. In addition, the companies that make the player systems may factory-install them into brands that they own; for example, QRS Pianomation into the Story & Clark brand, and PianoDisc into the Mason & Hamlin brand. When installed this way, the difference in price between the piano alone and the piano plus player system may be quite moderate. The next more expensive options are when the player system is installed at an intermediate distribution point before reaching the dealer, or when a larger dealer, in his own shop, installs a system in a piano already on the showroom floor—with most brands of piano, either of these can be done. More expensive yet is when the smaller dealer must hire a local independent installer to install a system in a piano that is on the dealer's showroom floor. The most expensive option is to have a system installed in a piano you already own. In that situation you also incur the expense of having the piano moved to and from the installer's shop. The resulting retail price of the most expensive option can be double that of the least.

The cost can also vary because player systems are often used by dealers as an incentive to buy the piano. The dealer will charge well for an expensive piano, then "throw in" the player system at cost. Or vice versa—the dealer lets the piano go cheaply, then makes it up by charging list price for the system. The more modular systems can also vary in price, according to which options and accessories the dealer includes.

For all these reasons, quoting prices for player systems without knowing the context in which they're installed and sold is nearly futile. Nevertheless, as a rule of thumb, one of the more popular, typically configured, factory-installed QRS or PianoDisc systems with playback and accompaniment might add $5,000 to $6,000 to the street price of the piano, with recording capability adding another $1,500 or so. However, for the reasons given above, prices 30 percent lower or higher aren't unusual. A list of electronic player-piano add-on systems and their manufacturers' suggested retail prices follows the "**Model & Pricing Guide**" in this publication.

As for systems available only as factory installations, Yamaha Disklavier grands generally cost $8,000 to $20,000 (street price) more than the same Yamaha model without the player system. At the high end, a Bösendorfer CEUS will set you back $50,000 to $60,000 (street price). The retail prices of these systems are included under their companies' listings in the "**Model & Pricing Guide**."

THE SYSTEMS

BÖSENDORFER CEUS

Yamaha Corporation of America
P.O. Box 6600
Buena Park, California 90622
714-522-9415
info@boesendorferus.com
www.boesendorfer.com

Bösendorfer's SE Reproducer System, out of production for a number of years, has been replaced by an all-new design called CEUS (Create Emotions with Unique Sound), with updated electronics and solenoids. The visual display is discreetly located on the fallboard and is wireless, so the fallboard can be removed for servicing the piano without the need to disconnect any wires. Player controls for recording, playback, and data transfer are by means of a combination of keystrokes on the sharp keys aligned with the fallboard display, pedal movements, and four small, brass, touch-sensitive buttons on the left side of the fallboard. When the system is inactive, these four brass buttons are the only evidence that the CEUS system is installed in the piano. Optical sensors measure key and hammer movements at an extremely high sampling rate, for maximum accuracy and sensitivity to musical nuance. Bösendorfer has a library of recordings for CEUS, and the system will also play standard MIDI piano files. CEUS is available in every Bösendorfer grand model and adds about $70,000 to the piano's list price. Retrofitting of CEUS into previously sold Bösendorfers is available at the factory.

LIVE PERFORMANCE MODEL LX

Live Performance, Inc.
316 California Ave., Suite 825
Reno, Nevada 89509
775-331-5533
sales@live-performance.com
www.live-performance.com

Live Performance was founded in 1992 by Wayne Stahnke, one of the world's foremost authorities in the design of electronic player-piano systems. Stahnke is perhaps best known for designing the SE reproducing system, which Bösendorfer factory-installed in its pianos in the mid-1980s.

In 2007 Live Performance introduced its own player-piano system, the Model LX, providing playback performance the company says approaches that of the legendary SE system at a price competitive with other retrofittable player systems. The LX can now also be factory-installed to order in new Fazioli pianos.

Compatible with any grand piano, the LX employs the technical specifications of the SE's playback system, including a high keyboard sample rate (800 times per second), high-resolution note expression (1,020 dynamic levels for each note), support for 96 notes (to cover the extended keyboards of some concert grands), and proportional pedaling (256 positions). Among the LX's unique features is the immunity of its expression to variations in line voltage, using a patented proprietary method. The LX also features a closed-loop pedal servomechanism that enables it to reproduce with great accuracy a pianist's use of the sustain pedal—especially subtle half-pedaling effects. The sostenuto pedal is software emulated, but the LX is now available with a keyboard-shift (una corda pedal) option, providing proportional control of the shift with 256 positions. This makes available the added tonal colors that the una corda provides.

The black keys aligned with the fallboard display are among the controls used to operate the Bösendorfer CEUS.

The LX does not include a Record feature.

In the interest of being future-proof, the LX does not include a proprietary control unit. Instead, it is driven by a CD, DVD, or MP3 player, a wireless link, a home music-distribution system, or other source of stereo audio. This provides maximum flexibility and the ability to take advantage of advanced audio technologies as they appear.

The installed LX is more attractive than some other systems because the note solenoids are contained within the keybed slot and so do not protrude beneath the piano. The mounting rail is a rigid steel structure that restores the integrity of the keybed after the slot for the solenoid rail has been cut into it. Because of the solenoid rail's shallow profile, the piano's conventional pedal trapwork doesn't need to be moved or modified to accommodate the system.

The Live Performance Model LX plays all non-encrypted CDs for player pianos, as well as its own high-resolution format. Ten high-resolution albums from a growing catalog are included with the purchase of each LX system. Software is available to translate MIDI and ESEQ (a Yamaha format) files into native LX format, extending the benefits of the LX's high-resolution performance to these files, too.

PIANODISC

PianoDisc
4111 North Freeway Blvd.
Sacramento, California 95834
800-566-3472
916-567-9999
www.pianodisc.com

PianoDisc makes retrofit systems —including its popular player systems—that can be added to virtually any piano, grand or vertical, new or used. PianoDisc systems maintain full manual functionality of all pedals, and record and play

back all 88 notes. Piano manufacturers offer factory-installed PianoDisc products, and piano dealers also have installations done at their own locations by trained and certified PianoDisc technicians.

Introduced in 2010, PianoDisc's high-resolution playback technology, SilentDrive HD, features a faster processor and streamlined architecture that improve timing, velocity, and dynamics. With SilentDrive HD, each note has 1,024 levels of expression, so trills, for example, play back with much more accuracy than was possible before. SilentDrive HD is standard equipment on all current PianoDisc systems, and is available as an upgrade for legacy systems.

Also new in 2010 was PianoDisc's live, 24/7, free streaming radio, a feature available on all iQ-based PianoDisc systems, and free to all iQ customers as well (see below). This service is of special interest to hotels, restaurants, and other business establishments that use PianoDisc to provide their customers with non-stop royalty-free entertainment. In addition, each PianoDisc system includes a generous software package valued at $1,000.

PianoDisc's newest player system is **iQ**, "the Intelligent Player System." Hidden within the piano body, iQ can play back PianoDisc music using as a source almost any media player: iPad, iTouch, MP3, iPod, Xbox, DVD, CD player, etc. The most popular configuration is the iQ iPad Air, bundled with an Apple iPad and Airport Express for wireless control. With iQ, customers can operate all functions of the system from one familiar source. Using an iDevice, such as the iPad or iTouch, the customer can also take advantage of hundreds of apps offered through Apple's App Store for additional enhancement and enjoyment. Unique within the industry, iQ features a patented method of

iQ Flash, an entry-level system, is the latest addition to the PianoDisc line.

detecting changes to the volume of the music player, and automatically adjusts the piano volume to match.

When combined with the MIDI Record option, an iQ-equipped piano includes MIDI IN and OUT ports on the instrument itself. This allows for easy connection to a computer-based sequencer or other MIDI device. The Performance package consists of MIDI Record and a USB/MIDI Cable. The Mobile Performance package, which includes the MIDI Record option and the iRig interface, is designed to easily integrate with popular iDevices such as the iPad. The professional user would prefer the Studio Performance package, with MIDI Record and iConnect interface, which will integrate with an iDevice or other USB-connected device. A recommended app for record and playback of iQ (using either the Mobile or Studio Performance package connected to an iDevice) is Symphonix Evolution. Dozens of other interactive software apps for learning, practicing, and performing are available through the Apple App Store for free or for purchase. Examples include Garage Band, Music Studio, Home Concert Extreme, 50in1 Piano HD, Grinta Karaoke Lite, ForScore, Piano Notes Pro, Scorecerer, and Steinway Etude.

PianoDisc Remote is a utility app that supports the iQ system, available for purchase for $49.99 through the Apple App Store. Although piano and audio balance can be adjusted with the IQ Audio Balance Control, PianoDisc Remote permits the user to adjust the piano and audio balance wirelessly from an iPad or iTouch without leaving the couch. The app also performs other functions, such as scheduling start and stop times, creating playlists in a Music Chest, streaming PD Radio, setting presets and limits, and more.

iQ Flash, an entry-level system, is the latest addition to the PianoDisc line. Basic operation is accomplished by playing PianoDisc MP3 files from USB, SD, or MMC flash memory. All functions can be accessed either from the included remote control or via a few multi-function buttons on the face of the iQ Flash control box. As well, audio and piano balance control are easily adjusted with the wheel adjacent to the SD slot. An easy-to-read, high-contrast, backlit LCD display allows the user to view and make song selections, or to engage repeat and shuffle features. Incorporating the Studio Performance package into iQ Flash allows players to capture performances as MP3 files on their preferred media storage devices. With an additional mixer and a powered microphone, vocals can be added to the recording. The complimentary $1,000 software package is provided on a USB thumb drive.

For use with its systems, PianoDisc maintains a growing library of thousands of music titles available as digital downloads, CDs, DVDs, and high-definition Blu-ray discs. The library includes solo piano performances by famous artists, piano with instrumental accompaniment (most of it live), and vocals. Now, with the addition of iQ Flash, if a customer prefers to order a software selection rather than downloading

the music via MusiConnect, he or she will receive the album on an SD card packaged in a standard jewel case. PianoDisc systems also play any standard MIDI files (types 0 and 1), and some disc formats of other systems when converted to MP3 format using MusiConnect.

MusiConnect is a free PianoDisc application for Windows or Macintosh computers that allows consumers to download music purchased from PianoDisc's online music store. With MusiConnect, consumers can import PianoDisc album files or download purchases directly to a computer. MusiConnect also allows customers to load solo-piano or piano-with-orchestral-accompaniment MIDI files into iTunes. Once all the music is downloaded, MusiConnect gives the option of syncing a Piano-Disc album or playlist with iTunes. This process creates a matching playlist in iTunes, imports each PianoDisc song, and includes album, artist, and genre information (when available). From there, the music can be loaded into an iPod or burned to a CD. MusiConnect also includes a patented technology, Always Play, that allows the user to import any MIDI file, even if the recording contains no piano part, and guarantees that it will play back on the piano. Always Play recognizes the lead instrument (guitar, organ, flute, etc.) and substitutes the piano for it.

PianoSync is a MIDI-controlled piano performance that synchronizes with a commercially available audio CD of a major recording artist. PianoSyncs are purchased from PianoDisc's website as downloads or CD and stored using MusiConnect. The consumer also purchases the original artist's CD and loads it into iTunes, where the two are merged. The consumer plays the merged file on the PianoDisc and hears the original CD along with its new, live piano accompaniment.

PianoVideo HD, the first high-definition video format created specifically for modern player-piano systems, combines MIDI, audio, and video. The PianoVideo HD technology gives PianoDisc owners the ultimate entertainment experience: as they watch a high-definition video, their piano will play along with it live, in sync with the pianist on the screen. PianoVideo HD performances come on standard-definition DVD or Blu-ray discs.

PianoDisc also offers a stable of complementary products such as **Sync-A-Vision**, which brings the element of HD video to the PianoDisc experience. Sync-A-Vision comes with a high-definition monitor built into a piano music rack, and is powered by a computer, such as Apple's Mac mini or iMac, that comes preloaded with educational and entertainment programs. Included are 72 piano lessons, sing-and-play-along karaoke, cartoon and silent-film entertainment, concert performances, PianoDisc music, and PianoVideo HD performances. Most of these video performances are also available for separate purchase in either the Sync-A-Vision Educational or Entertainment bundle, which can be added to the popular iQ iPad Air system.

QuietTime MagicStar can mute an acoustic piano and let the user hear his or her performance through headphones via sampled sound. MagicStar has a control unit with 128 sampled instruments—a full General MIDI (GM) sound set—as well as 11 popular instrument presets, such as piano with strings. It also includes a built-in, adjustable metronome. A MIDI key sensor strip is installed under the keys, and a padded mute rail prevents the hammers from hitting the strings while retaining the motion and feel of the piano action. The mute rail is activated by moving a small lever under the keyboard, which also turns on the sampled sound. MagicStar comes with a control unit, power supply, MIDI cable, MIDI strip, pedal switches, headphones, and mute rail.

PIANOFORCE

Pianoforce LLC
476 Old Smizer Mill Rd. #136
Fenton, Missouri 63026
877-542-8807
sales@pianoforce.com
www.pianoforce.com

Pianoforce is a new entrant into the player-piano market under its own name, but the company that makes it—Ncode Ltd. of Bratislava, Slovakia—has been developing and manufacturing front-end controllers for the player-piano systems of other companies, such as Baldwin and QRS, since 1995. In 2005, Pianoforce was first offered as a complete system in the pianos of selected piano makers. In 2006, it was introduced as a retrofit kit installable in any piano, new or old. Designed and built by Ncode in Europe, the kit is ordered through a piano dealer and is typically installed in a new piano either at a distribution point or at the dealer location.

Pianoforce says that its system differs from those of its competitors in that the main rail component also contains all the controlling electronics, eliminating the need for a lot of complicated wiring and making for a neater and simpler installation. Also, a technician can plug a laptop computer into a USB port on the rail and, using software supplied by Pianoforce, can customize the system to the piano and to the customer's preferences through the control of many playing parameters, such as solenoid force, note release, and pedal release. These custom settings can then be archived on the laptop. The system automatically calibrates itself to the piano's sound with the help of a small sensor mounted on the soundboard. The combination

of automatic calibration with manual setup ensures the best playback performance for each individual piano following installation.

In 2007 Pianoforce introduced its latest controller, the Performance. Expanding on the company's past experience in supplying control components for other companies, the new controller contains some of the newest, most advanced features in the player-piano arena, such as the ability to read the software of other systems, including Yamaha Disklavier, QRS (except SyncAlong), and Web Only software, plus standard MIDI files; and onboard connections to the Internet via an Ethernet or wireless hookup, through which the user can download music from Pianoforce or even have system problems diagnosed. There are three USB ports for greater versatility, such as plugging in flash memory or a WiFi key. There is an optical digital stereo output and a dedicated subwoofer output line.

The system can now be controlled remotely via the user's iPod Touch or iPhone, and Internet streaming radio is available 24/7 with piano accompanied by original audio tracks.

The system comes with 500 MB of internal memory, pre-loaded with approximately 20 hours of piano music and expandable to 8 GB. The units are also shipped with approximately 400 Star Track piano recordings. A Star Track is a piano file in MIDI format synchronized to an original audio CD. When the audio CD is inserted, the corresponding Star Track is activated and plays a 30-second sampler accompaniment on the piano.

Keescan, an optional recording feature, uses optical sensors to record key and sustain-pedal movement. Also available is the **AMI** box, which facilitates connection of a microphone, iPod, and other USB devices. In addition to the system's ability to play other makers' software,

Pianoforce is building its own library of CDs.

QRS PNOmation

QRS Music Technologies, Inc.
269 Quaker Drive
Seneca, Pennsylvania 16346
800-247-6557
814-676-6683
www.qrsmusic.com

PNOmation II is the latest generation of QRS Music's flagship player-piano product, PNOmation, formerly called Pianomation. In addition to PNOmation, QRS has released a family of products under the PNO trademark, including PNOscan, Silent-PNO, and others.

PNOmation II is an electronic player-piano system that can be installed in virtually any piano, grand or vertical, new or used. Most manufacturers endorse the PNOmation system, and will install it, at a dealer's request, at one of their manufacturing or distribution points. QRS installs the system in many major brands of piano at its own U.S. factory, and it can also be installed at a dealer location by a QRS-trained technician.

Traditionally, electronic player pianos have been defined by the type of control box at the front of the piano, or by the controller's capabilities. PNOmation II differs in integrating the core features of every controller, including the music, into the PNOmation engine, thereby eliminating confusing options as well as the need to have a box hanging under the piano. Instead of offering a modular approach to the equipment required for various features, PNOmation offers all features standard, and a modular approach to their use. For example, the user can log in to the PNOmation system through any web-enabled device, pull up the system's embedded web-app user interface, and begin to play the piano; or, for those who are more comfortable with inserting their

The QRS PNOmation II web app gives the user full control of all parameters of the system and how music is played.

music selections into the device, music can be delivered via a USB thumb key; then you need only push Play on the system's remote control, or the Play button on the unit itself.

Key to PNOmation II's flexibility is the fact that it is delivered in a standalone-network mode, with its own network serving its own user interface, or web app. The big advantage of this approach is that a web app gives the user full control of all parameters of the system and how music is played. Some customers are concerned only with whether a song is a solo performance or a performance with background music, which they can determine from the web-app screen. Other customers may want to manipulate a MIDI file to change the tempo or tuning, and some may want to upload a recorded performance to view or change. None of this is possible with an off-the-shelf MP3 playback engine, but all of it is easily done with QRS's PNOmation II web app.

The web app also offers the customer several new control capabilities over the PNOmation II engine, including controlled release of the sustain pedal, to give it a soft landing and eliminate the potential thump heard with the release of the damper tray. The same controlled-release technology has also been applied to the keys, improving the PNOmation's already quiet playback while adding much more lifelike fingering. Other features include trill timing compensation, delay compensation, pitch correction, and MIDI-output curve maps. While most customers will use the default settings, those who want to dial in the perfect performance will be able to do so.

All of the data that controls the movements of the piano keys and pedals is in a non-compressed MIDI format (a high-definition MIDI format will soon be released). All music available for the new PNOmation II—currently over 6,300 tracks and growing—can be purchased one song at a time or by the album, giving listeners great flexibility in hearing what they want to hear.

While not required, connecting PNOmation II to a home network is easy to do. As a device on a home network, a PNOmation-equipped piano can be updated and/or controlled remotely via the Internet by accessing the web-app user interface via iPhone, iPad, iTouch, Android, Mac, Google Chrome browser, Kindle Fire, or any other similar piece of technology.

SyncAlong is a patented means of delivering music, whereby a MIDI-controlled piano performance synchronizes with a commercially available audio MP3 of a major recording artist. SyncAlong allows the listener to hear the original artist's content while the piano plays along. **Qsync** is a DVD interface designed to implement QRS's patented DVD SyncAlong technology. With the addition of Qsync, a PNOmation II player piano will be able to play along with selected popular, commercially available concert DVDs.

PNOmation II can also integrate with the **PNOscan** optical sensor strip, a leading technology for recording performances on an acoustic piano that is standard on all Story & Clark pianos. The PNOscan strip doesn't touch the keys, using only reflected light to continuously measure key and pedal movements. By integrating PNOscan with PNOmation II, one need only push the Record button on the web app to record. When recorded, the file is automatically saved and named according to your preferences. The file can also be sent to your favorite editing program, or e-mailed to a friend—all without boxes or wires.

SilentPNO consists of the PNOscan record strip, a piano sound module, and a stop rail for muting the acoustic piano. By muting the piano and turning on the sound card, the pianist can play in privacy with headphones. See the article on "**Hybrid Pianos**" for more information.

Upgrades from existing Pianomation systems to PNOmation II require replacing the Pianomation processor, and installing a WiFi adapter and a port extender—altogether, about a two-hour operation. PNOmation II can also be added to competitors' systems, allowing them to have PNOmation-type capabilities and music.

YAMAHA DISKLAVIER

Yamaha Corporation of America
P.O. Box 6600
Buena Park, California 90622
714-522-9011
800-854-1569
infostation@yamaha.com
www.yamaha.com

Disklaviers are Yamaha pianos that have been outfitted with an electronic player-piano system. These mechanisms are installed only in new Yamahas, and only at the Yamaha factory. They cannot be retrofitted into older Yamahas or any other brand.

Disklavier differs from most aftermarket systems in that Disklavier is not modular. Whatever Disklavier features come with a particular model of piano is what you get (although software upgrades are possible). The sophistication of the key, hammer, and pedal sensing also varies, depending on which Disklavier (E3 or Mark IV) is associated with that particular piano model.

Some of the highlights of the **Mark IV Disklavier** include:

- 80 Gigabyte hard drive capable of holding all Disklavier software ever written (and then some)
- CD drive
- floppy drive

The Yamaha Mark IV Disklavier comes with hard, CD, and floppy-disk drives; headphones, and pocket wireless remote control, among other features.

- pocket remote control to communicate wirelessly with the Disklavier
- built-in Ethernet for connecting to your network and downloading MIDI files
- grayscale (continuous) hammer-shank sensors (on 6' 1" and larger models) for more sensitive recording capabilities
- XG tone generator with hundreds of synthesized and sampled sounds
- dedicated digital piano sound chip
- Articulation Element Modeling (AEM) voices for greater realism in orchestrated backgrounds
- built-in speaker system
- karaoke capability
- 16-track recording capabilities
- Silent Mode: silences the acoustic piano for listening through headphones
- Quiet Mode: silences the acoustic piano and directs the sound to speakers
- Quick Escape Action: maintains correct action regulation when using Silent Mode or Quiet Mode
- headphones
- SmartKey: a teaching device
- CueTime: a smart accompaniment feature
- PianoSmart Audio Synchronization: the ability to link a piano track in MIDI format with selected popular CDs on the general market for synchronized playback
- PianoSmart Video Synchronization: videotape a piano performance and the Disklavier will play the performance back perfectly on the piano whenever you play back the video of the performance
- Disklavier Radio: a group of streaming MIDI music stations, available on a subscription basis

The Version 3.0 operating system for the Mark IV includes the ability to make audio recordings of the piano and anything coming into the mic input, and enables control of the Mark IV via a PC or Macintosh computer through the use of a Web browser.

The current Mark IV Version 4.0 operating system provides Disklavier owners with the ability to control their system with an iPhone or iPod Touch, and the potential to take part in the new Remote Lesson feature (piano-to-piano connection via the Internet), described later in this article. Yamaha has also, for the first time, released its code to software developers so they can develop third-party Disklavier controllers.

The performance level of the standard Mark IV Disklavier is the same as formerly found in the Mark III PRO series. The Mark IV PRO provides the highest level of performance in the Disklavier line. The PRO series has a much higher internal recording resolution and a greater dynamic range in playback.

Introduced recently, the **Disklavier E3** offers many of the most popular capabilities of the Mark IV at a lower price. The E3 is offered only on Yamaha's smaller grands, from the 5' model GB1K through the 5' 8" model C2, and on the 48" U1 upright. The following are the differences between the E3 and Mark IV Disklaviers:

- The E3 has no internal hard drive. However, it does support a user-supplied USB hard drive.
- The E3 has no floppy-disk drive, though one can be added.
- The E3's ensemble electronic voices do not include Yamaha's Articulation Element Modeling (AEM) voices.
- The E3 has flash memory.
- The E3 does not have a dedicated digital piano sound chip, instead using the piano sound in the XG tone generator.

- The upright version of the E3 (DU1E3) does not come with built-in speakers.
- The E3 has only 2-track recording capability instead of 16-track.
- The E3 does not support Silent Mode, Quiet Mode, or Quick Escape Action.
- The E3 does not come with headphones.

Current E3 Version 3.0 adds the same capabilities as described earlier for the Mark IV Version 4.0.

Models DGC1B and DC2B, recently discontinued, are Mark III Disklaviers with some limits in their functionality. They don't support Silent Mode, Quiet Mode, or Quick Escape Action, and headphones and a digital piano sound chip are not included (instead, they use the piano sound in the tone generator). The playback-only model DGB1CD is being discontinued in favor of the E3 version, the DGB1KE3. Owners of Mark IIXG and Mark III systems can access many of the advanced features found in the E3 system by purchasing replacement control unit DKC-850.

For simple playback, most player-piano systems now on the market are probably equally recommended. The Disklavier, however, has a slight edge in quality control, and its recording system is more sophisticated than most of the others, especially in the larger grands. For this reason, it is often the system of choice for professional applications such as performance and teaching, and much of Yamaha's marketing efforts are directed at that audience.

Two examples are especially noteworthy. Yamaha sponsors regular piano "e-competitions" in which contestants gather in several cities and play Disklavier concert grands. Their performances are recorded using PianoSmart Video Synchronization, then sent to judges in another location, who,

The Bösendorfer
Klimt Special Edition

The Klimt model, made in cooperation with the Belvedere Museum of Vienna, uses the image of the "Kiss" on the inside of the lid. Craftsmen further customize it by applying additional elements of real gold leaf.

rather than listen to recordings, watch and listen to the music reproduced perfectly on other Disklavier pianos.

A similar concept is a technology called Remote Lesson, which debuted in spring 2010 after years of development and testing. A student takes a lesson on one Disklavier while a teacher located far away teaches and critiques on a second Disklavier connected via the Internet, student and teacher communicating with each other in real time via videoconferencing. Initially, this feature will be made available only to selected universities and at additional cost. Details and timing regarding availability of this feature to individuals is still under discussion.

Yamaha maintains a large and growing library of music for the

Disklavier, including piano solo, piano with recorded "live" accompaniment, piano with digital instrumental accompaniment, and PianoSmart arrangements. The system will also play Standard MIDI files types 0 and 1.

Yamaha also makes a line of **Silent Pianos**, formerly called MIDI-Pianos. Technically, these are not Disklaviers because they don't use solenoids for playback; they're included here because they are closely related products that have some similar features. Like the Disklaviers, Silent Pianos have sensors associated with the keys, hammers, and pedals that record their movements in MIDI format and output the information through a digital piano sound chip to headphones or

speakers, or to a computer for editing. With the addition of Yamaha's piano mute rail, the acoustic piano can be silenced and the instrument used as a digital piano with a real piano action. A new vertical silent system, called SG is now available. The SG system offers nine additional sounds, can record, and has USB capability to preserve recorded performances. See also the article on "**Hybrid Pianos**" in this issue for additional information. 🎹

Mike Kemper, a Los Angeles-based piano technician and expert on electronic player-piano systems, contributed to this article.

THIS SECTION contains brief descriptions of most brands of new piano distributed nationwide in the United States. Brands that are associated with only a single dealer, or otherwise have marginal distribution, are omitted unless I believe them to be significant in some respect. These profiles contain, sometimes verbatim, material from the fourth edition of *The Piano Book* where still relevant and accurate, accumulated changes from past *Supplements*, and new material gleaned from interviews with manufacturers and industry professionals. The contact information listed for each brand is that of the brand's U.S. distributor, or of the manufacturer itself if there is no separate U.S. distributor. Most manufacturers had an opportunity to see, comment on, and correct for factual accuracy the descriptions of their products. To keep the size manageable, however, much historical and technical information was abbreviated or omitted, including information on older, discontinued models, and on problems and defects that have long since been rectified. Although the information in this publication will usually be sufficient to help guide you in purchasing a new piano, you may wish, at your leisure, to peruse *The Piano Book* for additional commentary on the brands you're considering. Just be aware that, particularly where it conflicts with information in this publication, *The Piano Book* may no longer be accurate. In most cases, brands included in *The Piano Book* but not here, are either out of business or no longer distributed in the United States.

As in *The Piano Book*, the articles here are a bit quirky—that is, they vary in length, and in the thoroughness with which they treat their subjects. Some companies have more interesting histories, some instruments have more unusual technical features, some brands have more controversial issues associated with them, and some manufacturers were more helpful than others in providing access to interesting material. The comments are more descriptive than evaluative. For a "road map" depicting how I think the piano industry views the different brands relative to one another, see the article "The New-Piano Market Today."

Note: Electronic player-piano systems are covered in "**Buying an Electronic Player-Piano System**," elsewhere in this issue.

ALTENBURG, OTTO
Wyman Piano Company
P.O. Box 506
Colusa, California 95932
908-351-2000
info@wymanpiano.com
www.altenburgpiano.com

Pianos made by: Beijing Hsinghai Piano Group, Ltd., Beijing, China

This is the house brand of Altenburg Piano House, a New Jersey piano retailer in business for over 150 years, at one time as a manufacturer. This brand is sold via the Internet and through other dealers, in addition to the company's own stores. For many years, Otto Altenburg pianos have been made by Samick in Korea or Indonesia, though sometimes to musical and cabinet designs different from Samick's own. More recently, Altenburg has engaged the Beijing Hsinghai Piano Group in China to make a new line of pianos, some of which are exclusive to Altenburg, with individually hitched strings. The Beijing models are the ones shown in the Model & Pricing Guide of this issue. Grand models up to 5' 3" use a laminated soundboard, larger models use solid spruce.

Warranty: 12 years, parts and labor, transferable to future owners within the warranty period.

ASTIN-WEIGHT

Astin-Weight Piano Makers
P.O. Box 65281
Salt Lake City, Utah 84165
801-487-0641
astinweight@yahoo.com

Astin-Weight pianos have been made in Salt Lake City since 1959. The company continues to engage in limited production at several temporary locations due to storm damage at the factory.

Astin-Weight vertical pianos, 50" in height, are unusual from a technical standpoint because they have no backposts, instead relying on a massive full-perimeter plate; and also because the soundboard takes up the entire back of the piano, behind the pinblock, resulting in a much greater volume of sound than from a conventional piano (see *The Piano Book* for an illustration of this feature). Many of the cabinet finishes are simple, hand-rubbed oil finishes. The 41" console has been discontinued.

The Astin-Weight 5'9" grand is produced in very limited quantities. It has an unusual symmetrical shape and is hinged on the treble side instead of the bass. The company says this shape allows for much longer strings and a greater soundboard area.

Warranty: 25 years, parts and labor.

BALDWIN

For current, Chinese-made pianos:
North American Music, Inc.
11 Holt Drive
Stony Point, New York 10980
845-429-0106

For older and U.S.-made pianos:
Baldwin Piano Company
309 Plus Park Boulevard
Nashville, Tennessee 37217
615-871-4500
800-876-2976
800-444-2766 (Baldwin 24/7 consumer hotline)
www.baldwinpiano.com

Pianos made by: Baldwin Dongbei (Yingkou) Piano and Musical Instrument Co., Ltd., Yingkou, Liaoning Province, China; Baldwin (Zhongshan) Piano and Musical Instrument Co., Ltd., Zhongshan, Guangdong Province, China; both owned by Gibson Guitar Corporation, Nashville, Tennessee.

Baldwin Piano & Organ Co. was established in Cincinnati in 1862 as a retail enterprise and began manufacturing its own line of pianos in 1890. Throughout most of the 20th century, the company was considered one of the most successful and financially stable piano makers in the United States. Beginning in the 1980s, however, the quality declined, especially as a result of the relocation of action manufacturing to Mexico. In 2001, a combination of foreign competition and management problems resulted in bankruptcy, and purchase by Gibson Guitar Corporation.

Baldwin currently manufactures pianos for the U.S. market in two factories it owns in China, where it also maintains a major presence in the Chinese domestic, and other international, piano markets. The company ceased regular piano production at its only remaining U.S. factory, in Trumann, Arkansas, at the end of 2008, though the facility remains open as a U.S. distribution and service center. Pianos sold in the U.S. now bear only the Baldwin name; all other piano names Baldwin owns and has used recently, such as Hamilton, Wurlitzer, Chickering, Howard, and D.H. Baldwin, have been retired, although some pianos bearing those names may remain on showroom floors for quite some time until sold. To distinguish new Baldwin pianos made in China from ones made in the U.S., a small *c* over the *i* in *Baldwin* on the fallboard indicates Chinese manufacture.

Baldwin has re-created versions of most of its former U.S. vertical models at its facility in Zhongshan, China. These are the model numbers beginning with B (formerly BZ). Initial reports suggest they are competently made. Model B242 is a 42" console, in attractive furniture styles (and model B242E in continental style), similar to the former model Classic 660 console. Models B342 and B442 are the same piano, but with fancier cabinets. Models B243 and B247 are similar to the famous Baldwin Hamilton studio, the most popular school piano ever built, with toe-block construction, the 243 in school style and the 247 with slightly curved legs. Model B252 is a replica of the former 52" model 6000 upright, complete with original features such as sostenuto and Accu-just hitch pins. In addition to re-creating versions of former U.S. vertical models, Baldwin is also in the process of creating a number of new models to fill various price points and meet consumer demand. At the moment, the model lineup is in flux. See Baldwin's website and the **Model & Pricing Guide** in this book for more information.

Baldwin grands are made at the Dongbei piano factory in Yingkou, China, which Gibson purchased in 2007 (models beginning with BD, formerly with BH). These are technically nearly identical to Dongbei's grands made for other distributors (see **Dongbei**), although the cabinets may have features that mimic the appearance of Baldwin's U.S.-made Artist-series grands. The

Artist grands are still available from existing U.S. inventory. In addition to standard cabinet finishes, they are also available in striking—sometimes wild—artcase cabinets.

Baldwin sells an electronic player-piano system called ConcertMaster, available only on Baldwin pianos.

Warranty: U.S.-made Baldwin grands—lifetime on parts, 10 years on labor. Imported Baldwin grands and verticals—10 years on parts and labor.

BECHSTEIN, C.

including W. Hoffmann

Bechstein America LLC
Box 87
Manalapan, New Jersey 07726
212-581-5550
info@bechstein-america.com
www.bechstein.de

Pianos made by: C. Bechstein Pianoforte Fabrik GmbH, Berlin and Seifhennersdorf, Germany; and C. Bechstein Europe Ltd. (former Bohemia Piano Ltd.), Hradec Králové, Czech Republic

Bechstein was founded in 1853 by Carl Bechstein, a young German piano maker who, in the exploding world of piano technology of his day, had visions of building an instrument that the tradition-bound pianomaking shops of Berlin were not interested in. Through fine workmanship and the endorsement of famous pianists, Bechstein soon became one of the leading piano makers in Europe, producing over 5,000 pianos annually by 1900. The two World Wars and the Depression virtually destroyed the company, but it was successfully rebuilt. In 1963 it was acquired by Baldwin, and in 1986 Baldwin sold it to Karl Schulze, a leading West German piano retailer and master piano technician, who undertook a complete technical and financial reorganization of the company. In the early 1990s, Bechstein acquired the names and factories of Euterpe, W. Hoffmann, and Zimmermann. Pianos with these names are currently being sold in Europe, but only W. Hoffmann is sold in North America. In 2006 Bechstein purchased a controlling interest in the Czech piano maker Bohemia, and integrated it into a new entity called C. Bechstein Europe Ltd.

Bechstein says that all Bechstein-branded pianos are manufactured in Seifhennersdorf, Germany, and that W. Hoffmann pianos are made in the Czech Republic. However, Bechstein recently announced a technical-cooperation agreement with the Chinese piano maker Hailun, and it is widely believed in the industry that major components for some Bechstein or W. Hoffmann models are made by Hailun. With few exceptions, Bechstein prefers not to divulge where the components for its instruments are made, a policy that frustrates some industry observers who seek transparency. However, the company says that, whatever the origin, all parts are inspected and made to conform to its rigid standards, and, in my experience, all models, including the less expensive ones, continue to receive praise for their high quality.

All Bechstein pianos use Abel or Renner hammers, solid European spruce soundboards, and beech or beech and mahogany for grand rims and some structural parts. American maple pinblocks are used in the most expensive grand and vertical pianos, Delignit in the others. Three pedals are standard on all pianos, the grands with sostenuto and the verticals with practice pedal (sostenuto optional). Over the past few years, all Bechstein grands have been redesigned with a capo bar (eliminating the agraffes in the treble), higher tension scale, and front and rear duplex scales for better tonal projection and tonal color. Also, unlike older Bechsteins, which had an open pinblock design, in the redesigned grands the plate covers the pinblock area. For better tuning control, the higher-level pianos are without tuning-pin bushings.

Bechstein pianos are available in two levels of quality. The regular verticals and partially redesigned versions of the old grand models are a lower-priced line known as the Academy series and say only "Bechstein" on the fallboard. The 51½" Concert 8 (one of my all-time favorite verticals), several smaller verticals, and the fully redesigned grands (models D, C, B, M/P, and L), are the higher-priced line and say "C. Bechstein" on the fallboard. The company says both lines are made in Germany, though for cost-effectiveness some parts and components may originate in the Czech Republic.

The differences between the two lines appear to be primarily in tonal philosophy and cabinetry. C. Bechstein grands were designed with a higher tension scale for better projection, and with various components that the company believed would result in the greatest usable palette of tonal color (tapered soundboard, vertically laminated bridges, hornbeam hammer shanks, solid keybed, thicker rim, and hammers with walnut moldings and AAA felt). The grand soundboard is installed after the inner and outer rims are joined. The ribs are tapered after being glued to the soundboard, and the heavy-duty rim posts are dovetailed and embedded in the rim.

The Academy-series grands have an untapered soundboard, solid beech bridge with beech cap, maple hammer shanks, expansion-type keybed, and hammers with mahogany moldings and AA felt. The same quality wood and strings are used in both. The rim parts are joined, and the soundboard and ribs installed, in a more efficient, less time-consuming manner than with the C. Bechstein. C. Bechstein keys still use leather key bushings, whereas the Academy-series keys use the more conventional cloth bushings. Bone keytops are an option on the C. Bechstein pianos, and genuine ebony sharps are used on both series.

Bechstein uses its own Silver Line action in the Academy series and, in the C. Bechstein series, its Gold Line action, which has slightly stricter tolerances. As part of its global strategy, the company uses multiple suppliers for nearly all parts; parts for the Gold Line action come from Renner in Germany, while Silver Line parts come from China. Both actions appear to be well made, and both are of the Renner design, with the smooth, responsive touch characteristic of that design. Of course, the parts from Renner are more time-tested than the others.

The C. Bechstein cabinetry is much sleeker and more sophisticated than the plain Academy series, though both cabinets are finished to the same standards. The C. Bechstein plates receive the royal hand-rubbed finish; the Academy-series plates are just spray-finished in the conventional manner.

C. Bechstein grands are impeccably made in Europe with the customary brighter tone that Europeans prefer, and may need considerable voicing to suit the American musical taste. (However, several of my colleagues had high praise for the wide dynamic range, tonal color, and responsive action of the recently redesigned 7'8" model C grand.) The company maintains that since voicing is a matter of overall piano design, their pianos are voiced at the factory to their tonal standard and should not be altered. Some customers may still prefer the slightly warmer sound of the Academy grands, which are also about half the price.

Bechstein engineers oversee production of the Bechstein-designed W. Hoffmann line of pianos in the company's Czech facility. This is a mid-priced line intended to compete with other mid-priced pianos from Eastern Europe. Currently it consists of five grand and four vertical models in two series. The Tradition series is completely made in the Czech Republic. The Vision series is assembled in the Czech Republic, but the strung back (structural and acoustical elements) is imported from China.

Warranty: 5 years, parts and labor, to original purchaser.

BEIJING HSINGHAI

Beijing Hsinghai Piano Group, Ltd., part of the Beijing Hsinghai Musical Instruments Co., has been producing pianos in Beijing, China, since 1949. It manufactures more than 50,000 vertical and grand pianos annually, mostly for domestic Chinese consumption. In 2005 the company consolidated its three older plants into a new facility of 1.2 million square feet. The pianos are available throughout the world under the Otto Meister and Hsinghai (or Xinghai) labels, as well as under various other labels as joint ventures with other manufacturers and distributors, including Wyman and Altenburg. Kawai also has a joint venture with Beijing, though the pianos (formerly under the name Linden) are distributed only in Canada and Europe.

BERGMANN — See Young Chang.

BLÜTHNER
including Haessler. See also Irmler.
Blüthner USA LLC
5660 W. Grand River
Lansing, Michigan 48906
517-886-6000
800-954-3200
info@bluthnerpiano.com
www.bluthnerpiano.com
In Canada, contact Bluethner Piano Canada Inc.
604-264-1138
rrgarvin@telus.net
www.bluethner.ca
Pianos made by: Julius Blüthner Pianofortefabrik GmbH, Leipzig, Germany

Blüthner has been making pianos of the highest quality in Leipzig, in the eastern part of Germany, since 1853, and though nationalized in 1972, always remained under the management of the Blüthner family. Until 1900, Blüthner was Europe's largest piano factory. During World War II, the factory was bombed, but after the war the East German government allowed the Blüthner family and workers to rebuild it because the Blüthner piano was considered a national treasure (and because the Soviet Union needed quality pianos). With the liberation of Eastern Europe, Blüthner is again privately owned by the Blüthner family.

Blüthner pianos have beech rims (grands), solid spruce soundboards, Delignit pinblocks, Renner actions, Abel hammers, and polyester finishes. Pianos for export have three pedals, including sostenuto on the grands, and celeste (practice) on the verticals. Blüthner builds about 100 verticals a year in four sizes, and 500 grands a year in six sizes.

In addition to numerous specialized furniture styles and finishes, Blüthner has two recently issued special editions. In honor of the company's 150th anniversary, Blüthner introduced a Jubilee model with a commemorative cast-iron plate in the style of the special-edition pianos of a century ago. It is available in several sizes, in any style or finish. A Julius Blüthner edition honoring the founder of the company, now operated by the fifth generation of his family, is available in most grand sizes, and features, among other embellishments, brass inlays in the lid, round Victorian legs, and a very fancy, elaborately carved music desk in the styling designed by the founder.

Blüthner pianos incorporate several unique technical features. With aliquot stringing, the notes in the highest treble section (about the top two octaves) have four strings each instead of three. The extra string is raised slightly above the others and vibrates only sympathetically. The effect, heard mainly in medium to forte playing, is similar to that of a duplex scale, adding tonal color to the treble and aiding the singing tone. Another feature concerns the angled hammers, which may at first look odd, though the reason may not be readily apparent. It turns out that the angled hammers are actually cut at an angle to match the string line and mounted straight on the shanks instead of being cut straight and mounted at an angle like other brands. The company says that the effect is to more evenly distribute the force of the blow across both the strings and the hammers, and to make a firmer connection with the backchecks, which are also positioned in a straight line. Visually, the effect is an even, rather than a staggered, hammer line.

In what is perhaps a world's first, Blüthner has designed and built a piano for left-handed pianists. This is a completely backward piano, with the treble keys, hammers, and strings on the left and the bass on the right. When it was introduced, a pianist gave a concert on it after only a couple of hours of practice! It is currently available in the 6'10" and 9'2" sizes by special order (price not available).

With voicing, Blüthner pianos have a very full sound that is warm, romantic, and lyrical, generally deeper and darker than some of their German counterparts. Sustain is good, but at a low level of volume, giving the tone a refined, delicate character. The action is a little light, but responsive. The pianos are built of superb materials, and are favorably priced compared to some of their competitors.

In the 1990s a Haessler line of pianos was added to the Blüthner line. (Haessler is a Blüthner family name.) Created to better compete in the American market, Haessler pianos have more conventional technical and cosmetic features than Blüthner pianos and cost about 25 percent less. For example, the grands are loop-strung instead of single-strung, there is no aliquot stringing, and the hammers are cut and mounted in the conventional way. Case and plate cosmetics are simpler. The pianos are made in the Blüthner factory in Germany to similarly high quality standards.

Warranty: Blüthner and Haessler—10 years, parts and labor, to original purchaser.

BOHEMIA

German American Trading, Inc.
P.O. Box 17789
Tampa, Florida 33682
813-961-8405
germanamer@msn.com

Pianos made by: C. Bechstein Europe Ltd. (former Bohemia Piano Ltd.), Hradec Králové, Czech Republic

The factory that makes Bohemia pianos began production in 1871, and after World War II became part of the Czech state-owned enterprise that included the better-known Petrof. Privatized in 1993, the factory now makes 1,500 verticals and 400 grands per year. Originally it exported to the U.S. under the name Rieger-Kloss, a name now used only for Czech pipe organs. The name Bohemia is derived from the original term used by the ancient Romans for the part of Europe that is now the Czech Republic.

In 2006, C. Bechstein purchased a controlling interest in Bohemia Piano Ltd. and integrated it into a new entity called C. Bechstein Europe. Production was moved to a new state-of-the-art factory in Hradec Králové. However, Bohemia pianos continue to be sold through Bohemia's own dealer network, as before. Bechstein also makes the W. Hoffmann line of pianos there (see **Bechstein, C.**). All the components for Bohemia pianos are made in the Czech Republic or elsewhere in Europe. The pianos use Czech actions with Abel or Renner hammers. All grands have a slow-close fallboard. Bohemia pianos play very well, with a nice, bright, singing treble tone.

Bohemia makes four sizes of vertical piano from 45" to 52", and four sizes of grand from 5' 3" to 6' 1". In 2010, a new collection, Rhapsody (vertical model numbers beginning with R and grand model numbers beginning with BT), replaced several discontinued models.

Warranty: 5 years, parts and labor, to original purchaser.

BÖSENDORFER

Yamaha Corporation of America
P.O. Box 6600
Buena Park, California 90622
714-522-9415
info@boesendorferus.com
www.boesendorfer.com

Pianos made by: L. Bösendorfer Klavierfabrik GmbH, Vienna, Austria

Bösendorfer was founded in 1828 in Vienna, Austria, by Ignaz Bösendorfer. The young piano maker rose to fame when Franz Liszt endorsed his concert grand after being unable to destroy it in playing, as he had every other piano set before him. Ignaz died in 1858 and the company was taken over by his son, Ludwig. Under Ludwig's direction, the firm greatly prospered and the pianos became even more famous throughout Europe and the world. Ludwig, having no direct descendants, sold the firm to a friend, Carl Hutterstrasser, in 1909. Carl's sons, Wolfgang and Alexander, became partners in 1931. Bösendorfer was sold to Kimball International, a U.S. manufacturer of low- and medium-priced pianos, in 1966. In 2002 Kimball, having left the piano business, sold Bösendorfer to BAWAG Bank, Austria's third largest financial institution. The bank encountered financial troubles unrelated to Bösendorfer and sold the piano company to Yamaha in 2008. Yamaha says it will not be making any changes to Bösendorfer's location or methods of production, and that its sales network will continue to be separate from Yamaha's. Bösendorfer manufactures fewer than 500 pianos a year, with close to half of them sold in the U.S.

Bösendorfer makes a 52" upright and eight models of grand piano, from 5' 1" to the 9' 6" Imperial Concert Grand, one of the world's largest pianos. The 5' 1" grand, new in 2012 and unusually small for a Bösendorfer, has the same keyboard as the 5' 8" grand, ensuring a good touch despite the instrument's small size. The company also makes slightly less expensive versions of four grand models known as the Conservatory Series (CS). Conservatory Series grands are like the regular grands except that the case receives a satin finish instead of a high polish, and some cabinet details are simpler. Previously, the CS models also had a satin-finished plate, and were loop-strung instead of single-strung, but in 2009, regarding these features, the specifications of the regular models were restored. All Bösendorfer grand pianos

have three pedals, the middle pedal being a sostenuto.

One of the most distinctive features of the grands is that a couple of models have more than 88 keys. The 7' 4" model has 92 keys and the 9' 6" model has 97 keys. The lowest strings vibrate so slowly that it's actually possible to hear the individual beats of the vibration. Piano technicians say that it is next to impossible to tune these strings by ear, although electronic tuning aids can help accomplish this. Of course, these notes are rarely used, but their presence, and the presence of the extra-long bridge and larger soundboard to accommodate them, add extra power, resonance, and clarity to the lower regular notes of the piano. In order not to confuse pianists, who rely on the normal keyboard configuration for spatial orientation while playing, the keys for these extra notes are usually covered with a black ivorine material.

The rim of the Bösendorfer grand is built quite differently from that of all other grands. Instead of veneers bent around a form, the rim is made in solid sections that are then jointed together. It is also made of spruce instead of the usual maple or beech. Spruce is better at transmitting sound than reflecting it, and this, along with the scale design, may be why Bösendorfers tend to have a more delicate treble, and a bass that features the fundamental tone more than the higher harmonics. Although the stereotype that "Bösendorfers are better for Mozart than Rachmaninoff" may be an exaggeration (as evidenced by the number of performing artists who successfully use the piano in concert for a wide variety of music), the piano's not-so-"in-your-face" sound is certainly ideally suited for the classical repertoire, in addition to whatever else it can do. In recent years Bösendorfer has made some refinements to its designs to increase tonal projection. The relatively newer 6' 1", 7', and 9' 2" models have been designed specifically to appeal to pianists looking for a more familiar sound. In all models, however, the distinctive Bösendorfer difference is still readily apparent.

In the past few years, Bösendorfer has introduced a number of interesting instruments in new cabinet styles. These include a Porsche-designed modern piano in aluminum and polished ebony (or special-ordered in any standard Porsche finish color); the Liszt and Vienna models of Victorian-styled pianos; and a model, Yacht, in a decorative veneer finish with brass inlay that can be ordered without casters so that it can be bolted to the deck of a ship! Edge, a modern piano designed by a group of industrial designers, was the winner of a design competition. The Liszt Anniversary model, a limited edition of 25 instruments, commemorates the 200th anniversary of the great composer's birth. Gold-leaf inlays decorate the pedal lyre and legs, and a silhouette of Liszt, outlined in gold leaf, adorns the music desk. Perhaps not to be outdone by Porsche, in 2009 Bösendorfer produced a model commissioned and designed by Audi on the occasion of that automaker's 100th anniversary.

Bösendorfer makes a unique electronic player-piano system called CEUS. See "**Buying an Electronic Player-Piano System**," elsewhere in this issue, for more information. The Bösendorfer model 200 is optionally available with a Yamaha Disklavier E3 installed.

Perhaps the world's most expensive piano inch for inch, Bösendorfer grands make an eloquent case for their prices. They are distinctive in both appearance and sound, and are considered to be among the finest pianos in the world.

Warranty: 10 years, parts and labor, transferable to future owners within the warranty period.

BOSTON

Steinway & Sons
One Steinway Place
Long Island City, New York 11105
718-721-2600
800-366-1853
boston@steinway.com
www.steinway.com/boston

Pianos made by: Kawai Musical Instrument Mfg. Co., Ltd., Hamamatsu, Japan and Karawan, Indonesia

---

In 1992 Steinway launched its Boston line of pianos, designed by Steinway & Sons and built by Kawai. Steinway's stated purpose in creating this line was to supply Steinway dealers with a quality, mid-priced piano containing some Steinway-like design features for those customers "who were not yet ready for a Steinway." In choosing to have a piano of its own design made in Japan, Steinway sought to take advantage of the efficient high-technology manufacturing methods of the Japanese while utilizing its own design skills to make a more musical piano than is usually available from that part of the world. In 2009, Steinway launched the Performance Edition of the Boston piano with enhancements to the instruments' design and specifications, including a grand inner rim of maple for increased structural integrity and improved tone, the patented Octagrip® pinblock for smoother tuning and more consistent torque, and improvements to hardware and keytop material, among other things. Performance Edition models have model numbers ending in PE. Sold only through select Steinway dealers, Boston pianos are currently available in three sizes of vertical and five sizes of grand. All are made in Japan, except the model UP-118S PE, which is made in Kawai's Indonesian factory.

Boston pianos are used by a number of prestigious music schools and festivals, including Aspen, Bowdoin, Brevard, Ravinia, and Tanglewood.

The most obvious visible feature of the Boston grand piano's design (and one of the biggest differences from Kawai pianos) is its wide tail. Steinway says this allows the bridges to be positioned closer to the more lively central part of the soundboard, smoothing out the break between bass and treble. This, plus a thinner, tapered soundboard and other scaling differences, may give the Boston grands a longer sustain though less initial power. The wide-tail design may also endow some of the grands with the soundboard size normally associated with a slightly larger piano. The verticals are said to have a greater overstringing angle, for the same purpose. Over the last few years, the Boston verticals have been redesigned for greater tuning stability and musical refinement.

A number of features in the Boston piano are similar to those in the Steinway, including the above-mentioned maple inner rim, vertically laminated bridges for better tonal transmission, duplex scaling for additional tonal color, rosette-shaped hammer flanges to preserve hammer spacing, and radial rim bracing for greater structural stability. The Boston grand action is said to incorporate some of the latest refinements of the Steinway action. Cabinet detailing on the Boston grands is similar to that on the Steinway. Boston hammers are made differently from both Kawai and Steinway hammers, and voicers in the Kawai factory receive special instruction in voicing them. All Boston grand models come with a sostenuto pedal; all verticals have a practice (mute) pedal, except for the model UP-118S PE, which has a bass sustain.

Boston grands also have certain things in common with Kawai RX-series grands: tuning pins, grand leg and lyre assemblies, radial rim bracing, sostenuto pedal, and the level of quality control in their manufacture. The same workers build the two brands in the same factories. One important way they differ is that Kawai uses carbon-fiber–reinforced ABS Styran plastic for most of its action parts, whereas Boston uses only traditional wooden parts. Although similarly priced at the wholesale level, Kawai pianos tend to be a little less expensive to the retail customer than comparably sized Bostons due to the larger discounts typically given by Kawai dealers.

Steinway guarantees full trade-in value for a Boston piano at any time a purchaser wishes to upgrade to a Steinway grand.

Piano technicians are favorably inclined toward Boston pianos. Some find them to have a little better sustain and more tonal color than Kawais, while being otherwise similar in quality. When comparing the two brands, I would advise making a choice based primarily on one's own musical perceptions of tone and touch, as well as the trade-up guarantee, if applicable.

Warranty: 10 years, parts and labor, to original purchaser.

BRODMANN

including Taylor London

Piano Marketing Group, LLC
752 East 21st Street
Ferdinand, Indiana 47532
812-630-0978
christian.hoeferl@brodmann.at
www.brodmann-pianos.com
www.taylor-pianos.com

Company Headquarters: J. B. Piano GmbH, Kudlichgasse 24, A-1100 Vienna, Austria. Phone: +43-1-890-3203;
christian.hoeferl@brodmann-pianos.com

Pianos made by: various makers (see text)

Joseph Brodmann was a well-known piano maker in Vienna in the late 18th and early 19th centuries. Ignaz Bösendorfer apprenticed in Brodmann's workshop and eventually took it over, producing the first Bösendorfer pianos there. Today's Brodmann is a new company, headquartered in Vienna, and founded in 2004 by two former Bösendorfer executives, pursuing a direction they say was planned as a possible second line for Bösendorfer a number of years ago, but never acted upon.

Brodmann says its mission is to produce a piano with high-end performance characteristics at an affordable price by using European components in key areas, strict quality control, and manufacturing in countries with favorable labor rates.

There are three lines of Brodmann piano. The Professional Edition (PE) pianos, made in China, are designed in Vienna and use European components such as Strunz soundboards, Abel hammers, Röslau strings, and Langer-designed actions (Renner in the model 228, a Chinese action in the verticals). For quality control, Brodmann has its own employees from Europe in the factory. The scale design of the 6' 2" model PE 187 is said to be similar to that of a Steinway model A and is often singled out for praise.

The Conservatory Edition (CE), for the more price-conscious buyer, is also made in China, and comprises all Chinese parts (except for Japanese hammer felt), and receives Brodmann quality control.

The Artist Series (AS), introduced in 2011 and available only in the larger grand sizes, is partially made in China and then shipped to Germany, where the strings and action are installed and all musical finishing work is performed. The rim is made of maple; the soundboard, ribs, and pinblock are from Bolduc in Canada; and the piano uses a Renner action, Kluge keyboard, and Abel or Renner hammers.

The Brodmann company also makes an entry-level piano line called Taylor London, made in China with Asian parts, and subject to Brodmann's quality control.

Warranty: 10 years, parts and labor, transferable to future owners within the warranty period.

BURGER & JACOBI

Ciampi USA
1520 Appian Way
Montebello, California 90640
323-236-2446
g.ciampi@ciampi.it
www.burgerjacobi.com/en

Pianos made by: Burger & Jacobi, Hradec Králové, Czech Republic

In 1872, Christian Burger began making pianos in his workshop in Burgdorf, Switzerland, later moving to larger quarters in Biel. He was joined in 1879 by his son-in-law, Herman Jacobi. For more than a century, aided by good workmanship, thousands of satisfied customers, and the endorsement of Johannes Brahms, Burger, Jacobi, and four generations of their descendants continued making pianos in Switzerland. In 1990, the company was purchased by the Ciampi Group, of Rome, Italy, a leading European distributor of musical instruments, whose founder had once worked at Burger & Jacobi. Ciampi moved production to the Petrof factory in the Czech Republic, where their pianos continued to be produced until recently, with distribution primarily limited to Europe. In 2010, Ciampi purchased its own factory in the same town as Petrof's, and is now expanding distribution to North America.

For North American distribution, Burger & Jacobi is starting with three vertical and three grand models, with prices and features aimed at the middle to upper level of the piano market. The company says that the pianos are entirely made in the Czech Republic, and that all components are European in origin. Czech-made Detoa actions are used in all models except the concert grand, which has a Renner action. All models contain a solid spruce soundboard, Röslau strings, and Abel or Renner hammers. The 50" upright has a true sostenuto pedal.

Warranty: 5 years, parts and labor.

CABLE, HOBART M. — See Sejung.

CABLE-NELSON — See Yamaha.

CHASE, A.B. — See Everett.

CONCERTMASTER — See Baldwin.

CONOVER CABLE — See Samick.

CRISTOFORI

Jordan Kitt's Music
12303 Twinbrook Parkway
Rockville, Maryland 20852

301-770-9081
(Chris Syllaba)
info@cristoforipianos.com

Schmitt Music
2400 Freeway Blvd.
Brooklyn Center,
Minnesota 55430
763-566-4560 x5075
(Wayne Reinhardt)
www.cristoforipianos.com

Pianos made by: Guangzhou Pearl River Piano Group Ltd.,
Guangzhou, Guangdong Province, China

Originally issued under the name Opus II, the Cristofori and Lyrica brands are a joint undertaking by Jordan Kitt's Music, which owns and operates four piano dealerships in the D.C. and Atlanta markets; and Schmitt Music, which has more than a dozen locations throughout the Midwest and in Denver. Nearly ten years ago, wanting to improve their entry-level product offerings, the two companies combined forces to negotiate upgrades of product features and quality control directly with the factory. Today, although the brands are identical, Cristofori is sold only in Jordan Kitt's stores, Lyrica in Schmitt Music stores. Bartolomeo Cristofori (1655–1731) was, of course, the inventor of the piano.

The Cristofori and Lyrica lines are manufactured by China's largest piano manufacturer, Guangzhou Pearl River Piano Group. The uprights come in numerous sizes, styles, and finishes, including 42½" continental consoles and 43" decorator consoles in traditional and French cherry cabinets. The 48" professional upright, appropriate for home or institutional use, has double front legs and toe blocks for strength, and a large soundboard and long strings for bigger sound. Grands come in lengths of 4' 10", 5' 3", 5' 7", and 6' 2". The 5' 3" and 5' 7" sizes are wide-tail designs, which gives these mid-sized grands a larger soundboard area and, thus, a bigger sound.

The Cristofori and Lyrica pianos are differentiated from Pearl River's own line of pianos by upgraded specifications such as the use of highest-quality Mapes strings from the U.S.; all-spruce veneered soundboards of premium Siberian spruce; a different selection of cabinet styles; and a full, transferable warranty. U.S. technicians inspect every Cristofori and Lyrica piano at the Pearl River factory prior to crating and shipping.

Warranty: 12 years, parts and labor, transferable to future owners within the warranty period.

CUNNINGHAM

Cunningham Piano Company
5427 Germantown Avenue
Philadelphia, Pennsylvania 19144
800-394-1117
215-438-3200
www.cunninghampiano.com

Pianos made by: Ningbo Hailun Musical Instruments Co. Ltd., Ningbo, Zhejiang Province, China; with Cunningham Piano Company, Philadelphia, Pennsylvania

Cunningham Piano Company began manufacturing pianos in 1891 and, in its time, was the largest piano maker in Philadelphia. The original Cunningham factory ceased production in December 1943. The company was reopened in December 1945 as a piano rebuilder and retailer. Today, Cunningham specializes in the restoration of high-quality American and European pianos, and produces the new Matchless Cunningham.

Designed by Frank Emerson, the Matchless Cunningham is based on the original Cunningham scale designs. "Matchless" is used in reference to an offer made by Patrick Cunningham over a century ago: that he would pay $10,000 to anyone who could build a better piano. Because no one ever took him up on his offer, Cunningham labeled his piano the Matchless. Today, Matchless also refers to a unique combination of high-quality parts and a successful American scale design, assembled in China at the world-class Hailun factory, and with quality control overseen by Cunningham in Philadelphia. Currently, the line consists of four grand pianos from 5' to 7', and two verticals, 44" and 50".

Cunningham grands have maple rims (arguably necessary for best sound), custom-designed German Abel Hammers, German music wire, agraffes, duplex scaling, and slow-close mechanisms on both the fallboard and lid. Cunningham regularly sends technical staff to the Ningbo Hailun factory to oversee production, and each piano undergoes a thorough final preparation by Cunningham in Philadelphia.

The special Heritage Series incorporates art cases that reflect late Victorian styling. Handcrafted cabinet parts are made and installed in Cunningham's Philadelphia facility, making each instrument unique. Customers have the option of customizing certain aspects of the cabinetry based on their personal preferences.

Warranty: 10 years, parts and labor.

DONGBEI

Pianos made by: Baldwin Dongbei (Yingkou) Piano and Musical Instrument Company, Ltd., Yingkou, Liaoning Province, China

The Dongbei Piano Company in China is owned by Baldwin Piano Company, a subsidiary of Gibson Guitar Corporation, and makes pianos that are sold in North America by various distributors and under a variety of names, including **Baldwin**, **Everett**, and **Hallet, Davis & Co.** (see listings under those names). Pianos made under the names Nordiska and Weinbach are no longer distributed in the U.S.

Dongbei is Chinese for "northeast." In 1952 Dongbei was formed by splitting off from a government-owned piano factory in Shanghai and establishing a new government-owned factory in the northeastern part of the country. Dongbei began a process of modernization in 1988 when it purchased the designs and manufacturing equipment for a vertical piano model from the Swedish company Nordiska when that company went out of business. The Swedish-designed model 116 vertical was strikingly more advanced than Dongbei's own Prince and Princess piano lines. (At that time, Dongbei made only vertical pianos.)

In 1991 Dongbei entered into an agreement with Korean piano maker Daewoo whereby Daewoo would assist Dongbei in improving its production of vertical pianos. In 1996 that relationship was extended to the design and production of grand pianos. In 1997, when Daewoo decided to leave the piano business, Dongbei purchased nearly all of Daewoo's grand-piano manufacturing equipment and began making grands. Export to the U.S. began in 1994 under the brand name Sagenhaft, at first only of vertical pianos. When the export of grand pianos began in 1998, other brand names such as Nordiska, Everett, and Story & Clark, began to become available, and over the next 10 years production for both domestic use and for export grew enormously.

In early 2007 Gibson Musical Instruments, parent of Baldwin Piano Company, acquired Dongbei Piano and renamed it Baldwin Dongbei (Yingkou) Piano and Musical Instrument Co., Ltd., thus creating a major piano-manufacturing power in China with two plants. (The other plant, Baldwin (Zhongshan) Piano and Musical Instrument Co., Ltd., is in southern China.) Baldwin has greatly expanded its presence in China over the last five years, and the company says it will use the manufacturing capacity of Dongbei to service the Chinese domestic market as well as the world market (see also under **Baldwin**). In the four years since Baldwin acquired Dongbei, both the workforce and the production output have been considerably reduced to make the former government-owned operation more efficient and profitable.

When Daewoo left the piano business in 1997, some of the technicians and designers sent by Daewoo to advise Dongbei stayed on with Dongbei for many years, during which they designed numerous new piano models. Some of these technicians had trained in both Korea and Germany. In the opinion of many technicians who have examined a variety of pianos from China, the Dongbei grand-piano designs are among the best and most successful musically.

EDELWEISS

Edelweiss Piano Company
1066 Pianos (USA) Inc.
P.O. Box 7728
Kalispell, Montana 59904
406-863-1066
ustrade@edelweiss-piano.com
www.edelweiss-piano.com

Pianos made by: various Chinese suppliers

Edelweiss Piano Company is a subsidiary of 1066 Pianos, a long-established family-owned U.K. firm specializing in high-end rebuilding and custom-made designer pianos. Although all of the rebuilding and custom manufacture are carried out in 1066's own workshops in Cambridge, England or in the U.S., the company also sells new instruments, under the Edelweiss brand, which it sources from various Chinese suppliers, who build them to 1066's designs. The pianos feature German Strunz soundboards and Abel hammers, among other quality components.

Edelweiss model G50 pianos have the distinction of being, at only 4' 2" (127 cm) long, the shortest grand pianos on the market; and with only 85 notes, they are also a little narrower than other grands. The piano rim, instead of being straight on one side and curved on the other, is symmetrical, and comes in two furniture styles: "half moon" and "butterfly." With half moon, the semi-circular lid is hinged at the front and propped up at the rear. A semi-circular music rack mirrors the lid's shape. With butterfly, the lid is hinged at the middle, creating two mini-lids like butterfly wings, each propped up on the side. The instrument's small size and unusual shape may permit it to fit in places others will not. Stock colors are polished ebony and polished white; custom colors are available.

Other, more standard, models of Edelweiss piano will soon be available in the U.S., but specifications and prices were not available at press time. See the company's website for current information.

Warranty: 5 years parts and labor, to original purchaser

ESSEX

Steinway & Sons
One Steinway Place
Long Island City, New York 11105
718-721-2600
800-366-1853
essex@steinway.com
www.steinway.com/essex

Pianos made by: Guangzhou Pearl River Piano Group Ltd., Guangzhou, Guangdong Province, China

Essex pianos are designed by Steinway & Sons engineers and are made in China by Pearl River. Steinway introduced its Essex line of pianos in early 2001 with a limited offering of models made by Young Chang, and the brand kept an unusually low profile in the piano market for a number of years. In 2006, a major relaunch of Essex included a new and very complete line comprising 35 grand and 31 vertical models and finishes.

Today, two grand sizes and three vertical scales are made. The 42" model EUP-108 is a continental-style version of the 44" model EUP-111 console. The 46" model EUP-116 studio is available in 10 different and striking cabinets designed by Steinway & Sons and renowned furniture designer William Faber. Styles include: Classic, Queen Anne, Italian Provincial, French Country, Formal French, English Country, English Traditional, Contemporary, and Sheraton Traditional. These models incorporate various leg designs (including cabriole leg, spoon leg, and canopy-styled tapered leg and arm designs) and hand-carved trim (such as Acanthus leaf and tulip designs, and vertical bead molding), highly molded top lids, picture-frame front panels, and stylized, decorative music desks. The 48" model EUP-123 upright comes in a traditional style in four finishes, along with Empire and French styles; an all-new school

model, the EUP-123S, is offered in ebony polish only.

The Essex grands are available in 5' 1" (EGP-155) and 5' 8" (EGP-173) sizes in Classic and French Provincial styles. They come in a variety of regular and exotic veneers in high polish polyester and satin luster (semi-gloss) finishes.

Like Steinway's Boston pianos, the Essex line was designed with a lower tension scale and incorporates many Steinway-designed refinements. Included in these are a wide tail design that allows the bridges to be positioned closer to the more lively, central part of the soundboard, smoothing out the break between bass and treble. This and a thinner, tapered soundboard, and other scaling differences, produce a tone with a longer sustain. Other Steinway-designed features include an all-wood action with Steinway geometry, and with rosette-shaped hammer flanges, like those used in Steinway grands, to preserve hammer spacing; pear-shaped hammers with reinforced shoulders and metal fasteners; vertically laminated bridges with a solid maple cap; duplex scale; radial bracing (in grands); and staggered backposts (in verticals).

Steinway has put an immense amount of time and effort into the relaunch of Essex. The pianos are entirely new designs by Steinway engineers, not warmed-over designs from other companies. Steinway has a permanent office in Shanghai, China, and full-time employees who inspect the pianos made in the Asian factory. I expect that the quality of the Essex pianos will be toward the upper end of what these factories are capable of producing. So far, feedback from piano technicians confirms this expectation.

Steinway guarantees full trade-in value for an Essex piano toward the purchase of a Steinway grand within 10 years.

Warranty: 5 years, parts and labor, to original purchaser.

ESTONIA

Laul Estonia Piano Factory Ltd.
7 Fillmore Drive
Stony Point, New York 10980
845-947-7763
laulestoniapiano@aol.com
www.estoniapiano.com

Pianos made by: Estonia Klaverivabrik AS, Tallinn, Estonia

Estonia is a small republic in northern Europe on the Baltic Sea, near Scandinavia. For centuries it was under Danish, Swedish, German, or Russian domination, and finally gained its independence in 1918, only to lose it again to the Soviet Union in 1940. Estonia became free again in 1991 with the collapse of the Soviet Union.

Piano-making in Estonia goes back over 200 years under German influence, and from 1850 to 1940 there were nearly 20 piano manufacturers operating in the country. The most famous of these was Ernst Hiis-Ihse, who studied piano making in the Steinway Hamburg and Blüthner factories and established his own company in 1893. His piano designs gained international recognition. In 1950 the Communist-dominated Estonian government consolidated many smaller Estonian piano makers into a factory managed by Hiis, making pianos under the Estonia name for the first time. The instruments became prominent on concert stages throughout Eastern Europe and, amazingly, more than 7,400 concert grands were made. However, after Hiis's death, in 1964, the quality of the pianos gradually declined, partly due to the fact that high-quality parts and materials were hard to come by during the Communist occupation of the country. After Estonia regained its independence in 1991, the factory struggled to maintain production. In 1994 Estonia pianos were introduced to the U.S. market.

In 1994 the company was privatized under the Estonia name, with the managers and employees as owners. During the following years, Indrek Laul, an Estonian recording artist with a doctorate in piano performance from the Juilliard School of Music, gradually bought shares of the company from the stockholders until, in 2001, he became sole owner. Dr. Laul lives in the U.S. and represents the company here. In 2005, at its 100th-anniversary celebration, the Juilliard School named him one of the school's top 100 graduates. Estonia makes about 350 pianos a year, all grands, mostly for sale in the U.S.

Estonia pianos have rims of laminated birch, sand-cast plates, Renner actions and hammers, laminated red beech pinblocks, and European solid spruce soundboards. They come in 5' 6", 6' 3", 7' 4" (introduced in 2011), and 9' sizes. All have three pedals, including sostenuto, and come with a slow-close fallboard and an adjustable artist bench.

When I reported on Estonia pianos for the fourth edition of *The Piano Book* (2001), it was a good piano with much potential, but as the company was still rebounding from problems suffered during the Communist era, some caution was advised. Since becoming sole owner in 2001, Dr. Laul has made so many improvements to the piano that it is practically a different instrument. These include: rescaling the bass, and upgrading the machinery for producing hand-wound bass strings; improving the method of drilling pinblocks; stronger plates and improved plate finishes; thicker inner and outer rims; improved fitting of soundboard to rim; concert-grand–quality soundboard spruce on all models; quartersawn maple bridge caps; adjustable front and rear duplex scales; wood for legs and keyslips heat-treated to better resist changing climatic conditions; Renner Blue hammers on all models; better-quality metal hardware that resists oxidation; suede-covered music-desk tray; improved, more scratch-resistant satin finishes; establishing a quality-control department headed by Dr. Laul's father (both of his parents are professional musicians); higher-grade and artistically matched veneers; and establishing a U.S. service center for warranty repairs. All pianos are now accompanied by a quality-control certificate signed by a member of the Laul family, and each piano is played and checked by them.

The Estonia factory has recently introduced a new custom line of pianos, offering exotic veneers such as rosewood, bubinga, and pyramid mahogany, and is willing to finish instruments to fit the desires of individual customers. The custom line also features a number of different Victorian-style legs and ornamental music desks.

In the short time Estonia pianos have been sold here, they have gathered an unusually loyal and devoted following. Groups of owners of Estonia pianos, completely independent of the company, frequently hold musical get-togethers at different locations around the country. The pianos have a rich, warm, singing tone; are very well constructed and well prepared at the factory; and there is hardly a detail that the company has not examined and impressively perfected. The price has risen over the years, but they are still an unusually good value among higher-end instruments.

Warranty: 10 years, parts and labor, to original purchaser.

EVERETT

including A.B. Chase and Vose & Sons

Wrightwood Enterprises, Inc.
717 St. Joseph Drive
St. Joseph, Michigan 49085
616-828-0618
www.everett-piano.com

Pianos made by: Dongbei Piano Company, Ltd., Yingkou, Liaoning Province, China

The Everett Piano Company originated in Boston in 1883 and moved to South Haven, Michigan, in 1926. It was acquired by Yamaha in 1973. Until mid-1986, Yamaha made a line of Everett vertical pianos in the Michigan factory alongside its U.S.-made Yamaha pianos. When Yamaha moved its U.S. piano manufacturing to Thomaston, Georgia, in 1986, it contracted with Baldwin to continue making Everett pianos. The contract terminated in 1989, and Yamaha dropped the line permanently. See the entry for Everett in *The Piano Book* for more information about pianos from that era.

The Everett name has been used by Wrightwood Enterprises, Inc. since 1995. The pianos are made in China by the Dongbei Piano Company (see **Dongbei**). The grands have duplex scaling and a bass scale that is custom made for the Everett brand, the company says. The same pianos are also sold under the A.B. Chase and Vose & Sons labels.

Warranty: 10 years, parts and labor, to original purchaser.

FALCONE — See Sejung.

FANDRICH & SONS

Fandrich & Sons Pianos
7411 Silvana Terrace Road
Stanwood, Washington 98292
360-652-8980
877-737-1422
fandrich@fandrich.com
www.fandrich.com

Pianos made by: Bohemia, Heintzman & Co., Dongbei (see text)

In the late 1980s, Darrell Fandrich, an engineer, pianist, and piano technician, developed a vertical piano action designed to play like a grand, for which 10 patents have been issued. You can see an illustration of the Fandrich Vertical Action™, an explanation of how it works, and some history of its development in the third and fourth editions of *The Piano Book* and on the Fandrich & Sons website. Since 1994, Fandrich and his wife, Heather, have been installing Renner-made Fandrich actions in selected new pianos, selling them under the Fandrich & Sons label. They also sell some grands (with regular grand actions) under that name.

Over the years, the Fandrichs have installed their actions in over 200 instruments, including ones from Pearl River, Wilh. Steinberg, Klima, Feurich, and Bohemia. At present, the action is being installed in Bohemia models R126 (49.6") and R132 (52"), designed by Bohemia's owner, Bechstein, and sold under the Fandrich & Sons label. The converted pianos are available directly from the Fandrichs.

Playing a piano outfitted with a Fandrich Vertical Action is a very interesting experience. The action easily outperforms that of most other vertical pianos on the market, and some grands as well. The Fandrichs have now had years of experience in refining and servicing the action, and reports suggest that customers are very satisfied with them.

Fandrich & Sons grand pianos are made in China by Dongbei, now owned by Gibson Guitar Corp. (see **Dongbei**), and remanufactured at the Fandrich & Sons facility in Stanwood, Washington. The company offers three sizes of grand piano: models 165 (5' 5"), 185 (6' 1"), and 215 (7' 1"), in three configurations: S, S-H, and HGS-H. The S model retains all the original factory components, including Delignit pinblock, solid spruce soundboard, Röslau music wire, and Abel hammers; the S-H models additionally feature Heller bass strings from Germany; and the HGS-H models feature Heller bass strings, Renner hammer shanks, and Ronsen hammers with Würzen Weickert felt. All models also feature redesigned pedal-lyre and trapwork systems, precision touchweighting using the Fandrichs' proprietary method, and a very lengthy and extensive high-end preparation. All Fandrich & Sons pianos come with a Dampp-Chaser dehumidifier system and an adjustable bench.

The Fandrichs are passionate about their craft and choose the brands they work with carefully for musical potential. In addition to making standard modifications and refinements to remedy perceived shortcomings in the original Chinese-made instruments, the Fandrichs are inveterate tinkerers always searching for ways to make additional improvements, however subtle. As a result, many who play the pianos find them to be considerably more musical than their price and origin would suggest.

Warranty: 12 years, parts and labor, to original purchaser.

Note: Do not confuse the Fandrich & Sons pianos with the 48" Fandrich upright that was once manufactured with a Fandrich Vertical Action by Darrell Fandrich's brother, Delwin Fandrich. That piano has not been made since 1994.

FAZIOLI

Fazioli Pianoforti srl
Via Ronche 47
33077 Sacile (Pn), Italy
+39-0434-72026
info@fazioli.com
www.fazioli.com

In 1978, musician and engineer Paolo Fazioli of Rome, Italy, began designing and building pianos, with the object of making the finest-quality instruments possible. Now even the most famous piano makers of Western Europe are recognizing his accomplishment, and artists throughout the world are using the instruments successfully on the concert stage and elsewhere.

As a youth, Fazioli studied music and engineering, receiving advanced degrees in both subjects. He briefly attempted to make a living as a concert pianist, but instead joined his family's furniture company, rising to the position of factory manager in the Rome, Sacile, and Turin factories. But his creative ambitions, combined with his personal search for the perfect piano, finally led him to conclude that he needed to build his own piano. With advice and financial backing from his family, in 1977 Fazioli assembled a group of experts in woodworking, acoustics, and piano technology to study and scientifically analyze every aspect of piano design and construction. The following year, prototypes of his new instruments in hand, he began building pianos commercially in a factory housed at one end of the family's Sacile furniture factory, a top supplier in Italy of high-end office furniture.

In 2001, Fazioli built a new, expanded, modern piano-production facility, and in 2005 opened an adjoining 198-seat concert hall with a stage large enough for a chamber orchestra, where he maintains a regular concert schedule of well-known musicians who perform there. The concert hall is designed so that it can be adjusted acoustically with movable panels and sound reflectors to optimize the acoustics for performing, recording, or testing, and for different kinds of music, musical ensembles, and size of audience. The hall is used for the research and testing of pianos—every instrument Fazioli makes is tested here. In addition to the research activities in the concert hall, the new factory also contains a research department for ongoing research in musical acoustics in cooperation with a number of educational institutions.

Fazioli builds only grands, about 120 per year, in six sizes from 5'2" to 10'2", the last one of the largest pianos in the world, with the further distinction of having four pedals. Three are the usual sustain, sostenuto, and una corda. The fourth is a "soft" pedal that brings the hammers closer to the strings—similar to the function in verticals and some older grands—to soften the sound without altering the tonal quality, as the una corda often does. A unique compensating device corrects for the action irregularity that would otherwise occur when the hammers are moved in this manner. The fourth pedal is available as an option on the other models. Fazioli also offers two actions and two pedal lyres as options on all models. Having two actions allows for more voicing possibilities without having to constantly revoice the hammers. A second pedal lyre containing only three pedals can be a welcome alternative for some pianists who might be confused by the presence of a fourth pedal.

All Fazioli pianos have inner and outer rims of maple. Pinblocks are of Delignit, except for the largest two models, which use five-ply maple pinblocks from Bolduc, in Canada. The pianos have Renner actions, Kluge keyboards, and either Renner or Abel hammers. The bronze capo d'astro bar is adjustable in the factory for setting the strike point and treble string length for best high-treble tone quality, and is removable for servicing if necessary; and the front and rear duplex scales can be tuned to maximize tonal color. The company says that a critical factor in the sound of its pianos is the scientific selection of its woods, such as the "resonant spruce" obtained from the Val di Fiemme, where Stradivari reportedly sought woods for his violins. Each piece of wood is said to be carefully tested for certain resonant properties before being used in the pianos. Similarly, three different types of wood are used for the bridge caps, each chosen for the most efficient transmission of tonal energy for a particular register.

An incredible level of detail has gone into the design and construction of these pianos. For instance, in one small portion of the soundboard where additional stiffness is required, the grain of the wood runs perpendicular to that of the rest of the soundboard, cleverly disguised so as to be almost unnoticeable. The pianos are impeccably prepared at the factory, including very fine voicing—even perfect tuning of the duplex scales.

A series of stunning art-case pianos is a testament to the ability of the Fazioli artisans to execute virtually any custom-ordered artistic variation on the six Fazioli models.

Those most familiar with Fazioli pianos describe them as combining great power with great warmth in a way that causes music played on them to "make sense" in a way made possible by few other pianos.

Warranty: 10 years, parts and labor, transferable to future owners within the warranty period.

FEURICH

Feurich USA
1771 Post Road East
Suite 239
Westport, Connecticut 06880
203-858-5979
usinfo@feurich.com
www.feurich.com

Pianos made by: Feurich Klavier-u.Fluegelfabrikation GmbH, Gunzenhausen, Germany; and Ningbo Hailun Musical Instruments Co. Ltd., Ningbo, Zhejiang Province, China

This German piano manufacturer was founded in Leipzig in 1851 by Julius Feurich. At its height in the early part of the 20th century, the company employed 360 people, annually producing 1,200 upright and 600 grand pianos. Like many German manufacturers, however, Feurich lost its factory during World War II. Following the war, the fourth generation of the Feurich family rebuilt in Langlau, in what became West Germany.

In 1991 Bechstein purchased Feurich and closed the Langlau factory, but in 1993 the name was sold back to the Feurich family. For a time, production was contracted out to other German manufacturers, including Schimmel, while the Feurich family marketed and distributed the pianos. In 1995 Feurich opened a new factory in Gunzenhausen, Germany. Under the direction of Julius Feurich, the fifth generation, the family-owned company is once again building its own pianos, and is currently making about 50 to 60 high-quality instruments per year in two sizes of grand and two sizes of vertical. All pianos and parts are made in Germany.

In 2011, Feurich entered a cooperative relationship with Wendl & Lung, which marketed, primarily in Europe, a line of Wendl & Lung pianos manufactured under contract by Hailun in China. Under the agreement, this line will now be marketed under the Feurich name, and several new and redesigned models will be added. Use of the Wendl & Lung brand name will be discontinued. The two vertical and two grand models currently made in Germany under the Feurich label will continue to be produced there, using only the highest-quality German parts and materials, and over the next few years three larger grand models will be introduced. In addition to being differentiated from the Chinese pianos by designs, sizes, and model numbers, the German pianos will contain the inscription "Handmade in Germany." See the review of Feurich (Ningbo) pianos in **this issue** of Piano Buyer.

Feurich offers an optional Harmonic Pedal on its Chinese-made grand pianos. This fourth pedal is essentially the inverse of a sostenuto—instead of holding up the dampers of notes pressed prior to depressing the pedal, it holds up all *but* those notes. The effect, known as "remanence harmony," is to allow the overtones of the depressed notes to sing out in a sustained fashion.

Warranty: 5 years, parts and labor, to original purchaser.

FÖRSTER, AUGUST

German American Trading Co., Inc.
P.O. Box 17789
Tampa, Florida 33682
813-961-8405
germanamer@msn.com
www.august-foerster.de

Pianos made by: August Förster GmbH, Löbau, Germany

The Förster factory was founded by Friedrich August Förster in 1859 in Löbau, Germany, after Förster studied the art of piano building with others. During the years of control by the government of East Germany, the factory was managed by the fourth-generation piano maker Wolfgang Förster and his daughter, Annekatrin. Since the reunification of Germany and privatization, Wolfgang and his family once again own the company.

With a workforce of 40 using a great deal of hand labor, Förster makes about 120 grands a year in four sizes, and 150 verticals a year in three sizes. The pianos are very well built structurally, and the cabinets are elegant. Rims and pinblocks are of beech, soundboards of solid mountain-grown spruce, and bridges are of hardrock maple (without graphite). Each string is individually terminated (single-strung). The actions are made by Renner with Renner hammers. A sostenuto pedal is standard on all grand models.

The tone of August Förster grands is unique, with a remarkable bass: dark, deep, yet clear. As delivered from the factory, the treble is often quite bright, and for some American tastes might be considered a bit thin— it is a less complex sound that emphasizes clarity. This, however, can be modified somewhat with voicing and a good dealer preparation. The instruments are quite versatile, at home with Mozart or Prokofiev, classical or jazz. The 6'4" model is often said to have an especially good scale. The concert-quality 7'2" and 9'1" models are well balanced tonally, and over the years have been endorsed by many famous artists. The Renner actions are very responsive and arrive in exacting regulation. The new 53" model 134K anniversary upright, intended for pianists who don't have space for a grand, has such grand-piano–like features as a full sostenuto; a large, adjustable music desk; and black keys of real ebony.

Most of the comments regarding the quality of materials and workmanship of the Förster grands also apply to the verticals. The cabinet of the vertical is of exceptional width, with extra-thick side panels of solid-core stock. Counter bridges are used on the outside of the soundboard to increase its mass. The verticals have a full set of agraffes, and all the hardware and handmade wood parts are of elegant quality. The actions are built by Renner. The verticals possess the same warm, rich, deep bass tone as the grands.

Warranty: 10 years, parts and labor, to original purchaser.

GROTRIAN

Grotrian Piano Company GmbH
P.O. Box 5833
D-38049 Braunschweig, Germany
+49-531-210100
+49-531-2101040 (fax)
contact@grotrian.de
www.grotrian.de

Friedrich Grotrian was born in 1803 in Schöningen, Germany, and as a young man lived in Moscow, where he ran a music business and was associated with piano manufacturing. Later in his life he teamed up with C.F. Theodor Steinweg, son of Heinrich Steinweg, to build pianos. Heinrich had emigrated to the U.S. about 1850, soon to establish the firm of Steinway & Sons. Theodor followed in 1865, selling his share in the partnership to Wilhelm Grotrian, son of Friedrich, who had died in 1860. Thereafter, the firm became known as Grotrian-Steinweg. (In a legal settlement with Steinway & Sons, Grotrian-Steinweg agreed to use only the name Grotrian on pianos sold in North America.)

Even as early as the 1860s, Grotrian pianos were well known and highly respected throughout Europe. Each successive generation of the Grotrian family maintained the company's high standards and furthered the technical development of the instrument. Today the company is owned by the sixth generation of Grotrians. Housed in an up-to-date factory, and using a combination of modern technology and traditional craftsmanship, Grotrian makes about 500 verticals and 100 grands a year. In 2010, the company celebrated its 175th anniversary.

Grotrian grands have beech rims, solid spruce soundboards, laminated beech pinblocks, Renner actions, and are single-strung. Grotrian prides itself on what it calls its "homogeneous soundboard," in which each piece of wood is specially chosen for its contribution to the tone of the soundboard. The cast-iron plate is attached with screws along the outer edges of the rim, instead of on top of the rim, which the company says allows the soundboard to vibrate more freely. The vertical pianos have a unique star-shaped wooden back structure and a full-perimeter plate. Grotrian makes five sizes of grand and six sizes of vertical piano.

To commemorate the company's 175th anniversary, Grotrian has issued the 46½" model Composé Exclusif. Limited to only 50 instruments, this elegant model includes such unusual features as 24-karat gold-plated hardware, inner cabinet veneer of red bird's-eye maple, white keys of satin-finish acrylic glass, and a hygrometer embedded in the case.

Grotrian also makes a lower-cost line, called Friedrich Grotrian, with a beech back frame but no back posts, and a simpler cabinet. It's available in a 43½" model in polished ebony with legs, and in 43½" and 45" models for institutional use, with satin finishes but without legs. The Friedrich Grotrian models are also completely made at the Grotrian factory in Braunschweig, Germany.

The treble of Grotrian pianos has extraordinary sustaining characteristics. It also has a pronounced sound of attack, subtle and delicate. The tenor is darker than many other brands. The bass can be powerful, but without stridency. Overall, Grotrian pianos have a unique, expressive sound and are a pleasure to play. Over the years, many well-known pianists have endorsed or expressed appreciation for Grotrian pianos.

Warranty: 5 years, parts and labor, transferable to future owners.

HAESSLER — See Blüthner.

HAILUN

Hailun USA
P.O. Box 1130
Richland, Washington 99352
509-946-8078
877-946-8078
info@hailun-pianos.com
www.hailun-pianos.com

Pianos made by: Ningbo Hailun Musical Instruments Co. Ltd., Ningbo, Zhejiang Province, China

Ningbo Hailun began making piano parts and components in 1986 under the Ningbo Piano Parts Factory name, and began assembling entire pianos in 1995. Its assembly facility converted to a full-scale piano manufacturing facility in 2000. Today, the Hailun factory has over 400,000 square feet of production capacity and 800 employees. A 200,000-square-foot expansion project is underway to accommodate distribution in the U.S. market. Additionally, a new cabinet factory is now complete and began production in 2008. In addition to making pianos under the Hailun name, the company also makes the Wendl & Lung brand (now changing to the Feurich brand—see **Feurich**). Hailun also makes pianos or components under contract for several other manufacturers and distributors.

Currently, the Hailun line consists of eight vertical sizes (mostly larger uprights) and six grand sizes. In 2010, the company introduced the 52" model HU7 (formerly called PE 33), with a duplex scale, agraffes, and a steel capo bar for, the company says, a "lush and powerful sound in the American tradition"; and a 51" model HU3 (formerly called K 5), "which reflects a brighter, more 'European,' sound philosophy." Both have a middle pedal that operates a true sostenuto mechanism.

Hailun is in the process of introducing several new grand and vertical models it calls the Vienna Series. Available only through select Hailun dealers known as Hailun Vienna Merchants, these instruments are intended to address the need of customers for an exacting, quality instrument that "reflects the European tradition of piano building" at a more favorable price, and to "create a warm tonal experience in the tradition of the Viennese sound." To that end, the pianos use soundboard wood sourced from the North Austrian Alps, and the grands are designed with a wide tail, vertically laminated maple bridges, and a slightly firmer touch and faster action speed. The vertical has a duplex scale, agraffes, a full-perimeter plate, and an enhanced soundboard design. Each purchaser of a Vienna Series piano may, within 18 months of purchase, request that a special highly qualified technician, known as a Vienna Concert Technician, spend a full day of concert-level regulation and voicing on the piano at the customer's home.

In 2011, Hailun introduced a slow-close piano lid in all its grand piano models. Graphically named the Hailun Limb Protection System (HLPS), this is a version of the Safety-Ease retrofit system, described **elsewhere** in this publication, built into the piano at the factory. HLPS allows even a child to easily lift the otherwise heavy lid of a grand piano without danger, and prevents a falling lid from crashing down onto arms and hands. Hailun has exclusive rights to use this system in the manufacture of new pianos. A version of HLPS, called HLPS Plus, and available only in the Vienna models, allows the user to adjust a grand piano lid to any position without the need for a lid propstick. Apart from the safety benefit, HLPS Plus allows the user to modulate sound projection by adjusting the lid position.

Hailun is a little different from most of the other Chinese companies selling pianos in the U.S.: Its founder

and owner, Chen Hailun, is an entrepreneur in the Western style, and deeply involved in every aspect of the business. Originally a maker of molds for industrial use, Chen got into the piano business when piano manufacturers started to use his services to make piano parts. In 1998 he bought out the government's position in his company to better control quality and hiring decisions.

While modern manufacturing methods are fully utilized, the factory also uses a large amount of skilled manual labor. Chen seeks out the best workers by paying considerably higher wages than other piano makers in China, he says, and provides an in-depth training program for his workers, conducted by piano builders and technicians from the U.S. and Europe. He also assists in the training of future piano technicians through an association with a local university. His greatest aspiration, Chen says, is to make the best piano in Asia.

Over the years, much of Chen's technical efforts have gone into maximizing the precision and stability of the pianos and parts his company makes. This is evidenced by the substantial investment in computer-controlled machinery used for precision cutting; the design of keys, keybeds, and other parts to resist warping; and the fact that grand piano actions are actually interchangeable between instruments of the same model (this requires an unusually high level of precision). The pianos themselves exhibit good quality control and intelligence in design. In terms of materials, the company uses maple in grand piano rims, a feature indicative of higher quality and arguably necessary for the best sound. In 2011, the company began sourcing its own supply of the highest-quality Austrian spruce, and plans to make its own soundboards with this spruce for select piano models. *Piano Buyer*'s reviewers have tried out several Hailun grands (see reviews in the **Fall 2009**, **Fall 2010**, and **Fall 2011** issues) and have been impressed with their musicality.

To help it reach the highest quality standards, Hailun has also hired an impressive group of experts from Japan (Ema Shigeru), Europe (Stephen Paulello, Claire Trichet, Sibin Zlatkovic, Peter Veletzky), and the U.S. (Frank Emerson). In 2009, to oversee and assist with quality control, Hailun hired Rolf Ibach, owner of Rud. Ibach Sohn, one of the oldest and most reputable European piano companies, which closed its doors in 2008 after more than 200 years in business.

Hailun USA has initiated several support programs designed to increase the speed at which service requests are handled, and to measure customer satisfaction. It has also introduced the Hailun Dream Assurance Program, in which the company guarantees, subject to certain limitations, that the sound of any purchased Hailun piano will be to the customer's liking or, within 90 days of purchase, the company will exchange the piano for another of the same model.

Warranty: 15 years, parts and labor, transferable to future owners within the warranty period; except for action parts, cast-iron plate, and metal case hardware, which are warranted for the lifetime of the original purchaser. See also the Dream Assurance Program, described above.

HALLET, DAVIS & CO.
North American Music, Inc.
11 Holt Drive
Stony Point, New York 10980
845-429-0106
www.namusic.com

Pianos made by: Dongbei Piano Company, Ltd., Yingkou, Liaoning Province, China

This famous old American piano brand dates back to at least 1843 in Boston, and has changed hands many times over the years. It eventually became part of the Aeolian group of piano brands, and instruments bearing the name were manufactured at Aeolian's Memphis plant until that company went out of business in 1985. At present, most Hallet, Davis & Co. grands are made in China by the Dongbei Piano Company (see **Dongbei**). The company appears to have changed manufacturer for its verticals and some of its grand models, but prefers not to reveal the source.

HARDMAN, PECK & CO.
Hardman Pianos
11 Holt Drive
Stony Point, New York 10980
845-429-0106
info@hardmanpiano.com
www.hardmanpiano.com

Pianos made by: Beijing Hsinghai Piano Group, Ltd., Beijing, China

Hugh Hardman established the Hardman Piano Company in New York City in 1842. Leopold Peck joined the company in 1880, and became a partner in 1890, at which time the company was renamed Hardman, Peck & Company. In the early 20th century, Hardman, Peck was sold to the Aeolian Corporation, which eventually moved to Memphis, where it remained until it went out of business in 1985. Today's Hardman, Peck & Company pianos are manufactured in China by the Beijing

Hsinghai Piano Group (see **Beijing Hsinghai**). The piano line offers a selection of vertical and grand pianos in a variety of styles and finishes to meet the needs of entry-level and mid-level pianists.

HEINTZMAN & CO.
including Gerhard Heintzman

Heintzman Distributor Ltd.
210-2106 Main Street
Vancouver, British Columbia V5T 3C5
Canada
604-801-5393
778-420-0029
info@hzmpiano.com
www.hzmpiano.com

Pianos made by: Heintzman Piano Company, Ltd., Beijing, China

Heintzman & Co. Ltd. was founded by Theodore August Heintzman in Toronto in 1866. By 1900, Heintzman was one of Toronto's larger manufacturing concerns, building 3,000 pianos per year and selling them throughout Canada and abroad through a network of company stores and other distributors. The pianos received high praise and won prizes at exhibitions. Even today, technicians frequently encounter old Heintzman pianos built in the early part of the 20th century and consider them to be of high quality. In the latter decades of the century, Heintzman, like other North American brands, struggled to compete with cheaper foreign imports. The factory finally closed its doors in 1986 and relocated to China. (For a few years thereafter, some pianos continued to be sold in Canada under the Heintzman and Gerhard Heintzman names.) At first the company was a joint venture with the Beijing Hsinghai Piano Group (see **Beijing Hsinghai**), but when the Chinese government began allowing foreign ownership of manufacturing concerns, the Canadian partner bought back majority ownership and took control.

The new company, known as Heintzman Piano Company, Ltd., is Canadian owned and managed and has a private, independent factory dedicated to producing Heintzman-brand pianos. Heintzman makes pianos to the original Canadian Heintzman designs and scales using some of the equipment from Canada. James Moffat, plant manager of the Canadian Heintzman factory for 40 years, has been retained as a consultant and visits the factory in China several times a year. The company even uses some components from Canada, such as Bolduc soundboards, in grands and larger verticals. The factory makes about 5,000 pianos per year.

The smallest vertical made under the Heintzman name is 43½" tall, but pianos for export to North America typically start at 47½" and contain a mixture of Chinese and imported parts, such as pinblocks and treble strings from Germany and Mapes bass strings from the U.S. Verticals 48½" and taller use Renner Blue hammers, and the largest two sizes have Canadian Bolduc solid Eastern white spruce soundboards. All verticals have a middle pedal that operates a bass-sustain mechanism, as well as a Silent Switch that operates a mute bar for silent practice.

The grands—5' 6", 6' 1", 6' 8", and 9' in size—also use German pinblocks and strings, Mapes bass strings, Renner Blue hammers, and Canadian Bolduc soundboards. The 9' concert grand comes with a full Renner action and Kluge keys from Germany. A Renner action is a higher-priced option on the other models. All grands come with a sostenuto pedal. A 6' 1" model patterned on the old Heintzman model D was introduced in 2007.

Heintzman Piano Company also makes the slightly less expensive Gerhard Heintzman brand. This line uses less expensive materials and components, such as Japanese hammers and a veneer-laminated spruce soundboard in the verticals (a Bolduc soundboard in some of the grands). The polished ebony grands have a silver plate and trim.

Warranty: Heintzman and Gerhard Heintzman—10 years, parts and labor, from the factory, transferable to future owners within the warranty period.

HOFFMANN, W. — See Bechstein, C.

HSINGHAI — See Beijing Hsinghai.

IRMLER
including Schiller

Blüthner USA LLC
5660 W. Grand River
Lansing, Michigan 48906
517-886-6000
800-954-3200
916-337-1086
info@irmler-piano.com
www.irmler-piano.com
In Canada, contact Bluethner Piano Canada Inc.
604-264-1138
rrgarvin@telus.net
www.bluethner.ca

Pianos made by: Irmler Piano GmbH, Leipzig, Germany, and other factories (see text)

Irmler is a sister company of Blüthner, and Irmler pianos are distributed through the Blüthner dealer network. The brand has recently been reintroduced to the market in two series: Studio and Professional.

The Studio series is largely made in a factory in China owned by Irmler. The pianos are then shipped to the Blüthner factory in Germany, where Abel hammers are installed and the pianos are inspected and adjusted as needed, prior to shipping to dealers. The pianos have Delignit pinblocks and veneer-laminated spruce soundboards. The grand rims are of Chinese oak and the grand actions are made with Renner parts. The Studio-series verticals include a number of models with interesting, modern cabinet designs.

The Professional series, also known as Irmler Europe, is assembled in Germany using strung backs (structural and acoustical elements) from Samick in Indonesia and cabinets from Poland (suppliers are subject to change). The pianos have Delignit pinblocks and solid spruce soundboards. Grands have rims of maple and beech, action parts by Renner (U.S. distribution only), and duplex scaling. Vertical actions are by Detoa.

The Irmler Studio series is also available from some dealers under the Schiller brand name, with a slightly modified cabinet; prices are comparable to those for Irmler.

Warranty: 10 years, parts and labor, to original purchaser.

KAWAI

including Shigeru Kawai

Kawai America Corporation
2055 East University Drive
Rancho Dominguez, California 90220
310-631-1771
800-421-2177
310-223-0900 (Shigeru Kawai)
acoustic@kawaius.com
www.kawaius.com
www.shigerukawai.com

Pianos made by: Kawai Musical Instrument Mfg. Co., Ltd.; Hamamatsu, Japan, and Karawan, Indonesia

Kawai was founded in 1927 by Koichi Kawai, an inventor and former Yamaha employee who was the first person in Japan to design and build a piano action. While Kawai is second in size to Yamaha among Japanese piano manufacturers, it has a well-deserved reputation all its own for quality and innovation. Nearly all Kawai grands and taller uprights are made in Japan; most consoles and studios are made in Indonesia. The company closed its North Carolina factory in 2005.

One of Kawai's most important innovations is the use of ABS Styran plastic in the manufacture of action parts. More than 40 years of use and scientific testing have shown this material to be superior to wood for this purpose. ABS does not swell and shrink with changes in humidity, so actions made with it are likely to maintain proper regulation better than wood actions. The parts are stronger and without glue joints, so breakage is rare. These parts are present in every Kawai piano. In the current Millennium III action found in some models, the ABS is reinforced with carbon fiber so it can be stronger with less mass. Having less mass to move (that is, less inertia), the action can be more responsive to the player's intentions, including faster repetition. Certain contact surfaces on the action parts are also micro-engineered for ideal shape and texture, resulting in a more consistent touch. Although it took a number of years to overcome the idea that plastic parts must be inferior, there is essentially no dispute anymore among piano technicians on this subject.

Kawai's vertical piano offerings change frequently and are sometimes confusing. At present there are three basic series of Kawai verticals. The console series begins with the 44½" model 506N, a basic entry-level console in an institutional-style cabinet (legs with toe blocks). Model K-15 is a 44" version of this in a continental-style cabinet (no legs), and model 508 is a 44½" version in a simple furniture-style cabinet (freestanding legs). Model 607 is the same piano in a fancier furniture-style cabinet. All have the same internal workings. The action in this series is slightly smaller than a full-size action, so it will be slightly less responsive. However, it is more than sufficient for beginner or casual use.

Kawai has replaced both of its former studio models, the UST-7 and UST-8, with the 46" model UST-9, made in Indonesia. This model has the stronger back of the UST-7, rather than that of the UST-8, which was not known for its tuning stability. The UST-9 also contains the Millennium III action; an angled, leather-lined music desk to better hold music; and a stylish, reinforced bench. The 46½" model 907 is essentially the UST-9 in a fancy, furniture-style cabinet. Rounding out the Kawai studios is the new Japanese-made FINO Interior Design Series of three models—the Gilda, Rosina, and Lauretta—that Kawai says are "European in style."

Kawai's K series of upright models comprises the K-2 (45"), K-3 (48"), K-5 (49"), K-6 (52"), and K-8 (52"). All have the Millennium III action; a soft-close fallboard; a wide, leather-lined music desk; a somewhat stylish cabinet; and come with an adjustable bench. The K-5 has Neotex synthetic-ivory keytops. The 52" models also feature agraffes, duplex scaling, Neotex keytops, and various kinds of tone escape mechanisms. The K-8 has a true sostenuto pedal.

Kawai makes three series of grand pianos: RX, GE, and GM. The RX, now in a version known as the RX BLAK series, is the most expensive and has the best features. It is designed for the best performance, whereas the GE and GM series are designed more for efficiency in manufacturing, with fewer refinements. The RX pianos are the only Kawai grands with a radial beam structure, focused and connected to the plate using a cast-iron bracket at the tenor break. This system makes for a more rigid structure, which translates into better tone projection. The soundboard of the RX models is tapered for better tonal response, and the rim is thicker and stronger than in the GE and GM models. The RX BLAK pianos use a new version of the Millennium III action with hammer-shank stabilizers, designed to retain power by keeping the shank from wavering under a heavy blow; have agraffes, duplex scaling, lighter hammers (less inertia), and Neotex synthetic ivory keytops; and come with a slow-close fallboard. The RX grands get more precise key weighting, plus more tuning, regulating, and voicing at the factory. The cabinetry is nicer looking and of better quality than that of the GE and GM series pianos, with the polished ebony models in the new RX BLAK series receiving a UV-cured, scratch-resistant coating on the music rack and music shelves.

Some of the RX features are also found in the GM and GE pianos, but it varies by model. The GM-10K is the only Kawai grand made in Indonesia. It has Kawai's standard ABS action, no agraffes or duplex scaling, standard keytops, and a regular fallboard. The model GM-12, made in Japan, has the regular Millennium III action (without hammer-shank stabilizers), no agraffes or duplex scaling, standard keytops, and a slow-close fallboard. The GE models, also made in Japan, have the regular Millennium III action, agraffes, duplex scaling, Neotex keytops, and a slow-close fallboard.

Kawai's quality control is excellent, especially in its Japanese-made pianos. Major problems are rare, and other than normal maintenance, after-sale service is usually limited to fixing the occasional minor buzz or squeak. Kawai's warranty service is also excellent, and the warranty is transferable to future owners within the warranty period (a benefit that is not common these days). The tone of most Kawai pianos, in my opinion, is not as ideal for classical music as some more expensive instruments, but when expertly voiced, it is not far off, and in any case is quite versatile musically. In part because the touch is so good, Kawai grands are often sought by classical pianists as a less-expensive alternative to a Steinway or other high-end piano. Kawai dealers tend to be a little more aggressive about discounting than their competition (Yamaha). There is also a thriving market for used Kawais. (If you're considering buying a used Kawai, please read "Should I Buy a Used 'Gray Market' Yamaha or Kawai Piano?" on pages 176–177 of *The Piano Book*, or the shorter version in "**Buying a Used or Restored Piano**" in this publication.)

The Shigeru Kawai line of grands represents Kawai's ultimate effort to produce a world-class piano. Named after Kawai's former chairman (and son of company founder Koichi Kawai), the limited-edition (fewer than 300 per year) Shigeru Kawai grands are made at the separate facility where Kawai's EX concert grands are built.

Although based on the Kawai RX designs, the Shigeru Kawai models are "hand made" in the extreme. Very high-grade soundboard spruce is air-dried for multiple years, then planed by hand by a worker who knocks on the wood and listens for the optimum tonal response. Ribs are also hand-planed for correct stiffness. String bearing is set in the traditional manner by planing the bridges by hand instead of having pre-cut bridges pinned by machine. Bass strings are wound by hand instead of by machine. Hammers are hand-pressed without heat for a wider voicing range, and the hammer weights are carefully controlled for even touch. Hammer shanks are thinned along the bottom so that their stiffness is matched to the hammer mass. These procedures represent a level of detail relatively few manufacturers indulge in.

In 2012, Kawai updated the Shigeru Kawai grands, changing the cabinet styling and some of the pianos' construction features. The inside of the rim is now finished with bird's-eye maple veneer, and the round legs have been changed to straight legs with brass trim. The rim itself is now made of alternating layers of rock maple and mahogany, which Kawai says provides more power without losing warmth in the tone. The structure at the front of the piano has been made stronger, and the beams underneath are now made from spruce instead of the laminated mahogany Kawai uses in its other models. The keys have been lengthened for a better touch, especially on the smaller models.

Each buyer of a Shigeru Kawai piano receives a visit within the first year by a Kawai master technician from the factory in Japan. These are the same factory technicians who do the final installation of actions in pianos, as well as the final voicing and regulation. According to those who have watched them work, these Japanese master technicians are amazingly skilled. Because the Shigeru Kawai pianos have been on the market only ten years and in very limited quantities, many piano technicians have yet to service one. Those who have, however, tend to rank them among the world's finest instruments, and Shigeru Kawai pianos are often chosen by pianists participating in international piano competitions.

Warranty: Kawai and Shigeru Kawai—10 years, parts and labor, transferable to future owners within the warranty period.

KIMBALL

Kimball Piano USA, Inc.
1819 North Major Avenue
Chicago, Illinois 60639
312-212-3635
kimballpiano@gmail.com
www.kimballpianousa.com

Kimball, a name with a long history in the piano world (see *The Piano Book* for details), is now being produced by Kimball Piano USA, Inc., which acquired the rights to the Kimball name in 2005. Kimball International, which previously owned the Kimball brand and produced Kimball pianos from 1959 to 1996, was primarily a furniture maker that mass-produced a very average piano.

In contrast, Kimball is now controlled by a Registered Piano Technician (RPT) who has returned Kimball to its historical roots in Chicago and says he is placing the company's focus on the musical instrument and on technical details of American piano design and construction. The result of this focus is two new collections of Kimball pianos: Classic and Artist.

The Kimball Classic Collection consists of the 5'1" model K1 and 6'2" model K3 grands. Parts and components for these models are being sourced primarily from China and Europe. They include a rim made of maple and oak (grands); full-length back posts (vertical); bridges planed and notched by hand in the traditional manner; a wet-sand cast plate; Herrburger Brooks keys, action, and hammers; Röslau strings; Delignit pinblock; and a solid spruce soundboard.

The Kimball Artist Collection includes the 5'8" model A2 grand and the 49" model A49 vertical. The company says that the Artist Collection embodies its commitment to producing high-quality performance pianos by paying great attention to the design of the scale, soundboard, and action, and to proper execution and attention to details. High-end components, primarily from Germany, include a rim of European beech (grand), Renner action (grand), Strunz premium solid spruce soundboard and ribs, Delignit pinblock, Röslau strings, Klinke agraffes, and Abel hammers. The vertical has full-length spruce back posts and a Herrburger Brooks action; cabinets are from China.

In the U.S., Kimball is doing final assembly and detailing of the instruments, with a major focus on proper action, hammer, and key installation to ensure superb playability. At its facility in Chicago, Kimball now has a showroom where, by appointment, both individual customers and dealers are welcome to see and play the new pianos.

Warranty: 10 years, parts and labor, to original purchaser.

KINGSBURG

Doremi USA Inc.
5036 Dr. Phillips Boulevard, Suite 288
Orlando, Florida 32819
866-322-5986
info@kingsburgusa.com
www.kingsburgusa.com

Pianos made by: Yantai Kingsburg Piano Co., Ltd., Yantai, Shandong Province, China

Yantai Kingsburg, formerly known as Yantai Longfeng, was established in 1988, and at various times made pianos under the Steigerman and Perzina brand names. It is located in a temperate area of northern China that, the company says, is ideal for piano making because of its moderate humidity level.

All Kingsburg pianos have been designed by well-known piano designer Klaus Fenner, and include components sourced from around the world, such as Röslau piano wire, Abel hammers, Detoa or Renner actions, and Japanese tuning pins. Interesting design features include longer keys on upright models for more grand-like performance, brass-bar duplex scale, and the company's exclusive Tri Board solid spruce soundboard, which, for better bass tone and improved tuning stability, is unattached to the piano back at the bottom.

At present, the Kingsburg line comprises larger uprights and two sizes of grand, with plans to possibly expand into the market for home console pianos. Custom styles and finishes are also available.

A key focus of Yantai Kingsburg is that the final factory preparation of the pianos be done in such a manner that the dealer can deliver the instrument to the customer's home with very little additional work being required. To that end, the U.S. distributor's Japanese affiliate sends highly trained technicians to the factory to fully tune, voice, and regulate each Kingsburg piano to their high standards before it is crated for shipment.

Warranty: 12 years, parts and labor, to original purchaser.

KNABE, WM.

See also Samick.

Samick Music Corp. (SMC)
1329 Gateway Drive
Gallatin, Tennessee 37066
615-206-0077
info@smcmusic.com
www.knabepianos.com

Pianos made by: Samick Musical Instrument Mfg. Co. Ltd., Inchon, South Korea; and Bogor, West Java, Indonesia

Founded in Baltimore in 1837 by Wilhelm (William) Knabe, a German immigrant, Wm. Knabe & Co. established itself in the 19th and early 20th centuries as one of the finest piano makers in America. Over the years, Knabe pianos have left an important mark on the music field, including over 40 years as the official piano of the Metropolitan Opera, sponsoring Tchaikovsky's appearance at the opening of Carnegie Hall, and their places inside the White House and Graceland. Today, Knabe is the official piano of the American Ballet Theatre at the Met. 2012 marks the company's 175th anniversary.

As part of the consolidation of the American piano industry in the early 20th century, Knabe eventually became part of the Aeolian family of brands. Following Aeolian's demise in 1985, the Knabe name became part of Mason & Hamlin, which was purchased out of bankruptcy in 1996 by the owners of PianoDisc. For a time, a line of Knabe pianos was made for PianoDisc by Young Chang in Korea and China. When the line was discontinued, Samick acquired the Wm. Knabe & Co. name. (Note: "Knabe" is pronounced using the hard K sound followed by "nobby.")

SMC (Samick's U.S. distribution subsidiary) began by using the Wm. Knabe name on some of the pianos formerly sold as the World Piano premium line of Samick instruments. In 2002, SMC developed the Concert Artist series for the Knabe name. Highlighting this series are the 5' 8" and 6' 4" grand models, which have been redesigned, based on the original 19th- and early 20th-century Knabe scale designs and cabinet styles in use when the company was based in Baltimore. Features include sand-cast plates, lacquer semigloss wood finishes, Renner actions on larger grands, German hammers, and rims of maple and oak. The company has added 5' 3", 7' 6", and 9' 2" models for the American market. The verticals feature unique cabinet designs with bird's-eye maple and mahogany inlays, rosewood key inserts, and tone escapement. The 52" upright includes a full sostenuto, hand-activated mute rail, and agraffes throughout the bass section of the piano.

For two years, SMC completed assembly of Concert Artist grands at its Tennessee facility, with strung backs made in Indonesia or Korea. Now, most Knabe pianos are made in their entirety in Indonesia but are still uncrated in the U.S., where they are inspected, tuned, regulated, and voiced before being shipped to dealers.

In 2011, SMC unveiled two additional product lines within the Knabe family: the Academy and Baltimore series. The Academy series has many of the same features and specifications as the popular, upper-end, Kohler & Campbell Millennium brand, also made by Samick: a maple or beech inner rim (grands); a premium soundboard of solid white spruce; German hammers; a Samick Premium Action; satin lacquer semigloss wood finishes; and a Samick-made hornbeam action rail (larger verticals). (See **Samick** for more about Kohler & Campbell.) The Academy series also boasts two institutional studio uprights, the WMV245 and WMV247, both with full-length music racks, the WMV247 also with agraffes through the bass section.

The Baltimore series offers a more modestly priced alternative to the institutional Academy series or upper-end Concert Artist series. This line features an all-spruce "surface tension" (veneered) soundboard. The grands provide a full sostenuto pedal, slow-close fallboard, fully adjustable music desk and rack, multiple finishes in both satin ebony and wood tones, and, recently, a new designer grand with accents of Bubinga or African Pommele. The verticals showcase a wide range of sizes and cabinet styles, including wood tones in French cherry, traditional mahogany, and Renaissance walnut.

Warranty: 10 years, parts and labor, transferable to future owners within the warranty period.

KOHLER & CAMPBELL — See Samick.

MAMMOTH
Mammoth Piano Co.
Monroe, Washington
877-957-4266
mammothpiano@comcast.net
www.mammothpiano.com

Reminiscent of some piano designs attempted 200 years ago, the Mammoth is one of the most unusual pianos being built today. Dubbed a Vertical Concert Grand, Mammoth's model VCG stands 7' 2" tall, weighs 1,200 pounds, and has the scale design and sound of a 9' concert grand.

The piano's immense structure includes six laminated wooden back posts and a welded steel frame, yet despite its bulk, the instrument appears quite attractive in its custom-made cabinet of Brazilian cherry. The soundboard and ribs are of Sitka spruce. The action, invented specifically for this piano, appears superficially to be like that of a vertical, but actually contains the double-escapement feature of a grand piano action.

Inventor-builder Chris Chernobieff got his start assembling dulcimer and harpsichord kits, and branched out into piano service and rebuilding about 15 years ago. Inspired by other technicians who built their own pianos, Chernobieff asked, "Why not me?" Having spent the last several years designing and building the Mammoth, he now has plans for a 6' vertical and some innovative grand models.

Mammoth model VCG retails for $98,000.

MASON & HAMLIN

Mason & Hamlin Piano Company
35 Duncan Street
Haverhill, Massachusetts 01830
916-567-9999
www.masonhamlin.com

Pianos made by: Mason & Hamlin Piano Co., Haverhill, Massachusetts

Mason & Hamlin was founded in 1854 by Henry Mason and Emmons Hamlin. Mason was a musician and businessman and Hamlin was an inventor working with reed organs. Within a few years, Mason & Hamlin was one of the largest makers of reed organs in the U.S. The company began making pianos in 1881 in Boston, and soon became, along with Chickering, among the most prestigious of the Boston piano makers. By 1910, Mason & Hamlin was considered Steinway's chief competitor. Over the next 85 years, Mason & Hamlin changed hands many times. (You can read the somewhat lengthy and interesting history in *The Piano Book*.) In 1996 the Burgett brothers, owners of PianoDisc, purchased Mason & Hamlin out of bankruptcy and set about reestablishing manufacturing at the six-story factory in Haverhill, Massachusetts. The company emphasizes limited-quantity, handbuilt production, and currently manufactures from 200 to 350 pianos per year. Daily tours are offered to visitors.

Since acquiring the company, the Burgetts have brought back most of the piano models from the company's golden Boston era (1881–1932) that originally made the company famous. Refinements have been made to the original scale designs and other core design features. First came the 5' 8" model A and 7' model BB, both of which had been manufactured by the previous owner. Then, in fairly rapid succession, came the 6' 4" model AA, the 9' 4" model CC concert grand, and the 5' 4" model B. The development of these three models was an especially interesting and costly project: in the process, the engineering staff resurrected the original design of each model, constructed new rim presses, standardized certain features, refined manufacturing processes, and modernized jigs, fixtures, templates, and machinery, improvements that afterward were applied to the company's other models. The 50" model 50 vertical piano has also been reintroduced and redesigned, with longer keys for a more grand-like touch, and improved pedal leverage. Internal parts for the verticals are made in Haverhill, then assembled in the company's Sacramento factory, where it also installs PianoDisc systems.

All Mason & Hamlin grands have certain features in common, including a wide-tail design; a full-perimeter plate; an extremely thick and heavy maple rim; a solid spruce soundboard; a seven-ply, quartersawn maple pinblock; and the patented tension-resonator Crown Retention System. The tension resonator (illustrated in *The Piano Book*), invented by Richard Gertz in 1900, consists of a series of turnbuckles that connect to specific points on the inner rim. This system of turnbuckles, sometimes called "the spider," is said to lock the rim in place so that it cannot expand with stress and age, thereby preserving the soundboard crown (curvature). (The soundboard is glued to the inner rim and would collapse if the rim expanded.) While there is no modern-day experimental evidence to confirm or deny this theory, anecdotal evidence and observations by piano technicians tend to validate it because, unlike most older pianos, the soundboards of old Mason & Hamlins almost always have plenty of crown.

In the early part of the 20th century, Wessell, Nickel & Gross was a major supplier of actions to American piano manufacturers, including Mason & Hamlin. Over the years, the name fell into disuse. In 2004 Mason & Hamlin revived the name by registering the trademark, which now refers to the design and specifications of Mason & Hamlin actions. The company manufactures a new line of carbon fiber and nylon-based composite action parts of strikingly innovative design, which the company makes available to its dealers and to rebuilders as a high-performance upgrade to the traditional wood action. The company explained that it has moved to using composite parts because of the inherent shortcomings of wood: it's prone to breakage under constant pounding, the parts vary in strength and mass from one piece of wood to the next, and wood shrinks and swells with changing temperature and humidity. Composite parts, on the other hand, are more than ten times as strong as wood; are built to microscopic tolerances, so they are virtually identical; and are impervious to weather. According to the company, material scientists predict that in the benign environment of a piano, the minimum life expectancy of composite parts is 100 years. The Wessell, Nickel & Gross composite action is now standard on all new Mason & Hamlin pianos.

Mason & Hamlin grands are available in ebony and several standard and exotic wood finishes, in both satin and high polish. Satin finishes are lacquer, the high-polish finishes are polyester. Most sizes are also available in a stylized case design called Monticello, which has fluted, conical legs, similar to Hepplewhite style, with matching lyre and bench. In 2009 Mason & Hamlin introduced the Chrome art-case design, in polished ebony with chrome and stainless-steel case hardware replacing the traditional brass hardware. This design also has art-deco case styling, a silver plate, and a new fallboard logo in a modern font. This modern-font logo, along with a new slow-close fallboard, is standard on all new Mason & Hamlin grands.

The tone of Mason & Hamlin pianos is typically American—lush, singing, and powerful, not unlike the Steinway in basic character, but with an even more powerful bass and a clearer treble. The designers have done a good job of making a recognizable Mason & Hamlin sound that is consistent throughout the model line. The 5' 8" model A has a particularly powerful bass for a piano of its size. The treble, notably weak in prior versions, has been beefed up, but the bass is still the showpiece of the piano. The new 5' 4" model B also has a large-sounding bass for its size. The "growling" power of the Mason & Hamlin bass is most apparent in the 7' model BB. The 6' 4" model AA is a little better balanced between bass and treble, one reason why it is a favorite of mine.

The basic musical design of Mason & Hamlin pianos is very good, as is most of the workmanship. As with other American-made pianos, musical and cabinet detailing, such as factory voicing and regulation and plate and cabinet cosmetics, are reasonable but lag somewhat behind the company's European competitors in finesse. The company says it is standard procedure for final voicing and regulation to be finished off by thorough and competent dealer prep.

In recent years many companies have turned to China and other international sources for parts and materials, for several reasons: a domestic source is no longer available, to save money, to increase the security of supply, and, in some cases, to increase quality. Among makers of high-end pianos, Mason & Hamlin has been pioneering in this regard, though it is not the only company to do so. The company's worldwide sourcing of parts and materials, along with its investment in modernized equipment, has made the Mason & Hamlin a better instrument while keeping the piano's price at a reasonable level. It's a very good value among high-end instruments.

Warranty: 5 years, parts and labor, transferable to future owners within the warranty period.

MAY BERLIN — See Schimmel.

MILLER, HENRY F.

Henry F. Miller
236 West Portal Avenue #568
San Francisco, California 94127
888-516-6528
info@henryfmiller.com

Henry F. Miller was the name of an old American piano maker, established in 1863 near Boston, which eventually became part of the Aeolian Corporation, and was discontinued in 1985. The name is now owned by the Sherman Clay chain of piano stores and is used on a mid-priced line of pianos carried by these and other major piano retailers around the country. Current Henry F. Miller pianos are made by Pearl River in China. The product line consists of five vertical models from 44" to 52" and four grand models from 4' 10" to 6' 2".

PALATINO

The Music Link
P.O. Box 57100
Hayward, California 94545
888-552-5465
piano@palatinousa.com
www.palatinousa.com

Pianos made by: AXL Musical Instrument Co., Ltd. Corp., Shanghai, China

Although Palatino may be a relatively new name to the piano world, it is not a newcomer to the music business. For almost 20 years, parent company AXL has been manufacturing a full range of musical instruments under its own name and under a variety of other, recognizable brand names. The company has a highly automated factory, employing CNC routers from Japan and Germany, and importing high-quality materials and components for its pianos from around the world.

Palatino makes about 7,000 pianos annually in two categories: Classic and Professional. The Professional series includes the 50" vertical Messina model (PUP-126TU) and the 5' 9" grand Palermo model (PGD-59). The Classic series includes a number of models based on traditional designs. Features common to all Palatino pianos include solid spruce soundboard, high-quality Japanese hammers, hard rock maple bridges and pinblock, German Röslau strings, wet-sand-cast plate, Renner-style action, slow-close fallboard, solid brass hardware, and adjustable artist bench. In addition, Professional series pianos have higher-grade Canadian white solid spruce soundboards and German Abel hammers. Beginning in 2012, Palatino is offering a Renner action as an option in some models.

The Renner vertical actions are assembled in Shanghai from German-made Renner parts under the supervision of Renner personnel.

Based on personal observation and dealer reports, Palatino pianos appear to have good quality control and are prepared well at the factory before being shipped to dealers. Our own reviewer tested a couple of the grand models and found them to be very musical and a pleasure to play (see **review** in the Fall 2009 issue).

Warranty: 10 years, parts and labor, transferable to future owners within the warranty period.

PEARL RIVER

including Ritmüller

GW Distribution, LLC
135 Fisher Road
Mahwah, New Jersey 07430
845-429-3712
www.pearlriverusa.com
junewang@pearlriverpiano.com

Pianos made by: Guangzhou Pearl River Piano Group Ltd., Guangzhou, Guangdong Province, China

Established in 1954 through the consolidation of several piano-making facilities, Pearl River is now the largest piano manufacturer in the world, with a production of over 125,000 pianos annually by more than 4,000 workers. The government-owned company says the average length of service of its workers is 17 years. Pianos are made under the Pearl River and Ritmüller names, and under a few other names for OEM contracts with distributors, such as **Cristofori** (with Jordan Kitt's), **Henry F. Miller** (with Sherman Clay) and **Essex** (with Steinway). (See separate listings under those names.) Pearl River is the best-selling piano brand in China, and is exported to more than 100 countries.

Over the past couple of years, Pearl River has revised and streamlined its model lineup with the assistance of Lothar Thomma, a well-respected German scale designer. Some new models have been introduced, and older models have been reviewed and modified. Currently, Pearl River verticals begin with the 42½" console model 108 in continental style (no legs) and a style with legs and toe blocks, and with the 43" model 110 in a variety of American furniture styles. They continue with a series of studio models, including the 45" model 115 in a traditional institutional style (legs with toe blocks), and the 45" model 115E in a school-friendly institutional style. Finally, there are the upright models, including the newly designed 48" model EU122 and the 51½" model 130, both in institutional style.

Pearl River grands come in six sizes, from 4' 11" to 9', including three new models: GP160 (5' 3"), GP170 (5' 7"), and GP188A (6' 2").

Prior to 2008, Pearl River's Ritmüller line used the same strung back (structural and acoustical components) as the Pearl River line, but with different cabinets. Lothar Thomma, mentioned above, was hired in 2006 to design, from the ground up, a line of higher-end pianos that would be distinct from the Pearl River line. These instruments were introduced in North America in 2009 under the Ritmüller name. In most other parts of the world, the pianos are branded Kayserburg. All the new UH and GH models feature solid spruce soundboards, Renner hammers, hornbeam wood actions, and real ebony sharps, among other higher-quality features. *Piano Buyer*'s reviewers have tried out several of the new grand models and have been very impressed (see reviews in the **Fall 2009**, **Fall 2010**, and **Fall 2011** issues).

A new lower-cost line of Ritmüller pianos, introduced in 2011, consists of vertical models 43½" UP-110RB in several furniture styles, 47" UP-120RE (educator studio), and 47½" UP-121RB, and new grand models R-8 (4' 11") and R-9 (5' 3"). These models, also designed by Lothar Thomma, feature an all-spruce veneered and tapered soundboard, and Röslau strings; the grands use Abel hammers.

Warranty: 10 years, parts and labor, to original purchaser.

PERZINA, GEBR.

Piano Empire, Inc.
3035 E. La Mesa Street
Anaheim, California 92806
800-576-3463
714-408-4599
info@pianoempire.com
www.perzinapianos.com

Pianos made by: Yantai-Perzina Piano Manufacturing Co., Ltd., Yantai, Shandong Province, China

The Gebr. Perzina (Perzina Brothers) piano company was established in the German town of Schwerin in 1871, and was a prominent piano maker until World War I, after which its fortunes declined. In more recent times, the factory was moved to the nearby city of Lenzen and the company became known as Pianofabrik Lenzen GmbH. In the early 1990s the company was purchased by Music Brokers International B.V. in the Netherlands. Eventually it was decided that making pianos in Germany was not economically viable, so manufacturing was moved to Yantai, China, where both verticals and grands were made for a number of years by the Yantai Longfeng Piano Co. under the Perzina name. In 2003 Music Brokers International established its own factory in Yantai, called Yantai-Perzina, where it now builds Perzina pianos. The Carl Ebel and Gerh. Steinberg brands made at this factory are no longer distributed in the U.S.

Perzina verticals have several interesting features rarely found in other pianos, including a "floating" soundboard that is unattached to the back at certain points for freer vibration, and a reverse, or concave soundboard crown. (There may be something to this; the Perzina verticals sound very good, their bass being particularly notable.) Soundboards are of solid Austrian white spruce. A premium series of verticals (model numbers ending in R) come with Renner AA or Abel Deluxe hammers.

A new line of Perzina grand pianos was introduced in 2011, designed and manufactured by Perzina in cooperation with a major European manufacturer. All contain solid Austrian white spruce soundboards, duplex scaling, and Renner AA or Abel hammers, among other high-quality components. A Perzina action is standard, with Detoa and Renner actions optionally available at additional cost. All models come with a slow-close fallboard, and most come with an adjustable artist bench.

The company's European headquarters says it ships many European materials to Yantai, including Degen copper-wound strings, Röslau strings, Delignit pinblocks, Renner hammers, English felts, European veneers, and Austrian white spruce soundboards. New machinery is from Germany, Japan, and Italy. According to the company, all the piano designs are the original German scales. The Renner actions used by Perzina are ordered complete from Germany, not assembled from parts.

Warranty: 10 years, parts and labor, to original purchaser.

PETROF

Petrof USA, LLC
5400 Lawrenceville Hwy., Suites B1 & 2
Lilburn, Georgia 30047
877-9-PETROF (877-973-8763)
770-564-4974
sales@petrofpianosusa.com
www.petrof.com
Pianos made by: Petrof, spol. s.r.o., Hradec Králové, Czech Republic

The Petrof piano factory was founded in 1864 by Antonin Petrof in Hradec Králové, an industrial town 100 kilometers east of Prague, in the present Czech Republic. Five generations of the Petrof family owned and managed the business, during which time the company kept pace with technical developments and earned prizes for its pianos at international exhibitions. The Czechs have long been known for their vibrant musical-instrument industry, which also includes makers of brass, woodwind, and stringed instruments.

In 1947, when all businesses in the Czech Republic were nationalized by the state, the Petrof family was forced out of the business. In 1965 Petrof, along with other piano manufacturers, was forced to join Musicexport, the state-controlled import-export company for musical instruments. Since the fall of the Soviet Union and the liberation of Eastern Europe, the various factories that were part of Musicexport have been spun off as private businesses, including Petrof, which is once again owned and controlled by the Petrof family. Currently Petrof manufactures 5,000 vertical pianos and 900 grands annually.

Petrof recently introduced a series of six new grand piano models, named (in size order) Bora, Breeze, Storm, Pasat, Monsoon, and Mistral, from 5'2" to 9'2" in length. Most component parts are produced by Petrof or other Czech factories, including the hardware, plates, and cabinetry. Soundboards are of solid Bohemian spruce, grand rims are of laminated beech and birch, pinblocks are of compressed beech, plates are cast in wet sand, and hammers are from Renner or Abel. These pianos also boast several interesting features: The soundboard is custom-tapered and asymmetrically crowned for optimal resonance; the treble bridge is capped with genuine ebony for better transmission of treble tone; front and rear duplexes are tuned for tonal color; pianos are single-strung for tuning stability; an adjustable bolt has been added from the plate to the wooden cross block for additional tuning stability; and a decorative veneer has been added to the inner rim. The earlier series of Petrof grands with model numbers containing roman numerals will coexist with the new models as long as supplies last.

Actions in Petrof pianos are standard Detoa on the smaller verticals, Renner on the larger grands and larger verticals, and either Renner parts on a Petrof action frame or Petrof Original Actions made by Detoa on mid-size instruments.

Petrof has also invented and patented a version of its new grand action that uses tiny opposing magnets on the wippens and wippen rail. These magnets allow for the removal of the usual lead counterweights in the keys and, according to the company, significantly alter the action's dynamic properties. The new action also furthers the European Union's stated environmental goal of phasing out the use of lead in pianos. The action is adjusted in the factory for a standard touchweight and is serviced in exactly the same way as a standard action. The Magnetic Accelerated Action, as it is known, is a special-order option on the grands. Petrof also offers as an option the Magnetic Balanced Action, which allows the player to quickly and easily change the touchweight in the range of ±4–5 grams simply by turning a knob.

Petrofs are known for their warm, rich, singing tone, full of color. The pianos are solidly built and workmanship is good. After careful preparation, the pianos can sound and feel quite beautiful and hold their own against other European brands. Wages in the Czech Republic have risen in recent years, and with it the price of Petrof pianos, but the company has placed a greater emphasis on quality control and enhanced features in the new models in order to meet the higher expectations that come with higher prices.

Note: For years, Weinbach pianos were made by the Petrof company and were virtually identical to Petrof brand pianos. The Weinbach name is no longer being used in North America.

Warranty: 10 years, parts and labor, to original purchaser, from the manufacturer.

PRAMBERGER

See also Samick.

Samick Music Corp. (SMC)
1329 Gateway Drive
Gallatin, Tennessee 37066
615-206-0077
info@smcmusic.com
www.smcmusic.com

Pianos made by: Samick Musical Instrument Mfg. Co. Ltd., Bogor, West Java, Indonesia

The Pramberger name was used by Young Chang for its premium-level pianos under license from the late piano engineer Joseph Pramberger, who at one time was head of manufacturing at Steinway & Sons. When Pramberger died, in 2003, his estate terminated its relationship with Young Chang and signed up with Samick. However, since Young Chang still holds the rights to its piano designs, Samick has designed new pianos to go with the name.

The J.P. Pramberger Platinum piano is a higher-end instrument, formerly made in Korea, and now made in Indonesia under Korean supervision using the CNC equipment acquired by Samick during its partnership with Bechstein. It is then shipped to the U.S. for inspection, tuning, regulating, and voicing before being shipped to dealers. Several American technicians who had known and worked with Joe Pramberger went to Korea at Samick's request to design this piano. Benefiting by work previously done by Bechstein engineers at the Samick factory, they began with a modified Bechstein scale, then added several features found on current or older Steinways, such as an all-maple (or beech) rim, an asymmetrically tapered white spruce soundboard, vertically laminated and tunneled maple and mahogany bridges with maple cap, duplex scaling, a Renner/Pramberger action, and Renner or Abel hammers. One of the technicians told me that the group feels its design is an advancement of Pramberger's work that he would have approved of.

The Pramberger Signature (formerly known as J. Pramberger) is a more modestly priced instrument from Indonesia whose design is based on the former Korean-built Young Chang version. This line uses Samick's Pratt-Reed Premium action, Renner or Abel hammers, and a Bolduc (Canadian) solid spruce soundboard. The institutional verticals in this line have all-wood cabinet construction and agraffes in the bass section, and the decorator versions include Renner hammers and a slow-close fallboard.

The Pramberger Legacy, the newest addition to the Pramberger line, has a veneer-laminated "surface tension" soundboard, and provides a reasonably priced option for the budget-minded consumer. These models were formerly sold under the Remington label. (The Remington brand is no longer a regular part of the Pramberger lineup, but is available to dealers on special order.)

[Note: Samick's Pratt-Reed Premium action should not be confused with the Pratt-*Read* action used in many American-made pianos in the mid to late 20th century and eventually acquired by Baldwin. Samick says its Pratt-Reed action, designed by its research and development team and based on the German Renner action, is made in Korea.]

See **Samick** for more information.

Warranty: 10 years, parts and labor, transferable to future owners within the warranty period.

RAVENSCROFT

Spreeman Piano Innovations, LLC
7898 East Acoma Drive, Suite 105
Scottsdale, Arizona 85260
480-664-3702
info@spreemanpianoinnovations.com
www.RavenscroftPianos.com

Handcrafted in Scottsdale, Arizona by piano builder Michael Spreeman, the Ravenscroft piano entered the market for high-end performance pianos in 2006. Two models are available, the 7' 3" model 220 and the 9' model 275. The 220 made its debut in 2007 in the Manufacturers' Showcase of the 50th Annual Convention of the Piano Technicians Guild. A custom-built model 275 is currently the official piano at the Tempe Center for the Arts.

While the general trend in the industry seems to be toward outsourcing to less expensive suppliers, Spreeman says his concept is the exact opposite. Appealing to the niche market of high-end consumers, Spreeman's approach is more along the lines of the early European small-shop builders, with an emphasis on quality and exclusivity.

The case and iron frame of the Ravenscroft piano are constructed in Germany by Sauter to Ravenscroft specifications and shipped to the Arizona facility. The Renner action and Kluge keys of each piano are computer-designed to optimize performance. The rib scale, soundboard, bridges, and string scale are designed by Spreeman, who meticulously hand-builds each instrument with his three-person team.

Currently, only four to six pianos are produced yearly, with pricing beginning at $230,000 for a model 220, and up to $550,000 for a model 275 with "all the extras," including titanium string terminations, exotic veneers, intarsia, artwork, and inlays of precious stones. Most instruments are custom ordered and can take up to a year to complete.

RITMÜLLER — See Pearl River.

SAMICK

including Kohler & Campbell.
See separate listings for Wm. Knabe, Pramberger, and Seiler.
Samick Music Corp. (SMC)
1329 Gateway Drive
Gallatin, Tennessee 37066
615-206-0077
info@smcmusic.com
www.smcmusic.com

Pianos made by: Samick Musical Instrument Mfg. Co. Ltd., Inchon, South Korea; and Bogor, West Java, Indonesia

Samick was founded by Hyo Ick Lee in 1958 as a Baldwin distributor in South Korea. Facing an immense challenge in an impoverished and war-torn country, in the early 1960s Lee began to build and sell a very limited quantity of vertical pianos using largely imported parts. As the economy improved, Lee expanded his operation, and in 1964 began exporting to other parts of the world, eventually becoming one of the world's largest piano manufacturers, now making most parts in-house. Over the next several decades, Samick expanded into manufacturing guitars and other instruments and opened factories in China and Indonesia, where it shifted much of its production as Korean wages rose. The Asian economic crisis of the late 1990s forced Samick into bankruptcy, but the company emerged from bankruptcy in 2002 and is now on a sound financial footing.

The company says that "Samick" means "three benefits" in Korean, symbolizing the wish that the activities of the company benefit not only the company itself, but also the customers and the Korean economy.

Samick Music Corporation (SMC), the North American sales and marketing arm of the Korean company, distributes Samick, Kohler & Campbell, Pramberger, Wm. Knabe, and Seiler pianos in North America (see separate listings for **Wm. Knabe, Pramberger**, and **Seiler**). Samick no longer distributes pianos under the Bernhard Steiner, Conover Cable, Hazelton Bros., Remington, and Sohmer & Co. names. SMC has a manufacturing, warehousing, and office facility in Tennessee, at which it uncrates, inspects, tunes, regulates, and voices its upper-level Wm. Knabe, J.P. Pramberger, and Kohler & Campbell Millennium-series pianos before shipping them to dealers. While Samick says it will continue to make some pianos in Korea, it is gradually moving most of its production to Indonesia.

Until just a few years ago, Samick primarily made pianos under the Samick and Kohler & Campbell brand names. (For historical information about the original Kohler & Campbell piano company, see *The Piano Book*.) In the 1980s Klaus Fenner, a German piano designer, was hired to revise the Samick scale designs and make them more "European." Most of the Samick and Kohler & Campbell pianos now being made are based on these designs.

Although in most respects the Samick and Kohler & Campbell pianos are similar in quality, so as not to compete with one another the grands are available in different sizes and have some different features. The two lines are primarily differentiated by the fact that Kohler & Campbell grands (except the smallest model) have solid spruce soundboards and individually hitched stringing (also known as single stringing), whereas the Samick grands have veneer-laminated soundboards and conventional loop stringing. A veneer-laminated soundboard (which Samick calls a "surface tension soundboard") is essentially a solid spruce soundboard surrounded by two very thin veneers. Samick pioneered the use of this soundboard with Klaus Fenner's technical advice in early 1980, and it is now used by others as well. Tonally, it behaves much more like a solid spruce soundboard than the old kind of laminated soundboard, which was essentially plywood. Like the old kind, however, it won't crack or lose its crown. The solid spruce soundboard may have a slight tonal advantage, but the laminated one will last longer, so take your pick. Likewise, single stringing is more elegant to those who know pianos, but otherwise offers little or no advantage over loop stringing. The two brands' vertical pianos are more alike: They have the same difference in soundboards as the grands, but are all loop-strung and come more or less in the same sizes.

Kohler & Campbell's upper-level Millennium pianos have higher-quality features than the regular series, now called New Yorker. The Millennium grands have a maple rim, premium Canadian Bolduc tapered solid spruce soundboard, Renner action and hammers, and satin wood finishes available in lacquer semigloss. The verticals have Renner parts on a Samick-made Pratt-Reed hornbeam action rail, Bolduc solid spruce soundboard, Renner hammers, lacquer semigloss wood finishes, and a sostenuto pedal on the 52" model. All Samick and New Yorker–series Kohler & Campbell pianos are made in Indonesia for the U.S. market. Smaller Millennium verticals and grands are made in Indonesia, larger ones in Korea. However, all Millennium-series pianos are shipped to the U.S. for inspection and tone and action regulation before being shipped to dealers.

[Note: Samick's Pratt-Reed Premium action should not be confused with the Pratt-*Read* action used in many American-made pianos in the mid to late 20th century and eventually acquired by Baldwin. Samick says its Pratt-Reed action is made in Korea and designed after the German Renner action.]

In the Kohler & Campbell price list, KC models are Indonesian-made, New Yorker–series verticals; KM are Indonesian-made Millennium-series verticals; KMV are Korean-made Millennium-series verticals; KCG and KIG are Indonesian-made New Yorker–series grands; KCM are Indonesian-made Millennium-series grands; and KFM are Korean-made Millennium-series grands.

Quality control in Samick's Korean and Indonesian factories has steadily improved, especially in the last few years, and the Indonesian product is said to be almost as good as the Korean. Many large-scale issues have been addressed and engineers are now working on smaller refinements. The company says that new CNC machinery installed in 2007 has revolutionized the consistency and accuracy of its manufacturing. Climate control in the tropically situated Indonesian factory, and issues of action geometry, are also among the areas that have recently seen improvement. Samick's upper-level pianos—Kohler & Campbell Millennium series, J.P. Pramberger, and Wm. Knabe—have met with a very positive response from technicians as to their musical design and performance, exceeding comparably priced pianos from Japan in those regards. Workmanship is good, although still not quite as consistent as in the Japanese pianos. Many of Samick's Indonesian pianos are priced similarly to low-cost pianos from China, and technicians often report finding the Samicks to be more consistent than some of the Chinese. With dealer prep, Samick-made pianos are a good value for most typical uses.

[Note: Samick-made pianos have an odd system of serial numbers consisting of a series of letters and numbers. The system appears to vary from factory to factory. Please contact SMC for information on the date of manufacture of a Samick-made piano.]

Warranty: 10 years, parts and labor, transferable to future owners within the warranty period.

SAUTER

Sauter USA
P.O. Box 1130
Richland, Washington 99354
509-946-8078
877-946-8078
+49-7424-94820 (factory)
info@sauteramerica.com
info@sauter-pianos.de
www.sauter-pianos.de
www.sauterforum.com

Pianos made by: Carl Sauter Pianofortemanufaktur GmbH & Co. KG, Max-Planck-Strasse 20, 78549 Spaichingen, Germany

The Sauter piano firm was founded in 1819 by Johann Grimm, stepfather to Carl Sauter I, and has been owned and managed by members of the Sauter family for six generations, currently by Ulrich Sauter. The factory produces about 800 vertical pianos and 120 grand pianos a year in its factory in the extreme south of Germany, at the foot of the Alps. Structural and acoustical parts are made of high-quality woods, including solid Bavarian spruce soundboards and beech pinblocks. Actions are made by Renner, and Sauter makes its own keys. The keybed is reinforced with steel to prevent warping, and all pianos are fully tropicalized for humid climates. The larger verticals use an action, designed and patented by Sauter, that contains an auxiliary jack spring to aid in faster repetition. Sauter calls this the R2 Double Escapement action. (Although the term *double escapement* does not apply here as it has historically been used, the mechanism has some of the same effects.)

Sauter pianos are especially known for the variety of finishes and styles in which they are available, many with intricate detail and inlay work. It is common to find such rare woods as yew, burl walnut, pyramid mahogany, and genuine ebony in the cabinets of Sauter pianos, as well as special engravings, which can be customized to any customer's desires. Sauter's M Line of vertical pianos features exclusive cabinet detailing and built-in features such as a hygrometer to measure relative humidity. New Masterline institutional uprights, sold directly to institutions and not through dealers, include protective sidebars, industrial-grade casters, and locking mechanisms. Amadeus is a special-edition 6' 1" grand honoring the 250th anniversary of Mozart's birth, with styling reminiscent of that in Mozart's time. The natural keytops are of polished bone, the sharps of rosewood with ebony caps. Only 36 are to be made, one for each year of Mozart's life.

The company also has introduced versions of its 48" upright and 6'11" and 7'6" grands with cabinets designed by the famous European designer Peter Maly.

Some recent designs include the 48" upright Vitrea, after the Latin word for glass, with a veneer of greenish glass covering the front of the cabinet; and Ambiente, a 7'6" grand that is asymmetrically curved on both the bass and treble sides. In the recent past, Sauter has won several prestigious design awards for its Peter Maly–designed pianos.

A couple of extremely unusual models bear mentioning. The 7'3" model 220 has colored lines painted on the soundboard and white inlays on the tops of the dampers as guides for musicians performing music for "prepared piano," ultramodern music requiring the insertion of foreign objects between the strings, or the plucking or striking of strings directly by the performer. The 1/16-tone microtonal piano is an upright with 97 keys that has a total pitch range, from its lowest to its highest note, of only one octave, the pitch difference from key to key being only 1/16 of a tone (1/8 of a semitone). You can read more about these strange instruments in *The Piano Book*.

Sauter pianos are high-quality instruments with a lush, full, singing tone, closer to an "American" sound than most other European pianos.

Warranty: 5 years, parts and labor, to original purchaser.

SCHILLER — See Irmler.

SCHIMMEL

including Vogel and May Berlin

Schimmel Piano Corporation
329 N. New Street
Lititz, Pennsylvania 17543
800-426-3205
schimmel@ptd.net
www.schimmel-piano.de

Pianos made by: Wilhelm Schimmel Pianofortefabrik GmbH, Braunschweig, Germany (Schimmel) and Kalisz, Poland (Vogel); unspecified factory in China (May Berlin)

Wilhelm Schimmel began making pianos in Leipzig in 1885, and his company enjoyed steady growth through the late 19th and early 20th centuries. The two World Wars and the Depression disrupted production several times, but the company has gradually rebuilt itself over the past 60 years with a strong reputation for quality. Today, Schimmel is managed by Hannes Schimmel-Vogel, the husband of Viola Schimmel. Schimmel makes about 2,500 verticals and 500 grands per year and is one of Europe's most important piano makers.

Among European piano manufacturers, Schimmel has been a pioneer in the use of computer-aided design and manufacturing. The company has used its Computer Assisted Piano Engineering (CAPE) software to research, design, and implement virtually every aspect of making a piano, from keyboard layout and action geometry to soundboard acoustics and scale design. According to Schimmel, the combination of CNC machinery and handcraftsmanship leads to better results than handwork alone. Schimmel also believes that precision is aided by controlling as much of the production process as possible. For that reason, Schimmel produces its own piano-cabinet components and its own keyboards, which it also supplies to other German piano makers.

Over the last few years, Schimmel has reorganized its model lineup into two categories: Schimmel Konzert (models beginning with K) and Schimmel Classic (models beginning with C). The Konzert series consists of some of the newer and larger vertical models, and the six most recently designed and advanced grand models. The company says that the purpose of the Konzert series was to expand the Schimmel line upward to a higher level of quality than it had previously attained, in order to compete with other brands of the highest quality. The Classic series consists of the rest of the verticals, the 6' model 182 grand, and the 6' 10" model 208 grand. This series represents models that have been tested over time and are solid, traditional, high-quality instruments, but without the latest refinements.

The Konzert series uprights—48" model K122, 49" model K125, and 52" model K132—are based on a more sophisticated philosophy of construction than the Classics. These models also incorporate triplex scaling and other advanced design features. Schimmel's philosophy for these uprights was to design them to be as much like the grands as possible. The treble scales, in fact, are exactly the same as in the Konzert grands. All uprights have adjustable casters (to adjust to unevenness in the floor) and come with a matching adjustable bench.

The Konzert grands consist of two model groups. The Trilogy I group consists of the 7' 6", 8' 4", and 9' 2" semi-concert and concert grand models. In this group, all three models have the same keyboard and action as the concert grand. In the Trilogy II group, Schimmel has married the front-end (keyboard) of its 7' grand to two smaller models: 5' 7" and 6' 3". The smaller models have the same treble scale, keyboard, and action as the 7' grand, so all three have a similar sound and touch. On all Konzert grand models, the case sides are angled slightly to obtain a larger soundboard, and all have tunable front and rear duplex scales for greater tonal color, real ebony sharps, and mineral white keytops to mimic the feel of ivory, among other advanced features. The largest grands have reinforced keys for optimal energy transmission.

The 6' 3" model K189 and 7' model K213 are currently available in a Nikolaus W. Schimmel (NWS) model. Built to commemorate the retirement of the elder Nikolaus Schimmel, this model has many small technical and cosmetic refinements, uses top-quality soundboard material, and receives greater final preparation at the factory to create a really superior instrument.

Schimmel grand pianos have historically had a tone that was very bright and clear, but a bit thin and lacking in color in the treble. The grands were redesigned, in part, to add additional color to the tone, and the result is definitely more interesting than before. Sustain is also very good. The pianos are being delivered to U.S. dealers voiced less bright than previously, as this is what the American ear tends to prefer. As for the verticals, the smaller ones tend to have a very big bass for their size, with a tone that emphasizes the fundamental, giving the bass a warmer character. The 52" model K132, which features a grand-shaped soundboard, has a very big sound; listening to it, one might think one was in the presence of a grand.

In 2002, Schimmel acquired the PianoEurope factory in Kalisz, Poland, a piano restoration and manufacturing facility. Schimmel is using this factory to manufacture its Vogel brand, a moderately priced line named after the company's president. Schimmel says that although the skill level of the employees is high, lower wages and other lower costs result in a piano approximately 30 percent less costly than the Schimmel. Vogel grand pianos feature full Renner actions, with other parts mainly made by Schimmel in Braunschweig or by the Kalisz factory. The Vogel pianos, though designed by Schimmel, don't have all the refinements and advanced features of the latest Schimmel models. Nevertheless, the Vogels have received praise from many quarters for their high-quality workmanship and sound.

Schimmel now imports an entry-level series of pianos from China under the name May Berlin. The pianos are made by a selected, but unspecified, supplier. The company says it sends soundboard wood and hammer felt for grand pianos to the factory in China. When completed, the pianos are inspected in the factory by a top Schimmel technician who travels to China every few weeks.

Warranty: Schimmel, Vogel, May Berlin—10 years, parts and labor, to original purchaser.

SCHULZE POLLMANN

North American Music Inc.
11 Holt Drive
Stony Point, New York 10980
845-429-0106
www.schulzepollmann.com
www.namusic.com

Pianos made by: Schulze Pollmann s.r.l., Borgo Maggiore, San Marino

Schulze Pollmann was formed in 1928 by the merger of two German piano builders who had moved to Italy. Paul Pollmann had worked first with Ibach, then with Steinway & Sons (Hamburg), before opening his own piano factory in Germany. He later moved to Italy, where he met up with Albert Schulze, another relocated German piano builder. Pollmann managed the combined firm until 1942, and was followed by his son Hans, who had managed the piano-maker Schimmel before returning to his father's firm. Recently the company relocated a short distance to San Marino, a tiny city-state completely surrounded by Italy.

Schulze Pollmann uses both sophisticated technology and handwork in its manufacturing. The pianos contain Delignit pinblocks, solid European spruce soundboards, and Renner actions and hammers. Interesting features include a one-piece solid lock (laminated) back made of beech on the verticals, agraffes on the larger vertical, and finger-jointed construction of all soundboards to prevent cracking. Many of the cabinets have beautiful designs and inlays.

The uprights are well built and have a sound that is warm and colorful with a good amount of sustain. The treble is not nearly as brittle sounding as in some of the other European uprights. Schulze Pollmann grands are likewise very nicely crafted and arrive at the dealer in good condition. However, they need solid preparation by the dealer to sound their best.

In 2005, Italian auto manufacturer Ferrari Motor Car selected Schulze Pollmann as a partner in the launch of its new Ferrari 612 Scaglietti series of automobiles. For the occasion, Schulze Pollmann crafted a limited-edition version of its 6'7" model 197/G5 grand piano, still available, with a case that sports the Ferrari racing red and a cast-iron plate in Ferrari gray carbon, the same color as the engine of the Scaglietti. The car and the piano have been exhibited together in cities around the world.

Warranty: 10 years, parts and labor, transferable to future owners within the warranty period.

SEILER

Samick Music Corp. (SMC)
1329 Gateway Drive
Gallatin, Tennessee 37066
800-592-9393
615-206-0077
info@smcmusic.com
www.seilerpianousa.com

Pianos made by: Ed. Seiler Pianofortefabrik, Kitzingen, Germany; with Samick Musical Instrument Mfg. Co. Ltd., Bogor, West Java, Indonesia

Eduard Seiler, the company's founder, began making pianos in 1849, in Liegnitz, Silesia, then part of Prussia. By 1923, the company had grown to over 435 employees, was producing up to 3,000 pianos per year, and was the largest piano manufacturer in Eastern Europe. In 1945 and after World War II, when Liegnitz became part of Poland, the plant was nationalized by the Polish Communist government, and the Seiler family left their native homeland with millions of other refugees. In 1954, Steffan Seiler reestablished the company in Copenhagen under the fourth generation of family ownership, and began making pianos again. In 1962 he moved the company to Kitzingen, Bavaria, in Germany, where it resides today. Steffan Seiler died in 1999; the company was managed by his widow, Ursula, until its sale to Samick in 2008. Seiler produces about 1,000 pianos annually. Samick says it plans to continue Seiler's tradition of making the highest-quality pianos.

Seiler uses a combination of traditional methods and modern technology in building pianos. The scale designs are of relatively high tension, producing a brilliant, balanced tone that is quite consistent from one Seiler to the next. Although brilliant, the tone also sings well, due to, the company says, a unique soundboard feature called the Membrator system, used in all Seiler pianos. The Membrator is a patented construction feature in which the perimeter of the soundboard is sculpted to be thicker and heavier in mass than the interior, to form a frame within the soundboard. The lighter inner area becomes the vibrating membrane—a diaphragm on its own—unimpeded by the larger soundboard's attachment to the inner rim. The company says that use of the Membrator system, as well as effective rib positioning, improves the soundboard's efficiency in radiating sound. It's easy to identify the Membrator by the tapered groove around the perimeter of the board.

The grands have wide tails for greater soundboard area and string length. The pianos feature Bavarian spruce soundboards, multi-laminated beech pinblocks, quartersawn beech bridges, Renner actions, and slow-close fallboards. A few years ago, the grands were redesigned with a duplex scale for greater treble tonal color, and with longer keys and a lighter touch. Musically, these redesigns were very successful. They retained the typical Seiler clarity, but with longer sustain and a marvelously even-feeling touch.

In 2011, Samick expanded the Seiler line to cover three price points. The top-level instruments continue to be handcrafted at the Seiler factory in Kitzingen, just as they have been for many years. They come in two styles, Classic and Trend. The construction and specifications of the two styles are the same, but the Trend looks a bit more modern, and sports a silver-colored plate and chrome hardware, whereas the Classic has the traditional gold- or bronze-colored plate and brass hardware. Both are available in dozens of special furniture styles with beautiful, exotic woods and inlays.

The mid-level Seiler pianos, designated the ES models, and the more affordable ED models, are together known as the Eduard Seiler line. These have cabinet parts and sound bodies (strung backs) constructed at Samick's Indonesian factory using German CNC machinery, and to the exact scales and specifications of the hand-built German models. The ES models are then shipped to Kitzingen, where assembly is completed, full Renner actions and German hammers are installed, and the final musical finishing of the instruments is performed. Final assembly of the ED models takes place in Indonesia, using Renner wippen assemblies and a Samick hornbeam or Delignit action rail. All Seiler pianos distributed in North America, regardless of origin, come with the Seiler name on the fallboard.

At both the Kitzingen and Indonesian factories, strung backs are inspected to make sure that all specifications have been met to the strictest tolerances. Soundboard mass distribution and rib positioning are under strict quality control in order to achieve consistency in the soundboard's acoustical properties. Pre-stretching of the strings is done several times, followed by multiple tunings, to ensure maximum stability. Hammer alignment, voicing, and key weighting and balancing are all carefully performed by experienced Seiler technicians. Renner actions are regulated for maximum performance. All cabinet parts are carefully fitted to exact specifications.

Seiler's 52" upright is available with the optional Super Magnet Repetition (SMR) action, a patented feature that uses magnets to increase repetition speed. During play, tiny magnets attached to certain action parts of each note repel each other, forcing the parts to return to their rest position faster, ready for the next keystroke.

Warranty: 10 years, parts and labor, to original purchaser.

SEJUNG

including Falcone, Hobart M. Cable, Geo. Steck

Welkin Sound
1590 S. Milliken Ave., Unit H
Ontario, California 91761
909-484-7498
866-473-5864
sales@sejungusa.com
www.sejungusa.com

Pianos made by: Sejung Corporation, Qingdao, Shandong Province, China

Sejung is a Korean-based company established in 1974. The musical instrument division of the business began production in 2001 with the creation of a partnership with Qingdao Sejung Musical Instruments in China. They began by building a 700,000-square-foot factory in Qingdao, a port city on the eastern coast with a temperate climate; hired dozens of managers who had once worked for Young Chang and Samick; and staffed the factory with some 2,000 workers. In order to attract skilled labor and reduce turnover, the company built dormitories to house and feed this labor force. The company has invested substantially in automated production equipment to achieve high quality standards, and produces just about every piano component in its own factories.

Sejung currently manufactures the Falcone, George Steck, and Hobart M. Cable brand names. These lines are technically similar and are differentiated mostly by their cabinet styles. Most of the models have a solid spruce soundboard, slow-close fallboard, cast pedals, and maple trapwork. In addition, an upscale Falcone Georgian (FG) series includes such features as Abel hammers on grands 5'4" and larger, upgraded soundboard material, bubinga veneer on the inside of the grand rim, real ebony sharps, and gold-plated hardware.

The first pianos from Sejung were sold in the U.S. in fall 2002, less than one year after production began. A number of their first offerings were examined by technicians, and although still a little rough, they were definitely satisfactory, and remarkably good for such a new company. Since then, the factory has grown to become one of China's largest exporters of musical instruments, production has been refined, and quality has improved. After proper regulation and tuning, the pianos offer good value in an entry-level instrument. The 4'8" grand and the continental console are most appropriate for those buyers whose primary considerations are price or appearance.

For model and price information, see under Sejung in the "Model & Pricing Guide."

Warranty: 12 years on parts, 10 years on labor, to original purchaser.

SOHMER

Persis International, Inc.
2647 N. Western Ave. #8030
Chicago, Illinois 60647
773-342-4212
www.sohmerpianos.com

Founded by German immigrant Hugo Sohmer in 1872, Sohmer & Co. was owned and managed by the Sohmer family in New York City for 110 years. Having no descendants to take over the business, the founder's grandsons sold the company in 1982. As the company changed hands several times over the following decade, limited production of Sohmer pianos took place in Connecticut and Pennsylvania, finally ceasing in 1994 (see the Sohmer entry in *The Piano Book* for a more detailed recent history).

Pianos are once again being made under this venerable name, once considered among the finest of American-built instruments. Sohmer pianos from Persis International are manufactured by Royale, a Korean firm descended from a former joint venture between the German manufacturer Ibach and the Korean manufacturer Daewoo, neither of which any longer makes pianos. During the German-Korean joint venture, the string scales, bridges, soundboards, rib dimensions, actions, keys, and hammers were redesigned by Ibach to German standards. Models include a 50" vertical and 5' 3", 5' 10", and 7' 2" grands. The pianos have high-quality European components, such as Renner actions, Abel hammers, Delignit pinblocks, Röslau strings, and Ciresa solid spruce soundboards.

Note that, for a number of years, there was a legal dispute over the ownership of the Sohmer trademark, and from 2003 to 2010, Sohmer-branded pianos were distributed by both Persis International and Samick Music Corporation (SMC). That dispute has been settled in favor of Persis, and SMC stopped selling Sohmer pianos in 2010. However, the Samick-made pianos can be expected to remain on dealers' showroom floors for the near future, until sold, and Samick will continue to honor the warranties of the instruments it manufactured. (Note: Persis's pianos are labeled "Sohmer," and SMC's are labeled "Sohmer & Co.")

Warranty: 10 years, parts and labor, to original purchaser.

STECK, GEO. — See Sejung.

STEINBERG, WILH.

Unique Pianos
Brian Gatchell
25 South Wickham Rd.
Melbourne, Florida 32904
888-725-6633
321-725-5690
brianatlantic@bellsouth.net
www.Wilh-Steinberg.com

Pianos made by: Thüringer Pianoforte GmbH, Eisenberg, Germany

This company, formerly known as Wilh. Steinberg Pianofortefabrik, was formed after the reunification of Germany by the merger of several East German piano companies that collectively trace their origins back to 1877. In addition to its own pianos, Steinberg makes several other European piano brands under OEM agreements. The company also specializes in custom cabinets and finishes. Piano production is about 700 verticals and 80 grands per year.

In 2009, Steinberg introduced a new marketing concept that involves selling pianos at three levels of quality. The first level, IQ, is the traditionally crafted piano that the company has made entirely in Germany for many years. These high-quality instruments have beech rims with spruce bracing (grands), solid Bavarian spruce soundboards, maple bridges with maple caps, Renner actions and hammers, and Kluge keys. The second level, AC (Advanced Craftsmanship), uses some nonacoustical components manufactured in China, but the instruments are assembled, regulated, and voiced in Germany. The third level, P (Premium), consists of instruments entirely made in China, with only final preparation done in Germany. This level is not currently being imported into the U.S.

Warranty: 5 years, parts and labor, to original purchaser.

STEINGRAEBER & SÖHNE

Steingraeber & Söhne
Steingraeberpassage 1
95444 Bayreuth, Germany
+49-921-64049
+49-921-58272 (fax)
steingraeber@steingraeber.de
www.steingraeber.de

Bayreuth is famous the world over for its annual summer Wagner festival. But tucked away in the old part of town is a second center of Bayreuth musical excellence and one of the piano world's best-kept secrets: Steingraeber & Söhne. Founded in Bayreuth in 1852, and in its present factory since 1872, Steingraeber is one of the smaller piano manufacturers in the world, producing fewer than 80 grands and 60 verticals per year for the top end of the market. It is owned and operated by sixth-generation family member Udo Steingraeber, who still makes pianos using the traditional methods of his forebears.

Steingraeber makes three sizes of vertical piano: 48", 51", and 54". An interesting option on the vertical pianos is their "twist and change" panels: two-sided top and bottom panels, one side finished in polished ebony, the other in a two-toned combination of a wood veneer and ebony. The panels can be reversed as desired by the piano owner to match room décor, or just for a change of scenery.

The company also makes five sizes of grand piano: 5' 7", 6' 3", 7', 7' 7", and 8' 11". The 5' 7" model A-170 grand has an unusually wide tail, allowing for a larger soundboard area and longer bass strings than are customary for an instrument of its size. The 7' model C-212, known as the Chamber Concert Grand, and recently redesigned from the model 205, was intended to embody the tone quality of the Steingraeber Liszt grand piano of circa 1873, but with more volume in the bass register. The 8' 11" model E-272 concert grand was introduced in 2002 for Steingraeber's 150th anniversary. Unique features include a drilled capo bar for more sustain in the treble, unusually shaped rim bracing, and a smaller soundboard resonating area in the treble to better match string length. In 2007 Steingraeber introduced a new 7' 7" D-232 concert grand to provide an additional smaller, concert-size instrument. Its design features many of the innovations of the E-272. New in 2012 is the 6' 3" model B-192, which follows the design enhancements of the D-232 and C-212 in a size more comfortable for homes and smaller concert halls.

Steingraeber pianos have a unique sound, with an extensive tonal palette derived from a mixture of clarity and warmth.

Steingraeber is known for its many innovative technical improvements to the piano. One new one is a cylindrical, revolving knuckle (grand piano action part). It acts like a normal knuckle until the hammer reaches the let-off position. After that point, in soft playing, the knuckle revolves, reducing friction and making pianissimo playing easier, smoother, and more accurate. Another innovation is a new action for upright pianos. This SFM action, as it is called, contains no jack spring, instead using magnets to return the jack more quickly under the hammer butt for faster repetition. It is available in all three models of vertical piano. Steingraeber also specializes in so-called ecological or biological finishes, available as an option on most models. This involves the use of only organic materials in the piano, such as natural paints and glues in the case, and white keytops made from cattle bone.

In addition to its regular line of pianos, Steingraeber makes a piano that can be used by physically handicapped players who lack the use of their legs for pedaling. A wireless (bluetooth) pedal actuator in the form of a denture is actuated by biting on the denture.

The Steingraeber engineering department has designed and manufactured prototypes of new piano models for a number of other European piano manufacturers. These designs are not the same as Steingraeber's own current models.

Warranty: 10 years, parts and labor, to original purchaser.

Steingraeber Phoenix System Pianos

Unique Pianos
Brian Gatchell
25 South Wickham Rd.
Melbourne, Florida 32904
888-725-6633
321-725-5690
brianatlantic@bellsouth.net
www.atlanticmusiccenter.com

Pianos made by: Steingraeber & Söhne, Bayreuth, Germany

Steingraeber's most innovative technical improvement is the Steingraeber Phoenix system, introduced in 2008. Phoenix, initially developed by U.K. engineer Richard Dains and further developed by Steingraeber and used under license, is a system of tonal transmission that includes a soundboard made of a sheet of carbon fiber, and bridge agraffes that hold the strings to the bridge without compressing the soundboard. With the soundboard free of compression, and given the low-density, low-mass nature of the carbon fiber and its resistance to absorbing energy, a great amount of sound energy is conserved—so much that pianos outfitted with this system sound in certain respects like much larger instruments, with both increased sustain and greater volume of sound. A side benefit of the carbon fiber soundboard is that it is resistant to humidity changes, so the piano needs tuning much less often.

The bridge agraffes are quite complex in construction and completely unlike the simple ones sometimes used, with mixed success, in unusual pianos of the past. They provide very efficient transmission of tonal energy from the string to the bridge, with little downward pressure on the soundboard. To minimize downbearing, the precise setting of downbearing is aided by vertical, adjustable hitch pins. One challenge to the development of the Phoenix system has been the much greater production of higher harmonics once the impediments to sound transmission are removed. These harmonics are moderated by voicing.

All Phoenix-system pianos are equipped with a revolutionary new soft pedal that operates both an una corda (shift) mechanism, and a mechanism that allows for hammer blow-distance reduction, for different types of volume-reduction effects.

Steingraeber is now making the Phoenix system available by special order in each of its grand piano models. Both the carbon fiber soundboard (without the bridge agraffes), and the new soft pedal, are also available as options on regular Steingraeber models.

More information about the Phoenix system can be found at www.hurstwoodfarmpianos.co.uk, as well as on the Steingraeber website.

STEINWAY & SONS

Steinway & Sons
One Steinway Place
Long Island City, New York 11105
718-721-2600
800-366-1853
www.steinway.com

Heinrich Engelhardt Steinweg, a cabinetmaker and piano maker from Seesen, Germany, emigrated with his family to the United States in 1850, and established Steinway & Sons in 1853. Within a relatively short time, the Steinways were granted patents that revolutionized the piano, and which were eventually adopted or imitated by other makers. Many of these patents concerned the quest for a stronger frame, a richer, more powerful sound, and a more sensitive action. By the 1880s, the Steinway piano was in most ways the modern piano we have today, and in the next generation the standards set by the founder were strictly adhered to. (The early history of Steinway & Sons is fascinating, and is intimately connected to the history of New York City and the piano industry in general. You can read a summary of it in *The Piano Book;* there are also several excellent books devoted to the subject.)

In the 1960s the fourth generation of Steinways found themselves without any heirs willing or able to take over the business, and without enough capital to finance much-needed equipment modernization; eventually, in 1972, they sold their company to CBS. CBS left the musical instrument business in 1985, selling Steinway to an investment group. In 1995 the company was sold again, this time to Conn-Selmer, Inc., a major manufacturer of brass and woodwind instruments. The combined company, now known as Steinway Musical Instruments, Inc., is listed on the New York Stock Exchange under the symbol LVB. Steinway also owns a branch factory in Hamburg, Germany, which serves the world market outside of the Americas, and two major suppliers: the Herman Kluge company, Europe's largest maker of piano keys; and the O.S. Kelly company, the only remaining piano plate foundry in the U.S.

Steinway makes two types of vertical piano in three sizes: a 45" model 4510 studio, a 46½" model 1098 studio, and a 52" model K-52 upright. Models 4510 and 1098 are technically identical, with differences only in the cabinets: the former is in a period style for home use, the latter in an institutional cabinet for school use or less furniture-conscious home use. In all three models, the middle pedal operates a sostenuto mechanism. All Steinway verticals use a solid spruce soundboard, have no particleboard, and in many other ways are similar in design, materials, and quality of workmanship to Steinway grands. Actions are made by Renner. Model K-52 in ebony, and model 1098 in ebony, mahogany, and walnut, come with an adjustable artist bench, the others with a regular bench.

Technicians have always liked the performance of Steinway verticals, but used to complain that the studio models in particular were among the most difficult pianos to tune and would unexpectedly jump out of tune. In recent years, Steinway has made small design changes to alleviate this problem. The pianos are now mechanically more normal to tune and are stable, but an excess of false beats (tonal irregularities) still make the pianos at times difficult to tune.

Steinway makes six sizes of grand piano, two of which are new within the last several years. All ebony, mahogany, and walnut grand models come with an adjustable artist bench, the others with a regular bench.

The 5'1" model S is very good for a small grand, but has the usual limitations of any small piano and so is recommended only where space considerations are paramount. The 5'7" model M is a full six inches longer, but costs little more than the S. Historically one of Steinway's more popular models, it is found in living rooms across the country. Its medium size makes the tone in certain areas slightly less than perfect, but it's an excellent home instrument.

The 5'10½" model L has been replaced with the model O of the same size. Model O was first produced in 1902, but discontinued in 1924 in favor of the model L. Changes over time in both engineering and musical taste, as well as a desire to better synchronize the offerings of the New York factory with Hamburg (where the model O was never abandoned), seemed to dictate a return to the O. The main difference between the two models is in the shape of the tail—the L has a squared-off tail, the O a round tail—but this can also affect the soundboard and bridges and therefore the tone.

Reintroduction of the model O followed by one year the reintroduction of the legendary 6'2" model A. First offered in 1878 and discontinued in New York in 1945, the model A revolutionized piano making by featuring, for the first time, the radial rim bracing and one-piece bent rim construction now used in all Steinway grands. Over the years the model A has gone through several makeovers, each of slightly different size and scaling. The version being reintroduced was made in New York from 1896 to 1914 and is the same size as the model A that has been made at the Hamburg factory for more than a century. Models O and A are suitable for larger living rooms, and for many school and teaching situations.

The 6'10½" model B is the favorite of many piano technicians. It is the best choice for the serious pianist, recording or teaching studio, or small recital hall. Small design changes and other refinements to this model in recent years have brought a steady stream of accolades. The 8'11¾" model D, the concert grand, is the flagship of the Steinway line and the piano of choice for the overwhelming majority of concert pianists. It's too large for most places other than the concert stage.

Steinway uses excellent materials and construction techniques in the manufacture of its grands. The rims, both inner and outer, are made in one continuous bend from layers of maple, and the beams are of solid spruce. The keybed is of quartersawn spruce planks freely mortised together, and the keys are of Bavarian spruce. The pinblock consists of seven laminations of maple with successive grain orientations of 45 and 90 degrees. The soundboard is of solid Sitka spruce, the bridges are vertically laminated of maple with a solid maple cap, and all models have duplex scaling.

It is well known that Steinway's principal competition comes from used and rebuilt Steinways, many of which come in exotic veneers or have elaborately carved or customized "art cases." The company has responded by expanding its product line to include modern-day versions of these collector's items. The Crown Jewel Collection consists of the regular models in natural (non-ebonized) wood veneers, many of them exotic. They are finished in a semigloss that Steinway calls Satin Lustre. In addition to satin and semigloss finishes, all regular Steinway grands are also now available in polyester high-polish ebony, lacquer high-polish ebony, and polyester high-polish white.

Limited Edition models, issued at irregular intervals, are reproductions of turn-of-the-century designs, or pianos with artistic elements that make them unique. The newest Limited Edition model, honoring the 70th anniversary of the birth of John Lennon, is the Imagine Series, a white piano that incorporates artwork by Lennon, along with other design elements.

During the early 1900s, ownership of art-case Steinways became a symbol of wealth and culture. Steinway has resumed this tradition by regularly commissioning noted furniture designers to create new art-case designs, usually around a theme. For example, in 1999 Frank Pollaro designed an art case called Rhapsody to commemorate the 100th anniversary of the birth of George Gershwin. The piano featured a blue-dyed maple veneer adorned with more than 400 hand-cut mother-of-pearl stars and a gilded silver plate. Each year sees new art-case pianos from Steinway, and they are truly stunning.

As another way of capitalizing on the popularity of older Steinways, the company also operates at its factory the world's largest piano rebuilding facility for the restoration of older Steinways. *The Piano Book* contains a great deal of additional information on the purchase of older or restored Steinways. See also "Buying a Used or Restored Piano" in this publication.

The underlying excellence of the Steinway musical designs and the integrity of the construction process are the hallmarks of the Steinway piano. Steinway pianos at their best have the quintessential American piano sound: a powerful bass, a resonant midrange, and a singing treble with plenty of tonal color. Although other brands have some of these characteristics, it is perhaps the particular combination of harmonics that comprise the Steinway's tonal coloration that, more than anything else, distinguishes it from other brands and gives it its richness, depth, and power. The construction process creates a very durable and rigid framework that also contributes to the power of its sound.

Musical and cabinet detailing, such as factory voicing and regulation, and plate and cabinet cosmetics, are reasonable, but have traditionally lagged somewhat behind the company's European competitors in finesse. Over the last couple of years, however, the company has been making a determined effort to remedy this by paying close attention to many small details, and by applying lessons learned from its European operations. Examples include: rounding the edges and corners of satin ebony models so they will better hold the finish and not prematurely wear through; more careful woodworking on the bottom of the piano, and applying a clear coat of lacquer to the bottom instead of painting it to cover imperfections; protecting the case and plate during stringing and other manufacturing operations so they don't have to be touched up, often imperfectly, later on; additional time spent playing-in pianos during manufacture in order to naturally harden the hammers so they don't need quite so much chemical hardening and voicing in the field; and other improvements too numerous to mention here. (See discussion and photo essay on this subject in the **Spring 2011 issue of *Piano Buyer*.**)

Steinway pianos require more preparation by the dealer than most pianos in their class, but, as mentioned above, the factory preparation has greatly improved, so the work required by the dealer is no longer excessive. Still, some dealers are more conscientious than others, and I occasionally hear of piano buyers who "can't find a good Steinway." How much of this is due to inherent weaknesses in some pianos, how much to lack of dealer preparation, and how much to customer bias or groundless complaining is hard to tell. I suspect it is a little of each. Piano technicians who work on these pianos do sometimes remark that some seem to have more potential than others. Many dealers do just enough regulating and voicing to make the instruments acceptable to the average customer, but reserve the highest level of work for those situations where a fussy customer for one of the larger models is trying to decide between a few particular instruments. Most customers for a Steinway will probably find one they like on the sales floor. However, if you are a discriminating buyer who has had trouble finding a Steinway that suits your preferences, I recommend letting the salesperson know, as precisely as you can, what you're looking for. Give the salesperson some time to have a few instruments prepared for you before making a decision. It may also help to tactfully let the salesperson know that you are aware that other options are available to you in the market for high-end pianos.

By the way, customers seeking to purchase a model B or D Steinway who have not found the piano they are looking for at their local dealer can make arrangements with that dealer to visit the Steinway factory in New York, where a selection of the larger models is kept on hand for this purpose.

As mentioned earlier, Steinway owns a branch factory in Hamburg, Germany, established in 1880. The "fit and finish" (detailing) of the pianos at this factory is reputed to be better than at the one in New York, although pianists sometimes prefer the sound of the New York Steinway. Traditionally, the Hamburg factory has operated somewhat autonomously, but more recently the company has been synchronizing the two plants through technical exchanges, model changes, jointly built models, and materials that are shipped from New York to Hamburg. It's possible to special-order a Hamburg Steinway through an American Steinway dealer; or an enterprising American customer could travel to Europe, buy one there, and have it shipped back home.

In 2008 Steinway underwent a change in management, the first in 23 years. For the first time, the company's top executives have been recruited from its European operations rather than from America. It is speculated that this may signal a subtle change of direction with regard to quality issues, and may be one of the reasons that European quality standards are appearing to be more strictly applied to the American-made instruments.

Warranty: 5 years, parts and labor, to original purchaser.

STORY & CLARK

Story & Clark Piano Co.
269 Quaker Drive
Seneca, Pennsylvania 16346
800-247-6557
814-676-6683
www.qrsmusic.com

Owned by: QRS Music Technologies, Inc.

Pianos made by: various Asian manufacturers

Hampton Story began making pianos in 1857 and was joined by Melville Clark in 1884. The business settled in Grand Rapids, Michigan, in 1901, where it remained, under various owners, until about 1986. Around 1990, a new owner moved the company to its present location in Seneca, Pennsylvania. Over the years, pianos were manufactured under a number of different names, including, in recent years, Story & Clark, Hobart M. Cable,

Hampton, and Classic. In 1993 QRS Piano Rolls, Inc., now QRS Music Technologies, Inc., purchased Story & Clark. (Ironically, QRS itself was founded in 1901 by Melville Clark, of the Story & Clark Piano Co. of old.) QRS, historically the nation's major source of music rolls for traditional player pianos, now manufactures an electronic player-piano system, called PNOmation, that can be retrofitted into any piano (see "**Buying an Electronic Player-Piano System**").

Story & Clark offers two series of vertical and grand pianos, which are made to its specifications by various Asian manufacturers. The Heritage Series is a popularly priced line of verticals and grands with a Storytone II soundboard—Story & Clark's name for a veneer-laminated, all-spruce soundboard.

The Signature Series also comes in both vertical and grand models. These pianos feature premium Renner hammers, Röslau strings, maple and mahogany rims, solid brass hardware, Bolduc tapered soundboards of solid spruce, sand-cast plates, and advanced low-tension scales. The pianos have cabinet designs that offer lots of detail for the money and coordinate with major furniture trends. In spite of their beauty, the company says, these pianos are also appropriate for school and commercial applications.

In keeping with the tradition begun by Hampton Story and Melville Clark of integrating technology into pianos, all Story & Clark pianos are now equipped with an exclusive feature called PNOscan™. PNOscan is an optical sensor strip attached to the key frame directly under the keys. It senses the entire movement of each key so that it can precisely re-create every detail of an original performance, including the force, speed, and duration of each note played, without affecting the touch or response of the keyboard. The data captured by PNOscan is then transmitted through either a USB connection or MIDI output to a computer, general MIDI sound module, or other digital device. PNOscan and PNOmation are both HD MIDI ready. The addition of PNOscan to every Story & Clark acoustic piano gives customers the potential to have all the features of a digital piano. When combined with various accessories, PNOscan gives users the ability to learn, record, compose, practice in silence, and more. In addition, the ability of PNOscan to interface seamlessly with an iPad, tablet, or other computing device allows for their integration with the web-enabled PNOmation system recently introduced, with SilentPNO (a hybrid digital/acoustic piano), and with programs such as Music Minus One.

Warranty: 15 years, parts, and 5 years, labor, to original purchaser.

TAYLOR — See Brodmann.

VOGEL — See Schimmel.

VOSE & SONS — See Everett.

WALTER, CHARLES R.

Walter Piano Company, Inc.
25416 CR 6
Elkhart, Indiana 46514
574-266-0615
www.walterpiano.com

Charles Walter, an engineer, was head of Piano Design and Developmental Engineering at C.G. Conn in the 1960s, when Conn was doing important research in musical acoustics. In 1969 Walter bought the Janssen piano name from Conn, and continued to make Janssen pianos until 1981. In 1975 he brought out the Charles R. Walter line of consoles and studios, based on his continuing research in piano design. Walter began making grands in 1997.

The Walter Piano Company is fairly unique among U.S. piano manufacturers in that it is a family business, staffed by Charles and his wife, several of their grownup children, and various in-laws, in addition to unrelated production employees. The Walters say that each piano is inspected and signed by a member of their family before being shipped. Dealers and technicians report that doing business with the Walters is a pleasure in itself.

The Charles R. Walter line consists of 43" and 45" studio pianos in various decorator and institutional styles, and 5'9" and 6'4" grands. Note that both vertical models have full-size actions and therefore are studio pianos, not consoles, as I define those terms. In fact, they are identical pianos inside different cabinets. Walter calls the 43" model a console because of its furniture styling, but due to its larger action, it will outplay most real consoles on the market.

Although Mr. Walter is not oblivious to marketing concerns, his vertical piano bears the mark of being designed by an engineer who understands pianos and strives for quality. The pianos are built in a traditional manner, with heavy-duty, full-length spruce backposts; a solid spruce soundboard; and Delignit pinblock. Exceptionally long, thick keys that are individually lead-weighted provide a very even feel across the keyboard.

The scale design is well thought out and the bass sounds good most of the way to the bottom. The cabinetry is substantial, contains no particleboard, and is beautifully finished. Some of the fancy consoles in particular, such as the Queen Anne models, are strikingly beautiful. The pianos are well prepared at the factory and so need minimal preparation by the dealer.

The vertical pianos now use Renner actions, but a Chinese-made action is available as a lower-cost option, reducing the price of the piano by about $1,500. The Chinese parts are virtually indistinguishable from the Renner parts, but they make the action feel just slightly lighter due to differing spring tensions.

The Walter 5'9" and 6'4" grands were designed by Del Fandrich, one of the nation's most respected piano-design engineers. Both models have high-quality features such as a maple rim, Renner action, Kluge keys, Delignit pinblock, tapered solid spruce soundboard, and Abel hammers (Ronsen hammers in the 5' 9" model). The 5' 9" grand also has a number of innovative features: A portion of the inner rim and soundboard at the bass end of the piano are separated from the rest of the rim and allowed to "float." Less restricted in its movement, the soundboard can reproduce the fundamental frequencies of the lower bass notes more as a larger piano does. A special extension of the tenor bridge creates a smoother transition from bass to treble. Eight plate nosebolts increase plate stability, helping to reduce energy loss to the plate and thus increase sustain. Inverted half-agraffes embedded in the capo bar maintain string alignment and reduce unwanted string noise. The Walter grands are competently built and play very well.

Warranty: 12 years, parts and labor, transferable to future owners within the warranty period.

WEBER — See Young Chang.

WEINBACH — See Petrof.

WENDL & LUNG — See Feurich.

WYMAN

Wyman Piano Company
P.O. Box 506
Colusa, California 95932
513-543-0909
206-350-7912 (fax)
info@wymanpiano.com
www.wymanpiano.com

Pianos made by: Beijing Hsinghai Piano Group, Ltd., Beijing, China

Wyman Piano Company was created by experienced former Baldwin executives with more than 60 years of combined piano industry experience. Although a relatively new company, Wyman distribution has grown to include the U.K., Germany, and Japan, as well as the U.S.

The regular Wyman line consists of six vertical piano sizes and four grand models in a variety of cabinet styles and finishes. All are based on German scale designs and are manufactured in China by the Beijing Hsinghai Piano Group (see **Beijing Hsinghai**) at that company's new 1.2-million-square-foot factory.

Wyman offers the model CD2 player-piano system by Pianoforce, a new entrant in the field of player-piano systems (see **Pianoforce in the article on electronic player-piano systems**). The optional CD system features a unique stamped rail designed specifically for these pianos that, according to the company, allows a much lower profile than other player systems that use universal rails to fit any piano. These are installed at the Beijing factory.

Wyman says that its executives make frequent trips to the factory in Beijing to monitor manufacturing and inspect finished instruments.

Warranty: 10 years, parts and labor, transferable to future owners within the warranty period. Lifetime warranty on the soundboard.

XINGHAI — See Beijing Xinghai.

YAMAHA

including Cable-Nelson. See separate listing for Disklavier in "Buying an Electronic Player-Piano System."

Yamaha Corporation of America
P.O. Box 6600
Buena Park, California 90622
714-522-9011
800-854-1569
infostation@yamaha.com
www.yamaha.com

Pianos made by: Yamaha Corporation, Hamamatsu, Japan and other locations (see text)

Torakusu Yamaha, a watchmaker, developed Japan's first reed organ, and founded Yamaha Reed Organ Manufacturing in 1887. In 1899 Yamaha visited the U.S. to learn to build pianos. Within a couple of years he began making grand and vertical pianos under the name Nippon Gakki, Ltd. Beginning in the 1930s, Yamaha expanded its operations, first into other musical instruments, then into other products and services, such as sporting goods and furniture, and finally internationally.

Export of pianos to the U.S. began in earnest about 1960. In 1973 Yamaha acquired the Everett Piano Co., in South Haven, Michigan, and made both Yamaha and Everett pianos there until 1986. In that year, the company moved its piano manufacturing to a plant in Thomaston, Georgia, where it made Yamaha consoles, studios, and some grands until 2007, when a depressed piano market and foreign competition forced it to close its doors. Since then, the company has introduced new models, made in other Yamaha factories, to replace those formerly made in Thomaston.

Yamaha is probably the most international of the piano manufacturers. In addition to its factories in Japan, Yamaha has plants and partnerships with other companies in Germany (with Schimmel), Mexico, China, and Indonesia. Yamaha pianos sold in the U.S. are made in Japan, China, and Indonesia. In 2009, Yamaha closed its factories in England (with Kemble) and Taiwan. Models formerly made in those factories will in the future be produced in Yamaha's other Asian plants.

Yamaha's console line consists of 44" models M460 and M560 in furniture style (freestanding legs) with increasing levels of cabinet sophistication and price. All are internally the same and have a compressed action typical of a console, so the action will not be quite as responsive as with larger models.

The studio line consists of the popular 45" model P22 in institutional style (legs with toe blocks) with school-friendly cabinet; the furniture-style version P660; and the 47" model T118 in a less-expensive, traditional institutional-style cabinet. All are more or less the same internally, with a full-size action. All Yamaha verticals under 48" tall are now made in China.

The uprights are the very popular 48" model U1; the 48" model T121SC, made in China, with a slow-close fallboard; and the 52" model U3. Model U3 joins model U5 (now available only as a Super U model—see below) in the use of a "floating" soundboard—the soundboard is not completely attached to the back at the top, allowing it to vibrate a little more freely to enhance tonal performance. A new Super U series of uprights (YUS1, YUS3, and YUS5) have different hammers and get additional tuning and voicing at the factory, including voicing by machine to create a more consistent, more mellow tone. Model YUS5 uses German Röslau music wire instead of Yamaha wire, also for a mellower tone. This top-of-the-line 52" upright also has agraffes, duplex scaling, and a sostenuto pedal (all other Yamaha verticals have a practice/mute pedal). Except for the model T121SC, made in China, the uprights are all made in Japan.

Yamaha vertical pianos are very well made for a mass-produced piano. The taller uprights in particular are considered a "dream" to service by technicians, and are very much enjoyed by musicians. Sometimes the pianos can sound quite bright, though much less so now than in previous years. The current version of the model P22 school studio is said to have been redesigned to sound less bright and have an improved spectrum of tonal color. Double-striking of the hammer in the low tenor on a soft or incomplete stroke of the key is a problem occasionally mentioned in regard to Yamaha verticals by those who play with an especially soft touch. This tendency is a characteristic of the action design, the tradeoff being better-than-normal repetition for a vertical piano. It's possible that a technician can lessen this problem if necessary with careful adjustment, but at the risk of sacrificing some speed of repetition.

Yamaha grands come in five levels of sophistication and size. The Classic Collection consists of the 5' model GB1K, the 5'3" model GC1M, and the 5'8 model GC2. The GB1K has simplified case construction and cabinetry, no duplex scale, and the middle pedal operates a bass-sustain mechanism. It does have a soft-close fallboard. It is currently the only Yamaha grand sold in the U.S. that is made in Indonesia. The GC1M and GC2 have regular case construction, duplex scale, soft-close fallboards, and sostenuto pedal (the sostenuto was restored this year to the GC1, which was then renamed the GC1M), making them in most respects just like the models C1 and C2 (see below).

The Conservatory Collection consists of the 5'3" model C1, the 5'8" model C2, the 6'1" model C3, and the 6'7" model C5. The Conservatory Concert Collection comprises the 7' model C6 and the 7'6" model C7. Both collections have the advanced construction, scaling, and cabinetry mentioned above, including a true sostenuto pedal and a soft-close fallboard. Both now have vertically laminated bridges with maple or boxwood cap. The vertically laminated design is similar to that found in Steinways and other fine pianos, and is considered to give the bridges greater strength and resistance to cracking and better transmission of vibrational energy. All Conservatory grands have keytops of Ivorite™, Yamaha's ivory alternative.

Finally, the new CF Series Concert Grand Pianos (replacing the current Handcrafted Concert Collection) consist of the 9' model CFX (replacing the model CFIIIS), and the 6' 3" model CF4 and 7' model CF6 (replacing, in the U.S., the models S4B and S6B, which will remain available by special order only). The pianos in this collection are made in a separate factory to much higher standards and with some different materials. For example, they use maple and mahogany in the rim, which is made more rigid, for greater tonal power, than in the other collections; higher-grade soundboard material; a treble "bell" (as in the larger Steinways) to enhance treble tone; German strings, and hammer and scaling changes, for a more mellow tone; as well as the more advanced features of the other collections. The result is an instrument capable of greater dynamic range, tonal color, and sustain than the regular Yamahas. The new CF-series pianos have a thicker rim and more substantial structure than their predecessors for greater strength and tonal projection, and the method for developing the soundboard crown has been changed to allow the soundboard to vibrate more freely and with greater resonance. The models CF4 and CF6 have an open pinblock design reminiscent of some European pianos, which gives the tuner slightly greater control over the tuning pins. Yamaha says that the CF series represents 19 years of research and development conducted by its craftsmen, designers, and engineers. The Yamaha concert grand is endorsed and used by a number of notable musicians, including Michael Tilson Thomas, Chick Corea, and Elton John.

In Fall 2011, Yamaha introduced two new models —6' 1" model C3XA and 7' model C6XA—that incorporate some of the design elements of the limited-production CF series into the higher-production C-series pianos to create a similar sound. Features include a European spruce soundboard crowned using CF-series technology, a thicker rim and bracing, German music wire, additional time spent voicing, regulating, and tuning by very skilled craftsmen, and some cabinet design changes.

Other than the special grands just described, historically Yamaha grands have been a little on the percussive side and have been said not to "sing" as well as some more expensive pianos. The tone has been very clear and often bright, especially in the smaller grands, although the excessive brightness that once characterized Yamaha has seemed to be a thing of the past. The clarity and percussiveness are very attractive, but are sometimes said to be less well suited for classical music, which tends to require a singing tone and lush harmonic color. On the other hand, Yamaha is the piano of choice for jazz and popular music, which may value clarity and brightness more than the other qualities mentioned. More recently, however, Yamaha has been trying to move away from this image of a "bright" piano whose sound is limited to jazz. First with the larger grands, and more recently with the smaller ones, Yamaha has changed bridge construction and hammer density, and provided more custom voicing at the factory, to bring out a broader spectrum of tonal color in its pianos.

Both Yamaha's quality control and its warranty and technical service are legendary in the piano business. They are the standard against which every other company is measured. For general home and school use, piano technicians probably recommend Yamaha pianos more often than any other brand. Their precision, reliability, and performance make them a very good value for a consumer product.

Yamaha now makes a piano under the name Cable-Nelson. It is made in Yamaha's factory in Hangzhou, Zhejiang Province, China, southwest of Shanghai, where the company also makes guitars. The Cable-Nelson 45" model CN116 is identical in musical specifications to Yamaha's former model T116 (no longer available), except that the Cable-Nelson has a laminated soundboard, whereas all Yamaha pianos sold in the U.S. have a solid spruce soundboard. The Cable-Nelson model CN216 is a furniture-style version of the 116.

Cable-Nelson is the name of an old American piano maker whose roots can be traced back to 1903. Yamaha acquired the name when it bought the Everett Piano Company in 1973, and used the name in conjunction with Everett pianos until 1981.

There is a thriving market for used Yamahas. If you're considering buying a used Yamaha, please read "Should I Buy a Used, 'Gray Market' Yamaha or Kawai Piano?" on pages 176–177 of *The Piano Book*, and "**Buying a Used or Restored Piano**" in this publication.

To help its dealers overcome competition from "gray market" pianos, Yamaha has begun an Heirloom Assurance program that provides a five-year warranty on a used Yamaha piano less than 25 years old purchased from an authorized Yamaha dealer. See a Yamaha dealer for details.

Yamaha also makes electronic player pianos called Disklaviers, as well as a hybrid acoustic/digital instrument called Silent Piano (formerly called MIDIPiano), that account for a substantial percentage of the company's sales. These products are reviewed separately in the articles "**Buying an Electronic Player-Piano System**" and "**Hybrid Pianos.**"

Warranty: Yamaha and Cable-Nelson—10 years, parts and labor, to original purchaser.

YOUNG CHANG
including Weber and Albert Weber

Young Chang North America, Inc.
6000 Phyllis Drive
Cypress, California 90630
657-200-3470
800-874-2880
www.youngchang.com
www.weberpiano.com

Pianos made by: Young Chang Co., Ltd., Incheon, South Korea; and Tianjin, China

In 1956, three brothers—Jai-Young, Jai-Chang, and Jai-Sup Kim—founded Young Chang and began selling Yamaha pianos in Korea under an agreement with that Japanese firm. Korea was recovering from a devastating war, and only the wealthy could afford pianos. But the prospects were bright for economic development, and as a symbol of cultural refinement the piano was much coveted. In 1962 the brothers incorporated as Young Chang Akki Co., Ltd.

In 1964 Yamaha and Young Chang entered into an agreement in which Yamaha helped Young Chang set up a full-fledged manufacturing operation. Yamaha shipped partially completed pianos from Japan to the Young Chang factory in Incheon, South Korea, where Young Chang would perform final assembly work such as cabinet assembly, stringing, and action installation. This arrangement reduced high import duties. As time went by, Young Chang built more of the components, to the point where they were making virtually the entire piano. In 1975 the arrangement ended when Young Chang decided to expand domestically and internationally under its own brand name, thus becoming a competitor. Young Chang began exporting to the U.S. in the late 1970s, and established a North American distribution office in California in 1984. In addition to making pianos under its own name, Young Chang also made pianos for a time for Baldwin under the Wurlitzer

name, for Samsung under the Weber name, and private-label names for large dealer chains and distributors worldwide.

Weber & Co. was established in 1852 by Albert Weber, a German immigrant, and was one of the most prominent and highly respected American piano brands of the late 19th and early 20th centuries. During the consolidation of the American piano industry in the early 20th century, Weber became part of the Aeolian family of brands. Following Aeolian's demise in 1985, Young Chang acquired the Weber name.

In 1995, in response to rising Korean wages and to supply a growing Chinese domestic market, Young Chang built a 750,000-square-foot factory in Tianjin, China, and gradually began to move manufacturing operations there for some of its models. Today, the Tianjin facility produces Young Chang and Weber pianos, and components for the Albert Weber line, which is assembled in South Korea.

Hyundai Development Company, a Korean civil-engineering and construction firm, acquired Young Chang in 2006. The company says that Hyundai Development has brought the necessary capital for factory renovations and has instituted new advanced industrial quality-control systems.

In 2008 Young Chang hired noted American piano designer Delwin D. Fandrich to undertake a redesign of the entire Young Chang and Weber piano line. Highlights include extensively redesigned cast-iron plates, new string scales, and new rib designs. New directly-coupled bass bridges, along with unique "floating soundboard" configurations, improve soundboard mobility around the bass bridge for better bass tonal response. At the same time, a revised hammer-making process, in which the hammers are cold-pressed with less felt compression, provides for greater hammer resilience and improved tone, with less voicing required. Fandrich says that all of these features and processes contribute to his goal of building instruments with improved tonal balance and musicality, and provide opportunities to standardize manufacturing processes for better quality control. The new designs are being phased in gradually throughout 2011 and 2012.

Until recently, the Young Chang and Weber piano lines, each with three levels of quality, were identical: The top level instruments were the Young Chang Platinum Edition (models beginning with YP) and the Albert Weber (AW), made in Korea; the mid-level lines were the Young Chang Professional Artist (PE, PF, PG) and the Weber Sovereign (WSE, WSF, WSG), also made in Korea; and the entry-level lines were the Young Chang Traditional/Gold (T, AF, GS), the Weber Legend

(WLE, WLG), and, at one time, Bergmann, a name no longer used, all made in China.

Now, along with being redesigned by Mr. Fandrich, the multiple piano lines are being consolidated into just three lines: the Young Chang Y series (models beginning with Y) and Weber W series (W) are entry-level instruments made in China, and the Albert Weber (AW) is an upper-level line made in Korea. The Albert Weber grands have maple rims and Renner actions, and higher-quality hammer felt, soundboard material, and veneers (on wood-veneer models). The Y and W series grands have lauan rims and Young Chang actions. The Albert Weber verticals use slightly better materials than the other verticals for the cabinets, hardware, music wire, and keys, though in general the differences are smaller than with the grands. In addition, the Young Chang and Weber pianos will distinctly differ from each other: the Weber and Albert Weber lines with a low-tension scale and softer hammers, and the greater warmth and romantic tonal characteristics that often accompany that type of scale; the Young Chang line with a higher-tension scale and firmer hammers, and the greater brightness and stronger projection of a more modern sound.

Quality control in Young Chang's Korean factory has improved little by little over the years, and is now nearly as good as that in Japan. Most of the problems currently encountered are minor ones that can be cured by a good dealer make-ready and a little follow-up service, and the pianos hold up well in the field, even in institutions. The Albert Weber pianos, in particular, have great musical potential and respond well to expert voicing. Pianos from the factory in China, like other pianos from that country, have been uneven in quality, but in recent years have greatly improved. Young Chang says that Hyundai Development Group has upgraded the factories in both countries, and that the pianos made at the Tianjin factory are now on a par with those made in Korea.

Young Chang also owns Kurzweil Music Systems, a manufacturer of professional keyboards and home digital pianos, which it acquired in 1990.

Warranty: *New Fandrich-designed models:* Young Chang and Weber—10 years, parts and labor, to the original purchaser; Albert Weber—15 years, parts and labor, transferable to future owners during the warranty period, plus a lifetime warranty on parts to the original owner. *Older models:* Young Chang Platinum Edition and Albert Weber—15 years, parts and labor, transferable to future owners. Young Chang Professional Artist series and Weber Sovereign series—12 years, parts and labor, to original owner. Young Chang Gold/Traditional series and Weber Legend series—10 years, parts and labor, to original owner. Parts are further warranted for the lifetime of original owner. 🎹

[*Online Edition readers*: After reading the following introduction, please click below to access the free searchable database of acoustic piano models and prices.]

[Acoustic Piano Database]

This guide contains price information for nearly every brand, model, style, and finish of new piano that has regular distribution in the United States and, for the most part, Canada. Omitted are some marginal, local, or "stencil" brands (brands sold only by a single dealership). Prices are in U.S. dollars and are subject to change. Prices include an allowance for the approximate cost of freight from the U.S. warehouse to the dealer, and for a minimal amount of make-ready by the dealer. The prices cited in this edition were compiled in February 2012 and apply only to piano sales in the U.S. Prices in Canada are often very different due to differences in duty, freight, sales practices, and competition.

Note that the prices of European pianos vary with the value of the dollar against the euro. For this edition, the exchange rate used by most manufacturers was approximately €1 = $1.30–1.40. Prices of European pianos include import duties and estimated costs of airfreight (where applicable) to the dealer. However, actual costs will vary depending on the shipping method used, the port of entry, and other variables. Also keep in mind that the dealer may have purchased the piano at an exchange rate different from the current one.

Unless otherwise indicated, cabinet styles are assumed to be traditional in nature, with minimal embellishment and straight legs. Recognizable furniture styles are noted, and the manufacturer's own trademarked style name is used when an appropriate generic name could not be determined. Please see the section on "Furniture Style and Finish" in the article "**Piano-Buying Basics**" for descriptions or definitions of terms relating to style and finish.

"Size" refers to the height of a vertical or the length of a grand. These are the only dimensions that vary significantly and relate to the quality of the instrument. The height of a vertical piano is measured from the floor to the top of the piano. The length of a grand piano is measured from the very front (keyboard end) to the very back (tail end) with the lid closed.

About Prices

The subject of piano pricing is difficult, complicated, and controversial. One of the major problems is that piano dealers tend to prefer that list prices be as high as possible so they can still make a profit while appearing to give very generous discounts. Honesty about pricing is resisted.

But even knowing what is "honest" is a slippery business because many factors can have a dramatic effect on piano pricing. For one thing, different dealerships can pay very different wholesale prices for the same merchandise, depending on:

- the size of the dealership and how many pianos it agrees to purchase at one time or over a period of time
- whether the dealer pays cash or finances the purchase
- the degree to which the dealer buys manufacturer overstocks at bargain prices
- any special terms the dealership negotiates with the manufacturer or distributor.

In addition to these variations at the wholesale level, retail conditions also vary from dealer to dealer or from one geographic area to another, including:

- the general cost of doing business in the dealer's area
- the level of pre- and post-sale service the dealer provides
- the level of professionalism of the sales staff and the degree to which they are trained and compensated
- the ease of local comparison shopping by the consumer for a particular type of piano or at a particular price level.

Besides the variations between dealerships, the circumstances of each sale at any particular dealership can vary tremendously due to such things as:

- how long a particular piano has been sitting around unsold, racking up finance charges for the dealer
- the dealer's financial condition and need for cash at the moment

- competing sales events going on at other dealerships in the area
- whether or not the customer is trading in a used piano.

As difficult as it might be to come up with accurate price information, confusion and ignorance about pricing for such a high-ticket item is intolerable to the consumer, and can cause decision-making paralysis. I strongly believe that a reasonable amount of price information actually greases the wheels of commerce by giving the customer the peace of mind that allows him or her to make a purchase. In this guide I've tried to give a level of information about price that reasonably respects the interests of both buyer and seller, given the range of prices that can exist for any particular model.

Prices include a bench except where noted. (Even where a price doesn't include a bench, the dealer will almost always provide one and quote a price that includes it.) Most dealers will also include delivery and one or two tunings in the home, but these are optional and a matter of agreement between you and the dealer. Prices do not include sales tax.

In this guide, two prices are given for each model: Manufacturer's Suggested Retail Price (MSRP) and Suggested Maximum Price (SMP).

Manufacturer's Suggested Retail Price (MSRP)

The MSRP is a price provided by the manufacturer or distributor and designed as a starting point from which dealers are expected to discount. I include it here for reference purposes—only rarely does a customer pay this price. The MSRP is usually figured as a multiple of the wholesale price, but the specific multiple used differs from company to company. **For that reason, it's fruitless to compare prices of different brands by comparing discounts from the MSRP.** To see why, consider the following scenario:

Manufacturer A sells brand A through its dealer A. The wholesale price to the dealer is $1,000, but for the purpose of setting the MSRP, the manufacturer doubles the wholesale price and sets the MSRP at $2,000. Dealer A offers a 25 percent discount off the MSRP, for a "street price" of $1,500.

Manufacturer B sells brand B through its dealer B. The wholesale price to the dealer is also $1,000, but manufacturer B triples the wholesale price and sets the MSRP at $3,000. Dealer B offers a generous 50 percent discount, for a street price of, again, $1,500.

Although the street price is the same for both pianos, a customer shopping at both stores and knowing nothing about the wholesale price or how the MSRPs are computed, is likely to come away with the impression that brand B, with a discount of 50 percent off $3,000, is a more "valuable" piano and a better deal than brand A, with a discount of 25 percent off $2,000. Other factors aside, which dealer do you think will get the sale? It's important to note that there is nothing about brand B that makes it deserving of a higher MSRP than brand A—how to compute the MSRP is essentially a marketing decision on the part of the manufacturer.

Because of the deceptive manner in which MSRPs are so often used, some manufacturers no longer provide them. In those cases, I've left the MSRP column blank.

Suggested Maximum Price (SMP)

The Suggested Maximum Price (SMP) is a price I've created, based on a profit margin that I've uniformly applied to published wholesale prices. (Where the published wholesale price is believed to be bogus, as is sometimes the case, I've made a reasonable attempt to find out what a typical small dealer actually pays for the piano, and use that price in place of the published one.) Because in the SMP, unlike in the MSRP, the same profit margin is applied to all brands, the SMP can be used as a "benchmark" price for the purpose of comparing brands and offers. The specific profit margin I've chosen for the SMP is one that dealers often try—but rarely manage—to attain. Also included in the SMP, in most cases, are allowances for duty (where applicable), freight charges, and a minimal amount of make-ready by the dealer. Although the SMP is my creation, it's a reasonable estimate of the **maximum** price you should realistically expect to pay. However, **most sales actually take place at a discount to the SMP**, as discussed below.

Actual Selling or "Street" Price

As you should know by now from reading this publication, most dealers of new pianos are willing—and expect—to negotiate. Only a handful of dealers have non-negotiable prices. For more information on negotiating, please see **"Negotiating Price and Trade-Ins"** in the article **"Piano Buying Basics."** *The Piano Book* also gives advice about negotiating tactics.

How good a deal you can negotiate will vary, depending on the many factors listed earlier. But in order to make a budget, or to know which pianos are within your budget, or just to feel comfortable enough to actually make a purchase, you need some idea of what is considered normal in the industry. In most cases, discounts from the Suggested Maximum Price range from 10 to 30 percent. For budgeting purposes only, I suggest figuring a discount of about 15 or 20 percent. This will probably bring you within about 10 percent, one way or the other, of the final negotiated price. Important exception: Discounts on Steinway pianos generally range from 0 to 10 percent. For your convenience in figuring the effects of various discounts, a discount calculator is included in the model and price database, accessible through the electronic edition of this publication.

There is no single "fair" or "right" price that can be applied to every purchase. The only fair price is that which the buyer and seller agree on. It's understandable that you would like to pay as little as possible, but remember that piano shopping is not just about chasing the lowest price. Be sure you are getting the instrument that best suits your needs and preferences, and that the dealer is committed to providing the appropriate level of pre- and post-sale service.

For more information about shopping for a new piano and how to save money, please see pages 60–75 in *The Piano Book, Fourth Edition.*

[*Online Edition readers:* Click below to access the free searchable database of acoustic piano models and prices.]

[Acoustic Piano Database]

Model	Feet	Inches	Description	MSRP*	SMP*
ALTENBURG					
Verticals					
AV108		42.5	Continental Polished Ebony	5,000	3,690
AV108		42.5	Continental Polished Cherry/Mahogany	5,075	3,750
AV110		43	Classic Polished Ebony	5,500	4,090
AV110		43	Classic Polished Cherry/Mahogany	5,575	4,150
AV110		43	American Country Oak/Sable Brown Mahogany	6,300	4,690
AV110		43	French Provincial Cherry/Country French Oak	6,425	4,790
AV115		45	Polished Ebony	5,763	4,290
AV115		45	Polished Cherry/Mahogany	5,735	4,350
AV118		46	Institutional Polished Ebony	6,576	4,890
AV118		46	Institutional Satin Walnut	6,635	5,190
AV120		48	Polished Ebony	6,300	4,890
AV120		48	Polished Mahogany	6,375	4,950
AV132		52	Classic Polished Ebony	7,750	5,990
Grands					
AG145	4	9	Polished Ebony	11,563	8,790
AG145	4	9	Polished Mahogany/Cherry/White	12,088	9,190
AG160	5	3	Polished Ebony	13,975	10,780
AG160	5	3	Polished Mahogany/Cherry/White	14,475	11,180
AG170	5	7	Polished Ebony	15,550	11,990
AG170	5	7	Polished Mahogany/Cherry/White	16,075	12,390
AG185	6	1	Polished Ebony	18,188	13,790
AG185	6	1	Polished Mahogany/Cherry/White	18,725	14,190
			With Round or Curved Legs, add		1,000
			Satin Ebony/Mahogany/Cherry, add		800
ASTIN-WEIGHT					
Verticals					
U-500		50	Oiled Oak	17,180	16,180
U-500		50	Santa Fe Oiled Oak	18,580	17,580
U-500		50	Lacquer Oak	17,580	16,580
U-500		50	Oiled Walnut	17,780	16,780
U-500		50	Lacquer Walnut	18,180	17,180
Grands					
	5	9	Satin Ebony	39,500	38,500

*See pricing explanation on page 203.

Model	Feet	Inches	Description	MSRP*	SMP*
BALDWIN					
Verticals					
B242		42	Satin Cherry/Walnut	8,050	5,590
B342		43	Designer French Satin Cherry	8,750	5,990
B442		43	Designer Satin Mahogany	8,750	5,990
BJ120		46	Polished Ebony	6,995	4,990
BJ120		46	Polished Rosewood	7,295	5,190
BH122		47	Polished Ebony	7,695	5,390
B243		47	Satin Ebony/Walnut (school piano)	8,750	5,990
B247		47	Polished Ebony	8,750	5,990
BH125		49	Polished Ebony	8,750	5,990
B49		49	Polished Ebony w/sostenuto	9,795	6,590
B252		52	Satin Ebony	11,195	7,390
B252E		52	Euro-style Polished Ebony	11,195	7,390
China Grands					
BD146	4	8	Satin Ebony	15,750	9,990
BD146	4	8	Polished Ebony	15,395	9,790
BD146	4	8	Polished Mahogany/White	16,100	10,190
BD152	5		Satin Ebony	16,795	10,590
BD152	5		Polished Ebony	16,450	10,390
BD152	5		Polished Mahogany/White	17,150	10,790
BD165	5	5	Satin Ebony	17,850	11,190
BD165	5	5	Polished Ebony	17,495	10,990
BD165	5	5	Polished Mahogany/White	18,195	11,390
BD185	6	1	Satin Ebony	19,950	12,390
BD185	6	1	Polished Ebony	19,595	12,190
BD185	6	1	Polished Mahogany/White	20,295	12,590
BD215	7		Polished Ebony	51,450	30,390
BD215	7		Polished White	54,950	32,390
BD275	9		Polished Ebony	104,995	60,990
U.S. Grands					
M1	5	2	Satin Ebony	43,800	30,200
M1	5	2	Polished Ebony	44,100	30,400
M1	5	2	Satin and Polished Mahogany	44,700	30,800
225E	5	2	French Provincial Satin Cherry	43,500	30,000
R1	5	8	Satin Ebony	45,600	31,400
R1	5	8	Polished Ebony	48,300	33,200
R1	5	8	Satin Mahogany	48,600	33,400
R1	5	8	Satin Walnut	45,450	31,300
R1	5	8	Polished Walnut	48,750	33,500
226E	5	8	French Provincial Satin Cherry	49,500	34,000
226E	5	8	French Provincial Polished Cherry	53,400	36,600
L1	6	3	Satin Ebony	48,480	33,320
L1	6	3	Polished Ebony	50,700	34,800
L1	6	3	Satin Mahogany	47,190	32,460
L1	6	3	Satin Walnut	47,640	32,760
SF10E	7		Satin Ebony	67,584	46,056
SF10E	7		Polished Ebony	76,500	52,000

*See pricing explanation on page 203.

PIANOBUYER.COM

Model	Feet	Inches	Description	MSRP*	SMP*

BECHSTEIN, (C.)

Models beginning with "A" say only "Bechstein" on the fallboard. Others say "C. Bechstein."

Bechstein Verticals

Model	Feet	Inches	Description	MSRP*	SMP*
A112		44	Satin and Polished Ebony	18,100	16,833
A3		45.5	Polished Ebony	18,700	18,700
A3		45.5	Satin Mahogany/Walnut/Cherry	18,700	18,700
A3		45.5	Polished Mahogany/Walnut/Cherry/White	19,900	19,900
A3		45.5	Satin Alder/Beech	18,700	18,700
A2		47.5	Polished Ebony	19,900	19,900
A2		47.5	Satin Mahogany/Walnut/Cherry	19,900	19,900
A2		47.5	Polished Mahogany/Walnut/Cherry/White	21,200	21,200
A2		47.5	Satin Alder	19,900	19,900
A1		49.5	Polished Ebony	21,200	21,200
A1		49.5	Satin Mahogany/Walnut/Cherry	21,200	21,200
A1		49.5	Polished Mahogany/Walnut/Cherry/White	23,000	23,000

C. Bechstein Verticals

Model	Feet	Inches	Description	MSRP*	SMP*
M116		45.5	Polished Ebony	22,800	22,800
M116K		45.5	Polished Ebony	23,400	23,400
Classic 124		49	Polished Ebony	35,000	35,000
Classic 124		49	Satin Walnut/Mahogany/Cherry	35,000	35,000
Classic 124		49	Polished Walnut/Mahogany/Cherry	36,600	36,600
Elegance 124		49	Polished Ebony	37,400	37,400
Elegance 124		49	Satin Walnut/Cherry	37,400	37,400
Elegance 124		49	Polished Walnut/Mahogany/Cherry	41,600	41,600
Concert 8		51.5	Polished Ebony	52,800	52,800
Concert 8		51.5	Satin Walnut/Mahogany/Cherry	52,800	52,800
Concert 8		51.5	Polished Walnut/Mahogany	55,000	55,000
Concert 8		51.5	Special Woods	62,400	62,400

Bechstein Grands

Model	Feet	Inches	Description	MSRP*	SMP*
A160	5	3	Polished Ebony	51,400	51,400
A160	5	3	Polished Mahogany	54,800	54,800
A160	5	3	Polished White	58,200	58,200
A160	5	3	Special Woods	69,600	69,600
A190	6	3	Polished Ebony	61,400	61,400
A190	6	3	Polished Mahogany	64,800	64,800
A190	6	3	Polished White	64,800	64,800
A190	6	3	Special Woods	79,600	79,600
A208	6	8	Polished Ebony	65,800	65,800
A208	6	8	Polished Mahogany	69,000	69,000
A208	6	8	Polished White	72,000	72,000
A228	7	5	Polished Ebony	75,400	75,400

C. Bechstein Grands

Model	Feet	Inches	Description	MSRP*	SMP*
L167	5	6	Satin and Polished Ebony	93,600	93,600
L167	5	6	Satin Mahogany/Walnut/Cherry	93,600	93,600
L167	5	6	Polished Mahogany/Walnut/Cherry/White	100,000	100,000
L167	5	6	Special Woods	112,800	112,800
MP192	6	4	Satin and Polished Ebony	108,600	108,600
MP192	6	4	Satin Mahogany/Walnut/Cherry	108,600	108,600
MP192	6	4	Polished Mahogany/Walnut/Cherry/White	115,000	115,000
MP192	6	4	Special Woods	127,600	127,600
L, MP			Classic Style, add'l	16,600	16,600
L, MP			Chippendale, add'l	15,300	15,300
B212	7		Satin and Polished Ebony	130,000	130,000
C234	7	7	Polished Ebony	163,000	163,000
B, C			Classic Style, add'l	18,800	18,800
D282	9	2	Polished Ebony	212,600	212,600

*See pricing explanation on page 203.

Model	Feet	Inches	Description	MSRP*	SMP*

BLÜTHNER

Prices do not include bench.

Verticals

Model	Feet	Inches	Description	MSRP*	SMP*
D		45	Satin and Polished Ebony	28,455	26,362
D		45	Satin and Polished White	29,737	27,504
C		46	Satin and Polished Ebony	30,084	27,814
C		46	Satin and Polished Walnut	31,825	29,366
C		46	Satin and Polished Mahogany	31,517	29,092
C		46	Satin and Polished Cherry	31,676	29,232
C		46	Satin and Polished White	31,589	29,156
C		46	Satin and Polished Bubinga/Yew/Rosewood/Macassar	33,588	30,938
C		46	Saxony Polished Pyramid Mahogany	39,109	35,858
C		46	Polished Burl Walnut/Camphor	39,488	36,196
A		49	Satin and Polished Ebony	38,321	35,156
A		49	Satin and Polished Walnut	40,533	37,128
A		49	Satin and Polished Mahogany	40,149	36,786
A		49	Satin and Polished Cherry	40,342	36,956
A		49	Satin and Polished White	40,233	36,860
A		49	Satin and Polished Bubinga/Yew/Rosewood/Macassar	42,777	39,128
A		49	Saxony Polished Pyramid Mahogany	49,810	45,396
A		49	Polished Burl Walnut/Camphor	50,293	45,826
B		52	Satin and Polished Ebony	43,749	39,994
B		52	Satin and Polished Walnut	46,279	42,250
B		52	Satin and Polished Mahogany	45,842	41,860
B		52	Satin and Polished Cherry	46,057	42,052
B		52	Satin and Polished White	45,937	41,944
B		52	Satin and Polished Bubinga/Yew/Rosewood/Macassar	48,839	44,532
B		52	Saxony Polished Pyramid Mahogany	56,877	51,694
B		52	Polished Burl Walnut/Camphor	57,419	52,178
S		57	Satin and Polished Ebony	55,649	50,600
Verticals			Sostenuto pedal, add	2,063	2,063

Grands

Model	Feet	Inches	Description	MSRP*	SMP*
11	5	1	Satin and Polished Ebony	77,588	70,154
11	5	1	Satin and Polished Walnut	82,073	74,152
11	5	1	Satin and Polished Mahogany	81,292	73,456
11	5	1	Satin and Polished Cherry	81,683	73,804
11	5	1	Satin and Polished White	81,465	73,610
11	5	1	Satin and Polished Bubinga/Yew/Rosewood/Macassar	86,618	78,204
11	5	1	Saxony Polished Pyramid Mahogany	100,862	90,898
11	5	1	Polished Burl Walnut/Camphor	101,832	91,764
11	5	1	"President" Polished Ebony	85,346	77,068
11	5	1	"President" Polished Mahogany	88,762	80,114
11	5	1	"President" Polished Walnut	89,610	80,870
11	5	1	"President" Polished Bubinga	90,507	81,668
11	5	1	Louis XVI Satin and Polished Ebony	89,214	80,526
11	5	1	Louis XVI Satin and Polished Mahogany	93,686	84,504
11	5	1	Louis XVI Satin and Polished Walnut	92,793	83,706
11	5	1	"Nicolas II" Satin Walnut with Burl Inlay	104,743	94,358
11	5	1	Louis XIV Rococo Satin White with Gold	112,506	101,276
11	5	1	"Alexandra" Polished Ebony	86,896	78,450
11	5	1	"Alexandra" Polished Mahogany	91,242	82,324
11	5	1	"Alexandra" Polished Walnut	90,373	81,550
11	5	1	Julius Blüthner Edition	104,743	94,358
10	5	5	Satin and Polished Ebony	89,442	80,720
10	5	5	Satin and Polished Walnut	94,614	85,330
10	5	5	Satin and Polished Mahogany	93,710	84,524
10	5	5	Satin and Polished Cherry	94,164	84,928
10	5	5	Satin and Polished White	93,913	84,706

*See pricing explanation on page 203.

PIANOBUYER.COM

Model	Feet	Inches	Description	MSRP*	SMP*
BLÜTHNER (continued)					
10	5	5	Satin and Polished Bubinga/Yew/Rosewood/Macassar	99,850	89,996
10	5	5	Saxony Polished Pyramid Mahogany	112,185	100,990
10	5	5	Polished Burl Walnut/Camphor	113,627	102,276
10	5	5	"President" Polished Ebony	98,385	88,690
10	5	5	"President" Polished Mahogany	102,320	92,200
10	5	5	"President" Polished Walnut	103,306	93,078
10	5	5	"President" Polished Bubinga	108,221	97,458
10	5	5	"Senator" French Satin Walnut with Leather	107,328	96,662
10	5	5	"Senator" Jacaranda Satin Rosewood w/Leather	114,486	103,042
10	5	5	Louis XVI Satin and Polished Ebony	102,857	92,678
10	5	5	Louis XVI Satin and Polished Mahogany	108,001	97,262
10	5	5	Louis XVI Satin and Polished Walnut	106,973	96,346
10	5	5	"Kaiser Wilhelm II" Polished Ebony	103,754	93,476
10	5	5	"Kaiser Wilhelm II" Polished Mahogany	107,903	97,174
10	5	5	"Kaiser Wilhelm II" Polished Walnut	108,941	98,100
10	5	5	"Kaiser Wilhelm II" Polished Cherry	108,419	97,634
10	5	5	"Ambassador" Satin East Indian Rosewood	120,743	108,618
10	5	5	"Ambassador" Satin Walnut	111,800	100,648
10	5	5	"Nicolas II" Satin Walnut with Burl Inlay	120,743	108,618
10	5	5	Louis XIV Rococo Satin White with Gold	129,695	116,598
10	5	5	"Alexandra" Polished Ebony	100,172	90,284
10	5	5	"Alexandra" Polished Mahogany	105,182	94,750
10	5	5	"Alexandra" Polished Walnut	104,180	93,856
10	5	5	Julius Blüthner Edition	115,390	103,848
6	6	3	Satin and Polished Ebony	97,551	87,948
6	6	3	Satin and Polished Walnut	103,194	92,976
6	6	3	Satin and Polished Mahogany	102,210	92,100
6	6	3	Satin and Polished Cherry	102,707	92,540
6	6	3	Satin and Polished White	102,430	92,296
6	6	3	Satin and Polished Bubinga/Yew/Rosewood/Macassar	108,910	98,072
6	6	3	Saxony Polished Pyramid Mahogany	123,403	110,990
6	6	3	Polished Burl Walnut/Camphor	124,846	112,276
6	6	3	"President" Polished Ebony	107,308	96,644
6	6	3	"President" Polished Mahogany	111,599	100,468
6	6	3	"President" Polished Walnut	112,665	101,420
6	6	3	"President" Polished Bubinga	118,035	106,206
6	6	3	"Senator" French Satin Walnut with Leather	117,057	105,334
6	6	3	"Senator" Jacaranda Satin Rosewood w/Leather	124,869	112,296
6	6	3	Louis XVI Satin and Polished Ebony	112,184	100,990
6	6	3	Louis XVI Satin and Polished Mahogany	117,796	105,992
6	6	3	Louis XVI Satin and Polished Walnut	116,671	104,990
6	6	3	"Kaiser Wilhelm II" Polished Ebony	113,162	101,862
6	6	3	"Kaiser Wilhelm II" Polished Mahogany	117,683	105,892
6	6	3	"Kaiser Wilhelm II" Polished Walnut	118,820	106,904
6	6	3	"Kaiser Wilhelm II" Polished Cherry	118,255	106,402
6	6	3	"Ambassador" Satin East Indian Rosewood	131,696	118,380
6	6	3	"Ambassador" Satin Walnut	121,938	109,684
6	6	3	"Nicolas II" Satin Walnut with Burl Inlay	131,696	118,380
6	6	3	Louis XIV Rococo Satin White with Gold	141,450	127,076
6	6	3	"Alexandra" Polished Ebony	109,256	98,380
6	6	3	"Alexandra" Polished Mahogany	114,723	103,254
6	6	3	"Alexandra" Polished Walnut	113,627	102,276
6	6	3	Julius Blüthner Edition	126,609	113,846
6	6	3	Jubilee Edition Plate, add	6,059	5,400
4	6	10	Satin and Polished Ebony	115,699	104,124
4	6	10	Satin and Polished Walnut	122,387	110,084
4	6	10	Satin and Polished Mahogany	121,224	109,048
4	6	10	Satin and Polished Cherry	121,806	109,566

*See pricing explanation on page 203.

Model	Feet	Inches	Description	MSRP*	SMP*
BLÜTHNER (continued)					
4	6	10	Satin and Polished White	121,480	109,276
4	6	10	Satin and Polished Bubinga/Yew/Rosewood/Macassar	129,170	116,130
4	6	10	Saxony Polished Pyramid Mahogany	144,622	129,902
4	6	10	Polished Burl Walnut/Camphor	145,840	130,988
4	6	10	"President" Polished Ebony	127,270	114,436
4	6	10	"President" Polished Mahogany	132,363	118,976
4	6	10	"President" Polished Walnut	133,634	120,108
4	6	10	"President" Polished Bubinga	139,998	125,780
4	6	10	"Senator" French Satin Walnut with Leather	138,841	124,750
4	6	10	"Senator" Jacaranda Satin Rosewood w/Leather	148,100	133,002
4	6	10	Louis XVI Satin and Polished Ebony	133,060	119,596
4	6	10	Louis XVI Satin and Polished Mahogany	139,713	125,526
4	6	10	Louis XVI Satin and Polished Walnut	138,372	124,332
4	6	10	"Kaiser Wilhelm II" Polished Ebony	134,212	120,624
4	6	10	"Kaiser Wilhelm II" Polished Mahogany	139,588	125,414
4	6	10	"Kaiser Wilhelm II" Polished Walnut	140,927	126,610
4	6	10	"Kaiser Wilhelm II" Polished Cherry	140,254	126,010
4	6	10	"Ambassador" Satin East Indian Rosewood	152,251	136,702
4	6	10	"Ambassador" Satin Walnut	147,443	132,416
4	6	10	"Nicolas II" Satin Walnut with Burl Inlay	156,193	140,216
4	6	10	Louis XIV Rococo Satin White with Gold	167,770	150,534
4	6	10	"Alexandra" Polished Ebony	129,586	116,502
4	6	10	"Alexandra" Polished Mahogany	136,065	122,276
4	6	10	"Alexandra" Polished Walnut	134,767	121,118
4	6	10	Julius Blüthner Edition	149,046	133,844
2	7	8	Satin and Polished Ebony	129,314	116,258
2	7	8	Satin and Polished Walnut	136,800	122,930
2	7	8	Satin and Polished Mahogany	135,489	121,762
2	7	8	Satin and Polished Cherry	136,144	122,346
2	7	8	Satin and Polished White	136,800	122,930
2	7	8	Satin and Polished Bubinga/Yew/Rosewood/Macassar	144,364	129,674
2	7	8	Saxony Polished Pyramid Mahogany	164,120	147,280
2	7	8	Polished Burl Walnut/Camphor	165,584	148,586
2	7	8	"President" Polished Ebony	144,364	129,674
2	7	8	"President" Polished Mahogany	150,144	134,824
2	7	8	"President" Polished Walnut	151,590	136,114
2	7	8	"President" Polished Bubinga	158,803	142,542
2	7	8	"Senator" French Satin Walnut with Leather	157,492	141,374
2	7	8	"Senator" Jacaranda Satin Rosewood w/Leather	167,989	150,730
2	7	8	Louis XVI Satin and Polished Ebony	150,927	135,522
2	7	8	Louis XVI Satin and Polished Mahogany	158,476	142,250
2	7	8	Louis XVI Satin and Polished Walnut	156,963	140,902
2	7	8	"Kaiser Wilhelm II" Polished Ebony	152,245	136,696
2	7	8	"Kaiser Wilhelm II" Polished Mahogany	158,336	142,126
2	7	8	"Kaiser Wilhelm II" Polished Walnut	159,853	143,478
2	7	8	"Kaiser Wilhelm II" Polished Cherry	159,096	142,804
2	7	8	"Ambassador" Satin East Indian Rosewood	170,642	153,094
2	7	8	"Ambassador" Satin Walnut	165,909	148,876
2	7	8	"Nicolas II" Satin Walnut with Burl Inlay	177,180	158,920
2	7	8	Louis XIV Rococo Satin White with Gold	190,306	170,622
2	7	8	"Alexandra" Polished Ebony	146,989	132,012
2	7	8	"Alexandra" Polished Mahogany	154,341	138,566
2	7	8	"Alexandra" Polished Walnut	152,878	137,260
2	7	8	Julius Blüthner Edition	169,162	151,776
2	7	8	Queen Victoria JB Edition Polished Rosewood	204,601	183,362
1	9	2	Satin and Polished Ebony	166,935	149,790
1	9	2	Satin and Polished Walnut	175,282	157,228
1	9	2	Satin and Polished Mahogany	173,613	155,742

*See pricing explanation on page 203.

PIANOBUYER.COM

Model	Feet	Inches	Description	MSRP*	SMP*
BLÜTHNER (continued)					
1	9	2	Satin and Polished Cherry	174,450	156,488
1	9	2	Satin and Polished White	175,282	157,228
1	9	2	Satin and Polished Bubinga/Yew/Rosewood/Macassar	183,629	164,668
1	9	2	Saxony Polished Pyramid Mahogany	217,011	194,422
1	9	2	Polished Burl Walnut/Camphor	219,099	196,284
1	9	2	"President" Polished Ebony	186,161	166,926
1	9	2	"President" Polished Mahogany	193,604	173,560
1	9	2	"President" Polished Walnut	195,467	175,220
1	9	2	"President" Polished Bubinga	204,773	183,516
1	9	2	"Kaiser Wilhelm II" Polished Ebony	196,310	175,972
1	9	2	"Kaiser Wilhelm II" Polished Mahogany	204,168	182,976
1	9	2	"Kaiser Wilhelm II" Polished Walnut	206,128	184,724
1	9	2	"Kaiser Wilhelm II" Polished Cherry	205,156	183,856
1	9	2	"Ambassador" Satin East Indian Rosewood	228,474	204,640
1	9	2	"Ambassador" Satin Walnut	211,545	189,552
1	9	2	"Nicolas II" Satin Walnut with Burl Inlay	228,474	204,640
1	9	2	Julius Blüthner Edition	225,366	201,870
1	9	2	Queen Victoria JB Edition Polished Rosewood	255,118	228,388

BOHEMIA

Verticals

Model	Feet	Inches	Description	MSRP*	SMP*
R114		44.8	Polished Ebony	11,900	11,900
R114		44.8	Polished Mahogany/Walnut	12,840	12,840
R121		47.7	Polished Ebony	13,160	13,160
R121		47.7	Polished Mahogany/Walnut	13,940	13,940
R126		49.6	Polished Ebony	13,900	13,900
R132		52	Polished Ebony	15,900	15,900

Grands

Model	Feet	Inches	Description	MSRP*	SMP*
BT160	5	3	Polished Ebony	33,900	33,900
BT160	5	3	Polished Mahogany/Walnut	37,600	37,600
BT175	5	9	Polished Ebony	37,600	37,600
BT175	5	9	Polished Mahogany/Walnut	40,760	40,760
BT185	6	1	Polished Ebony	39,900	39,900
225R	7	4	Smetana Polished Ebony (Renner action)		53,520

BÖSENDORFER

Verticals

Model	Feet	Inches	Description	MSRP*	SMP*
130		52	Satin and Polished Ebony	61,599	58,300
130		52	Satin and Polished White, other colors	67,799	60,998
130		52	Polished, Satin, Open-pore: Walnut, Cherry, Mahogany, Pomele, Bubinga, Wenge	69,499	62,998
130		52	Polished , Satin, Open-pore: Pyramid Mahogany, Amboyna, Santos Rosewood, Burl Walnut, Birdseye Maple, Yew, Macassar, Yatoba, Aruba	72,799	66,100

Grands

Model	Feet	Inches	Description	MSRP*	SMP*
155	5	1	Satin and Polished Ebony	99,999	88,998
155	5	1	Satin and Polished White, other colors	110,899	101,598
155	5	1	Polished, Satin, Open-pore: Walnut, Cherry, Mahogany, Pomele, Bubinga, Wenge	116,299	104,798
155	5	1	Polished, Satin, Open-pore: Pyramid Mahogany, Amboyna, Santos Rosewood, Burl Walnut, Birdseye Maple, Yew, Macassar, Yatoba, Aruba	120,999	107,798
170CS	5	8	"Conservatory" Satin Ebony	93,399	84,998
170	5	8	Satin and Polished Ebony	103,699	99,598

*See pricing explanation on page 203.

Model	Feet	Inches	Description	MSRP*	SMP*
BÖSENDORFER (continued)					
170	5	8	Satin and Polished White, other colors	115,299	108,998
170	5	8	Polished, Satin, Open-pore: Walnut, Cherry, Mahogany, Pomele, Bubinga, Wenge	119,299	110,198
170	5	8	Polished, Satin, Open-pore: Pyramid Mahogany, Amboyna, Santos Rosewood, Burl Walnut, Birdseye Maple, Yew, Macassar, Yatoba, Aruba	124,399	115,198
170	5	8	"Chrome" Satin and Polished Ebony	131,234	108,930
170	5	8	"Edge"	131,234	108,930
170	5	8	"Johann Strauss"/"Franz Schubert"/Liszt Anniversary: Satin and Polished Ebony	131,234	104,960
170	5	8	"Johann Strauss"/"Franz Schubert": other finish	149,781	124,194
170	5	8	"Liszt"	149,781	124,194
170	5	8	"Senator"	142,320	116,404
170	5	8	Baroque/Louis XVI	160,201	132,754
170	5	8	"Chopin"	171,058	141,684
170	5	8	"Vienna"	186,372	154,278
170	5	8	"Artisan" Satin and Polished	216,330	178,916
185	6	1	"Conservatory" Satin Ebony	98,399	86,198
185	6	1	Satin and Polished Ebony	107,999	102,198
185	6	1	Satin and Polished White, other colors	119,899	110,998
185	6	1	Polished, Satin, Open-pore: Walnut, Cherry, Mahogany, Pomele, Bubinga, Wenge	124,199	112,998
185	6	1	Polished, Satin, Open-pore: Pyramid Mahogany, Amboyna, Santos Rosewood, Burl Walnut, Birdseye Maple, Yew, Macassar, Yatoba, Aruba	129,599	118,398
185	6	1	"Chrome" Satin and Polished Ebony	136,062	110,630
185	6	1	"Edge"	136,062	110,630
185	6	1	"Johann Strauss"/"Franz Schubert"/Liszt Anniversary: Satin and Polished Ebony	136,062	107,616
185	6	1	"Johann Strauss"/"Franz Schubert": other finish	153,620	127,342
185	6	1	"Liszt"	153,620	127,342
185	6	1	"Senator"	143,905	119,352
185	6	1	Baroque/Louis XVI	164,290	136,118
185	6	1	"Chopin"	175,154	145,052
185	6	1	"Vienna"	186,389	154,292
185	6	1	"Artisan" Satin and Polished	221,854	183,460
185	6	1	"Porsche Design," Satin and Polished Ebony	176,546	146,196
185	6	1	"Porsche Design," Polished Colors	188,756	156,238
200CS	6	7	"Conservatory" Satin Ebony	99,399	90,398
200CSDE3	6	7	"Conservatory" Satin Ebony with Disklavier	119,398	110,396
200	6	7	Satin and Polished Ebony	119,899	108,900
200DE3	6	7	Polished Ebony with Disklavier	139,898	128,898
200	6	7	Satin and Polished White, other colors	132,999	122,998
200	6	7	Polished, Satin, Open-pore: Walnut, Cherry, Mahogany, Pomele, Bubinga, Wenge	137,899	124,398
200	6	7	Polished, Satin, Open-pore: Pyramid Mahogany, Amboyna, Santos Rosewood, Burl Walnut, Birdseye Maple, Yew, Macassar, Yatoba, Aruba	143,899	130,198
200	6	7	"Chrome" Satin and Polished Ebony	145,596	120,744
200	6	7	"Edge"	145,596	120,744
200	6	7	"Klimt" Polished Ebony	145,596	123,798
200	6	7	"Johann Strauss"/"Franz Schubert"/Liszt Anniversary: Satin and Polished Ebony	145,596	123,798
200	6	7	"Johann Strauss"/"Franz Schubert": other finish	169,423	140,338
200	6	7	"Liszt"	169,423	140,338
200	6	7	"Senator"	158,711	131,528
200	6	7	Baroque/Louis XVI	181,191	150,018
200	6	7	"Chopin"	190,066	157,316

*See pricing explanation on page 203.

Model	Feet	Inches	Description	MSRP*	SMP*
BÖSENDORFER (continued)					
200	6	7	"Vienna"	193,825	160,408
200	6	7	"Artisan" Satin and Polished	244,676	202,230
214CS	7		"Conservatory" Satin Ebony	102,999	97,798
214	7		Satin and Polished Ebony	133,999	118,598
214	7		Satin and Polished White, other colors	147,399	128,198
214	7		Polished, Satin, Open-pore: Walnut, Cherry, Mahogany, Pomele, Bubinga, Wenge	154,199	138,398
214	7		Polished, Satin, Open-pore: Pyramid Mahogany, Amboyna, Santos Rosewood, Burl Walnut, Birdseye Maple, Yew, Macassar, Yatoba, Aruba	160,799	143,798
214	7		"Chrome" Satin and Polished Ebony	164,618	138,966
214	7		"Edge"	164,618	138,886
214	7		"Johann Strauss"/"Franz Schubert""/Liszt Anniversary: Satin and Polished Ebony	164,618	138,968
214	7		"Johann Strauss"/"Franz Schubert"": other finish	194,371	163,900
214	7		"Liszt"	194,371	163,900
214	7		"Senator"	184,288	155,452
214	7		Baroque/Louis XVI	208,764	175,964
214	7		"Chopin"	223,160	188,030
214	7		"Vienna"	230,360	194,064
214	7		"Artisan" Satin and Polished	274,456	231,022
214	7		"Porsche Design," Satin and Polished Ebony	230,360	194,064
214	7		"Porsche Design," Polished Colors	244,759	206,132
225	7	4	Satin and Polished Ebony	153,999	136,798
225	7	4	Satin and Polished White, other colors	169,399	149,398
225	7	4	Polished, Satin, Open-pore: Walnut, Cherry, Mahogany, Pomele, Bubinga, Wenge	177,099	152,198
225	7	4	Polished, Satin, Open-pore: Pyramid Mahogany, Amboyna, Santos Rosewood, Burl Walnut, Birdseye Maple, Yew, Macassar, Yatoba, Aruba	184,799	158,598
225	7	4	"Chrome" Satin and Polished Ebony	177,814	147,240
225	7	4	"Edge"	177,814	150,858
225	7	4	"Johann Strauss"/"Franz Schubert""/Liszt Anniversary: Satin and Polished Ebony	177,814	150,858
225	7	4	"Johann Strauss"/"Franz Schubert"": other finish	217,048	179,508
225	7	4	"Liszt"	217,048	179,508
225	7	4	"Senator"	205,794	170,252
225	7	4	Baroque/Louis XVI	233,127	192,730
225	7	4	"Chopin"	249,206	205,954
225	7	4	"Vienna"	257,243	212,564
225	7	4	"Artisan" Satin and Polished	298,815	246,754
280	9	2	Satin and Polished Ebony	199,999	177,398
280	9	2	Satin and Polished White, other colors	219,999	193,998
280	9	2	Polished, Satin, Open-pore: Walnut, Cherry, Mahogany, Pomele, Bubinga, Wenge	229,999	196,398
280	9	2	Polished, Satin, Open-pore: Pyramid Mahogany, Amboyna, Santos Rosewood, Burl Walnut, Birdseye Maple, Yew, Macassar, Yatoba, Aruba	239,999	205,798
280	9	2	"Johann Strauss"/"Franz Schubert"/Liszt Anniversary: Satin and Polished Ebony	240,533	198,822
280	9	2	"Johann Strauss"/"Franz Schubert": other finish	282,165	233,060
280	9	2	"Liszt"	282,165	233,060
280	9	2	"Senator"	267,536	221,030
280	9	2	Baroque/Louis XVI	303,066	250,252
280	9	2	"Chopin"	323,967	267,440
280	9	2	"Vienna"	334,417	276,034
280	9	2	"Artisan" Satin and Polished	355,316	293,224
280	9	2	"Porsche Design," Satin and Polished	334,417	276,034

*See pricing explanation on page 203.

Model	Feet	Inches	Description	MSRP*	SMP*
BÖSENDORFER (continued)					
280	9	2	"Porsche Design," Polished Colors	355,316	293,224
290	9	6	Satin and Polished Ebony	219,999	201,598
290	9	6	Satin and Polished White, other colors	241,999	220,198
290	9	6	Polished, Satin, Open-pore: Walnut, Cherry, Mahogany, Pomele, Bubinga, Wenge	252,999	224,398
290	9	6	Polished, Satin, Open-pore: Pyramid Mahogany, Amboyna, Santos Rosewood, Burl Walnut, Birdseye Maple, Yew, Macassar, Yatoba, Aruba	263,999	233,798
290	9	6	"Johann Strauss"/"Franz Schubert"/Liszt Anniversary: Satin and Polished Ebony	269,286	222,470
290	9	6	"Johann Strauss"/"Franz Schubert": other finish	320,977	264,980
290	9	6	"Liszt"	320,977	264,980
290	9	6	"Senator"	304,334	251,294
290	9	6	Baroque/Louis XVI	344,754	284,536
290	9	6	"Chopin"	368,529	304,090
290	9	6	"Vienna"	380,417	313,868
290	9	6	"Artisan" Satin and Polished	404,191	333,420
170-280			CEUS, add	83,999	69,278
290			CEUS, add	90,399	84,640

BOSTON

Boston MSRP is the price at the New York retail store.

Verticals

Model	Feet	Inches	Description	MSRP*	SMP*
UP-118E PE		46	Satin and Polished Ebony	11,400	11,400
UP-118E PE		46	Polished Mahogany	13,200	13,200
UP-118E PE		46	Satin and Polished Walnut	13,200	13,200
UP-118S PE		46	Satin Black Oak/Honey Oak	7,300	7,300
UP-118S PE		46	Satin Mahogany	8,900	8,900
UP-126E PE		50	Polished Ebony	13,700	13,700
UP-126E PE		50	Polished Mahogany	15,700	15,700
UP-132E PE		52	Polished Ebony	15,100	15,100

Grands

Model	Feet	Inches	Description	MSRP*	SMP*
GP-156 PE	5	1	Satin and Polished Ebony	20,700	20,700
GP-163 PE	5	4	Satin and Polished Ebony	25,300	25,300
GP-163 PE	5	4	Satin and Polished Mahogany	27,600	27,600
GP-163 PE	5	4	Satin and Polished Walnut	27,900	27,900
GP-163 PE	5	4	Polished White	25,900	25,900
GP-178 PE	5	10	Satin and Polished Ebony	29,600	29,600
GP-178 PE	5	10	Satin and Polished Mahogany	31,900	31,900
GP-178 PE	5	10	Satin and Polished Walnut	32,300	32,300
GP-193 PE	6	4	Satin and Polished Ebony	38,400	38,400
GP-215 PE	7	1	Satin and Polished Ebony	50,400	50,400

*See pricing explanation on page 203.

PIANOBUYER.COM

Model	Feet	Inches	Description	MSRP*	SMP*
BRODMANN					
Verticals					
PE 116		45	Polished Ebony	7,470	5,980
CE 118		46	Polished Ebony	6,590	5,390
PE 121		47	Polished Ebony	8,390	6,590
PE 121		47	Polished Mahogany/White	8,990	6,990
PE 123C		48	Italian Provincial Satin Walnut	8,990	6,990
PE 123M		48	French Provincial Polished Mahogany	8,990	6,990
PE 123W		48	Polished Walnut	8,990	6,990
PE 125		49	Polished Ebony	8,990	6,990
PE 125		49	Polished Mahogany/White	9,590	7,390
PE 130		51	Polished Ebony	12,590	9,390
AS 132		52	Polished Ebony	17,990	12,990
Grands					
CE 148	4	10	Polished Ebony	15,990	11,660
PE 150	4	11	Polished Ebony	19,490	13,990
PE 162	5	4	Polished Ebony	22,190	15,790
PE 162	5	4	Polished Mahogany/White	23,390	16,590
PE 162	5	4	Two-Tone	22,790	16,190
CE 175	5	9	Polished Ebony	18,590	13,390
PE 187	6	2	Polished Ebony	25,900	18,267
PE 187	6	2	Polished Mahogany/White	26,990	18,990
PE 187	6	2	"Strauss"	26,990	18,990
AS 187	6	2	Polished Ebony	49,990	34,327
PE 212	7		Polished Ebony	34,990	24,327
AS 212	7		Polished Ebony	59,990	40,990
PE 228	7	5	Polished Ebony	42,490	29,327
PE 228R	7	5	Polished Ebony w/Renner action	52,490	35,990
AS 228	7	5	Polished Ebony	69,990	47,660
AS 275	9		Polished Ebony	99,990	67,660
BURGER & JACOBI					
Verticals					
118M		44	Polished Ebony	11,255	11,255
118M		44	Polished Mahogany/Walnut	12,170	12,170
118M		44	Polished White	12,737	12,737
125EU		49	Polished Ebony	13,875	13,875
131 Anniversary		50	Polished Ebony	17,450	17,450
Grands					
GP170	5	7	Polished Ebony	30,645	30,645
GP170	5	7	Polished White	32,400	32,400
GP188	6	2	Polished Ebony	34,695	34,695
GP275 Majestic	9		Polished Ebony	109,700	109,700
CABLE, HOBART M. — see Sejung					
CABLE-NELSON					
Verticals					
CN 116		45	Polished Ebony	3,999	3,999
CN 216		45	Satin Walnut	3,999	3,999
Grands					
CN 151	5		Polished Ebony	9,399	9,399
CN 161	5	3	Polished Ebony	13,399	13,399

*See pricing explanation on page 203.

Model	Feet	Inches	Description	MSRP*	SMP*

CHASE, A.B. — see Everett

CRISTOFORI

Verticals

Model	Feet	Inches	Description	MSRP*	SMP*
CRV425		42.5	Continental Satin Ebony	3,569	3,569
CRV425		42.5	Continental Polished Ebony	3,569	3,569
CRV425		42.5	Continental Polished Mahogany	3,779	3,779
CRV430		43	French Provincial Satin Cherry	4,715	4,715
CRV430		43	Mediterranean Satin Oak	4,409	4,409
CRV430		43	Satin Cherry	4,610	4,610
CRV450S		45	Satin Ebony	5,765	5,093
CRV450S		45	Satin Walnut	5,765	4,988
CRV450S		45	Satin Oak	5,765	5,093
CRV480		48	Satin Ebony	6,605	6,248
CRV480		48	Polished Ebony	6,605	6,038
CRV480		48	Polished Mahogany	6,815	6,248

Grands

Model	Feet	Inches	Description	MSRP*	SMP*
CRG48	4	8	Polished Ebony	7,865	7,865
CRG48	4	8	Polished Mahogany	8,390	8,390
CRG410	4	10	Satin Ebony	9,965	9,083
CRG410	4	10	Polished Ebony	9,965	8,768
CRG410	4	10	Polished Mahogany	10,490	9,188
CRG410	4	10	French Provincial Satin Cherry	11,015	9,608
CRG53	5	3	Satin Ebony	12,590	10,973
CRG53	5	3	Polished Ebony	12,590	10,658
CRG53	5	3	Satin Walnut/Mahogany	13,115	11,078
CRG53	5	3	Polished Walnut/Mahogany	13,115	11,078
CRG53	5	3	French Provincial Satin Cherry	14,165	11,498
CRG53	5	3	Polished Bubinga	14,375	11,498
CRG53	5	3	Polished White	13,115	11,078
CRG57	5	7	Satin Ebony	15,215	11,813
CRG57	5	7	Polished Ebony	15,215	11,498
CRG57	5	7	Satin Walnut/Mahogany	15,740	11,918
CRG57	5	7	Polished Walnut/Mahogany	15,740	11,918
CRG57	5	7	French Provincial Satin Cherry	16,790	12,338
CRG57	5	7	Polished Bubinga	17,105	12,338
CRG57	5	7	Polished White	15,740	11,918
CRG62	6	2	Satin Ebony	17,315	13,283
CRG62	6	2	Polished Ebony	17,315	12,968
CRG62	6	2	Polished Mahogany	18,155	13,388

CUNNINGHAM

Verticals

Model	Feet	Inches	Description	MSRP*	SMP*
Liberty Console		44	Satin Ebony	4,690	4,690
Liberty Console		44	Polished Ebony	3,990	3,990
Liberty Console		44	Satin Mahogany	5,490	5,490
Liberty Console		44	Polished Mahogany	4,790	4,790
Studio		50	Satin Ebony	6,690	6,690
Studio		50	Polished Ebony	5,990	5,990
Studio		50	Satin Mahogany	7,590	7,590
Studio		50	Polished Mahogany	5,490	5,490

*See pricing explanation on page 203.

Model	Feet	Inches	Description	MSRP*	SMP*

CUNNINGHAM (continued)

Grands

Model	Feet	Inches	Description	MSRP*	SMP*
Baby Grand	5		Satin Ebony	12,990	12,990
Baby Grand	5		Polished Ebony	11,890	11,890
Baby Grand	5		Satin Mahogany	13,690	13,690
Baby Grand	5		Polished Mahogany	12,590	12,590
Baby Grand	5		Heritage Victorian Polished Mahogany	23,490	23,490
Studio Grand	5	4	Satin Ebony	14,790	14,790
Studio Grand	5	4	Polished Ebony	13,690	13,690
Studio Grand	5	4	Satin Mahogany	15,490	15,490
Studio Grand	5	4	Polished Mahogany	14,390	14,390
Studio Grand	5	4	Heritage Victorian Polished Mahogany	25,290	25,290
Parlour Grand	5	10	Satin Ebony	18,590	18,590
Parlour Grand	5	10	Polished Ebony	17,490	17,490
Parlour Grand	5	10	Satin Mahogany	19,290	19,290
Parlour Grand	5	10	Polished Mahogany	18,190	18,190
Parlour Grand	5	10	Heritage Victorian Polished Mahogany	28,490	28,490
Chamber Grand	7		Polished Ebony	30,790	30,790
Chamber Grand	7		Polished Mahogany	31,890	31,890
Concert Grand	9		Polished Ebony	59,990	59,990

DISKLAVIER — see Yamaha; see also Bösendorfer

EDELWEISS

Verticals

Model	Feet	Inches	Description	MSRP*	SMP*
UT-49		49	Transparent	17,250	17,250

Grands

Model	Feet	Inches	Description	MSRP*	SMP*
G50	4	2	Butterfly Polished Ebony	12,950	12,950
G50	4	2	Half Moon Polished Ebony	12,950	12,950
G50	4	2	Butterfly Polished White	13,400	13,400
GT-66	5	6	Transparent	35,995	35,995

ESSEX

Essex MSRP is the price at the New York retail store.

Verticals

Model	Feet	Inches	Description	MSRP*	SMP*
EUP-108C		42	Continental Polished Ebony	4,590	4,590
EUP-111E		44	Polished Ebony	5,390	5,390
EUP-111E		44	Polished Sapele Mahogany	5,790	5,760
EUP-116E		45	Polished Ebony	6,290	6,080
EUP-116E		45	Polished Walnut/Sapele Mahogany	6,590	6,180
EUP-116E		45	Polished White	6,790	6,320
EUP-116FC		45	French Country Cherry	6,390	6,180
EUP-116CT		45	Contemporary Sapele Mahogany	6,790	6,420
EUP-116IP		45	Italian Provincial Walnut	6,390	6,390
EUP-116QA		45	Queen Anne Cherry	6,390	6,390
EUP-116ST		45	Sheraton Traditional Sapele Mahogany	6,390	6,390
EUP-116EC		45	English Country Walnut	6,790	6,640
EUP-116ET		45	English Traditional Sapele Mahogany	6,790	6,640
EUP-116FF		45	Formal French Brown Cherry	6,790	6,640
EUP-116FF		45	Formal French Red Cherry	6,790	6,640
EUP-123E		48	Polished Ebony	6,790	6,540
EUP-123E		48	Satin Sapele Mahogany	7,190	6,760
EUP-123E		48	Polished Sapele Mahogany	7,190	6,640
EUP-123E		48	Satin Walnut	7,190	6,640

*See pricing explanation on page 203.

Model	Feet	Inches	Description	MSRP*	SMP*
ESSEX (continued)					
EUP-123CL		48	French Satin Sapele Mahogany	7,790	7,220
EUP-123FL		48	Empire Satin Walnut	7,790	7,220
EUP-123FL		48	Empire Satin Sapele Mahogany	7,790	7,220
EUP-123S		48	Institutional Studio Polished Ebony	6,290	6,290
Grands					
EGP-155	5	1	Satin and Polished Ebony	12,400	12,400
EGP-155	5	1	Polished and Satin Lustre Sapele Mahogany	13,200	13,200
EGP-155	5	1	Polished Kewazinga Bubinga	14,700	14,160
EGP-155	5	1	Polished White	15,700	14,160
EGP-155F	5	1	French Provincial Brown Cherry	15,900	15,840
EGP-173	5	8	Satin and Polished Ebony	15,900	15,900
EGP-173	5	8	Polished Sapele Mahogany	16,800	16,800
EGP-173F	5	8	French Provincial Brown Cherry	18,500	18,500

ESTONIA

The Estonia factory can make custom-designed finishes with exotic veneers; prices upon request.
Prices here include Jansen adjustable artist bench.

Grands

Model	Feet	Inches	Description	MSRP*	SMP*
L168	5	6	Satin and Polished Ebony	38,200	36,693
L168	5	6	Satin and Polished Mahogany/Walnut/White	41,325	39,221
L168	5	6	Satin and Polished Kewazinga Bubinga	44,824	42,877
L168	5	6	"Hidden Beauty" Polished Ebony w/Bubinga	42,276	39,999
L168	5	6	Polished Pyramid Mahogany	49,600	47,684
L190	6	3	Satin and Polished Ebony	46,436	43,764
L190	6	3	Satin and Polished Mahogany/Walnut/White	49,972	48,040
L190	6	3	Polished Pyramid Mahogany	59,654	54,847
L190	6	3	Polished Santos Rosewood	59,654	54,526
L190	6	3	Polished Kewazinga Bubinga	53,800	51,587
L190	6	3	"Hidden Beauty" Polished Ebony w/Bubinga	49,338	47,182
L225	7	4	Satin and Polished Ebony	69,500	65,064
L225	7	4	Satin and Polished Mahogany/Walnut/White	74,765	71,477
L225	7	4	Polished Pyramid Mahogany	82,990	81,674
L225	7	4	Polished Kewazinga Bubinga	75,088	76,735
L225	7	4	"Hidden Beauty" Polished Ebony w/Bubinga	73,815	70,190
L274	9		Satin and Polished Ebony	110,860	93,572
L274	9		Satin and Polished Mahogany/Walnut	121,600	103,960
L274	9		Polished Pyramid Mahogany	125,800	125,800
L274	9		Satin and Polished White	114,400	101,672

EVERETT

Verticals

Model	Feet	Inches	Description	MSRP*	SMP*
EV-112		44	Continental Polished Ebony		4,580
EV-112		44	Continental Polished Mahogany		4,700
EV-113		45	Polished Ebony		4,780
EV-113		45	Polished Mahogany		4,900
EV-115CB		45	Chippendale Polished Mahogany		5,100
EV-121		48	Polished Ebony		5,380
EV-121		48	Polished Mahogany		5,500

*See pricing explanation on page 203.

Model	Feet	Inches	Description	MSRP*	SMP*

EVERETT (continued)

Grands

Model	Feet	Inches	Description	MSRP*	SMP*
EV-146	4	9	Polished Ebony		8,980
EV-146	4	9	Polished Mahogany/White		9,480
EV-152	5		Polished Ebony		9,780
EV-152	5		Polished Mahogany/Sapele		10,280
EV-165	5	5	Polished Ebony		10,780
EV-165	5	5	Polished Mahogany/Walnut		11,280
EV-185	6	1	Polished Ebony		12,980

FALCONE — see Sejung

FANDRICH & SONS

These are the prices on the Fandrich & Sons website. Other finishes available at additional cost. See website for details.

Verticals

Model	Feet	Inches	Description	MSRP*	SMP*
126V		50	Polished Ebony	19,900	19,900
132V		52	Polished Ebony	21,900	21,900

Grands

Model	Feet	Inches	Description	MSRP*	SMP*
165S	5	5	Polished Ebony w/Mahogany	17,590	17,590
185S-H	6	1	Polished Ebony w/Mahogany	20,590	20,590
185HGS-H	6	1	Polished Ebony w/Mahogany	23,590	23,590
215S-H	7	1	Polished Ebony	34,790	34,790
215HGS-H	7	1	Polished Ebony	37,790	37,790

FAZIOLI

Fazioli is willing to make custom-designed cases with exotic veneers, marquetry, and other embellishments.
Prices on request to Fazioli.

Grands

Model	Feet	Inches	Description	MSRP*	SMP*
F156	5	2	Satin and Polished Ebony	95,800	95,800
F183	6		Satin and Polished Ebony	106,400	106,400
F212	6	11	Satin and Polished Ebony	120,600	120,600
F228	7	6	Satin and Polished Ebony	138,400	138,400
F278	9	2	Satin and Polished Ebony	179,200	179,200
F308	10	2	Satin and Polished Ebony	196,000	196,000
F308			Fourth pedal and two lyres included in price		
All but F308			Fourth pedal, add	11,400	11,400

FÖRSTER, AUGUST

Prices do not include bench. Euro = $1.32

Verticals

Model	Feet	Inches	Description	MSRP*	SMP*
116 C		46	Chippendale Polished Ebony		27,281
116 C		46	Chippendale Satin Mahogany		26,615
116 C		46	Chippendale Polished Mahogany		27,364
116 C		46	Chippendale Satin Walnut		27,932
116 C		46	Chippendale Polished Walnut		28,694
116 D		46	Continental Polished Ebony		22,180
116 D		46	Continental Satin Mahogany/Beech/Alder		20,198
116 D		46	Continental Polished Mahogany		22,291
116 D		46	Continental Satin Walnut/Pear/Oak/Cherry		21,570
116 D		46	Continental Polished Walnut/Pear/Oak/Cherry		23,677
116 D		46	Continental Polished White		23,719
116 E		46	Polished Ebony		25,728
116 E		46	Satin Mahogany/Beech/Alder		23,788

*See pricing explanation on page 203.

Model	Feet	Inches	Description	MSRP*	SMP*
FÖRSTER, AUGUST (continued)					
116 E		46	Polished Mahogany/Beech/Alder		25,825
116 E		46	Satin Walnut/Oak/Cherry/Pear		25,132
116 E		46	Polished Walnut/Oak/Cherry/Pear		27,156
116 E		46	Polished White		27,225
125 F		49	Polished Ebony		29,401
125 G		49	Polished Ebony		28,819
125 G		49	Satin Mahogany/Beech/Alder		26,796
125 G		49	Polished Mahogany/Beech/Alder		28,902
125 G		49	Satin Walnut/Oak/Cherry/Pear		28,681
125 G		49	Polished Walnut/Oak/Cherry/Pear		30,801
125 G		49	Polished White		30,330
125 G			With Medallion, add		1,300
134 K		53	Polished Ebony		42,624
Grands					
170	5	8	Polished Ebony		59,897
170	5	8	Satin and Polished Walnut		62,143
170	5	8	Satin and Polished Mahogany		59,994
170	5	8	Polished White		63,293
170	5	8	"Classik" Polished Ebony		67,021
170	5	8	"Classik" Polished Walnut		76,460
170	5	8	"Classik" Polished Mahogany		68,310
170	5	8	"Classik" Polished White		70,791
170	5	8	Chippendale Open-Pore Walnut		73,023
170	5	8	"Antik" Open-Pore Walnut		82,448
190	6	4	Polished Ebony		66,800
190	6	4	Satin and Polished Walnut		69,059
190	6	4	Satin and Polished Mahogany		66,952
190	6	4	Polished White		70,251
190	6	4	"Classik" Polished Ebony		73,910
190	6	4	"Classik" Polished Mahogany		75,240
190	6	4	"Classik" Polished White		77,735
190	6	4	Chippendale Open-Pore Walnut		79,925
190	6	4	"Antik" Open-Pore Walnut		89,364
170/190			Pyramid Mahogany, add		9,023
215	7	2	Polished Ebony		75,490
275	9	1	Polished Ebony		140,992

GROTRIAN

Prices do not include bench. Other woods available on request. Euro = $1.40

Verticals

Model	Feet	Inches	Description	MSRP*	SMP*
Studio 110		43.5	"Friedrich Grotrian" Satin Ebony	15,500	15,500
Studio 110		43.5	"Friedrich Grotrian" Polished Ebony	18,193	18,193
Cristal		44	Continental Satin Ebony	20,842	20,842
Cristal		44	Continental Polished Ebony	21,780	21,780
Cristal		44	Continental Open-pore Oak/Walnut/Beech	20,842	20,842
Cristal		44	Continental Polished Walnut/White	23,846	23,846
Canto		45	Continental Satin Ebony	23,846	23,846
Canto		45	Continental Open-pore Beech	23,846	23,846
Canto		45	Continental Polished Ebony	24,409	24,409
Carat		45.5	Polished Ebony	27,417	27,417
Carat		45.5	Open-pore Oak/Walnut	26,476	26,476
Carat		45.5	Polished Walnut/White	29,858	29,858
College		48	Satin Ebony	30,169	30,169
College		48	Polished Ebony	31,484	31,484
College		48	Open-pore Beech	30,169	30,169
Classic		49	Polished Ebony	36,932	36,932

*See pricing explanation on page 203.

220

PIANOBUYER.COM

Model	Feet	Inches	Description	MSRP*	SMP*
GROTRIAN (continued)					
Classic		49	Open-pore Oak/Walnut	35,428	35,428
Classic		49	Polished Walnut/White	40,314	40,314
Concertino		52	Polished Ebony	44,960	44,911
Uprights			Sostenuto pedal, add	1,600	1,382
Grands					
Chambre	5	5	Satin Ebony	66,465	65,000
Chambre	5	5	Polished Ebony	73,603	71,336
Chambre	5	5	Open-pore Oak/Walnut	68,717	66,999
Chambre	5	5	Polished Walnut/White	80,554	77,507
Cabinet	6	3	Satin Ebony	77,547	74,837
Cabinet	6	3	Polished Ebony	86,003	82,343
Cabinet	6	3	Open-pore Oak/Walnut	80,554	77,507
Cabinet	6	3	Polished Walnut/White	94,269	89,681
Charis	6	10	Satin Ebony	88,464	84,527
Charis	6	10	Polished Ebony	97,933	92,933
Concert	7	4	Satin Ebony	106,405	100,453
Concert	7	4	Polished Ebony	119,136	111,755
Concert Royal	9	1	Polished Ebony	147,728	137,136
All models			Chippendale/Empire, add	3,700	3,234
All models			CS Style, add	5,650	4,998
All models			Rococo, add	14,250	12,642

HAESSLER

Prices do not include bench.

Verticals

Model	Feet	Inches	Description	MSRP*	SMP*
115 K		45	Satin and Polished Ebony	19,505	18,730
115 K		45	Satin Beech/Ash/Waxed Alder	19,185	18,440
115 K		45	Satin and Polished White	20,249	19,410
118 K		47	Satin and Polished Ebony	21,393	20,450
118 K		47	Satin Ebony with Walnut Accent	23,029	21,930
118 K		47	Satin and Polished Mahogany	22,571	21,520
118 K		47	Satin and Polished Walnut	22,571	21,520
118 K		47	Satin and Polished Cherry	24,189	22,990
118 K		47	Satin and Polished Cherry with Yew Inlay	24,196	22,996
118 K		47	Satin Oak	20,466	19,604
118 K		47	Polished Bubinga	24,453	23,230
118 K		47	Satin and Polished White	22,308	21,280
118 KM		47	Satin and Polished Ebony	22,480	21,436
118 KM		47	Satin and Polished White	23,315	22,196
118 CH		47	Chippendale Satin and Polished Mahogany	24,123	22,930
118 CH		47	Chippendale Satin and Polished Walnut	24,123	22,930
124 K		49	Satin and Polished Ebony	24,419	23,200
124 K		49	Satin Ebony with Walnut Accent	23,910	22,736
124 K		49	Satin and Polished Mahogany	24,447	23,224
124 K		49	Satin and Polished Walnut	24,447	23,224
124 K		49	Satin and Polished Cherry	25,042	23,764
124 K		49	Satin and Polished Cherry with Yew Inlay	26,186	24,804
124 K		49	Satin and Polished White	23,589	22,444
124 KM		49	Satin and Polished Ebony	23,254	22,140
124 KM		49	Satin and Polished White	24,090	22,900
132		52	Satin and Polished Ebony	30,911	29,100

Grands

Model	Feet	Inches	Description	MSRP*	SMP*
175	5	8	Satin and Polished Ebony	59,984	54,540
175	5	8	Satin and Polished Mahogany	61,258	56,690
175	5	8	Satin and Polished Walnut	61,841	57,220

*See pricing explanation on page 203.

| --- | --- | --- | --- | --- | --- |

HAESSLER *(continued)*

Model	Feet	Inches	Description	MSRP*	SMP*
175	5	8	Satin and Polished Cherry	61,543	56,950
175	5	8	Polished Bubinga	64,788	59,900
175	5	8	Satin and Polished White	70,571	63,990
175	5	8	Saxony Polished Pyramid Mahogany	77,712	71,650
175	5	8	Saxony Polished Burl Walnut	78,462	72,330
175	5	8	"President" Polished Ebony	65,756	60,780
175	5	8	"President" Polished Mahogany	68,385	63,170
175	5	8	"President" Polished Walnut	69,047	63,770
175	5	8	"President" Polished Bubinga	72,335	66,760
175	5	8	Louis XV Ebony, Satin and Polished	68,738	63,490
175	5	8	Louis XV Mahogany, Satin and Polished	72,181	66,620
175	5	8	Louis XV Walnut, Satin and Polished	71,501	66,000
175	5	8	"Kaiser Wilhelm II" Polished Ebony	69,342	64,040
175	5	8	"Kaiser Wilhelm II" Polished Mahogany	72,115	66,560
175	5	8	"Kaiser Wilhelm II" Polished Walnut	72,807	67,190
175	5	8	"Kaiser Wilhelm II" Polished Cherry	72,466	66,880
175	5	8	"Ambassador" Satin East Indian Rosewood	80,706	74,370
175	5	8	"Ambassador" Satin Walnut	74,722	68,930
175	5	8	"Nicolas II" Satin Walnut w/Burl Inlay	80,697	74,360
175	5	8	Louis XIV Rococo Satin White w/Gold	86,680	79,800
175	5	8	"Classic Alexandra" Polished Ebony	66,946	61,860
175	5	8	"Classic Alexandra" Polished Mahogany	70,298	64,910
175	5	8	"Classic Alexandra" Polished Walnut	69,629	64,300
186	6	1	Satin and Polished Ebony	66,363	61,330
186	6	1	Satin and Polished Mahogany	69,014	63,740
186	6	1	Satin and Polished Walnut	69,674	64,340
186	6	1	Satin and Polished Cherry	69,343	64,040
186	6	1	Polished Bubinga	72,994	67,360
186	6	1	Satin and Polished White	69,674	64,340
186	6	1	Saxony Polished Pyramid Mahogany	87,558	80,600
186	6	1	Saxony Polished Burl Walnut	88,393	81,360
186	6	1	"President" Polished Ebony	74,085	68,350
186	6	1	"President" Polished Mahogany	77,042	71,040
186	6	1	"President" Polished Walnut	77,791	71,720
186	6	1	"President" Polished Bubinga	81,486	75,080
186	6	1	Louis XV Ebony, Satin and Polished	77,449	71,410
186	6	1	Louis XV Mahogany, Satin and Polished	81,321	74,930
186	6	1	Louis XV Walnut, Satin and Polished	80,552	74,230
186	6	1	"Kaiser Wilhelm II" Polished Ebony	78,123	72,020
186	6	1	"Kaiser Wilhelm II" Polished Mahogany	81,255	74,870
186	6	1	"Kaiser Wilhelm II" Polished Walnut	82,026	75,570
186	6	1	"Kaiser Wilhelm II" Polished Cherry	81,640	75,220
186	6	1	"Ambassador" Satin East Indian Rosewood	90,924	83,660
186	6	1	"Ambassador" Satin Walnut	84,192	77,540
186	6	1	"Nicolas II" Satin Walnut w/Burl Inlay	90,924	83,660
186	6	1	Louis XIV Rococo Satin White w/Gold	97,655	89,780
186	6	1	"Classic Alexandra" Polished Ebony	75,435	69,580
186	6	1	"Classic Alexandra" Polished Mahogany	79,199	73,000
186	6	1	"Classic Alexandra" Polished Walnut	78,440	72,310

*See pricing explanation on page 203.

Model	Feet	Inches	Description	MSRP*	SMP*
HAILUN					
Verticals					
HU116		45.5	Polished Ebony	7,605	6,630
HU120		47	Satin Walnut	7,680	6,830
HU121C		48	Polished Mahogany/Walnut (curved legs)	7,680	6,830
HU121TD		48	Polished Mahogany/Walnut w/Detail Trim	8,235	7,310
HU1-P		48	Polished Ebony	8,345	7,310
HU1-P		48	Polished Mahogany/Walnut	8,865	7,790
HU1-PS		48	Polished Ebony with Nickel Trim	8,550	7,550
HU1-EP		48	Polished Ebony w/mahogany leg, fallboard, cheekblocks	8,550	7,550
HU5-P		50	Polished Ebony	9,180	8,038
HU5-P		50	Polished Mahogany/Walnut	9,465	8,256
HU6-P		51.5	Polished Ebony	12,030	10,230
HU7-P		52	Polished Ebony	12,525	10,600
HU8		51	"Vienna" Polished Ebony	14,655	12,230
Grands					
HG151	4	11.5	Polished Ebony	16,035	13,850
HG151	4	11.5	Polished Mahogany/Walnut	16,995	14,598
HG151C	4	11.5	Chippendale Polished Mahogany/Walnut	19,155	15,684
HG161	5	4	Polished Ebony	18,435	15,750
HG161	5	4	Polished Mahogany/Walnut	20,025	14,350
HG161G	5	4	Georgian Polished Mahogany/Walnut	22,215	17,100
HG168	5	6	"Vienna" Polished Ebony	35,940	28,550
HG178	5	10	Polished Ebony	22,125	18,700
HG178	5	10	Polished Mahogany/Walnut	23,085	19,470
HG178B	5	10	Baroque Polished Ebony w/Birds-Eye Maple Accents	24,750	20,800
HG180	5	11	"Vienna" Polished Ebony	41,340	32,694
HG198	6	5	"Emerson" Polished Ebony	34,455	28,564
HG198	6	5	"Emerson" Polished Mahogany/Walnut	35,940	29,536
HG218	7	2	"Paulello" Polished Ebony	48,105	39,484
HALLET, DAVIS & CO.					
Heritage Collection Verticals					
H-C43R		43	Satin Cherry/Oak (Roung Leg)	5,775	4,300
H-C43F		43	French Provincial Satin Cherry/Oak	5,775	4,300
H-108		43	Continental Polished Ebony	4,750	3,710
H-108		43	Continental Polished Mahogany	4,950	3,810
H-116		46	Satin Ebony School Classic	5,950	4,390
H-117H		46	Polished Ebony Studio	5,250	3,990
H-118F		46	Demi-Chippendale Polished Mahogany	5,595	4,190
Signature Collection Verticals					
HS-112C		44	Continental Polished Ebony	5,250	3,990
HS-112C		44	Continental Polished Mahogany/Walnut/Cherry/White	5,425	4,100
HS-114E		45	Classic Studio Polished Ebony	5,775	4,300
HS-114E		45	Classic Studio Polished Mahogany/Walnut/Cherry	5,975	4,390
HS-115EC		45	Chippendale Polished Ebony	5,775	4,300
HS-115EC		45	Chippendale Polished Mahogany/Walnut/Cherry	5,975	4,390
HS-123E		48	Polished Ebony	6,275	4,590
HS-123E		48	Polished Mahogany/Walnut/Cherry	6,475	4,700
HS-125E		50	Polished Ebony	6,995	4,990
HS-125E		50	Polished Mahogany	7,175	5,100
HS-132E		52	Polished Ebony	8,750	5,990
HS-132E		52	Polished Mahogany	8,925	6,100

*See pricing explanation on page 203.

Model	Feet	Inches	Description	MSRP*	SMP*
HALLET, DAVIS & CO. (continued)					
Heritage Collection Grands					
H-142C	4	7	Polished Ebony	11,995	7,790
H-142C	4	7	Polished Mahogany	12,995	8,390
H-142F	4	7	Queen Anne Polished Mahogany	13,650	8,790
Signature Collection Grands					
HS-148A	4	10	Polished Ebony	13,295	8,590
HS-148A	4	10	Polished Mahogany	13,995	8,990
HS-152A	5		Polished Ebony	14,695	9,390
HS-175A	5	9	Polished Ebony	17,195	10,790
HS-186A	6	1	Polished Ebony	18,895	11,790
Imperial Collection Grands					
HD-146C	4	9	Satin Ebony	16,195	10,190
HD-146C	4	9	Polished Ebony	15,495	9,790
HD-146C	4	9	"Metropolitan" Polished Ebony/Silver Plate	16,195	10,190
HD-146C	4	9	Polished Mahogany/White	16,195	10,190
HD-146C	4	9	Satin Mahogany/Walnut	17,195	10,790
HD-146C	4	9	Polished Walnut	16,895	10,590
HD-146S	4	9	Queen Anne Polished Ebony	16,495	10,390
HD-146S	4	9	Queen Anne Polished Mahogany/Walnut	17,195	10,790
HD-152C	5		Satin Ebony	17,195	10,790
HD-152C	5		Polished Ebony	16,495	10,390
HD-152C	5		"Metropolitan" Polished Ebony/Silver Plate	17,195	10,790
HD-152C	5		Polished Mahogany/White	17,195	10,790
HD-152C	5		Satin Mahogany/Walnut	18,195	11,390
HD-152C	5		Polished Walnut	17,895	11,190
HD-152D	5		Victorian Polished Ebony	17,495	10,990
HD-152D	5		Victorian Polished Mahogany	18,195	11,390
HD-152D	5		Victorian Satin Mahogany/Walnut	19,295	11,990
HD-152D	5		Victorian Polished Walnut	18,895	11,790
HD-152S	5		Queen Anne Polished Ebony	17,495	10,990
HD-152S	5		Queen Anne Satin Mahogany/Walnut	19,295	11,990
HD-152S	5		Queen Anne Polished Mahogany	18,195	11,390
HD-152S	5		Queen Anne Polished Walnut	18,895	11,790
HD-165C	5	5	Satin Ebony	18,195	11,390
HD-165C	5	5	Polished Ebony	17,495	10,990
HD-165C	5	5	"Metropolitan" Polished Ebony/Silver Plate	18,195	11,390
HD-165C	5	5	Polished Mahogany/White	18,195	11,390
HD-165C	5	5	Satin Mahogany/Walnut	19,295	11,990
HD-165C	5	5	Polished Walnut	18,895	11,790
HD-165D	5	5	Period Polished Ebony	18,595	11,590
HD-165D	5	5	Period Satin Mahogany/Walnut	20,295	12,590
HD-165D	5	5	Period Polished Mahogany	19,295	11,990
HD-165D	5	5	Period Polished Walnut	19,995	12,390
HD-165S	5	5	Queen Anne Polished Ebony	18,595	11,590
HD-165S	5	5	Queen Anne Satin Mahogany/Walnut	20,295	12,590
HD-165S	5	5	Queen Anne Polished Mahogany	19,295	11,990
HD-165S	5	5	Queen Anne Polished Walnut	19,995	12,390
HD-185C	6	1	Satin Ebony	20,295	12,590
HD-185C	6	1	Polished Ebony	19,595	12,190
HD-185C	6	1	Polished Mahogany/Walnut	20,995	12,990
HD-185C	6	1	Satin Mahogany/Walnut	21,395	13,190
HD-215C	7	1	Polished Ebony	48,995	28,990

*See pricing explanation on page 203.

Model	Feet	Inches	Description	MSRP*	SMP*
HARDMAN, PECK & CO.					
Verticals					
R110S		44	Polished Ebony	4,750	3,710
R110S		44	Polished Mahogany	4,925	3,810
R45F		45	French Provincial Satin Cherry	6,145	4,490
R115LS		45	Polished Ebony	5,095	3,890
R115LS		45	Polished Mahogany	5,250	3,990
R116		46	School Polished Ebony	5,595	4,190
R116		46	School Satin Cherry	5,775	4,290
R117XK		46	Chippendale Polished Mahogany	5,595	4,190
R120LS		48	Polished Ebony	5,425	4,090
R120LS		48	Polished Mahogany	5,595	4,190
R132HA		52	Polished Ebony	8,395	5,790
Grands					
R143S	4	8	Satin Ebony	12,945	8,390
R143S	4	8	Polished Ebony	11,895	7,790
R143S	4	8	Polished Mahogany	12,945	8,390
R143S	4	8	Satin Cherry	12,945	8,390
R143F	4	8	French Provincial Polished Ebony	12,945	8,390
R143F	4	8	French Provincial Polished Mahogany	13,645	8,790
R143F	4	8	French Provincial Satin Cherry	13,645	8,790
R143R	4	8	Polished Ebony (round legs)	12,945	8,390
R143R	4	8	Polished Mahogany (round legs)	13,645	8,790
R143R	4	8	Satin Cherry (round legs)	13,645	8,790
R150S	5		Satin Ebony	13,995	8,990
R150S	5		Polished Ebony	13,295	8,590
R150S	5		Polished Ebony w/Chrome	14,695	9,390
R150S	5		Polished Mahogany	13,995	8,990
R150S	5		Satin Cherry	14,695	8,990
R150F	5		French Provincial Polished Ebony	13,995	8,990
R150F	5		French Provincial Polished Mahogany	14,695	9,390
R150F	5		French Provincial Satin Cherry	14,695	9,390
R150R	5		Polished Ebony (round legs)	13,995	8,990
R150R	5		Polished Mahogany (round legs)	14,695	9,390
R150R	5		Satin Cherry (round legs)	14,695	9,390
R158S	5	3	Satin Ebony	14,695	9,390
R158S	5	3	Polished Ebony	13,995	8,990
R158S	5	3	Polished Mahogany	14,695	9,390
R158S	5	3	Satin Cherry	14,695	9,390
R158F	5	3	French Provincial Polished Ebony	14,695	9,390
R158F	5	3	French Provincial Polished Mahogany	15,395	9,790
R158F	5	3	French Provincial Satin Cherry	15,395	9,790
R158R	5	3	Polished Ebony (round legs)	14,695	9,390
R158R	5	3	Polished Mahogany (round legs)	15,395	9,790
R158R	5	3	Satin Cherry (round legs)	15,395	9,790
R168S	5	7	Satin Ebony	16,095	10,190
R168S	5	7	Polished Ebony	15,395	9,790
R168S	5	7	Polished Mahogany	16,095	10,190
R168S	5	7	Satin Cherry	16,095	10,190
R185S	6	1	Satin Ebony	18,895	11,790
R185S	6	1	Polished Ebony	18,195	11,390
R185S	6	1	Polished Mahogany	18,895	11,790
R185S	6	1	Satin Cherry	18,895	11,790

*See pricing explanation on page 203.

HEINTZMAN & CO.

Heintzman Verticals

Model	Feet	Inches	Description	MSRP*	SMP*
121D/DL		48	Satin and Polished Mahogany	7,595	6,990
123B		48.5	Polished Mahogany	8,795	7,500
123F		48.5	French Provincial Polished Ebony	7,795	6,800
123F		48.5	French Provincial Polished Mahogany	7,995	6,900
126C		50	Polished Ebony	9,795	7,600
126C		50	Polished Mahogany	9,995	7,700
132D		52	Polished Ebony, Decorative Panel	11,795	8,370
132D		52	Polished Mahogany, Decorative Panel	11,995	8,480
132E		52	French Provincial Polished Ebony	11,795	8,370
132E		52	French Provincial Satin and Polished Mahogany	11,995	8,480
140CK		55	Polished Mahogany	14,995	10,500

Gerhard Heintzman Verticals

Model	Feet	Inches	Description	MSRP*	SMP*
G118		46.5	Polished Ebony w/Silver Plate and Trim		5,200
G118		46.5	Polished Mahogany w/Silver Plate and Trim		5,400
G120		47	Polished Ebony w/Silver Plate and Trim		5,600
G120		47	Polished Mahogany w/Silver Plate and Trim		5,800
G126		49.5	Polished Ebony w/Silver Plate and Trim		6,400
G126		49.5	Polished Mahogany w/Silver Plate and Trim		6,600

Heintzman Grands

Model	Feet	Inches	Description	MSRP*	SMP*
168	5	6	Polished Ebony/White	18,995	16,990
168	5	6	Satin and Polished Mahogany	19,995	17,390
186	6	1	Polished Ebony/White	23,995	18,780
186	6	1	Polished Mahogany	24,995	19,180
203	6	8	Polished Ebony/White	28,995	20,180
203	6	8	Polished Mahogany	29,995	20,780
277	9		Polished Ebony	89,995	60,995

Gerhard Heintzman Grands

Model	Feet	Inches	Description	MSRP*	SMP*
G152	5		Polished Ebony		11,600
G152	5		Polished Mahogany		12,200
G152R	5		Empire Polished Ebony		11,800
G152R	5		Empire Polished Mahogany		12,400
G168	5	6	Polished Ebony		12,800
G168R	5	6	Empire Polished Mahogany		13,600

HOFFMANN, W.

Vision Series Verticals

Model	Feet	Inches	Description	MSRP*	SMP*
V112		44	Polished Ebony	10,000	9,500
V112		44	Polished Mahogany/Walnut	10,800	10,300
V112		44	Polished White	11,100	10,600
V120		47	Polished Ebony	10,900	10,400
V120		47	Polished Mahogany/Walnut	11,400	10,900
V120		47	Polished White	11,700	11,200

Tradition Series Verticals

Model	Feet	Inches	Description	MSRP*	SMP*
T122		48	Polished Ebony	12,400	11,900
T122		48	Satin Mahogany/Walnut/Cherry/Alder	13,300	12,800
T122		48	Polished Mahogany/Walnut/Cherry/White	14,100	13,600
T128		50	Polished Ebony	13,900	13,400
T128		50	Satin Mahogany/Walnut/Cherry/Alder	14,700	14,200
T128		50	Polished Mahogany/Walnut/Cherry/Alder	15,600	15,100

*See pricing explanation on page 203.

Model	Feet	Inches	Description	MSRP*	SMP*

HOFFMANN, W. *(continued)*

Vision Series Grands

Model	Feet	Inches	Description	MSRP*	SMP*
V158	5	2	Polished Ebony	29,300	27,800
V158	5	2	Polished Mahogany/Walnut/White	32,500	31,000
V183	6	1	Polished Ebony/Mahogany/Walnut	35,100	33,600
V183	6	1	Polished White	38,100	36,600

Tradition Series Grands

Model	Feet	Inches	Description	MSRP*	SMP*
T161	5	3	Polished Ebony	35,300	33,800
T161	5	3	Polished Mahogany/Walnut/White	38,300	36,800
T177	5	9	Polished Ebony	39,900	38,400
T177	5	9	Polished Mahogany/Walnut/White	42,900	41,400
T186	6	2	Polished Ebony	41,300	39,800
T186	6	2	Polished Mahogany/Walnut/White	45,100	43,600

IRMLER

Studio Edition Verticals

Model	Feet	Inches	Description	MSRP*	SMP*
P108		42.5	Polished Ebony	5,962	5,962
P108		42.5	Polished Mahogany/Walnut	6,138	6,120
P108		42.5	Polished White	6,048	6,046
P110		43	Polished Ebony	5,790	5,790
P118I		46.5	"Ren Vindetti" Polished Ebony	5,296	5,296
P118L		46.5	"Ren Vindetti" Polished Mahogany	5,629	5,629
P118		47	Polished Ebony	6,220	6,188
P118		47	Polished Mahogany/Walnut	6,397	6,336
P118		47	Polished White	6,353	6,300
P121B		47.5	"Ren Vindetti" Polished Ebony	5,920	5,920
P121I		47.5	"Ren Vindetti" Polished Mahogany	5,379	5,379
P122		48	Polished Ebony	6,481	6,406
P122 Décor		48	Polished Ebony w/Burr Walnut Accents	6,837	6,704
P122		48	Polished Mahogany/Walnut	6,581	6,490
P122		48	Polished White	6,650	6,548
P132		52	Polished Ebony	7,378	7,154
P132		52	Polished Mahogany/Walnut	7,648	7,380
P132		52	Polished White	7,547	7,296

Art Design Verticals

Model	Feet	Inches	Description	MSRP*	SMP*
Mia		47.5	Polished Ebony	5,873	5,873
Gina		48.5	Polished Ebony	5,773	5,773
Monique		49	Polished Ebony	6,349	6,349
Louis		49	Polished Ebony	5,884	5,884
Titus		49	Polished Ebony	6,956	6,956
Alexa		49	Polished Ebony	7,516	7,516
Hugo		49	Polished Ebony	7,948	7,948
Paolo		49	Polished Ebony	8,372	8,372

Professional Edition Verticals

Model	Feet	Inches	Description	MSRP*	SMP*
P116E		46	Polished Ebony	8,596	8,286
P116E		46	Satin Mahogany/Walnut/Cherry	8,598	8,286
P116E		46	Polished Mahogany/Walnut/Cherry	8,731	8,400
P116E		46	Satin and Polished Bubinga	9,687	9,210
P122E		48	Polished Ebony	9,149	8,754
P122E		48	Satin Mahogany/Walnut/Cherry	9,147	8,752
P122E		48	Polished Mahogany/Walnut/Cherry	9,285	8,870
P122E		48	Satin and Polished Bubinga	10,218	9,660
P132E		52	Polished Ebony	10,248	9,686
P132E		52	Satin Mahogany/Walnut/Cherry	10,799	10,152
P132E		52	Polished Mahogany/Walnut/Cherry	11,350	10,620
P132E		52	Satin and Polished Bubinga	12,252	11,384

*See pricing explanation on page 203.

Model	Feet	Inches	Description	MSRP*	SMP*

IRMLER (continued)

Studio Edition Grands

Model	Feet	Inches	Description	MSRP*	SMP*
F142	4	8	Polished Ebony	16,448	14,720
F142	4	8	Polished Mahogany/Walnut/White	17,258	15,396
F160	5	3	Polished Ebony	19,353	17,144
F160	5	3	Polished Mahogany/Walnut	20,221	17,868
F160	5	3	Polished White	20,063	17,736
F188	6	2	Polished Ebony	27,674	24,086
F188	6	2	Polished Mahogany/Walnut	28,453	24,734
F188	6	2	Polished White	28,367	24,664
F213	7		Polished Ebony	33,214	28,706
F213	7		Polished White	34,466	29,750

Professional Edition Grands

Model	Feet	Inches	Description	MSRP*	SMP*
F160E	5	3	Polished Ebony	36,152	31,640
F160E	5	3	Satin Mahogany/Walnut/Cherry	36,152	31,640
F160E	5	3	Polished Mahogany/Walnut/Cherry	37,911	33,130
F160E	5	3	Satin and Polished Bubinga	41,046	35,788
F175E	5	9	Polished Ebony	38,795	33,880
F175E	5	9	Satin Mahogany/Walnut/Cherry	38,795	33,880
F175E	5	9	Polished Mahogany/Walnut/Cherry	40,778	35,560
F175E	5	9	Satin and Polished Bubinga	44,147	38,416
F190E	6	3	Polished Ebony	41,439	36,120
F190E	6	3	Satin Mahogany/Walnut/Cherry	41,439	36,120
F190E	6	3	Polished Mahogany/Walnut/Cherry	43,420	37,800
F190E	6	3	Satin and Polished Bubinga	46,153	40,116
F210E	6	10.5	Polished Ebony	51,138	44,340
F210E	6	10.5	Satin Mahogany/Walnut/Cherry	51,138	44,340
F210E	6	10.5	Polished Mahogany/Walnut/Cherry	53,559	46,392
F210E	6	10.5	Satin and Polished Bubinga	56,289	48,706
F230E	7	6.5	Polished Ebony	60,835	52,560

KAWAI

Verticals

Model	Feet	Inches	Description	MSRP*	SMP*
K-15		44	Continental Polished Ebony	4,495	4,495
K-15		44	Continental Polished Mahogany	4,695	4,695
506N		44.5	Satin Ebony/Mahogany/Oak	4,695	4,695
508		44.5	Satin Mahogany	5,495	5,390
607		44.5	Satin American Oak	5,995	5,790
607		44.5	French Provincial Satin Cherry	6,195	5,990
607		44.5	Queen Anne Satin Mahogany	6,195	5,990
K-2		45	Satin and Polished Ebony	5,995	5,790
K-2		45	Satin and Polished Mahogany	6,695	6,390
K-2		45	French Provincial Polished Mahogany	7,195	6,790
SI-15		45	FINO Modern Satin Walnut	11,495	10,190
UST-9		46	Satin Ebony/Oak/Walnut/Cherry	7,495	6,990
907N		46.5	English Regency Satin Mahogany	9,495	8,590
907N		46.5	French Provincial Satin Cherry	9,495	8,590
SI-16		47	FINO Traditional European Polished Cherry	13,195	11,590
SI-17		47	FINO Demi-Chippendale Polished Mahogany	15,995	13,790
K-3		48	Satin and Polished Ebony	8,995	8,190
K-3		48	Satin and Polished Mahogany	9,695	8,790
K-3		48	Polished Snow White	9,695	8,790
K-5		49	Satin and Polished Ebony	11,695	10,390
K-5		49	Polished Sapele Mahogany	13,495	11,790
K-6		52	Polished Ebony	16,195	13,990
K-8		52	Polished Ebony	19,195	16,390

*See pricing explanation on page 203.

Model	Feet	Inches	Description	MSRP*	SMP*

KAWAI (continued)
Grands

Model	Feet	Inches	Description	MSRP*	SMP*
GM-10K	5		Satin and Polished Ebony	14,195	12,390
GM-10K	5		Satin and Polished Mahogany	15,495	13,390
GM-10K	5		French Provincial Polished Mahogany	16,695	14,390
GM-12	5		Satin and Polished Ebony	18,495	15,790
GM-12	5		Polished Mahogany/Snow White	20,195	17,190
GE-30	5	5	Satin and Polished Ebony	24,495	20,590
GE-30	5	5	Polished Walnut/Sapele Mahogany	27,195	22,790
GE-30	5	5	Satin Walnut	26,695	22,390
GE-30	5	5	Polished Snow White	26,195	21,990
RX-1BLK	5	5	Satin and Polished Ebony	31,695	26,390
RX-1BLK	5	5	Satin Walnut	35,995	29,790
RX-1BLK	5	5	Polished Walnut/Sapele Mahogany	36,995	30,590
RX-1BLK	5	5	Polished Snow White	35,995	29,790
RX-2BLK	5	10	Satin and Polished Ebony	36,195	29,990
RX-2BLK	5	10	Satin Mahogany/Walnut/Cherry/Oak	40,495	33,390
RX-2BLK	5	10	Polished Walnut/Sapeli Mahogany	42,195	34,790
RX-2BLK	5	10	Polished Rosewood	47,495	38,990
RX-2BLK	5	10	Polished Snow White	38,995	32,190
RX-2BLK	5	10	French Provincial Polished Mahogany	46,995	38,590
RX-3BLK	6	1	Satin and Polished Ebony	46,995	38,590
CR40N	6	1	Plexiglass	192,495	154,990
RX-5BLK	6	6	Satin and Polished Ebony	53,195	43,590
RX-6BLK	7		Satin and Polished Ebony	59,495	48,590
RX-7BLK	7	6	Satin and Polished Ebony	68,995	56,190
EXG	9		Polished Ebony	167,495	134,990

KAWAI, SHIGERU
Grands

Model	Feet	Inches	Description	MSRP*	SMP*
SK-2	5	10	Polished Ebony	57,900	47,400
SK-2	5	10	Polished Sapele Mahogany	66,700	54,400
SK-3	6	1	Polished Ebony	67,500	55,000
SK-3	6	1	Polished Sapele Mahogany	77,500	63,000
SK-5	6	6	Polished Ebony	77,800	63,200
SK-6	7		Polished Ebony	87,500	71,200
SK-7	7	6	Polished Ebony	97,500	78,800
SK-EX	9		Polished Ebony	199,500	166,400

KIMBALL
Verticals

Model	Feet	Inches	Description	MSRP*	SMP*
A49		49	Polished Ebony	11,900	10,990

Grands

Model	Feet	Inches	Description	MSRP*	SMP*
K1	5	1	Polished Ebony	14,300	12,990
A2	5	8	Polished Ebony	32,500	30,800
K3	6	2	Polished Ebony	17,300	15,990

*See pricing explanation on page 203.

Model	Feet	Inches	Description	MSRP*	SMP*
KINGSBURG					
Verticals					
KU 120		48	Polished Ebony/Mahogany/Walnut	6,495	5,590
KU 120C		48	French Polished Ebony/Mahogany/Walnut	6,495	5,590
KG 125		50	Polished Ebony/Mahogany/Walnut	7,695	6,590
KG 133		52	Polished Ebony/Mahogany/Walnut	8,295	6,990
Grands					
KG 158	5	2	Polished Ebony/Mahogany/Walnut	13,995	12,990
KG 185	6	1	Polished Ebony/Mahogany/Walnut	16,995	13,990
KNABE, WM.					
Baltimore Series Verticals					
WV 142		42	Continental Polished Ebony	3,650	3,650
WV 142		42	Continental Satin Walnut/Cherry	3,780	3,780
WV 142		42	Continental Polished Mahogany/Walnut/Ivory	3,780	3,780
WV 043		42	Continental Polished Ebony	4,190	
WV 043		42	Continental Polished Mahogany/Walnut	4,390	
WV 243F		43	French Provincial Satin Cherry	4,720	4,720
WV 243T		43	Satin Mahogany/Walnut	4,720	4,720
WV 115		45	Polished Ebony	4,720	
WV 115		45	Polished Mahogany/Walnut	4,720	
WV 118H		46.5	Polished Ebony	5,347	4,780
WV 118H		46.5	Polished Mahogany/Walnut	5,481	4,900
Academy Series Verticals					
WMV 245		45	Satin Ebony	5,260	5,210
WMV 245		45	Polished Ebony	5,064	5,046
WMV 245		45	Satin Walnut/Cherry	5,064	5,046
WMV 245		45	Polished Mahogany/Walnut/Ivory	5,260	5,210
WMV 247		46.5	Satin Ebony	6,387	6,108
WMV 247		46.5	Polished Ebony	6,407	6,124
WMV 247		46.5	Satin Mahogany/Walnut	6,571	6,216
WMV 247		46.5	Polished Mahogany/Walnut	6,551	6,200
WMV 647F		46.5	French Provincial Satin Cherry	6,100	5,880
WMV 647R		46.5	Renaissance Satin Walnut	6,100	5,880
WMV 647T		46.5	Satin Mahogany	6,100	5,880
WMV 121F/M		48	Satin Ebony	6,702	6,214
WMV 121F/M		48	Polished Ebony	6,506	6,016
WMV 121F/M		48	Polished Mahogany	6,702	6,214
WMV 131		52	Polished Ebony	7,078	6,662
WMV 131		52	Polished Mahogany	7,373	6,906
Concert Artist Series Verticals					
WKV 118F		46.5	French Provincial Lacquer Semigloss Cherry	8,400	8,400
WKV 118R		46.5	Renaissance Lacquer Satin Ebony	8,800	8,800
WKV 118R		46.5	Renaissance Lacquer Semigloss Walnut	8,800	8,800
WKV 118T		46.5	Lacquer Semigloss Mahogany	8,800	8,800
WKV 121		48	Satin Ebony	9,300	9,300
WKV 121		48	Polished Ebony	8,700	8,700
WKV 121		48	Polished Mahogany	10,100	10,100
WKV 131		52	Satin Ebony	10,100	11,100
WKV 131		52	Polished Ebony	9,700	9,700
WKV 131		52	Polished Mahogany	11,100	11,100
WKV 131		52	Polished Rosewood	13,400	13,400
Baltimore Series Grands					
WG 48	4	8	Satin Ebony	11,241	10,538
WG 48	4	8	Polished Ebony	10,406	9,822

*See pricing explanation on page 203.

PIANOBUYER.COM

Model	Feet	Inches	Description	MSRP*	SMP*
KNABE (continued)					
WG 48	4	8	Satin and Polished Mahogany/Walnut	11,241	10,538
WG 50	5		Satin Ebony	12,160	11,000
WG 50	5		Polished Ebony	10,888	10,294
WG 50	5		Satin and Polished Mahogany/Walnut	12,160	11,000
WG 54	5	4	Satin Ebony	14,092	12,274
WG 54	5	4	Polished Ebony	13,084	11,468
WG 54	5	4	Satin and Polished Mahogany/Walnut	14,092	12,274
WG 54	5	4	Polished Bubinga/Pommele	15,791	13,146
WG 59	5	9	Satin Ebony	15,530	13,420
WG 59	5	9	Polished Ebony	14,530	12,620
WG 59	5	9	Lacquer Semigloss and Polished Mahogany/Walnut	15,530	13,420
WG 61	6	1	Satin Ebony	17,500	15,000
WG 61	6	1	Polished Ebony	16,380	14,100
WG 61	6	1	Lacquer Semigloss and Polished Mahogany/Walnut	17,500	15,000
Academy Series Grands					
WMG 600	5	9	Satin Ebony	17,580	15,060
WMG 600	5	9	Polished Ebony	16,380	14,100
WMG 600	5	9	Lacquer Semigloss and Polished Mahogany/Walnut	17,580	15,060
WMG 600SKAF	5	9	LXV French Provincial Lacquer Semigloss Cherry/Dark Walnut	18,512	15,810
WMG 650	6	1	Satin Ebony	19,630	16,700
WMG 650	6	1	Polished Ebony	18,500	15,800
WMG 650	6	1	Lacquer Semigloss and Polished Mahogany/Walnut	19,630	16,700
WMG 700T	6	10	Satin Ebony	27,040	21,800
WMG 700T	6	10	Polished Ebony	25,740	20,800
Concert Artist Series Grands					
WKG 53	5	3	Satin Ebony	21,400	21,400
WKG 53	5	3	Polished Ebony	20,800	20,800
WKG 53	5	3	Polished Mahogany/Walnut/Ivory/White	22,400	22,400
WKG 53	5	3	Polished Bubinga/Pommele	23,300	23,300
WKG 58	5	8	Satin Ebony	25,000	25,000
WKG 58	5	8	Polished Ebony	24,300	24,300
WKG 58	5	8	Polished Mahogany/Ivory/White	25,800	25,800
WKG 58	5	8	Polished Bubinga/Pommele	27,000	27,000
WKG 64	6	4	Satin Ebony	30,400	30,400
WKG 64	6	4	Polished Ebony	29,600	29,600
WKG 64	6	4	Polished Mahogany/Ivory/White	31,400	31,400
WKG 70	7		Satin Ebony	38,600	38,600
WKG 70	7		Polished Ebony	37,800	37,800
WKG 76	7	6	Satin Ebony	39,800	39,800
WKG 76	7	6	Polished Ebony	38,600	38,600
WKG 90	9		Satin Ebony	96,500	96,500
WKG 90	9		Polished Ebony	94,500	94,500
KOHLER & CAMPBELL					
New Yorker Series Verticals					
KC-142		42	Continental Polished Ebony	3,650	3,650
KC-142		42	Continental Satin Cherry/Walnut	3,780	3,780
KC-142		42	Continental Polished Mahogany/Walnut/Ivory	3,780	3,780
KC-243F		43	French Provincial Satin Cherry	4,720	4,720
KC-243M		43	Mediterranean Satin Brown Oak	4,720	4,720
KC-243T		43	Satin Mahogany/Walnut	4,720	4,720
KC-118C		46.5	Polished Ebony	5,347	5,347
KC-118C		46.5	Polished Mahogany/Walnut	5,481	5,481

*See pricing explanation on page 203.

KOHLER & CAMPBELL *(continued)*

Millenium Series Verticals

Model	Feet	Inches	Description	MSRP*	SMP*
KM-245		45	Polished Ebony	5,064	5,046
KM-245		45	Satin Cherry/Walnut	5,064	5,046
KM-245		45	Polished Mahogany/Walnut/Ivory	5,260	5,210
KM-247		46.5	Satin Ebony	6,387	6,108
KM-247		46.5	Polished Ebony	6,407	6,130
KM-247		46.5	Satin Mahogany/Walnut	6,571	6,216
KM-247		46.5	Polished Mahogany/Walnut	6,551	6,200
KM-647F		46.5	French Provincial Satin Cherry	6,100	5,880
KM-647R		46.5	Renaissance Satin Walnut	6,100	5,880
KM-647T		46.5	Satin Mahogany	6,100	5,880
KM-121M/F		48	Satin Ebony	6,702	6,214
KM-121M/F		48	Polished Ebony	6,506	6,016
KM-121M/F		48	Polished Mahogany	6,702	6,214
KMV-48SD		48	Satin Ebony	9,300	8,790
KMV-48SD		48	Polished Ebony	8,900	8,190
KMV-48SD		48	Polished Mahogany	10,400	9,390
KM-131		52	Polished Ebony	7,078	6,662
KM-131		52	Polished Mahogany	7,373	6,906
KMV-52MD		52	Satin Ebony	10,400	9,590
KMV-52MD		52	Polished Ebony	10,000	8,990
KMV-52MD		52	Polished Mahogany	11,800	10,390

New Yorker Series Grands

Model	Feet	Inches	Description	MSRP*	SMP*
KIG-48	4	8	Satin Ebony	10,490	9,100
KIG-48	4	8	Polished Ebony	9,790	8,550
KIG-48	4	8	Satin and Polished Mahogany/Walnut	10,490	9,100
KCG-450	4	9	Satin Ebony	11,390	9,790
KCG-450	4	9	Polished Ebony	10,490	9,190
KCG-450	4	9	Polished Mahogany/Walnut	11,390	9,790
KCG-450KAF	4	9	Queen Anne Lacquer Semigloss Cherry	13,850	11,900
KCG-450KAF	4	9	Queen Anne Polished Mahogany	13,850	11,900
KCG-450KBF	4	9	French Provincial Lacquer Semigloss Cherry	14,690	12,540
KCG-450KBF	4	9	French Provincial Polished Mahogany	14,690	12,540
KIG-50	5		Satin Ebony/Mahogany/Walnut	11,190	9,860
KIG-50	5		Polished Ebony	10,590	9,190
KIG-50	5		Polished Mahogany/Walnut	11,190	9,860
KCG-500	5	1.5	Satin Ebony	12,590	10,860
KCG-500	5	1.5	Polished Ebony	11,900	10,230
KCG-500	5	1.5	Satin and Polished Mahogany/Walnut	12,590	10,860
KCG-500KAF	5	1.5	Queen Anne Lacquer Semigloss Cherry	15,100	12,850
KCG-500KAF	5	1.5	Queen Anne Polished Mahogany	15,100	12,850
KCG-500KBF	5	1.5	French Provincial Lacquer Semigloss Cherry	15,790	13,390
KCG-500KBF	5	1.5	French Provincial Polished Mahogany	15,790	13,390
KIG-54	5	4	Satin Ebony	12,290	10,690
KIG-54	5	4	Polished Ebony	11,690	10,020
KIG-54	5	4	Satin and Polished Mahogany/Walnut	12,290	10,690
KIG-54	5	4	Polished Bubinga/Pommele	12,590	10,920
KIG-59	5	9	Satin Ebony	12,990	11,130
KIG-59	5	9	Polished Ebony	12,390	10,660
KIG-59	5	9	Polished Mahogany	12,990	11,130
KIG-600	5	9	Satin Ebony	13,090	12,100
KIG-600	5	9	Polished Ebony	12,390	11,430
KIG-600	5	9	Lacquer Semigloss Mahogany/Walnut	13,090	12,100
KIG-600	5	9	Polished Mahogany/Walnut	13,090	12,100
KIG-600SKAF	5	9	Louis XV Lacquer Semigloss Cherry/Dark Walnut	17,290	15,690
KCG-600	5	9	Satin Ebony	14,590	12,350
KCG-600	5	9	Polished Ebony	13,690	11,700

*See pricing explanation on page 203.

Model	Feet	Inches	Description	MSRP*	SMP*
KOHLER & CAMPBELL (continued)					
KCG-600	5	9	Lacquer Semigloss Mahogany/Walnut	14,590	12,350
KCG-600	5	9	Polished Mahogany/Walnut	14,590	12,350
KCG-600KBF	5	9	French Provincial Lacquer Semigloss Cherry	17,100	14,450
KCG-600SKAF	5	9	Louis XV Lacquer Semigloss Cherry/Dark Walnut	18,300	15,700
KCG-600L	5	9	Empire Polished Ebony	15,590	13,390
KIG-650	6	1	Satin Ebony	14,490	13,430
KIG-650	6	1	Polished Ebony	13,590	12,770
KIG-650	6	1	Lacquer Semigloss Mahogany/Walnut	14,490	13,430
KIG-650	6	1	Polished Mahogany/Walnut	14,490	13,430
KCG-650	6	1	Satin Ebony	15,990	13,390
KCG-650	6	1	Polished Ebony	14,990	12,790
KCG-650	6	1	Lacquer Semigloss Mahogany/Walnut	15,990	13,390
KCG-650	6	1	Polished Mahogany/Walnut	15,990	13,390
Millenium Series Grands					
KCM-500	5	1.5	Satin Ebony	14,990	12,550
KCM-500	5	1.5	Polished Ebony	14,190	11,880
KCM-500	5	1.5	Lacquer Semigloss Mahogany/Walnut	15,190	12,700
KCM-500	5	1.5	Polished Mahogany/Walnut	15,190	12,700
KCM-600	5	9	Satin Ebony	16,300	14,000
KCM-600	5	9	Polished Ebony	15,390	13,170
KCM-600	5	9	Lacquer Semigloss Mahogany/Walnut	16,300	14,000
KCM-600	5	9	Polished Mahogany/Walnut	16,300	14,000
KCM-600 KBF	5	9	French Provincial Lacquer Semigloss Cherry	18,700	15,700
KCM-600SKAF	5	9	Louis XV Lacquer Semigloss Cherry/Dark Walnut	19,500	16,330
KCM-650	6	1	Satin Ebony	17,390	15,000
KCM-650	6	1	Polished Ebony	16,500	14,220
KCM-650	6	1	Lacquer Semigloss Mahogany/Walnut	17,390	15,000
KCM-650	6	1	Polished Mahogany/Walnut	17,390	15,000
KFM-700 (Indo)	6	10	Satin Ebony	23,000	19,400
KFM-700 (Indo)	6	10	Polished Ebony	22,000	18,600
KFM-700	6	10	Polished Ebony	34,000	29,630
KFM-850	7	6	Polished Ebony	37,000	32,000
MASON & HAMLIN					
Verticals					
50		50	Satin and Polished Ebony	23,208	19,195
Grands					
B	5	4	Satin Ebony	52,788	41,507
B	5	4	Polished Ebony	53,587	43,893
B	5	4	Satin Mahogany/Walnut	55,218	44,291
B	5	4	Polished Pyramid Mahogany	63,039	50,422
B	5	4	Satin Rosewood	57,943	46,427
B	5	4	Polished Bubinga	60,083	48,107
B	5	4	Satin Macassar Ebony	61,728	49,395
B	5	4	Polished Macassar Ebony	63,039	50,422
A	5	8	Satin Ebony	60,071	47,216
A	5	8	Polished Ebony	61,916	50,422
A	5	8	Satin Mahogany/Walnut	63,383	50,694
A	5	8	Polished Pyramid Mahogany	77,050	61,406
A	5	8	Satin Rosewood	70,353	56,157
A	5	8	Polished Bubinga	72,814	58,088
A	5	8	Satin Macassar Ebony	74,443	59,363
A	5	8	Polished Macassar Ebony	77,050	61,406
A	5	8	"Monticello" Polished Ebony	67,155	53,651
A	5	8	"Monticello" Satin Mahogany	67,475	53,901

*See pricing explanation on page 203.

Model	Feet	Inches	Description	MSRP*	SMP*
MASON & HAMLIN (continued)					
A	5	8	"Monticello" Satin Walnut/Rosewood	81,799	65,131
AA	6	4	Satin Ebony	68,015	54,325
AA	6	4	Polished Ebony	69,524	56,387
AA	6	4	Satin Mahogany/Walnut	71,595	57,131
AA	6	4	Polished Pyramid Mahogany	82,247	65,483
AA	6	4	Satin Rosewood	75,551	60,234
AA	6	4	Polished Bubinga	78,012	62,162
AA	6	4	Satin Macassar Ebony	79,640	63,438
AA	6	4	Polished Macassar Ebony	82,247	65,483
AA	6	4	"Monticello" Polished Ebony	75,119	59,893
AA	6	4	"Monticello" Satin Mahogany	75,687	60,341
AA	6	4	"Monticello" Satin Walnut/Rosewood	92,385	73,430
BB	7		Satin Ebony	77,080	61,432
BB	7		Polished Ebony	79,299	63,170
BB	7		Satin Mahogany/Walnut	79,810	63,571
BB	7		Polished Pyramid Mahogany	95,023	75,499
BB	7		Satin Rosewood	89,342	71,045
BB	7		Polished Bubinga	91,558	72,782
BB	7		Satin Macassar Ebony	92,722	73,693
BB	7		Polished Macassar Ebony	95,023	75,499
BB	7		"Monticello" Polished Ebony	83,084	66,138
BB	7		"Monticello" Satin Mahogany	83,902	66,781
BB	7		"Monticello" Satin Walnut/Rosewood	102,969	81,728
CC	9	4	Satin Ebony	114,604	90,850
CC	9	4	Polished Ebony	119,801	94,925
CC	9	4	Satin Mahogany/Walnut	122,670	97,173
CC	9	4	Polished Pyramid Mahogany	139,656	110,490
CC	9	4	Satin Rosewood	129,642	102,640
CC	9	4	Polished Bubinga	133,987	106,046
CC	9	4	Satin Macassar Ebony	137,428	108,744
CC	9	4	Polished Macassar Ebony	139,656	110,490
			Chrome Art Case, add	4,000	3,200

MAY BERLIN

Verticals

Model	Feet	Inches	Description	MSRP*	SMP*
M 121		48	Tradition Polished Ebony w/brass hardware	6,690	6,690
M 121		48	Tradition Polished Mahogany/White w/brass hardware	6,890	6,890
M 121		48	Tradition Satin Walnut w/brass hardware	6,890	6,890
M 121		48	Tradition Polished Ebony w/chrome hardware	7,090	7,090
M 121		48	Tradition Polished White w/chrome hardware	7,090	7,090
M 121		48	"Modern Cubus" Polished Ebony	7,090	7,090
M 126		50	"Noblesse" Polished Ebony	7,090	7,090

Grands

Model	Feet	Inches	Description	MSRP*	SMP*
M 178	5	10	Polished Ebony	19,890	18,380

*See pricing explanation on page 203.

Model	Feet	Inches	Description	MSRP*	SMP*

MILLER, HENRY F.

Verticals

Model	Feet	Inches	Description	MSRP*	SMP*
HMV-043		43	Continental Polished Ebony	3,726	3,726
HMV-043		43	Continental Polished Mahogany	3,936	3,936
HMV-044		44	Continental Polished Ebony	3,726	3,726
HMV-045		45	Italian Provincial	4,934	4,934
HMV-045		45	French Provincial	4,934	4,934
HMV-045		45	Mediterranean Oak	4,934	4,934
HMV-046		45.5	Satin Ebony	4,934	4,934
HMV-046		45.5	Satin Walnut	5,039	5,039
HMV-046		45.5	Satin Oak	4,789	4,789
HMV-047		46.5	Satin Ebony	4,619	4,619
HMV-047		46.5	Polished Ebony	4,304	4,304
HMV-047		46.5	Polished Mahogany	4,829	4,829
HMV-048		48	Italian Provincial Cherry	5,301	5,301
HMV-048		48	French Provincial Cherry	5,301	5,301
HMV-52		52	Polished Ebony	6,824	6,824

Grands

Model	Feet	Inches	Description	MSRP*	SMP*
HMG-058S	4	10	Satin Ebony	10,866	10,866
HMG-058S	4	10	Polished Ebony	10,446	10,446
HMG-058S	4	10	Satin Mahogany	11,292	11,292
HMG-058S	4	10	Polished Mahogany	10,866	10,866
HMG-058S	4	10	French Provincial Satin Cherry	11,601	11,601
HMG-064S	5	4	Satin Ebony	13,124	13,124
HMG-064S	5	4	Polished Ebony	12,704	12,704
HMG-064S	5	4	Satin Mahogany	13,193	13,193
HMG-064S	5	4	Polished Mahogany	13,124	13,124
HMG-064S	5	4	French Provincial Satin Cherry	13,259	13,259
HMG-067S	5	7	Polished Ebony	15,434	15,434
HMG-067S	5	7	Polished Mahogany	15,749	15,749
HMG-074S	6	2	Satin Ebony	17,849	17,849
HMG-074S	6	2	Polished Ebony	17,586	17,586

PALATINO

Verticals

Model	Feet	Inches	Description	MSRP*	SMP*
PUP-123T		48	"Lucca" Polished Ebony	5,400	5,400
PUP-123T		48	"Lucca" Polished Ebony with Renner action	7,400	7,400
PUP-123C		48	"Carved Contessa" French Satin Brown Mahogany	5,600	5,600
PUP-126		50	"Messina" Polished Ebony	6,000	6,000
PUP-126		50	"Messina" Polished Ebony with Renner action	7,600	7,600

Grands

Model	Feet	Inches	Description	MSRP*	SMP*
PGD-46	4	6	"Cesaro" Polished Ebony	10,800	10,800
PGD-50	5		"Salerno" Polished Ebony	11,600	11,600
PGD-59	5	9	"Palermo" Polished Ebony	13,800	13,800
PGD-59	5	9	"Palermo" Polished Ebony with Renner action	18,000	18,000

*See pricing explanation on page 203.

Model	Feet	Inches	Description	MSRP*	SMP*
PEARL RIVER					
Verticals					
UP-108D3		42.5	Continental Polished Ebony	3,795	3,590
UP-108D3		42.5	Continental Polished Mahogany/Walnut	3,995	3,790
UP-108M		42.5	Polished Ebony	4,195	3,790
UP-108T2		42.5	Polished Ebony	4,195	3,790
UP-110P8		43	French Provincial Satin Cherry	5,495	4,550
UP-110P9		43	Mediterranean Satin Walnut	5,495	4,550
UP-110P10		43	Italian Provincial Satin Mahogany	5,495	4,550
UP-115E		45	Satin Ebony/Oak/Walnut (School)	5,495	4,550
UP-115M2/M5		45	Polished Ebony	4,595	3,990
UP-115M2/M5		45	Polished Mahogany/Walnut	4,895	4,190
T1		46	Polished Ebony	4,755	4,590
T1		46	Polished Mahogany	4,945	4,730
T2		47.25	Polished Ebony	5,125	4,870
T2		47.25	Polished Walnut	5,285	4,990
EU122		48	Polished Ebony	5,995	4,890
T3		48	Polished Ebony	5,495	5,150
UP-130T		51.5	Polished Ebony	6,995	5,190
Grands					
GP-150	4	11	Hand-rubbed Satin Ebony	11,495	8,490
GP-150	4	11	Polished Ebony	10,995	8,090
GP-150	4	11	Polished Mahogany/Walnut/White	11,495	8,490
GP-160	5	3	Polished Ebony	11,995	8,990
GP-160	5	3	Satin Mahogany/Walnut	12,495	9,390
GP-160A	5	3	European Renaissance Polished Ebony	12,995	9,790
GP-170	5	7	Polished Ebony	13,995	10,590
GP-188A	6	2	Polished Ebony	16,995	12,990
GP-188A	6	2	Polished White	17,995	14,590
GP-212	7		Polished Ebony	24,995	18,990
GP-275	9		Polished Ebony	74,995	56,990
PERZINA, GEBR.					
Verticals					
GP-112		44	Polished Ebony	8,090	6,390
GP-112		44	Polished Mahogany/Walnut	8,580	6,720
GP-112		44	Polished Ribbon Mahogany	8,790	6,860
GP-112		44	Queen Anne Polished Ebony (with molding)	8,580	6,720
GP-112		44	Queen Anne Polished Mahogany/Walnut (with molding)	9,290	7,190
GP-112		44	Queen Anne Polished Ribbon Mahogany (with molding)	9,580	7,390
GP-122		48	Polished Ebony	9,140	7,090
GP-122		48	Polished Mahogany/Walnut	9,640	7,430
GP-122		48	Polished Ribbon Mahogany	9,870	7,580
GP-122		48	Deco Leg Polished Ebony w/Chrome Nickel Hardware	9,290	7,190
GP-122		48	Deco Leg Polished Two-Tone Ebony w/Oak Trim	9,640	7,430
GP-122		48	Deco Leg Polished Mahogany	9,870	7,580
GP-122		48	Deco Leg Polished Two-Tone Ebony w/Bubinga or Pommele Front	10,190	7,790
GP-122		48	Queen Anne Polished Ebony w/Molding	9,640	7,430
GP-122		48	Queen Anne Polished Mahogany/Walnut w/Molding	10,190	7,790
GP-122		48	Queen Anne Polished Ribbon Mahogany w/Molding	10,470	7,990
GP-122R		48	GP-122 with Renner AA or Abel Deluxe Hammers, add	1,050	700
GP-129		51	Polished Ebony	10,190	7,790
GP-129		51	Polished Mahogany/Walnut	10,690	8,120
GP-129		51	Deco Leg Polished Ebony w/Chrome Nickel Hardware	10,350	7,900
GP-129		51	Deco Leg Polished Two-Tone Ebony w/Oak Trim	10,590	8,070
GP-129		51	Deco Leg Polished Mahogany	10,950	8,300
GP-129		51	Deco Leg Polished Two-Tone Ebony w/Bubinga or Pommele Front	11,890	8,930

*See pricing explanation on page 203.

Model	Feet	Inches	Description	MSRP*	SMP*
PERZINA, GEBR. (continued)					
GP-129		51	Queen Anne Polished Ebony w/Molding	10,440	7,960
GP-129		51	Queen Anne Polished Mahogany/Walnut w/Molding	11,280	8,520
GP-129R		51	GP-129 with Renner AA or Abel Deluxe Hammers, add	1,300	867
GP-130R		51	Satin Ebony	12,540	9,360
GP-130R		51	Polished Ebony	12,060	9,040
GP-130R		51	Polished Mahogany/Walnut	12,540	9,360
GP-133R		52.5	"Schwerin" Polished Ebony	12,400	9,270
Grands					
T-152	5		Polished Ebony	18,790	13,540
T-152	5		Polished Mahogany/Walnut	20,550	14,700
T-152	5		Polished Ebony (round leg)	19,560	13,840
T-152	5		Polished Mahogany/Walnut (round leg)	20,970	14,980
T-152	5		Queen Anne Polished Ebony	19,560	13,840
T-152	5		Queen Anne Polished Mahogany/Walnut	20,970	14,980
T-152	5		Designer Polished Ebony w/Bubinga Fallboard/Lid (straight leg)	20,760	14,840
T-152	5		Designer Polished Ebony w/Bubinga Fallboard/Lid (curved leg)	21,270	15,180
T-152	5		Designer Polished Ebony w/Bubinga Legs/Fallboard/Desk	21,270	15,180
T-161	5	3	Polished Ebony	23,980	16,990
T-161	5	3	Polished Mahogany/Walnut	25,780	18,190
T-161	5	3	Polished Ebony (round leg)	24,820	17,550
T-161	5	3	Polished Mahogany/Walnut (round leg)	26,550	18,700
T-161	5	3	Queen Anne Polished Ebony	24,820	17,550
T-161	5	3	Queen Anne Polished Mahogany/Walnut	26,550	18,700
T-161	5	3	Designer Polished Ebony w/Bubinga Fallboard/Lid (straight leg)	26,890	18,990
T-161	5	3	Designer Polished Ebony w/Bubinga Fallboard/Lid (round or curved leg)	27,570	19,380
T-161	5	3	Designer Polished Ebony w/Bubinga Legs/Fallboard/Desk	27,570	19,380
T-175	5	9	Polished Ebony	26,090	18,390
T-175	5	9	Polished Mahogany/Walnut	28,350	19,900
T-175	5	9	Polished Ebony (round leg)	26,670	18,780
T-175	5	9	Polished Mahogany/Walnut (round leg)	28,920	20,280
T-175	5	9	Queen Anne Polished Ebony	26,670	18,780
T-175	5	9	Queen Anne Polished Mahogany/Walnut	28,920	20,280
T-175	5	9	Designer Polished Ebony w/Bubinga Fallboard/Lid (straight leg)	28,920	20,280
T-175	5	9	Designer Polished Ebony w/Bubinga Fallboard/Lid (round or curved leg)	29,990	20,990
T-175	5	9	Designer Polished Ebony w/Bubinga Legs/Fallboard/Desk	29,990	20,990
T-188	6	1	Polished Ebony	29,280	20,520
T-188	6	1	Polished Mahogany/Walnut	30,450	21,300
T-188	6	1	Polished Ebony (round leg)	29,990	20,990
T-188	6	1	Polished Mahogany/Walnut (round leg)	30,990	21,660
T-188	6	1	Queen Anne Polished Ebony	29,990	20,990
T-188	6	1	Queen Anne Polished Mahogany/Walnut	30,990	21,660
T-188	6	1	Designer Polished Ebony w/Bubinga Fallboard/Lid (straight leg)	30,990	21,860
T-188	6	1	Designer Polished Ebony w/Bubinga Fallboard/Lid (round or curved leg)	32,990	22,990
T-188	6	1	Designer Polished Ebony w/Bubinga Legs/Fallboard/Desk	32,990	22,990

*See pricing explanation on page 203.

Model	Feet	Inches	Description	MSRP*	SMP*
PETROF					
Verticals					
P 116 E1		45.75	Continental Polished Ebony	15,438	13,350
P 118 C1		46.25	Chippendale Satin/Polished Ebony/Mahogany/Walnut	19,063	16,250
P 118 D1		46.25	Demi-Chippendale Satin/Polished Ebony/Mahogany/Walnut/Cherry	18,850	16,080
P 118 G1		46.25	Satin/Polished Ebony/Mahogany/Walnut	18,263	15,610
P 118 M1		46.25	Satin/Polished Ebony/Mahogany/Walnut	17,275	14,820
P 118 P1		46.25	Satin/Polished Ebony/Mahogany/Walnut/Cherry	16,738	14,390
P 118 R1		46.25	Rococo Satin White w/Gold Trim	20,238	17,190
P 123 K3		48.5	"Cabinet" Continental Modern	41,913	34,530
P 125 F1		49.25	Satin/Polished Ebony/Mahogany/Walnut	19,863	16,890
P 125 G1		49.25	Satin/Polished Ebony/Mahogany/Walnut	20,575	17,460
P 125 M1		49.25	Satin/Polished Ebony/Mahogany/Walnut	20,138	17,110
P 127 NB		49.25	Satin Ebony with Chrome Legs	35,038	29,030
P 127 NC		49.25	Satin Ebony/Anthracite with Chrome Legs	35,038	29,030
P 131 M1		51	Polished Ebony	25,750	21,600
P 131 E1		51	Polished Ebony	25,750	21,600
P 135 K1		53	Polished Ebony	31,425	26,140
Grands					
P V	5	2	Polished Ebony/Mahogany/Walnut	51,075	41,860
P V	5	2	Demi-Chippendale Polished Ebony/Mahogany/Walnut	54,738	44,790
P 159	5	2	"Bora" Polished Ebony/Mahogany/Walnut	52,075	42,660
P 173	5	6	"Breeze" Polished Ebony/Mahogany/Walnut	55,675	45,540
P IV	5	7	Polished Ebony/Mahogany/Walnut	55,000	45,000
P IV	5	7	"Klasik" Polished Ebony/Mahogany/Walnut	64,438	52,550
P IV	5	7	Chippendale Polished Ebony/Mahogany/Walnut	72,825	59,260
P IV	5	7	Demi-Chippendale Polished Ebony/Mahogany/Walnut	62,600	51,080
P IV	5	7	Rococo Satin White w/Gold Trim	70,725	57,580
P III	6	3	Polished Ebony/Mahogany/Walnut	57,525	47,020
P III	6	3	"Majestic" Polished Ebony/Mahogany/Walnut	64,950	52,960
P 194	6	3	"Storm" Polished Ebony/Mahogany/Walnut	62,850	51,280
P 210	6	10	"Pasat" Polished Ebony	94,313	76,450
P II	7	9	Polished Ebony	116,950	94,560
P 237	7	9	"Monsoon" Polished Ebony	138,300	111,640
P 284 - I	9	2	"Mistral" Polished Ebony	163,700	131,960
PRAMBERGER					
Legacy Series Verticals					
LV-108		42	Continental Polished Ebony	3,691	3,691
LV-108		42	Continental Polished Mahogany/Ivory	3,823	3,823
LV-110		42	Continental Polished Ebony		
LV-110		42	Continental Polished Mahogany		
LV-43F		43	French Provincial Satin Cherry/Oak	4,788	4,788
LV-43T		43	Satin Mahogany/Walnut	4,788	4,788
LV-118		46.5	Satin Ebony	5,626	5,500
LV-118		46.5	Polished Ebony	5,347	5,296
LV-118		46.5	Polished Mahogany	5,626	5,500
Signature Series Verticals					
PV-118F		46.5	French Provincial Satin Cherry	6,100	5,760
PV-118R		46.5	Renaissance Satin Walnut	6,100	5,760
PV-118T		46.5	Satin Mahogany	6,100	5,760
PV-118S		46.5	Satin Ebony	6,551	6,026
PV-118S		46.5	Polished Ebony	6,322	5,832
PV-118S		46.5	Satin Mahogany/Walnut	6,322	5,832
PV-118S		46.5	Polished Mahogany/Walnut	6,551	6,026
PV-121		48	Satin Ebony	7,143	6,726

*See pricing explanation on page 203.

Model	Feet	Inches	Description	MSRP*	SMP*
PRAMBERGER (continued)					
PV-121		48	Polished Ebony	6,958	6,634
PV-121		48	Polished Mahogany	7,143	6,726
PV-131		52	Satin Ebony	7,661	6,926
PV-131		52	Polished Ebony	7,423	6,706
PV-131		52	Polished Mahogany	7,661	6,926
J.P. Pramberger Platinum Series Verticals					
JP-118F		46.5	French Provincial Lacquer Semigloss Cherry	9,100	9,100
JP-118T		46.5	Lacquer Semigloss Mahogany	9,100	9,100
JP-125		49	Satin Ebony	10,800	10,800
JP-125		49	Polished Ebony	10,400	10,400
JP-125		49	Lacquer Semigloss Mahogany/Walnut	11,700	11,700
JP-125		49	Lacquer Polished Bubinga/Rosewood	12,000	12,000
JP-131		52	Satin Ebony	12,000	12,000
JP-131		52	Polished Ebony	11,600	11,600
JP-131		52	Lacquer Semigloss Mahogany/Walnut	13,000	13,000
JP-131		52	Lacquer Polished Bubinga/Rosewood	13,400	13,400
Legacy Series Grands					
LG-145	4	8	Polished Ebony	10,406	9,822
LG-145	4	8	Polished Mahogany/Walnut	11,241	10,012
LG-150	4	11.5	Satin Ebony	11,552	11,000
LG-150	4	11.5	Polished Ebony	10,888	10,294
LG-150	4	11.5	Polished Mahogany	11,552	11,000
LG-157	5	2	Satin Ebony	13,081	11,890
LG-157	5	2	Polished Ebony	12,224	11,184
LG-157	5	2	Polished Mahogany	13,081	11,890
LG-157	5	2	Polished Pommele/Bubinga w/Ebony	15,654	13,042
LG-175	5	9	Satin Ebony	16,371	14,096
LG-175	5	9	Polished Ebony	15,377	13,302
LG-175	5	9	Polished Mahogany	16,371	14,096
Signature Series Grands					
PS-157	5	2	Satin Ebony	16,240	13,990
PS-157	5	2	Polished Ebony	15,330	13,260
PS-157	5	2	Lacquer Satin and Polished Mahogany/Walnut	16,240	13,990
PS-157	5	2	Polished Pommele/Bubinga w/Ebony	18,326	15,096
PS-175	5	9	Satin Ebony	17,630	15,100
PS-175	5	9	Polished Ebony	16,630	14,300
PS-175	5	9	Lacquer Satin and Polished Mahogany/Walnut	17,630	15,100
PS-175F	5	9	French Provincial Lacquer Semigloss Cherry	17,892	15,190
PS-175SKAF	5	9	Louis XVI Lacquer Semigloss Cherry/Dark Walnut	18,512	15,810
PS-185	6	1	Satin Ebony	19,630	16,700
PS-185	6	1	Polished Ebony	16,800	15,800
PS-185	6	1	Lacquer Satin and Polished Mahogany/Walnut	19,630	16,700
PS-208	6	10	Satin Ebony	27,040	21,800
PS-208	6	10	Polished Ebony	25,740	20,800
J.P. Pramberger Platinum Series Grands					
JP-179F	5	10	French Provincial Lacquer Semigloss Mahogany/Walnut/Cherry	33,200	33,200
JP-179L	5	10	Satin Ebony	28,200	28,200
JP-179L	5	10	Polished Ebony	27,500	27,500
JP-179L	5	10	Lacquer Semigloss Mahogany/Walnut	29,600	29,600
JP-179L	5	10	Polished Bubinga/Pommele	29,600	29,600
JP-190A	6	3	Satin Ebony	32,700	32,700
JP-190A	6	3	Polished Ebony	32,000	32,000
JP-190A	6	3	Lacquer Semigloss Mahogany/Walnut	34,000	34,000
JP-190A	6	3	Polished Bubinga/Pommele	34,400	34,400
JP-208B	6	10	Satin Ebony	35,400	35,400
JP-208B	6	10	Polished Ebony	34,600	34,600

*See pricing explanation on page 203.

Model	Feet	Inches	Description	MSRP*	SMP*
PRAMBERGER (continued)					
JP-208B	6	10	Lacquer Semigloss Mahogany/Walnut	36,800	36,800
JP-228C	7	6	Satin Ebony	39,600	39,600
JP-228C	7	6	Polished Ebony	38,400	38,400
JP-280E	9	2	Polished Ebony	94,500	94,500

RITMÜLLER

Verticals

Model	Feet	Inches	Description	MSRP*	SMP*
UP-110RB1		43.5	Satin Walnut/Cherry	6,995	4,990
UP-110RB		43.5	French Provincial Satin Walnut/Cherry	6,995	4,990
UH-118R		46.5	Polished Ebony	8,995	6,390
UP-120RE		47.5	Satin Ebony/Mahogany	7,836	5,590
UP-121RB		47.5	Polished Ebony	6,995	5,190
UP-121RB		47.5	Polished Mahogany/White	7,495	5,390
UH-121R		48	Chippendale Polished Ebony	9,495	6,990
UH-121R		48	Chippendale Polished Mahogany/Sapele	9,995	7,190
UH-132R		52	Polished Ebony	11,995	8,190

Grands

Model	Feet	Inches	Description	MSRP*	SMP*
GH-148R	4	10	Polished Ebony (spade leg)	15,995	10,590
GH-148R	4	10	Polished Mahogany/Sapele (spade leg)	16,495	11,390
GH-148R2	4	10	Polished Ebony (round leg)	16,495	10,990
GH-148R2	4	10	Polished Mahogany/Sapele (round leg)	16,995	11,790
R8	4	11	Polished Ebony	12,995	8,990
R8	4	11	Polished Mahogany/White	13,495	9,590
GH-160R	5	3	Hand-rubbed Satin Ebony	18,495	13,190
GH-160R	5	3	Polished Ebony	17,995	12,390
GH-160R	5	3	Polished Mahogany/Sapele	18,495	13,190
R9	5	3	Polished Ebony	14,995	9,790
R9	5	3	Polished Mahogany	15,495	10,390
GH-170R	5	7	Polished Ebony	19,995	14,390
GH-188R	6	2	Polished Ebony	24,995	17,990
GH-212R	7		Polished Ebony	29,995	22,990
GH-275R	9		Polished Ebony	79,995	60,990

SAMICK

Verticals

Model	Feet	Inches	Description	MSRP*	SMP*
JS-042		42	Continental Polished Ebony	3,650	3,650
JS-042		42	Continental Polished Mahogany/Walnut/Ivory	3,780	3,780
JS-042		42	Continental Satin Cherry/Walnut	3,650	3,650
JS-043		42	Continental Polished Ebony	4,190	4,190
JS-043		42	Continental Polished Mahogany/Walnut/Ivory	4,390	4,390
JS-143F		43	French Provincial Satin Cherry	4,720	4,720
JS-143M		43	Mediterranean Satin Brown Oak	4,720	4,720
JS-143T		43	Satin Mahogany	4,720	4,720
JS-115		45	Satin Ebony	5,076	5,076
JS-115		45	Polished Ebony	4,768	4,768
JS-115		45	Satin Mahogany/Walnut/Cherry	4,768	4,768
JS-115		45	Polished Mahogany/Walnut	5,076	5,076
JS-118H		46.5	Satin Ebony	5,626	5,626
JS-118H		46.5	Polished Ebony	5,347	5,347
JS-118H		46.5	Polished Mahogany	5,626	5,626
JS-247		46.5	Satin Ebony	6,551	6,200
JS-247		46.5	Polished Ebony	6,322	6,056
JS-247		46.5	Satin Mahogany/Walnut	6,322	6,056
JS-247		46.5	Polished Mahogany/Walnut	6,551	6,200
JS-121M		48	Satin Ebony	6,702	6,214

*See pricing explanation on page 203.

PIANOBUYER.COM

Model	Feet	Inches	Description	MSRP*	SMP*
SAMICK (continued)					
JS-121M		48	Polished Ebony	6,506	6,016
JS-121M		48	Polished Mahogany	6,702	6,214
JS-131		52	Satin Ebony	7,373	6,906
JS-131		52	Polished Ebony	7,136	6,708
JS-131		52	Polished Mahogany	7,373	6,906
Grands					
SIG-48	4	8	Polished Ebony	10,406	9,822
SIG-48	4	8	Polished Mahogany/Walnut	11,241	10,538
SIG-50	4	11.5	Satin Ebony	11,552	11,000
SIG-50	4	11.5	Polished Ebony	10,888	10,294
SIG-50	4	11.5	Satin Lacquer Mahogany/Walnut	11,552	11,000
SIG-50	4	11.5	Polished Mahogany/Walnut	11,552	11,000
SIG-54	5	4	Satin Ebony	14,092	12,274
SIG-54	5	4	Polished Ebony	13,084	11,468
SIG-54	5	4	Satin Lacquer Mahogany/Walnut	14,092	12,274
SIG-54	5	4	Polished Mahogany/Walnut	14,092	12,274
SIG-54	5	4	Polished Bubinga/Pommele w/Ebony	15,791	13,146
SIG-57	5	7	Satin Ebony	15,380	13,300
SIG-57	5	7	Polished Ebony	14,380	12,500
SIG-57	5	7	Satin Lacquer Mahogany/Walnut	15,380	13,300
SIG-57	5	7	Polished Mahogany/Walnut	15,380	13,300
SIG-57L	5	7	Empire Satin Ebony	17,130	14,700
SIG-57L	5	7	Empire Polished Ebony	16,130	13,900
SIG-57L	5	7	Empire Satin Lacquer Mahogany	17,130	14,700
SIG-57L	5	7	Empire Polished Mahogany	17,130	14,700
SIG-59	5	9	Satin Ebony		13,052
SIG-59	5	9	Polished Ebony		12,244
SIG-59	5	9	Satin Lacquer Mahogany		13,052
SIG-59	5	9	Polished Mahogany		13,052
SIG-61	6	1	Satin Ebony	17,500	15,000
SIG-61	6	1	Polished Ebony	16,380	14,100
SIG-61	6	1	Polished Mahogany/Walnut	17,500	15,000
SIG-61L	6	1	Empire Satin Ebony	19,250	16,400
SIG-61L	6	1	Empire Polished Ebony	18,130	15,500
SIG-61L	6	1	Empire Polished Mahogany	19,250	16,400

SAUTER

Standard wood veneers are walnut, mahogany, oak, ash, and alder.

Verticals

Model	Feet	Inches	Description	MSRP*	SMP*
122		48	"Ragazza" Polished Ebony	32,347	32,347
122		48	"Ragazza" Satin Cherry	32,017	32,017
122		48	"Ragazza" Polished Cherry/Yew	37,970	37,970
122		48	"Vista" Polished Ebony	35,434	35,434
122		48	"Vista" Satin Maple	33,781	33,781
122		48	"Vista" Satin Cherry	35,258	35,258
122		48	"Master Class" Polished Ebony	41,652	41,652
122		48	Peter Maly "Artes" Polished Ebony	46,437	46,437
122		48	Peter Maly "Artes" Polished Palisander/Macassar	47,893	47,893
122		48	Peter Maly "Artes" Polished White	47,319	47,319
122		48	Peter Maly "Pure Noble" Polished Ebony/Veneers	43,416	43,416
122		48	Peter Maly "Pure Noble" Polished White/Red	44,607	44,607
122		48	Peter Maly "Pure Basic" Satin Ebony/Walnut	35,192	35,192
122		48	Peter Maly "Pure Basic" Satin White/Maple	35,192	35,192
122		48	Peter Maly "Rondo" Polished Ebony	38,610	38,610
122		48	Peter Maly "Rondo" Satin Wenge	35,655	35,655
122		48	Peter Maly "Vitrea" Colored Ebony with Glass	36,140	36,140

*See pricing explanation on page 203.

Model	Feet	Inches	Description	MSRP*	SMP*
SAUTER (continued)					
122		48	"Schulpiano" Satin Beech/Black Ash	28,202	28,202
130		51	"Master Class" Polished Ebony	47,209	47,209
130		51	"Competence" Polished Ebony	40,219	40,219
130		51	"Competence" Satin Walnut	38,169	38,169
130		51	Peter Maly "Cura" Satin Walnut	45,136	45,136
130		51	Peter Maly "Cura" Satin Cherry	46,614	46,614
Grands					
160	5	3	"Alpha" Polished Ebony	84,650	84,650
160	5	3	"Alpha" Satin Standard Wood Veneers	78,123	78,123
160	5	3	Chippendale Satin Cherry	87,781	87,781
160	5	3	Chippendale Satin Standard Wood Veneers	84,518	84,518
160	5	3	"Noblesse" Satin Cherry	94,176	94,176
160	5	3	"Noblesse" Polished Cherry	104,671	104,671
160	5	3	"Noblesse" Satin Burl Walnut	98,387	98,387
160	5	3	"Noblesse" Satin Standard Wood Veneers	90,934	90,934
160	5	3	"Noblesse" Polished Standard Wood Veneers	101,276	101,276
185	6	1	"Delta" Polished Ebony	94,284	94,284
185	6	1	"Delta" Polished Ebony w/Burl Walnut	96,666	96,666
185	6	1	"Delta" Polished Pyramid Mahogany	104,126	104,126
185	6	1	"Delta" Polished Bubinga	103,340	103,340
185	6	1	"Delta" Polished Rio Palisander	104,126	104,126
185	6	1	"Delta" Satin Maple with Silver	88,667	88,667
185	6	1	"Delta" Polished White	97,228	97,228
185	6	1	"Delta" Satin Standard Wood Veneers	86,689	86,689
185	6	1	Chippendale Satin Cherry	96,396	96,396
185	6	1	Chippendale Satin Standard Wood Veneers	93,093	93,093
185	6	1	"Noblesse" Satin Cherry	103,070	103,070
185	6	1	"Noblesse" Polished Cherry	114,799	114,799
185	6	1	"Noblesse" Satin Burl Walnut	107,204	107,204
185	6	1	"Noblesse" Satin Standard Wood Veneers	99,902	99,902
185	6	1	"Noblesse" Polished Standard Wood Veneers	111,990	111,990
210	6	11	Peter Maly "Vivace" Polished Ebony	131,089	131,089
210	6	11	Peter Maly "Vivace" Satin Wood Veneers	122,363	122,363
210	6	11	Peter Maly "Vivace" Polished White	133,048	133,048
220	7	3	"Omega" Polished Ebony	118,980	118,980
220	7	3	"Omega" Polished Burl Walnut	132,625	132,625
220	7	3	"Omega" Polished Pyramid Mahogany	131,423	131,423
220	7	3	"Omega" Satin Standard Wood Veneers	114,172	114,172
230	7	7	Peter Maly "Ambiente" Polished Ebony	150,656	150,656
230	7	7	Peter Maly "Ambiente" Polished Ebony w/Crystals	172,359	172,359
275	9		Concert Polished Ebony	204,227	204,227
SCHIMMEL					
Classic Series Verticals					
C 114		45	"Modern Junior" Polished Ebony	18,990	17,580
C 116		46	Tradition Polished Ebony	19,490	17,980
C 116		46	Tradition Polished Mahogany/White	21,990	20,180
C 116		46	Tradition Satin Walnut/Cherry	19,490	17,980
C 116		46	Tradition Satin Alder/Beech	19,490	17,980
C 116		46	"Modern" Polished Ebony	22,690	20,780
C 116		46	"Modern" Polished White	24,990	22,780
C 116		46	"Modern Cubus" Polished Ebony	22,690	20,780
C 116		46	"Modern Cubus" Polished White	24,990	22,780
C 120		48	Tradition Polished Ebony	21,490	19,780
C 120		48	Tradition Polished Mahogany/White	23,790	21,780
C 120		48	Tradition Satin Walnut/Cherry	21,490	19,780

*See pricing explanation on page 203.

PIANOBUYER.COM

Model	Feet	Inches	Description	MSRP*	SMP*
SCHIMMEL (continued)					
C 120		48	Tradition Satin Alder/Beech	21,490	19,780
C 120		48	"Tradition Marketerie" Polished Mahogany	26,590	24,180
C 120		48	"International" Polished Ebony	20,390	18,780
C 120		48	"International" Polished Mahogany/White	22,690	20,780
C 120		48	"Royal" Polished Ebony	24,990	22,780
C 120		48	"Royal Intarsie Flora" Polished Mahogany	27,490	24,980
C 126		49	Tradition Polished Ebony	25,690	23,380
C 126		49	Tradition Polished Mahogany	27,890	25,380
C 130		51	Tradition Polished Ebony	27,890	25,380
C 130		51	Tradition Polished Mahogany	30,490	27,580
Konzert Series Verticals					
K 122		48	"Elegance" Polished Ebony	30,490	27,580
K 125		49	Tradition Polished Ebony	33,690	30,380
K 125		49	Tradition Polished Mahogany	36,190	32,580
K 132		52	Tradition Polished Ebony	36,190	32,580
K 132		52	Tradition Polished Mahogany	38,490	34,580
K 132		52	"Wilhelmina" Satin Mahogany/Walnut	48,090	42,980
Classic Series Grands					
C 182	6		Tradition Polished Ebony	42,990	38,580
C 182	6		Tradition Polished Mahogany/White	46,690	41,780
C 182	6		"Art Nouveau" Polished Ebony	47,190	42,180
C 182	6		"Art Nouveau" Polished Mahogany/White	50,790	45,380
C 208	6	10	Tradition Polished Ebony	53,790	47,980
C 208	6	10	Tradition Polished Mahogany	57,490	51,180
C 208	6	10	"Art Nouveau" Polished Ebony	57,890	51,580
C 208	6	10	"Art Nouveau" Polished Mahogany	61,590	54,780
Konzert Series Grands					
K 169	5	7	Tradition Polished Ebony	55,590	49,580
K 169	5	7	Tradition Polished Mahogany/White	60,390	53,780
K 169	5	7	Tradition Polished Exquisite Woods	75,990	67,380
K 169	5	7	"Tradition Intarsie Harp" Polished Ebony	63,190	56,180
K 169	5	7	"Tradition Intarsie Vase" Polished Mahogany	75,990	67,380
K 169	5	7	"Belle Epoque" Polished Ebony	65,690	58,380
K 169	5	7	"Royal" Polished Ebony	58,190	51,780
K 169	5	7	"Royal" Polished Mahogany/White	62,990	55,980
K 169	5	7	"Royal Intarsie Flora" Polished Mahogany	75,990	67,380
K 189	6	3	Tradition Polished Ebony	60,690	53,980
K 189	6	3	Tradition Polished Mahogany/White	65,490	58,180
K 189	6	3	Tradition Polished Exquisite Woods	80,990	71,780
K 189	6	3	"Tradition Intarsie Harp" Polished Ebony	70,690	62,780
K 189	6	3	"Tradition Intarsie Vase" Polished Mahogany	80,990	71,780
K 189	6	3	"Belle Epoque" Polished Ebony	70,690	62,780
K 189	6	3	"Edition N.W. Schimmel" Polished Ebony	80,990	71,780
K 189	6	3	"Royal" Polished Ebony	63,190	56,180
K 189	6	3	"Royal" Polished Mahogany/White	67,990	60,380
K 189	6	3	"Royal Intarsie Flora" Polished Mahogany	80,990	71,780
K 213	7		Tradition Polished Ebony	64,590	57,380
K 213	7		Tradition Polished Mahogany/White	69,390	61,580
K 213	7		Tradition Polished Exquisite Woods	84,690	74,980
K 213	7		"Edition N.W. Schimmel" Polished Ebony	84,890	75,180
K 213	7		"Royal" Polished Ebony	67,090	59,580
K 213	7		"Royal" Polished Mahogany/White	71,890	63,780
K 213	7		"Glas" Clear Acrylic and White or Black	156,290	137,580
K 213	7		"Otmar Alt" Polished Ebony w/Color Motifs	179,390	157,780
K 230	7	6	Tradition Polished Ebony	88,390	78,180
K 256	8	4	Tradition Polished Ebony	98,390	86,980
K 280	9	2	Tradition Polished Ebony	128,890	113,580

*See pricing explanation on page 203.

SCHULZE POLLMANN

Verticals

Model	Feet	Inches	Description	MSRP*	SMP*
118/P8		46	Polished Ebony	14,190	14,190
118/P8		46	Polished Briar Walnut/Mahogany	14,790	14,790
118/P8		46	Polished Feather and Peacock Mahogany	14,790	14,790
126/P6		50	Polished Ebony	15,590	15,590
126/P6		50	Polished Peacock Ebony/Mahogany/Walnut/Cherry	16,590	16,590
126/P6		50	Polished Briar Mahogany/Walnut	16,590	16,590
126/P6		50	Polished Feather Mahogany	16,590	16,590

Grands

Model	Feet	Inches	Description	MSRP*	SMP*
160/GK	5	3	Polished Ebony (spade leg)	40,990	40,990
160/GK	5	3	Polished Ebony (round leg)	42,590	42,590
160/GK	5	3	Polished Briar Mahogany (spade leg)	43,990	43,990
160/GK	5	3	Polished Briar Mahogany (round leg)	45,990	45,990
160/GK	5	3	Polished Feather Mahogany (spade leg)	48,990	48,990
197/G5	6	7	Polished Ebony (spade leg)	56,190	56,190
197/G5	6	7	Polished Briar Mahogany (spade leg)	58,990	58,990
197/G5	6	7	Polished Feather Mahogany (spade leg)	60,990	60,990

SEILER

Veneers I, II, III, and IV are traditional and exotic veneers grouped by price.

Seiler Classic Line Verticals

Model	Feet	Inches	Description	MSRP*	SMP*
116 Primus		46	Polished Ebony	19,789	18,990
116 Primus		46	Satin Veneer I	20,449	19,590
116 Primus		46	Satin Veneer II	21,549	20,590
116 Favorit		46	Polished Veneer I	21,010	20,100
116 Favorit		46	Satin Veneer I	21,450	20,500
116 Mondial		46	Polished Ebony	22,440	21,400
116 Mondial		46	Polished Veneer I	28,380	26,800
116 Mondial		46	Satin Veneer I	22,880	21,800
116 Mondial		46	Polished Veneer II	29,700	28,000
116 Mondial		46	Satin Veneer II	23,540	22,400
116 Escorial		46	Satin Cherry Ribbon Intaria	26,400	25,000
116 Jubilee		46	Polished Ebony	21,989	20,990
122 Primus		48	Polished Ebony	24,640	23,400
122 Primus		48	Satin Veneer I	25,080	23,800
122 Konsole		48	Polished Ebony	27,720	26,200
122 Konsole		48	Polished Veneer I	31,240	29,400
122 Konsole		48	Satin Veneer I	25,300	24,000
122 Konsole		48	Polished Veneer II	32,780	30,800
122 Konsole		48	Satin Veneer II	26,180	24,800
122 Konsole Vienna		48	Mahogany with Flower Inlay	31,020	29,200
122 Konsole Vienna		48	Oval Paneling, Rootwood Pilaster Strips	29,920	28,200
126 Primus		50	Polished Ebony	27,280	25,800
126 Primus		50	Polished Veneer I	33,440	31,400
126 Primus		50	Satin Veneer I	27,940	26,400
126 Konsole		50	Polished Ebony	27,720	26,200
126 Konsole		50	Polished Veneer I	33,880	31,800
126 Konsole		50	Satin Veneer I	28,380	26,800
132 Konzert		52	Polished Ebony	30,800	29,000
132 Konzert		52	Ebony Pilaster Strips Metal	37,730	35,300
132 Konzert		52	Satin Veneer I	32,120	30,200
132 Konzert		52	Polished Veneer II	39,600	37,000
132 Konzert		52	Satin Veneer II	33,000	31,000

*See pricing explanation on page 203.

SEILER (continued)

Seiler Trend Line Verticals

Model	Feet	Inches	Description	MSRP*	SMP*
116 Impuls		46	Polished Ebony	21,780	20,800
116 Impuls		46	Satin Veneers	22,220	21,200
116 Focus		46	Polished Ebony	22,660	21,600
116 Clou		46	Polished Ebony	22,660	21,600
116 Accent		46	Polished Ebony	22,880	21,800
116 Pulsar		46	Ash Silver	27,720	26,200
126 Impuls		50	Polished Ebony	28,160	26,600
126 Impuls		50	Satin Veneers	28,600	27,000
126 Focus		50	Polished Ebony	27,720	26,200
126 Focus		50	Satin Veneers	29,260	27,600
126 Attraction		50	Ebony Pilaster Strips Metal	33,000	31,000
126 Attraction		50	Satin Veneer Wood Paneling	34,980	32,800
126 Pulsar		50	Ash Silver	39,600	37,000

Seiler Grands

Model	Feet	Inches	Description	MSRP*	SMP*
168 Virtuoso	5	6	Polished Ebony	64,680	59,800
168 Virtuoso	5	6	Polished White	71,500	66,000
168 Virtuoso	5	6	Polished Veneer I	72,160	66,600
168 Virtuoso	5	6	Satin Veneer I	64,680	59,800
168 Virtuoso	5	6	Polished Veneer II	73,260	67,600
168 Virtuoso	5	6	Polished Veneer III	74,140	68,400
168 Virtuoso	5	6	Polished Veneer IV	76,340	70,400
186 Maestro	6	1	Polished Ebony	67,980	62,800
186 Maestro	6	1	Polished White	74,800	69,000
186 Maestro	6	1	Polished Veneer I	75,460	69,600
186 Maestro	6	1	Satin Veneer I	68,200	63,000
186 Maestro	6	1	Polished Veneer II	76,560	70,600
186 Maestro	6	1	Polished Veneer III	77,440	71,400
186 Maestro	6	1	Polished Veneer IV	79,200	73,000
186 Vision	6	1	Polished Ebony (Trend Line)	58,300	54,000
186	6	1	Chippendale Open-Pore Walnut	83,600	77,000
186	6	1	"Westminster" Polished Mahogany, Intarsia	102,520	94,200
186	6	1	"Florenz" Polished Mahogany/Walnut/Myrtle, Intarsia	102,520	94,200
186	6	1	"Louvre" Polished Ebony	83,600	77,000
186	6	1	"Louvre" Polished Cherry, Intarsia	102,520	94,200
186	6	1	"Prado" Polished Burl Rosewood	102,520	94,200
186	6	1	"Prado" Polished Brown Ash	109,780	100,800
186	6	1	"Stella" Polished Flame Maple w/Marquetry	109,780	100,800
208	6	10	Polished Ebony	74,800	69,000
208	6	10	Polished White	83,380	76,800
242	8		Polished Ebony	98,560	90,600
242	8		Polished White	108,900	100,000
278	9		Polished Ebony	169,400	155,000

Eduard Seiler ED Series Verticals

Model	Feet	Inches	Description	MSRP*	SMP*
ED-126		49	"Primus" Satin Ebony	11,400	11,400
ED-126		49	"Primus" Polished Ebony	11,000	11,000
ED-126		49	"Primus" Polished Mahogany/Walnut/Ivory	11,400	11,400
ED-132		52	"Konzert" Satin Ebony	13,400	13,400
ED-132		52	"Konzert" Polished Ebony	12,000	12,000
ED-132		52	"Konzert" Polished Mahogany/Walnut/Ivory	13,400	13,400

Eduard Seiler ED Series Grands

Model	Feet	Inches	Description	MSRP*	SMP*
ED-168	5	6	"Virtuoso" Satin Ebony	25,600	25,600
ED-168	5	6	"Virtuoso" Polished Ebony	25,000	25,000
ED-168	5	6	"Virtuoso" Polished Mahogany/Walnut	25,600	25,600
ED-186	6	2	"Maestro" Satin Ebony	33,000	33,000

*See pricing explanation on page 203.

Model	Feet	Inches	Description	MSRP*	SMP*
SEILER (continued)					
ED-186	6	2	"Maestro" Polished Ebony	32,000	32,000
ED-186	6	2	"Maestro" Polished Mahogany/Walnut	33,000	33,000
Eduard Seiler ES Series Verticals					
ES-126		49	"Primus" Polished Ebony	20,388	20,388
ES-126		49	"Primus" Polished Mahogany/Walnut	21,588	21,588
ES-126		49	"Primus" Satin Alder/Beech	21,588	21,588
ES-132		52	"Konzert" Polished Ebony	23,000	23,000
ES-132		52	"Konzert" Polished Mahogany/Walnut	24,200	24,200
ES-132		52	"Konzert" Satin Alder/Beech	24,200	24,200
Eduard Seiler ES Series Grands					
ES-186	6	2	"Maestro" Polished Ebony	47,988	47,988
ES-186	6	2	"Maestro" Polished Mahogany/Walnut	50,388	50,388
ES-186	6	2	"Maestro" Satin Maple/Cherry	50,388	50,388

SEJUNG

Sejung makes pianos under the names Falcone, Hobart M. Cable, and Geo. Steck. The large variety of styles and finishes offered under the three brand names are very similar from one brand to the next, and in most cases the prices are the same. To save space, I have compiled one master list of models for all three brands. Although I have used the generic model prefixes ""U" and ""C" for the verticals and ""G" for grands, each brand actually has its own prefixes: UF, CF, and GF for Falcone; FV and FG for the Falcone Georgian series; UH, CH, and GH for Hobart M. Cable; and US, CS, and GS for Geo. Steck. Models with a slow-close fallboard have models numbers ending with ""D." However, most models, both grand and vertical, regardless of how listed here, are available with or without a slow-close fallboard at a cost of about $100 more or less than shown. The Falcone Georgian series has upgraded cosmetic and technical features. The Falcone Georgian verticals cost the same as the other-named verticals, but the Falcone Georgian grands cost from $140 to $400 more, depending on size. Not all models, styles, and finishes shown are available under all names. Falcone Georgian grand (FG) models are shown only where a particular style or finish is available only under that label.

Verticals

Model	Feet	Inches	Description	MSRP*	SMP*
U 09		43	Continental Polished Ebony	4,400	3,514
U 09		43	Continental Polished Other Finishes	4,600	3,614
U 09		43	Continental Satin Finishes	4,500	3,563
U 09A		43	Continental Polished Ebony (no back posts)	4,100	3,346
U 09A		43	Continental Polished Other Finishes (no back posts)	4,300	3,446
U 09L		43	Polished Ebony	4,500	3,563
U 09L		43	Polished Other Finishes	4,700	3,664
C 12F		44	French Provincial Satin Cherry/Brown Oak	5,100	3,904
C 12F1		44	French Provincial Satin Cherry/Brown Oak	4,900	3,819
C 12IP		44	Italian Provincial Satin Walnut/Mahogany/Cherry/Oak	5,500	4,162
C 12M		44	Mediterranean Satin Cherry/Brown Oak	5,100	3,904
C 12M1		44	Mediterranean Satin Cherry/Brown Oak/Sapele	4,900	3,819
U 12F		44	French Provincial Polished Ebony	5,000	3,837
U 12F		44	French Provincial Other Polished Finishes	5,100	3,939
U 12F		44	French Provincial Satin Finishes	5,100	3,888
U 12FC		44	12F Satin with Decorated Front Panel	5,100	3,922
U 12T		44	Polished Ebony	4,800	3,733
U 12T		44	Polished Other Finishes	5,000	3,837
U 12T		44	Satin Finishes	4,900	3,784
C 13FD		44.5	French Provincial Satin Cherry/Mahogany	5,700	4,264
C 13F1D		44.5	French Provincial Satin Cherry/Brown Oak/Mahogany	6,000	4,435
C 13MD		44.5	Designer Satin Cherry/Dark Cherry/Mahogany	5,700	4,264
C 13M1D		44.5	Designer Satin Cherry/Brown Oak/Mahogany	6,000	4,435
C 16AT		45.5	Satin Cherry/Brown Oak	5,800	4,333
C 16F		45.5	French Provincial Satin Cherry/Brown Oak/Walnut	5,400	4,075
C 16FP		45.5	French Provincial Satin Cherry/Brown Oak	5,500	4,128
C 16IP		45.5	Italian Provincial Satin Cherry/Walnut	5,500	4,128
C 16QA		45.5	Queen Anne Satin Cherry/Brown Oak/Mahogany	6,000	4,419
U 16IC		46	Italian Provincial Polished Ebony	4,900	3,784
U 16IC		46	Italian Provincial Other Polished Finishes	5,100	3,888

*See pricing explanation on page 203.

PIANOBUYER.COM

Model	Feet	Inches	Description	MSRP*	SMP*
SEJUNG (continued)					
U 16ST		46	Satin Finishes (school)	5,000	3,837
U 16STL		46	Polished Ebony (school with lock)	5,000	3,853
U 16STL		46	Polished Other Finishes (school with lock)	5,200	3,955
U 16STL		46	Satin Finishes (school with lock)	5,100	3,904
U 16TC		46	Polished Ebony w/Decorated Front Panel	5,000	3,853
U 16TC		46	Polished Other Finishes w/Decorated Front Panel	5,200	3,955
U 18MS		46.5	Designer Other Polished Finishes w/Front Inlay	5,100	3,939
C 19F		47	Country French Satin Cherry/Brown Oak/Mahogany	5,700	4,248
C 19F1D		47	Country French Satin Cherry/Brown Oak	5,900	4,350
C 19M		47	Mediterranean Satin Brown Oak/Cherry/Mahog.	5,700	4,248
C 19M1D		47	Mediterranean Satin Cherry/Oak/Brown Oak	5,900	4,350
C 19QAD		47	Queen Anne Satin Cherry/Brown Oak	6,500	4,693
C 47CI		47	Modern Designer C Polished Ebony	7,000	5,018
C 47CI		47	Modern Designer C Polished Other Finishes	7,200	5,122
C 47FD		47	French Provincial Satin Cherry/Mahogany	7,700	5,378
C 47MD		47	Mediterranean Satin Mahogany	7,700	5,378
C 47R		47	Modern Designer R Other Polished Finishes	7,400	5,206
C 47V		47	Modern Designer V Polished Ebony	7,800	5,446
U 19F		47	French Provincial Polished Ebony	5,100	3,904
U 19F		47	French Provincial Polished Other Finishes	5,300	4,008
U 19F		47	French Provincial Satin Finishes	5,200	3,955
U 19FC		47	Polished Other Finishes w/Decorated Front Panel	5,400	4,075
U 19PD		47	Designer Polished Finishes	5,400	4,059
U 19ST		47	Polished Ebony	4,900	3,819
U 19ST		47	Polished Other Finishes	5,100	3,922
U 19ST		47	Satin Finishes	5,000	3,870
U 19T		47	Polished Ebony	4,900	3,819
U 19T		47	Polished Other Finishes	5,100	3,922
U 19T		47	Satin Finishes	5,000	3,870
U 20T		47	Designer Polished Ebony	5,400	4,075
U 20T		47	Designer Other Polished Finishes	5,600	4,179
U 210MD		47.5	Designer Special Other Polished Finishes	5,600	4,179
U 22F		48	French Provincial Polished Ebony	5,400	4,093
U 22F		48	French Provincial Polished Other Finishes	5,600	4,195
U 22ITD		48	Italian Designer Polished Ebony	5,700	4,264
U 22T		48	Polished Ebony	5,200	3,990
U 22T		48	Polished Other Finishes	5,400	4,093
U 22T		48	Satin Finishes	5,300	4,042
U 22WTD		48	Metropolitan Designer Polished Ebony	5,700	4,264
U 23FD		48	French Provincial Polished Ebony	5,900	4,350
U 23FD		48	French Provincial Polished Other Finishes	6,000	4,453
U 23FD		48	French Provincial Satin Finishes	6,000	4,402
U 23TD		48	Designer Professional Polished Ebony	5,700	4,248
U 23TD		48	Designer Professional Polished Other Finishes	5,900	4,350
U 23TD		48	Designer Professional Satin Finishes	5,800	4,299
U 26T		48	Designer Polished Ebony	5,300	4,042
U 28D		48	Designer Special Polished Bubinga	6,800	4,899
U 28SD		48	Designer Special Polished Bubinga w/Inlay	7,000	5,018
U 230CD		48.5	Designer Medieval Special Satin Finishes	6,600	4,762
U 25BD		49.5	Designer w/HM on Front Panel Polished Ebony	6,000	4,419
U 25S		49.5	Designer w/BLK Oval Polished Ebony	5,700	4,264
U 25SM		49.5	Designer w/BSP Oval Polished Ebony	5,800	4,299
U 32E		52	Professional Designer LHM Polished Ebony	7,800	5,446
U 32F		52	French Provincial Polished Ebony	5,700	4,264
U 32FD		52	French Provincial Polished Other Finishes	6,100	4,470
U 32HD		52	Professional Designer Polished Bubinga	7,000	5,018
U 32T		52	Polished Ebony	5,500	4,162

*See pricing explanation on page 203.

Model	Feet	Inches	Description	MSRP*	SMP*
SEJUNG (continued)					
U 32T		52	Polished Other Finishes	5,700	4,264
U 32T		52	Satin Finishes	5,600	4,213
Grands					
G 42D	4	8	Satin Ebony	13,700	8,826
G 42D	4	8	Polished Ebony	13,400	8,656
G 42D	4	8	Satin Wood Finishes	14,300	9,162
G 42D	4	8	Polished Wood Finishes	14,000	8,994
G 42D	4	8	Polished Ivory/White	13,700	8,826
FG 42D	4	8	Polished Bubinga	15,100	9,614
G 42F	4	8	French Provincial Polished Ebony	13,900	8,960
G 42FD	4	8	French Provincial Satin Wood Finishes	14,800	9,565
G 42FD	4	8	French Provincial Polished Wood Finishes	14,500	9,397
FG 42LD	4	8	Louis XVI Polished Ebony	14,100	9,043
G 52D	5		Satin Ebony	15,500	9,834
G 52D	5		Polished Ebony	15,200	9,662
G 52D	5		Satin Wood Finishes	16,100	10,176
G 52D	5		Polished Wood Finishes	15,800	10,005
G 52D	5		Polished Bubinga	16,700	10,518
FG 52FD	5		French Provincial Polished Ebony	16,100	10,227
G 52FD	5		French Provincial Satin Wood Finishes	16,800	10,587
G 52FD	5		French Provincial Polished Wood Finishes	16,500	10,416
FG 52FD	5		French Provincial Polished Ivory/White	16,400	10,398
G 52FAD	5		FrenchAnn Polished Wood Finishes	17,000	10,691
G 52LD	5		Louis XVI Polished Ebony	15,600	9,936
G 52LD	5		Louis XVI Polished Wood Finishes	16,200	10,278
G 62D	5	4	Satin Ebony	17,000	10,691
G 62D	5	4	Polished Ebony	16,700	10,518
G 62D	5	4	Satin Wood Finishes	17,600	11,034
G 62D	5	4	Polished Wood Finishes	17,300	10,862
G 62D	5	4	Polished Ivory/White	17,000	10,691
G 62F	5	4	French Provincial Satin Ebony	17,500	10,998
G 62FD	5	4	French Provincial Polished Ebony	17,400	10,930
G 62FD	5	4	French Provincial Satin Wood Finishes	18,300	11,445
G 62FD	5	4	French Provincial Polished Wood Finishes	18,000	11,274
G 62FD	5	4	French Provincial Polished Ivory/White	17,700	11,102
G 62HLED	5	4	Louis XVI Polished Ebony (Hexagonal)	17,700	11,136
G 62HLED	5	4	Louis XVI Polished Sapele (Hexagonal)	19,200	11,992
FG 62HLED	5	4	Louis XVI Polished Wood Finishes (Hexagonal)	19,800	12,318
G 62PLBD	5	4	Louis XVI Polished Bubinga (Octagonal)	19,200	11,992
G 62QAD	5	4	Queen Anne Polished Wood Finishes	18,500	11,547
G 72D	5	8	Satin Ebony	18,500	11,547
G 72D	5	8	Polished Ebony	18,200	11,376
G 72D	5	8	Satin Wood Finishes	19,100	11,890
G 72D	5	8	Polished Wood Finishes	18,800	11,718
G 72D	5	8	Polished Bubinga	19,700	12,232
G 72D	5	8	Polished Ivory/White	18,500	11,547
G 72FD	5	8	French Provincial Polished Ebony	18,900	11,787
G 72FD	5	8	French Provincial Satin Wood Finishes	19,800	12,301
G 72FD	5	8	French Provincial Polished Wood Finishes	19,500	12,130
G 72FD	5	8	French Provincial Polished Ivory/White	19,200	11,958
FG 72FF	5	8	Rococo Polished Ivory/White	20,000	12,456
G 72HLD	5	8	Louis XVI Satin Wood Finish (Hexagonal)	20,000	12,405
G 72HLD	5	8	Louis XVI Polished Bubinga (Hexagonal)	22,400	13,774
G 72LD	5	8	Louis XVI Polished Ebony	18,600	11,650
FG 72LD	5	8	Louis XVI Satin Wood Finishes	20,100	12,490
G 72LD	5	8	Louis XVI Polished Wood Finishes	19,200	11,992
G 72PLD	5	8	Louis XVI Polished Wood Finishes (Octagonal)	19,700	12,232

*See pricing explanation on page 203.

PIANOBUYER.COM

Model	Feet	Inches	Description	MSRP*	SMP*
SEJUNG (continued)					
G 72PLSD	5	8	Louis XVI Polished Wood Finishes (Octagongal)	20,400	12,661
G 72PLSD	5	8	Louis XVI Polished Sapele (Octagonal)	21,300	13,174
G 72QAD	5	8	Queen Anne Satin Wood Finishes	20,100	12,507
G 87BCD	6	2	Polished Bubinga w/Rim Band/Beveled Lid	21,600	13,363
G 87D	6	2	Satin Ebony	20,000	12,405
G 87D	6	2	Polished Ebony	19,700	12,232
G 87D	6	2	Polished Wood Finishes	20,300	12,576
G 87D	6	2	Polished Bubinga	21,200	13,090
G 87D	6	2	Polished Ivory/White	20,000	12,405
G 87FD	6	2	French Provincial Polished Ebony	20,400	12,643
G 87FD	6	2	French Provincial Satin Wood Finishes	21,300	13,158
G 87FD	6	2	French Provincial Polished Wood Finishes	21,000	12,987
FG 87FFBD	6	2	Rococo Polished Wood Finishes	22,200	13,690
FG 87HLBCD	6	2	Louis XVI Polished Beech Ebony (Hexagonal)	24,300	14,888
G 87HLD	6	2	Louis XVI Satin Wood Finish (Hexagonal)	21,500	13,261
G 87LD	6	2	Louis XVI Satin Ebony	20,400	12,678
G 87LD	6	2	Louis XVI Polished Ebony	20,100	12,507
G 87LD	6	2	Louis XVI Satin Wood Finishes	21,000	13,021
G 87LD	6	2	Louis XVI Polished Wood Finishes	20,700	12,850
G 87LD	6	2	Louis XVI Polished Ivory/White	20,400	12,678
G 87PLD	6	2	Louis XVI Satin Wood Finishes (Octagonal)	21,500	13,261
G 87PLSD	6	2	Louis XVI Polished Wood Finishes/Inlays (Octagonal)	22,100	13,603
G 208D	6	10	Satin Ebony	24,300	14,872
G 208D	6	10	Polished Ebony	24,000	14,701
G 208D	6	10	Satin Wood Finishes	24,900	15,214
G 208HLBCD	6	10	Louis XVI Satin Wood Finish (Hexagonal)	26,300	16,003
G 208HLBCD	6	10	Louis XVI Polished Wood Finish (Hexagonal)	26,000	15,832
G 208HLD	6	10	Louis XVI Satin Wood Finish (Hexagonal)	25,800	15,728

SOHMER

Verticals

Model	Feet	Inches	Description	MSRP*	SMP*
S-126		50	Polished Ebony		10,800
S-126		50	Polished Mahogany		11,200

Grands

Model	Feet	Inches	Description	MSRP*	SMP*
S-160	5	3	Polished Ebony		20,190
S-160	5	3	Polished Mahogany		20,990
S-180	5	10	Polished Ebony		22,190
S-180	5	10	Polished Mahogany		22,990
S-218	7	2	Polished Ebony		31,980

STECK, GEO. — see Sejung

*See pricing explanation on page 203.

Model	Feet	Inches	Description	MSRP*	SMP*

STEINBERG, WILH.

Verticals

Model	Feet	Inches	Description	MSRP*	SMP*
IQ 16		46	Polished Ebony		17,890
IQ 16		46	Satin Beech/Oak/Alder		18,010
IQ 16		46	Satin Walnut/Mahogany		18,620
IQ 16		46	Polished White		19,780
AC 118		46.5	Polished Ebony		15,140
AC 118		46.5	Polished White		15,810
IQ 24		48	Polished Ebony		20,210
IQ 24		48	Satin Beech/Oak/Alder		20,210
IQ 24		48	Satin Walnut/Mahogany		20,880
IQ 24		48	Polished White		22,280
IQ 24		48	"Amadeus" Polished Ebony		21,950
IQ 24		48	"Amadeus" Satin Walnut/Mahogany		23,230
IQ 24		48	"Amadeus" Polished White		23,840
AC 123		48.5	Polished Ebony		16,420
AC 130		51	Polished Ebony		18,800
IQ 28		51	Polished Ebony		24,180
IQ 28		51	Satin Beech/Alder/Oak		24,180
IQ 28		51	Satin Walnut/Mahogany		24,660
IQ 28		51	Polished White		26,160
IQ 28		51	"Amadeus" Polished Ebony		26,800
IQ 28		51	"Amadeus" Satin Walnut/Mahogany		27,290
IQ 28		51	"Amadeus" Polished White		28,690
IQ 28		51	"Passione" Polished Ebony		28,880
IQ 28		51	"Passione" Satin Walnut/Mahogany		30,130

Grands

Model	Feet	Inches	Description	MSRP*	SMP*
IQ 77	5	8	Polished Ebony		59,070
IQ 77	5	8	Satin Walnut/Mahogany		63,160
IQ 77	5	8	Satin Cherry		64,110
AC 188	6	2	Polished Ebony		38,290
AC 188	6	2	Polished White		41,520
AC 212	6	11.5	Polished Ebony		46,100

STEINGRAEBER & SÖHNE

For pricing information on Steingraeber-Phoenix pianos, please contact the distributor.

Verticals

Model	Feet	Inches	Description	MSRP*	SMP*
122 T		48	Polished Ebony	39,767	39,767
122 T		48	Satin Sapele/Walnut	39,095	39,095
122 T		48	Polished Sapele/Walnut	45,553	45,553
130 PS		51	Polished Ebony	51,475	51,475
130 PS		51	Polished Ebony w/Twist & Change Panels	55,559	55,559
130 PS		51	Satin Sapele/Walnut	46,886	46,886
130 PS		51	Polished Sapele/Walnut	53,575	53,575
130 PS		51	Satin Special Veneers	49,102	49,102
130 PS		51	Polished Special Veneers	55,790	55,790
138 K		54	Classic Polished Ebony	56,704	56,704
138 K		54	Classic Polished Ebony w/Twist & Change	60,809	60,809
138 K		54	Classic Satin Sapele/Walnut	54,740	54,740
138 K		54	Classic Polished Sapele/Walnut	61,450	61,450
138 K		54	Classic Satin Special Veneers	57,008	57,008
138 K		54	Classic Polished Special Veneers	63,707	63,707

*See pricing explanation on page 203.

PIANOBUYER.COM

Model	Feet	Inches	Description	MSRP*	SMP*

STEINGRAEBER & SÖHNE (continued)

Grands

Model	Feet	Inches	Description	MSRP*	SMP*
A170	5	7	Polished Ebony	93,382	93,382
A170	5	7	Studio Anti-Scratch Lacquer Polished Ebony	90,883	90,883
A170	5	7	Satin Sapele/Walnut	106,003	106,003
A170	5	7	Polished Sapele/Walnut	110,109	110,109
A170	5	7	Satin Special Veneers	107,557	107,557
A170	5	7	Polished Special Veneers	111,621	111,621
A170 K	5	7	"Classicism"/Chippendale Polished Ebony	107,757	107,757
A170 K	5	7	"Classicism"/Chippendale Studio Anti-Scratch Lacquer Polished Ebony	105,258	105,258
A170 S	5	7	"Studio" Polished Ebony	88,668	88,668
A170 S	5	7	"Studio" Studio Anti-Scratch Lacquer Polished Ebony	86,169	86,169
A170 S	5	7	"Studio" Satin Sapele/Walnut	101,278	101,278
A170 S	5	7	"Studio" Polished Sapele/Walnut	105,373	105,373
A170 S	5	7	"Studio" Satin Special Veneers	102,822	102,822
A170 S	5	7	"Studio" Polished Special Veneers	106,885	106,885
B192 N	6	3	Polished Ebony	117,017	117,017
B192 N	6	3	Studio Anti-Scratch Lacquer Polished Ebony	114,182	114,182
B192 N	6	3	Satin Sapele/Walnut	130,331	130,331
B192 N	6	3	Polished Sapele/Walnut	134,237	134,237
B192 N	6	3	Satin Special Veneers	131,979	131,979
B192 N	6	3	Polished Special Veneers	135,917	135,917
B192 S	6	3	Polished Ebony	111,483	111,483
B192 S	6	3	Studio Anti-Scratch Lacquer Polished Ebony	108,774	108,774
B192 S	6	3	Satin Sapele/Walnut	124,115	124,115
B192 S	6	3	Polished Sapele/Walnut	127,821	127,821
B192 S	6	3	Satin Special Veneers	125,690	125,690
B192 S	6	3	Polished Special Veneers	129,428	129,428
C212 N	7		Polished Ebony	128,598	128,598
C212 N	7		Studio Anti-Scratch Lacquer Polished Ebony	125,427	125,427
C212 N	7		Satin Sapele/Walnut	143,298	143,298
C212 N	7		Polished Sapele/Walnut	147,593	147,593
C212 N	7		Satin Special Veneers	145,136	145,136
C212 N	7		Polished Special Veneers	149,441	149,441
C212 K	7		"Classicism"/Chippendale Polished Ebony	142,973	142,973
C212 K	7		"Classicism"/Chippendale Studio Anti-Scratch Lacquer Polished Ebony	139,802	139,802
C212 S	7		"Studio" Polished Ebony	122,466	122,466
C212 S	7		"Studio" Studio Anti-Scratch Lacquer Polished Ebony	119,463	119,463
C212 S	7		"Studio" Satin Sapele/Walnut	136,431	136,431
C212 S	7		"Studio" Polished Sapele/Walnut	140,526	140,526
C212 S	7		"Studio" Satin Special Veneers	138,195	138,195
C212 S	7		"Studio" Polished Special Veneers	142,269	142,269
D-232 N	7	7	Semi-Concert Polished Ebony	156,402	156,402
D-232 N	7	7	Semi-Concert Studio Anti-Scratch Lacquer Polished Ebony	152,990	152,990
D-232 N	7	7	Semi-Concert Satin Sapele/Walnut	164,571	164,571
D-232 N	7	7	Semi-Concert Polished Sapele/Walnut	177,108	177,108
D-232 N	7	7	Semi-Concert Satin Special Veneers	175,008	175,008
D-232 N	7	7	Semi-Concert Polished Special Veneers	179,849	179,849
E-272	8	11	Concert Polished Ebony	230,156	230,156
E-272	8	11	Concert Studio Anti-Scratch Lacquer Polished Ebony	226,733	226,733
E-272	8	11	Concert Satin Sapele/Walnut	248,017	248,017
E-272	8	11	Concert Polished Sapele/Walnut	253,750	253,750
E-272	8	11	Concert Satin Special Veneers	250,306	250,306
E-272	8	11	Concert Polished Special Veneers	256,018	256,018

*See pricing explanation on page 203.

Model	Feet	Inches	Description	MSRP*	SMP*

STEINWAY & SONS

These are the prices at the Steinway retail store in New York City, often used as a benchmark for Steinway prices throughout the country. Model K-52 in ebony; model 1098 in ebony, mahogany, and walnut; and grand models in ebony, mahogany, and walnut include adjustable artist benches. Other models include regular wood bench. Ebony models are in a satin finish; all other models are in a semigloss finish called "satin lustre."

Verticals

Model	Feet	Inches	Description	MSRP*	SMP*
4510		45	Sheraton Satin Ebony	25,700	25,700
4510		45	Sheraton Mahogany	28,900	28,900
4510		45	Sheraton Walnut	30,100	30,100
1098		46.5	Satin Ebony	24,200	24,200
1098		46.5	Mahogany	26,800	26,800
1098		46.5	Walnut	27,600	27,600
K-52		52	Satin Ebony	31,600	31,600
K-52		52	Mahogany	36,100	36,100
K-52		52	Walnut	37,200	37,200

Grands

Model	Feet	Inches	Description	MSRP*	SMP*
S	5	1	Satin Ebony	54,500	54,500
S	5	1	Polyester Polished Ebony	58,900	58,900
S	5	1	Lacquer Polished Ebony	59,900	59,900
S	5	1	Polyester Polished White	64,800	64,800
S	5	1	Mahogany	61,100	61,100
S	5	1	Walnut	63,800	63,800
S	5	1	Figured Sapele	66,500	66,500
S	5	1	Dark Cherry	67,700	67,700
S	5	1	Kewazinga Bubinga	69,500	69,500
S	5	1	Santos Rosewood	77,100	77,100
S	5	1	East Indian Rosewood	77,900	77,900
S	5	1	African Pommele	78,500	78,500
S	5	1	Macassar Ebony	85,600	85,600
M	5	7	Satin Ebony	59,700	59,700
M	5	7	Polyester Polished Ebony	64,500	64,500
M	5	7	Lacquer Polished Ebony	65,700	65,700
M	5	7	Polyester Polished White	71,100	71,100
M	5	7	Mahogany	67,500	67,500
M	5	7	Walnut	70,200	70,200
M	5	7	Figured Sapele	73,200	73,200
M	5	7	Dark Cherry	74,300	73,760
M	5	7	Kewazinga Bubinga	76,200	76,200
M	5	7	Santos Rosewood	83,700	82,320
M	5	7	East Indian Rosewood	85,100	85,100
M	5	7	African Pommele	85,500	85,500
M	5	7	Macassar Ebony	93,200	93,200
M 1014A	5	7	Chippendale Mahogany	81,400	83,580
M 1014A	5	7	Chippendale Walnut	83,400	85,520
M 501A	5	7	Louis XV Walnut	104,900	108,760
M 501A	5	7	Louis XV East Indian Rosewood	122,200	126,000
M	5	7	"John Lennon Imagine" Polished White	89,900	95,800
O	5	10.5	Satin Ebony	67,200	67,200
O	5	10.5	Polyester Polished Ebony	72,600	72,500
O	5	10.5	Lacquer Polished Ebony	76,800	76,220
O	5	10.5	Polyester Polished White	79,900	79,660
O	5	10.5	Mahogany	75,700	75,700
O	5	10.5	Walnut	78,500	77,700
O	5	10.5	Figured Sapele	81,600	80,780
O	5	10.5	Dark Cherry	82,800	82,220
O	5	10.5	Kewazinga Bubinga	84,900	84,900
O	5	10.5	Santos Rosewood	93,100	93,100
O	5	10.5	East Indian Rosewood	94,500	94,500

*See pricing explanation on page 203.

PIANOBUYER.COM

|---|---|---|---|---|---|
STEINWAY & SONS *(continued)*					
O	5	10.5	African Pommele	95,200	95,200
O	5	10.5	Macassar Ebony	104,900	104,660
O	5	10.5	"John Lennon Imagine" Polished White	98,200	104,600
A	6	2	Satin Ebony	77,400	75,980
A	6	2	Polyester Polished Ebony	83,600	81,980
A	6	2	Lacquer Polished Ebony	89,200	86,200
A	6	2	Polyester Polished White	92,100	90,080
A	6	2	Mahogany	86,500	86,140
A	6	2	Walnut	89,200	87,900
A	6	2	Figured Sapele	92,700	91,700
A	6	2	Dark Cherry	94,100	93,260
A	6	2	Kewazinga Bubinga	96,700	96,100
A	6	2	Santos Rosewood	106,100	106,100
A	6	2	East Indian Rosewood	107,600	107,600
A	6	2	African Pommele	108,400	108,400
A	6	2	Macassar Ebony	119,200	118,060
A	6	2	"William Steinway Limited Edition" Satin Ebony	93,900	93,900
A	6	2	"John Lennon Imagine" Polished White	117,300	117,300
B	6	10.5	Satin Ebony	87,500	85,160
B	6	10.5	Polyester Polished Ebony	94,500	91,900
B	6	10.5	Lacquer Polished Ebony	100,400	96,220
B	6	10.5	Polyester Polished White	104,100	101,000
B	6	10.5	Mahogany	97,400	96,320
B	6	10.5	Walnut	100,300	98,480
B	6	10.5	Figured Sapele	104,400	102,860
B	6	10.5	Dark Cherry	105,800	104,780
B	6	10.5	Kewazinga Bubinga	108,900	107,760
B	6	10.5	Santos Rosewood	119,300	119,300
B	6	10.5	East Indian Rosewood	121,200	121,100
B	6	10.5	African Pommele	122,200	121,580
B	6	10.5	Macassar Ebony	133,700	132,100
B	6	10.5	"William Steinway Limited Edition" Satin Ebony	108,900	108,900
B	6	10.5	"John Lennon Imagine" Polished White	132,300	130,620
D	8	11.75	Satin Ebony	137,400	131,980
D	8	11.75	Polyester Polished Ebony	148,400	142,460
D	8	11.75	Lacquer Polished Ebony	154,800	145,760
D	8	11.75	Polyester Polished White	163,300	156,620
D	8	11.75	Mahogany	153,100	143,580
D	8	11.75	Walnut	156,800	145,940
D	8	11.75	Figured Sapele	165,100	152,420
D	8	11.75	Dark Cherry	169,200	155,380
D	8	11.75	Kewazinga Bubinga	171,100	158,600
D	8	11.75	Santos Rosewood	188,100	176,140
D	8	11.75	East Indian Rosewood	190,600	177,740
D	8	11.75	African Pommele	192,200	178,240
D	8	11.75	Macassar Ebony	210,200	194,460
D	8	11.75	"John Lennon Imagine" Polished White	191,900	186,640

*See pricing explanation on page 203.

Model	Feet	Inches	Description	MSRP*	SMP*

Steinway (Hamburg) Grands

I frequently get requests for prices of pianos made in Steinway's branch factory in Hamburg, Germany. Officially, these pianos are not sold in North America, but it is possible to order one through an American Steinway dealer, or to go to Europe and purchase one there. The following list shows approximately how much it would cost to purchase a Hamburg Steinway in Europe and have it shipped to the United States. The list was derived by taking the published retail price in Europe, subtracting the value-added tax not applicable to foreign purchasers, converting to U.S. dollars (the rate used here is 1 Euro = $1.32, but is obviously subject to change), and adding approximate charges for duty, air freight, crating, insurance, brokerage fees, and delivery. Only prices for grands in polished ebony are shown here. Caution: This list is published for general informational purposes only. The price that Steinway would charge for a piano ordered through an American Steinway dealer may be different. (Also, the cost of a trip to Europe to purchase the piano is not included.)

Model	Feet	Inches	Description	MSRP*	SMP*
S-155	5	1	Polished Ebony	71,500	71,500
M-170	5	7	Polished Ebony	78,300	78,300
O-180	5	10.5	Polished Ebony	83,000	83,000
A-188	6	2	Polished Ebony	88,500	88,500
B-211	6	11	Polished Ebony	102,800	102,800
C-227	7	5.5	Polished Ebony	120,500	120,500
D-274	8	11.75	Polished Ebony	154,600	154,600

STORY & CLARK

All Story & Clark pianos include PNOscan, and USB and MIDI connectivity.

Heritage Series Verticals

Model	Feet	Inches	Description	MSRP*	SMP*
H6		44	Continental Polished Ebony	6,495	5,190
H6		44	Continental Polished Mahogany	6,495	5,190
H6		44	"Huntington" Satin Lacquer Oak/Mahogany	7,595	5,790
H6		44	"Calais" Satin Lacquer Cherry	7,595	5,790
H7		46	"Academy" Satin or Polished Ebony	8,295	6,095
H7		46	"Academy" Satin Oak	8,295	6,095
H8		48	"Deluxe" Polished Ebony/Mahogany/Walnut	6,495	5,390
H8		48	"Deluxe" Queen Anne Polished Ebony/Mahogany/Walnut	6,495	5,595
H9		51	"Artist" Polished Ebony	7,895	6,790
H9		51	"Artist" Polished Mahogany/Walnut	8,095	6,790

Signature Series Verticals

Model	Feet	Inches	Description	MSRP*	SMP*
S7		46	"Cosmopolitan" Hybrid Polished Ebony	7,895	6,790
S10		52	"Park West" Concert	11,895	8,930

Heritage Series Grands

Model	Feet	Inches	Description	MSRP*	SMP*
H50	4	9	"Prelude" Polished Ebony/Mahogany	13,695	9,590
H60	5	1	"Academy" Satin and Polished Ebony	16,195	10,790
H60	5	1	"Academy" Polished Mahogany/White	16,195	10,790
H60 QA	5	1	French Provincial Polished Ebony	17,095	11,790
H60 QA	5	1	French Provincial Satin and Polished Mahogany	17,095	12,390
H70	5	7	"Artist" Conservatory Polished Ebony	14,795	10,990
H70	5	7	"Artist" Conservatory Polished Mahogany/White	14,795	11,390
H80	6	1	"Artist" Professional Polished Ebony	18,695	15,590
H90	6	8	"Artist" Semi-Concert Polished Ebony	26,995	21,590

Signature Series Grands

Model	Feet	Inches	Description	MSRP*	SMP*
S500	4	11	"Manhattan" Semigloss Ebony w/Birdseye Maple Accents	21,995	17,790
S500	4	11	"Manhattan" Semigloss Teak w/Birdseye Maple Acents	21,995	17,790
S600	5	4	"Cosmopolitan" Polished Ebony	24,295	17,190
S600	5	4	"Melrose" Polished Ebony/Mahogany	24,295	19,390
S600	5	4	"Park West" Satin and Polished Ebony	24,295	16,590
S700	5	9	"Fairfax" Polished Ebony	24,295	19,190
S700	5	9	"Versailles" Satin Lacquer Cherry	24,295	18,990
S700	5	9	"Versailles" Satin Antique Ivory	24,295	19,590
S700	5	9	"Park West" Polished Ebony	24,295	17,590
S800	6	2	"Islander" British Colonial Satin Walnut	25,195	20,190
S800	6	2	"Park West" Polished Ebony	25,195	18,190
S900	7		"Park West" Satin Ebony	27,695	24,495

*See pricing explanation on page 203.

PIANOBUYER.COM

Model	Feet	Inches	Description	MSRP*	SMP*
TAYLOR LONDON					
Verticals					
TU 110		44	Satin Ebony	5,390	4,590
TU 110		44	Polished Ebony	5,090	4,390
TU 110		44	Satin and Polished Mahogany/Walnut	5,390	4,590
TU 123		48	Satin Ebony	6,290	5,190
TU 123		48	Polished Ebony	5,990	4,990
TU 123		48	Satin and Polished Mahogany/Walnut	6,290	5,190
TU 133		52	Satin Ebony	7,790	6,190
TU 133		52	Polished Ebony	7,490	5,990
TU 133		52	Polished Mahogany/Walnut	7,790	6,190
Grands					
TG 145	4	9	Satin Ebony	12,890	9,590
TG 145	4	9	Polished Ebony	11,990	8,990
TG 145	4	9	Satin and Polished Mahogany/Walnut	12,890	9,590
TG 145	4	9	Chippendale	14,250	10,500
TG 166	5	5	Satin Ebony	14,090	10,390
TG 166	5	5	Polished Ebony	13,490	9,990
TG 166	5	5	Satin and Polished Mahogany/Walnut	14,090	10,390
TG 166	5	5	Chippendale	15,890	11,590
TG 185	6	1	Satin Ebony	19,990	14,327
TG 185	6	1	Polished Ebony	19,109	13,739
TG 185	6	1	Polished Mahogany/Walnut	19,990	14,327
VOGEL					
Verticals					
V 115		45	Tradition Polished Ebony	13,290	12,580
V 115		45	Tradition Polished Mahogany/White	14,390	13,580
V 115		45	"Modern" Polished Ebony	13,290	12,580
V 115		45	"Modern" Polished White	14,390	13,580
V 121		48	Tradition Polished Ebony	14,890	13,980
V 121		48	Tradition Polished Mahogany/White	16,290	15,180
V 125		49	Tradition Polished Ebony	16,990	15,780
V 125		49	Tradition Polished Mahogany	18,090	16,780
Grands					
V 180	6		Tradition Polished Ebony	29,790	26,980
V 180	6		Tradition Polished Mahogany/White	32,290	29,180
V 180	6		Tradition Polished Mahogany Drapee Intarsie Liaison	42,990	38,580
V 180	6		Chippendale Polished Ebony	33,190	29,980
V 180	6		Chippendale Polished Mahogany/White	35,690	32,180
V 180	6		"Royal" Polished Ebony	33,890	30,580
V 180	6		"Royal" Polished Mahogany/White	36,390	32,780
V 180	6		"Royal" Polished Mahogany Drapee Intarsie Oval	42,990	38,580
V 180	6		"Royal Marketerie" Polished Flame Khaya Mahogany Coffer	42,990	38,580

VOSE & SONS — see Everett

*See pricing explanation on page 203.

WALTER, CHARLES R.

Verticals

Model	Feet	Inches	Description	MSRP*	SMP*
1520		43	Satin Ebony	14,540	12,632
1520		43	Semi-Gloss Ebony	14,673	12,738
1520		43	Polished Ebony	14,805	12,844
1520		43	Satin and Polished Walnut	14,270	12,416
1520		43	Satin and Polished Cherry	14,230	12,384
1520		43	Satin and Polished Oak	13,793	12,034
1520		43	Satin and Polished Mahogany	14,508	12,606
1520		43	Italian Provincial Satin Ebony	14,540	12,632
1520		43	Italian Provincial Semi-Gloss Ebony	14,673	12,738
1520		43	Italian Provincial Polished Ebony	14,805	12,844
1520		43	Italian Provincial Satin and Polished Walnut	14,295	12,436
1520		43	Italian Provincial Satin and Polished Mahogany	14,535	12,628
1520		43	Italian Provincial Satin and Polished Oak	13,805	12,044
1520		43	Country Classic Satin and Polished Cherry	14,110	12,288
1520		43	Country Classic Satin and Polished Oak	13,875	12,100
1520		43	French Provincial Satin and Polished Oak	14,295	12,436
1520		43	French Provincial Satin and Polished Cherry/Walnut/Mahogany	14,690	12,752
1520		43	Riviera Satin and Polished Oak	13,755	12,004
1520		43	Queen Anne Satin and Polished Oak	14,403	12,522
1520		43	Queen Anne Satin and Polished Mahogany/Cherry	14,690	12,752
1500		45	Satin Ebony	13,345	11,676
1500		45	Semi-Gloss Ebony	13,580	11,864
1500		45	Polished Ebony (Lacquer)	13,725	11,980
1500		45	Polished Ebony (Polyester)	13,990	12,192
1500		45	Satin and Polished Oak	12,748	11,198
1500		45	Satin and Polished Walnut	13,478	11,782
1500		45	Satin and Polished Mahogany	13,663	11,930
1500		45	Satin and Polished Gothic Oak	13,490	11,792
1500		45	Satin and Polished Cherry	13,620	11,896
Verticals			Chinese-made action instead of Renner, less	1,875	1,500

Grands

Model	Feet	Inches	Description	MSRP*	SMP*
W-175	5	9	Satin Ebony	57,105	46,684
W-175	5	9	Semi-Polished and Polished Ebony (Lacquer)	58,590	47,872
W-175	5	9	Polished Ebony (Polyester)	59,400	48,520
W-175	5	9	Satin Mahogany/Walnut/Cherry	59,698	48,758
W-175	5	9	Semi-Polished & Polished Mahogany/Walnut/Cherry	61,235	49,988
W-175	5	9	Open-Pore Walnut	58,240	47,592
W-175	5	9	Satin Oak	54,865	44,892
W-175	5	9	Chippendale Satin Mahogany/Cherry	61,560	50,248
W-175	5	9	Chippendale Semi-Polished & Polished Mahogany/Cherry	63,073	51,458
W-190	6	4	Satin Ebony	60,788	49,630
W-190	6	4	Semi-Polished and Polished Ebony (Lacquer)	62,340	50,872
W-190	6	4	Polished Ebony (Polyester)	63,180	51,544
W-190	6	4	Satin Mahogany/Walnut/Cherry	63,470	51,776
W-190	6	4	Semi-Polished & Polished Mahogany/Walnut/Cherry	65,068	53,054
W-190	6	4	Open-Pore Walnut	61,965	50,572
W-190	6	4	Satin Oak	58,455	47,764
W-190	6	4	Chippendale Satin Mahogany/Cherry	65,443	53,354
W-190	6	4	Chippendale Semi-Polished & Polished Mahogany/Cherry	66,975	54,580

*See pricing explanation on page 203.

Model	Feet	Inches	Description	MSRP*	SMP*
WEBER					
Weber Verticals					
W112		44	Continental Satin Ebony	4,705	4,582
W112		44	Continental Polished Ebony	4,438	4,406
W112		44	Continental Polished Mahogany/White	4,705	4,582
W112F		44	French Provincial Satin Cherry	5,070	4,840
W112F		44	Satin Mahogany	5,070	4,840
W114		45	Satin Ebony	5,338	5,017
W114		45	Polished Ebony	5,070	4,819
W114		45	Polished Mahogany/White	5,338	5,017
W114E		45	Polished Ebony w/Chrome	5,708	5,214
W121		48	Satin Ebony	5,873	5,532
W121		48	Polished Ebony	5,605	5,336
W121		48	Polished Mahogany	5,873	5,532
W121E		48	Polished Ebony w/Chrome	6,468	6,039
W121N		48	Polished Ebony	5,883	5,595
W131		52	Satin Ebony	6,408	6,008
W131		52	Polished Ebony	6,140	5,815
W131		52	Polished Mahogany	6,408	6,008
Albert Weber Verticals					
AW 121		48	Polished Ebony	9,998	8,648
AW 121		48	Satin Mahogany	10,373	8,978
AW 121E		48	Polished Ebony	11,248	9,678
AW 131		52	Satin Ebony	13,498	11,398
AW 131		52	Polished Ebony	12,348	10,528
Weber Grands					
W150	4	11	Satin Ebony	12,865	10,599
W150	4	11	Polished Ebony	12,415	10,228
W150	4	11	Polished Mahogany/White	12,865	10,599
W150E	4	11	Polished Ebony	14,113	11,465
W157	5	2	Satin Ebony	14,788	11,759
W157	5	2	Polished Ebony	14,238	11,332
W157	5	2	Polished Mahogany/White	14,788	11,759
W175	5	9	Satin Ebony	16,135	12,955
W175	5	9	Polished Ebony	15,468	12,447
W175	5	9	Polished Mahogany	16,135	12,955
W185	6	1	Satin Ebony	18,848	15,136
W185	6	1	Polished Ebony	18,038	14,567
W185	6	1	Polished Mahogany	16,054	15,136
Albert Weber Grands					
AW 185	6	1	Satin Ebony	33,998	27,194
AW 185	6	1	Polished Ebony	32,498	26,039
AW 208	6	10	Satin Ebony	43,998	34,312
AW 208	6	10	Polished Ebony	41,998	32,798
AW 228	7	6	Satin Ebony	60,998	48,144
AW 228	7	6	Polished Ebony	58,998	46,598
AW 275	9		Polished Ebony	104,998	81,998

*See pricing explanation on page 203.

Model	Feet	Inches	Description	MSRP*	SMP*
WYMAN					
Verticals					
WV108		42.5	Continental Polished Ebony	4,500	3,779
WV108		42.5	Continental Polished Mahogany/Cherry	4,575	3,840
WV110		43	Polished Ebony	5,000	4,057
WV110		43	Polished Mahogany/Cherry	5,075	4,118
WV115		45	Polished Ebony	5,263	4,225
WV115		45	Polished Mahogany/Cherry	5,325	4,281
WV118DL		46	Polished Ebony w/Chrome Hardware (double leg)	6,190	4,778
WV120		48	Polished Ebony	5,800	4,539
WV120		48	Polished Mahogany	5,875	4,601
WV127		50	Polished Ebony w/Mahogany Trim (straight leg)	8,575	6,585
WV127		50	Polished Ebony w/Mahogany Trim (curved leg)	8,665	6,650
WV132		52	Polished Ebony	7,250	5,713
Grands					
WG145	4	9	Polished Ebony	10,963	8,483
WG145	4	9	Polished Mahogany	11,488	8,903
WG160	5	3	Polished Ebony	13,375	9,973
WG160	5	3	Polished Mahogany	13,875	10,383
WG170	5	7	Polished Ebony	14,950	10,813
WG170	5	7	Polished Mahogany	15,475	11,233
WG185	6	1	Polished Ebony	17,588	12,825
WG185	6	1	Polished Mahogany	18,125	13,250
All models			Satin Finishes, add		300
YAMAHA					
Including Disklavier and Silent Piano					
Verticals					
M460		44	Satin Cherry/Brown Cherry	5,999	5,998
M560		44	Hancock Satin Brown Cherry	6,599	6,598
M560		44	Sheraton Satin Mahogany	6,599	6,598
M560		44	Queen Anne Satin Cherry	6,599	6,598
P22		45	Satin Ebony/Walnut/Oak/Cherry	5,999	5,999
P660		45	Sheraton Satin Brown Mahogany	7,999	7,798
P660		45	Queen Anne Satin Brown Cherry	7,999	7,798
T118		47	Satin Ebony	5,999	5,999
T118		47	Polished Ebony	5,499	5,499
T118		47	Polished Mahogany/Walnut	5,999	5,999
T121SC		48	Polished Ebony	6,499	6,499
U1		48	Satin and Polished Ebony	9,999	9,999
U1		48	Satin American Walnut	11,999	11,999
U1		48	Open-Pore American Walnut	11,999	11,999
U1		48	Polished American Walnut/Mahogany	11,999	11,999
U1		48	Polished White	11,999	11,999
YUS1		48	Satin and Polished Ebony	13,999	13,598
YUS1		48	Satin American Walnut	17,599	16,798
YUS1		48	Polished American Walnut/Mahogany	17,599	16,798
YUS1		48	Polished White	17,599	16,798
U3		52	Polished Ebony	12,999	12,398
U3		52	Satin American Walnut	14,999	14,998
U3		52	Polished Mahogany	14,999	14,998
YUS3		52	Polished Ebony	16,999	16,198
YUS3		52	Polished Mahogany	19,999	18,998
YUS5		52	Polished Ebony	18,999	17,798

*See pricing explanation on page 203.

PIANOBUYER.COM

Model	Feet	Inches	Description	MSRP*	SMP*
YAMAHA *(continued)*					
Disklavier Verticals					
DU1E3		48	Polished Ebony	25,999	23,998
Silent Verticals					
U1SG		48	Polished Ebony	15,799	14,598
YUS1SG		48	Polished Ebony	18,999	17,398
U3SG		52	Polished Ebony	20,799	18,798
YUS3SG		52	Polished Ebony	22,999	19,998
YUS5SG		52	Polished Ebony	25,999	21,998
Grands					
GB1K	5		Polished Ebony	13,499	12,598
GB1K	5		Polished American Walnut/Mahogany	15,999	14,998
GB1K	5		French Provincial Satin Cherry	17,499	16,398
GB1K	5		Georgian Satin Mahogany	16,999	15,998
GC1M	5	3	Satin and Polished Ebony	21,999	21,198
GC1M	5	3	Satin American Walnut	27,999	25,998
GC1M	5	3	Polished Mahogany	27,999	25,998
GC1M	5	3	Polished American Walnut	27,999	25,598
GC1M	5	3	Polished Ivory/White	27,999	25,998
C1	5	3	Satin and Polished Ebony	30,999	27,698
C1	5	3	Satin American Walnut	35,999	32,998
C1	5	3	Polished American Walnut	35,999	32,998
C1	5	3	Satin and Polished Mahogany	35,999	32,998
C1	5	3	Polished White	35,999	32,998
GC2	5	8	Satin and Polished Ebony	25,999	24,198
GC2	5	8	Satin American Walnut	30,999	28,998
GC2	5	8	Polished American Walnut	30,999	28,998
GC2	5	8	Satin Mahogany	30,999	28,998
GC2	5	8	Polished Mahogany	30,999	28,998
GC2	5	8	Polished Ivory/White	30,999	28,998
C2	5	8	Satin and Polished Ebony	34,999	31,598
C2	5	8	Satin American Walnut	38,999	34,998
C2	5	8	Polished American Walnut	38,999	34,998
C2	5	8	Satin and Polished Mahogany	38,999	34,998
C2	5	8	Satin Light American Oak	39,999	36,998
C2	5	8	Polished White	38,999	34,998
C3	6	1	Satin and Polished Ebony	46,599	41,998
C3	6	1	Satin American Walnut	57,999	52,998
C3	6	1	Polished Mahogany/American Walnut	57,999	52,998
C3	6	1	Polished White	57,999	52,998
C3XA	6	1	Polished Ebony	54,999	47,998
S4BB	6	3	Polished Ebony	64,999	60,998
CF4	6	3	Polished Ebony	87,999	87,999
C5	6	7	Satin and Polished Ebony	49,999	45,198
C5	6	7	Polished Mahogany	58,799	53,798
C6	7		Satin and Polished Ebony	55,999	50,398
C6	7		Polished Mahogany	64,999	59,198
C6XA	7		Polished Ebony	62,999	57,598
S6BB	7		Polished Ebony	79,999	70,998
CF6	7		Polished Ebony	99,999	99,798
C7	7	6	Satin and Polished Ebony	64,999	57,798
C7	7	6	Polished Mahogany	74,599	67,498
CFX	9		Polished Ebony	149,999	147,998

*See pricing explanation on page 203.

YAMAHA (continued)

Disklavier Grands

Model	Feet	Inches	Description	MSRP*	SMP*
DGB1KE3	5		Polished Ebony	23,999	20,998
DGB1KE3	5		Polished Mahogany/American Walnut	29,999	27,998
DGC1ME3	5	3	Satin Ebony	39,999	34,598
DGC1ME3	5	3	Polished Ebony	35,999	32,598
DGC1ME3	5	3	Satin American Walnut	41,999	38,998
DGC1ME3	5	3	Polished Mahogany/American Walnut	41,999	38,998
DGC1MM4	5	3	Satin and Polished Ebony	49,999	42,998
DGC1MM4	5	3	Satin American Walnut	55,999	48,998
DGC1MM4	5	3	Polished American Walnut/Mahogany	55,999	48,998
DGC1MM4	5	3	Polished Ivory/White	55,999	48,998
DC1E3	5	3	Satin and Polished Ebony	43,999	40,998
DC1E3	5	3	Polished American Walnut/Mahogany	50,999	44,998
DC1M4	5	3	Satin and Polished Ebony	57,999	48,998
DC1M4	5	3	Satin and Polished American Walnut	62,999	54,998
DC1M4	5	3	Satin and Polished Mahogany	62,999	54,998
DC1M4	5	3	Polished White	62,999	54,998
DGC2E3	5	8	Satin and Polished Ebony	41,999	38,998
DGC2E3	5	8	Polished Mahogany/American Walnut	48,999	42,998
DC2E3	5	8	Satin and Polished Ebony	45,999	42,998
DC2E3	5	8	Polished Mahogany/American Walnut	52,999	46,998
DC2M4	5	8	Satin and Polished Ebony	63,999	54,998
DC2M4	5	8	Satin American Walnut/Mahogany	68,999	60,998
DC2M4	5	8	Polished American Walnut/Mahogany	68,999	60,998
DC2M4	5	8	Polished White	68,999	60,998
DC3M4	6	1	Satin and Polished Ebony	77,999	65,998
DC3M4	6	1	Satin American Walnut	84,999	72,998
DC3M4	6	1	Polished American Walnut/Mahogany	84,999	72,998
DC3M4	6	1	Polished White	84,999	72,998
DC5M4	6	7	Satin and Polished Ebony	83,999	71,998
DC5M4	6	7	Polished Mahogany	91,999	78,998
DC6M4	7		Polished Ebony	88,999	75,998
DC6M4	7		Polished Mahogany	97,999	82,998
DC7M4	7	6	Polished Ebony	96,999	81,998
DC7M4	7	6	Polished Mahogany	102,999	88,998
DC7M4	7	6	Polished White	102,999	88,998

Disklavier Pro Grands

Model	Feet	Inches	Description	MSRP*	SMP*
DC3M4PRO	6	1	Polished Ebony	81,999	70,998
DS4M4PROBB	6	3	Polished Ebony	119,999	98,998
DC5M4PRO	6	7	Polished Ebony	88,999	76,998
DC6M4PRO	7		Polished Ebony	94,999	80,998
DS6M4PROBB	7		Polished Ebony	131,999	108,998
DC7M4PRO	7	6	Polished Ebony	99,999	86,998
DCFXM4PRO	9		Polished Ebony	229,999	190,998

Silent Grands

Model	Feet	Inches	Description	MSRP*	SMP*
GB1KS	5		Polished Ebony	19,999	18,398
C1SG	5	3	Polished Ebony	36,999	32,998
C2SG	5	8	Polished Ebony	38,999	34,998
C3SG	6	1	Polished Ebony	50,999	44,998
C5SG	6	7	Polished Ebony	54,999	48,998
C6SG	7		Polished Ebony	59,999	52,998
C7SG	7	6	Polished Ebony	68,999	60,998

*See pricing explanation on page 203.

Model	Feet	Inches	Description	MSRP*	SMP*

YOUNG CHANG

Verticals

Model	Feet	Inches	Description	MSRP*	SMP*
Y112		44	Continental Polished Ebony	4,273	4,248
Y112		44	Continental Polished Mahogany/Walnut/White	4,530	4,416
Y112F		44	French Provincial Satin Cherry	4,975	4,732
Y112F		44	Satin Mahogany	4,975	4,732
Y114		45	Polished Ebony	4,975	4,713
Y114		45	Polished Mahogany/Walnut/White	5,238	4,904
Y114E		45	Polished Ebony w/Chrome	5,238	4,870
Y118		47	Satin Ebony	5,488	5,118
Y118		47	Polished Ebony	5,218	4,910
Y118		47	Polished Mahogany	5,488	5,118
Y121		48	Satin Ebony	5,763	5,424
Y121		48	Polished Ebony	5,500	5,233
Y121		48	Polished Mahogany	5,763	5,424
Y131		52	Satin Ebony	6,288	5,844
Y131		52	Polished Ebony	6,025	5,656
Y131		52	Polished Mahogany	6,288	5,844

Grands

Model	Feet	Inches	Description	MSRP*	SMP*
Y150	4	11	Satin Ebony	12,410	10,109
Y150	4	11	Polished Ebony	11,970	9,750
Y150	4	11	Polished Mahogany/Walnut/White	12,410	10,109
Y150E	4	11	Polished Ebony w/Chrome	13,225	10,552
Y157	5	2	Satin Ebony	14,138	11,189
Y157	5	2	Polished Ebony	13,613	10,876
Y157	5	2	Polished Mahogany/Walnut/White	14,138	11,189
Y175	5	9	Satin Ebony	15,843	12,600
Y175	5	9	Polished Ebony	15,188	12,099
Y175	5	9	Polished Mahogany/Walnut	15,843	12,600
Y185	6	1	Satin Ebony	18,338	14,939
Y185	6	1	Polished Ebony	17,550	14,316
Y185	6	1	Polished Mahogany/Walnut	18,338	14,939

*See pricing explanation on page 203.

ELECTRONIC PLAYER-PIANO ADD-ON (RETROFIT) SYSTEMS AND PRICES

Prices for electronic player-piano add-on (retrofit) systems vary by installer, and by options and accessories chosen. The following are manufacturers' suggested retail prices for installed systems, options, and accessories. The usual dealer discounts may apply, especially as an incentive to purchase a piano. Prices for player-piano brands that are installed only by the piano manufacturer, such as Yamaha Disklavier and Bösendorfer CEUS, are included in the acoustic piano Models & Prices section of this publication.

Model/Option	MSRP
LIVE PERFORMANCE	**None provided**
PIANODISC	
SilentDrive HD w/1,024 levels of expression, Apple Airport Express included with Air Systems, plus $1,000 software package, unless otherwise stated.	
iQ—"Intelligent Player System," factory-installed or retrofitted:	
iQ iPad64G Air Platinum w/ Core MIDI Performance Package (MIDI Record, iRig, MuteRail & Headphones), $2,500 Preloaded Music & Video Package included	13,760
iQ iPad64G Air Premier–$2,500 Preloaded Music & Video Package included	11,360
iQ iPad64G Air	8,689
iQ iPad32G Air	8,457
iQ iPad16G Air	8,263
iQ iTouch Air—w/32G Wireless iPod Touch	8,060
iQ iPod Classic—w/160G iPod Classic	7,974
iQ Flash—MP3 Player w/ Remote Control	7,534
iQ Flex Air—Using Customer-Provided Playback Device	7,557
iQ Flex—Using Customer-Provided Playback Device	7,409
Add for Amplified PDS150 Speakers (Pair)	861
Performance Package—MIDI Record, USB/MIDI Cable (standalone or PC/Mac)	1,975
Mobile Performance Package—MIDI Record, iRig MIDI (standalone, iDevice)	2,155
Studio Performance Package—MIDI Record, iConnect MIDI (standalone, iDevice, or PC/Mac)	2,860
Sync-A-Vision iMac w/iQ (Ebony)—Integrated Music Desk, Wireless Keyboard & Mouse, w/SAV Content	16,631
Sync-A-Vision Mac mini w/iQ (Ebony)—Integrated Music Desk, Wireless Keyboard & Mouse, w/SAV Content	16,336
MIDI Record System	1,962
Add for Piano MuteRail	722
iQ Audio Balance Control—Dual Balance Piano/Audio Control	188
QuietTime MagicStar (Control Unit w/128 GM Sound Module, MuteRail, Optical Key Sensor MIDI Strip, MIDI Interface Board, Cable, Power Supply, and Headphones)	3,443
MIDI Controller (MIDI Strip, MIDI Interface Board, Pedal Switch, Cable, Power Supply)	2,158
Sync-A-Vision Software Bundle: Includes Educational & Entertainment Video Selections	1,299
Sync-A-Vision Entertainment Bundle: Includes Entertainment Video Selections	999

Model/Option	MSRP
PIANOFORCE	
Includes pedal solenoid, two amplified speakers, remote control	5,995
QRS PNOmation	
PNOmation II Playback, installation extra	6,195
PNOmation II Playback and Record, installation extra	8,095
PNOmation II Playback, Record, Perform, and Practice; installation extra	8,495
PNOmation II Upgrade Kit, installation extra	2,095
PNOmation II MIDI Upgrade Kit, installation extra	2,295
PNOscan II Key Sensor Strip, installation extra	1,895
Qsync	1,595

IF YOU'VE READ any of the "**Brand and Company Profiles**" on the acoustic side, you'll see that discussions of digital makes and models is of a very different nature. For one thing, although a few manufacturers of digital pianos can trace their roots back over 100 years, such histories, while occasionally fascinating, have little or no relevance to a type of instrument that has existed for only a few dozen years. For another, whereas acoustic piano makers may boast of using slowly grown spruce carefully harvested from trees on north-facing slopes in the Bavarian Alps, there are no stories from digital piano makers of silicon carefully harvested from isolated south-facing beaches during the second low tide of October; no tales of printed circuit boards still crafted by hand as they've been for generations, or descriptions of internal cable harnesses made of only the finest German wire. And while it's interesting to know who was the first to introduce a particular feature, digital pianos, like all modern electronic products, are very much a matter of "What have you done for me *lately*?"

Even more than in the section dedicated to acoustic pianos, the descriptions provided here are only half the story, and must be used in conjunction with the chart of "**Digital Piano Specifications and Prices**" if you are to have a clear picture of a given brand's offerings. In some cases, little information is available or forthcoming regarding a brand, and much that could have been included would simply be a reiteration of marketing statements. In others, specifications or descriptions available from a manufacturer have been in conflict, as when specifications on their website say one thing and the owner's manual says something else. While every effort has been made to ensure the accuracy of these listings and descriptions, some discrepancies will have undoubtedly slipped through.

Adagio

Kaysound
2165 46th Avenue
Lachine, Quebec H8T 2P1
Canada
514-633-8877
ussupport@kaysound.com
www.adagiopianos.com

Adagio is a division of Kaysound, a Canadian-based distributor of music products. There are six models of Adagio digitals, including verticals, grands, and ensembles. Kaysound also sells three models under the Kingston label.

Behringer

Behringer USA, Inc.
18912 North Creek Parkway, Suite 200
Bothell, Washington 98011
425-672-0816
www.behringer.com

Founded in Germany in 1989 by Uli Behringer, this company is primarily focused on professional audio products, but also makes electric guitars and digital pianos. Their digital pianos, available for some time in Europe, are now coming to North America. Four models are available: two grands, two verticals.

Bellissimo

See Symphony

Brodmann

Piano Marketing Group LLC
752 East 21st Street
Ferdinand, Indiana 47532
812-630-0978
gary.trafton@brodmann-pianos.com
www.brodmann-pianos.com

The Joseph Brodmann Group, based in Vienna, Austria, has entered the digital piano market with six models of vertical piano.

Blüthner

Blüthner USA LLC
5660 West Grand River
Lansing, Michigan 48906
517-886-6000
800-954-3200
info@bluthnerpiano.com
www.bluthnerpiano.com

Blüthner, one of the world's pre-eminent piano makers, has released its first digital piano, the e-Klavier. (For company background, see the Blüthner listing in the "Brand and Company Profiles" for acoustic pianos.) Engineered and manufactured entirely at the Blüthner factory in Leipzig, Germany, the e-Klavier is offered in three styles: slab, vertical, and professional performance keyboard.

Blüthner says it has developed a unique approach to sampling and sound modeling that allows the e-Klavier to reproduce the effect of the aliquot (fourth) string from the Blüthner piano, an approach the company calls Authentic Acoustic Behavior. This system also permits the reproduction of advanced harmonics, such as the coincidental partials produced when two notes are played simultaneously, and the sound the dampers make when lifting off the strings. The e-Klavier will include a digital editor that will allow the user to adjust the string resonance, aliquot effect, and damper performance. The user will also be able to download new sounds into the e-Klavier via the Internet, and to store the sounds of turn-of-the-century Blüthner pianos and other Blüthners of interest.

The speaker system and amplifier are unique to the e-Klavier and were designed by Günther Phillip of PCL Audio. The e-Klavier 2 model contains an actual piano soundboard, enabling the instrument to produce certain aspects of acoustic-piano tone that are difficult or impossible to simulate by purely electronic means.

Casio

Casio USA
570 Mount Pleasant Avenue
Dover, New Jersey 07801
973-361-5400
www.casio.com

Kashio Tadao established Casio in 1946. Originally a small subcontractor factory that made parts and gears for microscopes, Casio built Japan's first electric calculator in 1954, which began the company's transformation into the consumer-electronics powerhouse it is today. Perhaps best known for its calculators, digital cameras, and watches, Casio entered the musical instrument business with the launch of the Casiotone in 1980.

Casio's current line of digital pianos consists of four vertical and three slab models. The Privia line's PX-130 and PX-330 slabs are the least expensive ensemble models, and offer an optional stand-and-pedal module that turns them into three-pedal pianos with support for half-pedaling. The PX-130, at a mere 25 pounds, is also the lightest digital piano. Some vertical models are marketed under the Celviano label. Casio digital pianos are available at music retailers, consumer-electronics and club stores, and online. Casio has more models under $1,000 than any other manufacturer.

Galileo

Galileo Music Corporation
P.O. Box 633
Falmouth, Massachusetts 02541
508-457-6771
www.galileomusic.com

Galileo is the digital piano brand of Viscount, an Italian company that traces its roots back to accordion builder Antonio Galanti, who built his first instrument in 1890. The Galanti accordion factory was opened in 1898 by Antonio's son Egidio Galanti, whose own sons, Matteo and Marcello, became the driving forces behind General music and Viscount, respectively. Viscount began manufacturing electronic organs in the 1960s, with digital pianos following in the late 1980s. Today, Viscount is run by the fourth generation of the Galanti family, Marcello's son Mauro and daughter Loriana.

There are currently 13 models in the Galileo line, including one slab, five verticals, and seven grands. The grands use a 19-ply wood rim like that of an acoustic grand. Galileo offers its Concerto model in the most ornate traditional wood cabinet currently available.

Galileo also makes digital pianos under the brand names Princeton and Viscount.

Kaino

See Omega

Kawai

Kawai America Corporation
2055 East University Drive
Rancho Dominguez, California 90220
310-631-1771
800-421-2177
info@kawaius.com
www.kawaius.com

For company background, see the Kawai listing in the "**Brand and Company Profiles**" for acoustic pianos.

After 50 years as a piano builder, Kawai entered the market with its first digital piano in 1985. Today, Kawai's lineup for North America features 17 models, many of them new. Kawai's digital piano line comprises four groups: the Concert Performer (CP) ensemble pianos; the standard digital piano line, consisting of the Concert Artist (CA), Classic Series (CS), CL, and CN models; the ES and EP portable instruments; and Professional Products, including the CE220 and MP series.

Kawai created the first digital piano to use a transducer-driven soundboard for a more natural piano sound, a feature that is available on the flagship CA93. The CP ensemble models have undergone a complete makeover, with all models now sporting touchscreen technology and USB audio. The top-of-the-line CP209 ensemble grand is also available with two different levels of factory-installed PianoDisc player-piano system. If you're after a huge number of voices, the models at the upper end of the CP line come with over 1,000.

Kawai uses five different actions in its digital pianos. The two newest ones—the Responsive Hammer (RH) and top-of-the-line Realistic Material, Realistic Mechanism, Realistic Motion (RM3) actions—can be found in the CN, CA, CP, CS, and MP piano models. The RM3 action has wood keys, Ivory Touch (simulated ivory) keytops, and, on the MP10, CA93, CS6, CP209, and CP179 models, simulated escapement.

Kawai has initiated on its website an online store that allows customers to purchase certain models of digital piano formerly sold only through bricks-and-mortar piano dealers. The pianos are delivered by the closest stocking dealer. In Europe it has been possible for some time to purchase name-brand home digital pianos online; this marks the first time this arrangement is being tried in North America.

Ketron

CMC Distributors
1510 Bath Avenue
Brooklyn, New York 11228
800-554-5982
www.ketronusa.com

Italian producer Ketron, established in 1981, began by making portable organs. The company introduced its first digital pianos in 1998, and expanded that product line in 2002. Ketron currently offers five models, including slabs, verticals, and a grand.

Ketron did not respond to requests for information.

Kingston

See Adagio

Kohler

See Samick

Korg

Korg USA, Inc.
316 South Service Road
Melville, New York 11747
631-390-6800
www.korg.com

Korg was founded in 1962 to produce its first product, an automatic rhythm machine, and in 1972 entered the electronic-organ market. The LP-10 stage piano appeared in 1980, and its first digitally sampled piano, the SG1, was introduced in 1986. Korg now offers four models of 88-key digital piano, including the entry-level model SP-170 at only $500, plus several models with shorter keyboards. Following Kawai's lead, Korg recently announced plans to sell its home digital pianos online (see Kawai, above).

Kurzweil (Young Chang)

Kurzweil Music Systems
6000 Phyllis Drive
Cypress, California 90630
657-200-3470
800-874-2880
www.kurzweilmusicsystems.com

Legendary inventor Ray Kurzweil, perhaps best known for having developed a reading machine for the blind, launched Kurzweil Music Systems in 1983, following conversations with Stevie Wonder about the potential for combining the control and flexibility of the computer with the sounds of acoustic instruments. The result was the Kurzweil K250, launched in 1984. In 1990, Kurzweil Music Systems was purchased by Young Chang, which continues to operate the division today.

The new X-PRO series, which includes a vertical and a mini-grand, and the new MP series, are based on Kurzweil's powerful PC3X professional keyboard. Most Kurzweil products are now available through a combination of musical instrument dealers, piano dealers, and online sources. Most Kurzweil models employ Italian Fatar actions.

M-Audio

M-Audio
5795 Martin Road
Irwindale, California 91706
626-633-9050
www.m-audio.com

M-Audio (formerly Midiman) is a business unit of Avid Technology, Inc., founded in 1987. Avid also operates Digidesign, producer of the recording-industry standard Pro Tools software, the popular and powerful Sibelius notation software, and professional video-production products. M-Audio makes and sells a wide variety of music-production hardware, including audio/MIDI computer interfaces and monitor speakers. The company has withdrawn from its brief sojourn in the home digital piano market, leaving only the ProKeys88 slab model.

Nord

American Music & Sound
22020 Clarendon Street, Suite 305
Woodland Hills, California 91367
800-431-2609
nord@americanmusicandsound.com
www.americamusicandsound.com
www.nordkeyboards.com

The Nord Piano 2 HA88, successor to the Nord Piano 88, is a professional stage piano that comes with a library of more than 1,000 sounds on a DVD, or downloadable from the Nord Piano website to the instrument via USB. Nord Keyboards are made in Sweden by Clavia DMI AB.

Omega

Piano Empire, Inc.
3035 E. La Mesa Street
Anaheim, California 92806
800-576-3463
714-408-4599
info@omegapianos.com
www.omegapianos.com

Omega is the brand name used in the U.S. for Kaino digital pianos. Kaino, located in Guangzhou, China, began making portable keyboards in 1986, and digital pianos in 1997.

Princeton

See Galileo

Roland

Roland Corporation U.S.
5100 South Eastern Avenue
Los Angeles, California 90040
323-890-3700
www.rolandus.com

To simply say that Roland Corporation was established in 1972 would be to ignore one of the most compelling stories in the realm of digital pianos. Ikutaro Kakehashi started down the path to Roland Corporation at the age of 16, when he began repairing watches in postwar Japan. His enthusiasm for music soon evolved into repairing radios in addition to watches and clocks. At the age of 20, Kakehashi contracted tuberculosis. After three years in the hospital, he was selected for the trial of a new drug, streptomycin, and within a year he was out of the hospital.

In 1954, Kakehashi opened Kakehashi Musen (Kakehashi Radio). Once again his interest in music intervened, this time leading him to develop a prototype organ. In 1960, Kakehashi Radio evolved into Ace Electronic Industries. The FR1 Rhythm Ace became a standard offering of the Hammond Organ Company, and Ace Electronic Industries flourished. Guitar amplifiers, effects units, and more rhythm machines were developed, but as a result of various business-equity involvements, Ace was inadvertently acquired by a company with no interest in musical products, and Kakehashi left in March 1972. One month later, Kakehashi established Roland Corporation. The first Roland product, not surprisingly, was a rhythm box.

Fast-forward to 1986, when the introduction of the RD1000 stage piano was Roland's first entry in what would become the digital piano category. Today Roland offers more than two dozen models of digital piano covering every facet of the category: slabs, verticals, grands (including moving-key player pianos), ensembles, and stage pianos. Some Roland digital pianos are even assembled in the U.S. at the Roland-owned Rodgers Organ factory, in Hillsboro, Oregon.

Of particular interest to those looking for educational features are the HPi models, which include a substantial suite of educational capabilities supported by a music-desk–mounted LCD screen. The newly introduced model LX10 adds a traditional-looking vertical piano to the line. Roland can also lay claim to the most extensive collection of model designations in the world of digital pianos. While this is hardly a drawback, it does present a challenge when sorting through the model lineup; the chart of "**Digital Piano Specifications and Prices**" will help to clarify things.

The V-Piano is the first digital piano to rely entirely on physical modeling as its tonal source. Physical modeling breaks down a piano's sound into discrete elements that can be represented by mathematical equations, and creates the tone in real time based on a complex series of calculations. There are no acoustic piano samples. For more information about physical modeling, please see, elsewhere in this issue, "**Digital Basics, Part 1: Imitating the Acoustic Piano**" and "**My Other Piano Is a Computer: An Introduction to Software Pianos.**"

The HP models are the core of Roland's home digital piano offering, and the latest models share Roland's new SuperNATURAL® piano sound engine, differing from each other primarily in the specifications of their audio systems and actions.

Samick

Samick Music Corporation
1329 Gateway Drive
Gallatin, Tennessee 37066
800-592-9393
www.kohlerdigitalpianos.com
www.smcmusic.com

Samick is in the process of expanding its presence in the digital piano market. Its line consists of four grands and three verticals marketed under the Kohler brand, and three grands and nine verticals under the Samick label. Samick/Kohler tends to offer more finish options than many other brands. The Kohler KD165 grand is the only digital available with curved French Provincial–style legs.

Suzuki

Suzuki Corporation
P.O. Box 710459
Santee, California 92072
800-854-1594
www.suzukimusic.com

Suzuki sells its line of digital pianos on its website, through other online outlets, and through Costco. Models change frequently.

Symphony

Symphony Pianos
90-02 Atlantic Avenue
Ozone Park, New York 11416
718-322-0737
dbrandi@symphonypiano.com
www.symphonypiano.com

Symphony digitals are manufactured by Zhejiang Youyi Electronic Co. Ltd., one of China's larger digital piano makers, located in Zheijiang Province, China. A similar line of digital pianos appears to be distributed in Canada under the Bellissimo label.

Viscount

See Galileo

Williams

Williams Pianos
P.O. Box 5111
Thousand Oaks, California 91359
www.williamspianos.com

Williams digital pianos, a house brand of Guitar Center, are also available through Guitar Center's Musician's Friend e-commerce website and two other e-commerce sites. There are seven models from Williams, including four verticals, two slabs with optional stand, and one grand.

Yamaha

Yamaha Corporation of America
P.O. Box 6600
Buena Park, California 90622
714-522-9011
800-854-1569
infostation@yamaha.com
www.yamaha.com

For company background, see the Yamaha listing in the "Brands and Company Profiles" for acoustic pianos.

Yamaha Corporation is the world's largest producer of musical instruments—from the obvious (pianos) to the slightly obscure (bassoon), Yamaha makes it. Yamaha entered the world of electronic instruments in 1959, when it introduced the first all-transistor organ. In 1971, because no manufacturer would develop an integrated circuit (IC) for Yamaha's relatively low-volume demand, the company built its own IC plant. Jumping ahead to 1983, the introduction of the first Yamaha Clavinova, the YP-40, marked the beginning of what we now call the digital piano. Today, Yamaha's three dozen or so models of digital piano (not counting different finishes) constitute the broadest range of any manufacturer. The downside is that deciphering the variety of options—slabs, verticals, grands, stage pianos, ensemble pianos, designer digitals, hybrids—can be a bit daunting. And then there are the sub-brands: Clavinova, Modus, and Arius.

Clavinova digital pianos include the standard CLP line and the ensemble CVP line, and are available only through piano dealers. The new CLPS400 models sport a more traditional vertical-piano look while retaining the advantage of a small footprint. The Modus models (model numbers beginning with F, H, and R), Yamaha's series of designer digitals, are functionally similar to the CLP line but with modern-looking cabinets. (The Modus H01 and H11 are perhaps the most striking visual designs among digital pianos.) They are now available online through authorized dealers. Arius (model numbers beginning with YDP) represents Yamaha's economy line of digital verticals, with the long-popular YDP223 now replaced by the YDP181.

Yamaha has introduced physical modeling technology to its CP line of stage pianos. The CP1 is a physical-modeling instrument featuring Yamaha's new Spectral Component Modeling (SCM) technology. Its less expensive siblings, the CP5 and CP50, feature a combination of SCM and Advanced Wave Memory (AWM) sampling. The CP1 and CP5 also include the new NW-Stage action.

Yamaha's Internet Direct Connect (IDC) is unique in the digital-piano world. Available on most Clavinova and Modus models, IDC allows owners to download Yamaha's Digital Music Notebook sheet music, download new styles, listen to music (via a subscription service similar to Disklavier Radio), and take lessons.

Seven different actions are used in Yamaha digitals. In order of increasing quality, they are: Graded Hammer Standard (GHS), Graded Hammer Effect (GHE), Graded Hammer 3 (GH3), Natural Wood (NW), Natural Wood Stage (NW-Stage), Natural Wood Linear Graded Hammer (NW-LGH), and the grand piano action used in the AvantGrand models.

A few years ago Yamaha introduced its game-changing AvantGrand hybrid piano. Only time will tell how hybrid pianos will alter the piano landscape, but we predict that the AvantGrand will displace the sales of many similarly priced acoustic models—including Yamaha's own. For more information about the AvantGrand, see the article on "Hybrid Pianos" elsewhere in this issue.

In the chart that follows, we have included those features and specifications about which buyers, in our experience, are most likely to be curious. However, many models have more features than are shown here. Listings are sorted in the following order: first by brand; then, within each brand, by physical form (slab, vertical, or grand); within each form, by type (standard digitals, then ensemble digitals); and finally, by price or model number, whichever seems most appropriate. See the various articles on digital pianos elsewhere in this publication for more information about each of the terms defined below, shown in the order in which they appear in the chart.

Form The physical form of the model: G=Grand, V= Vertical (Console), S=Slab.

Ensemble A digital piano with easy-play accompaniments (not just rhythms).

Finish The wood finishes or colors available for a particular model (not specified for slab models unless multiple finishes are available). Multiple finish options are separated by a slash (/). A manufacturer's own color term is used where a generic term could not be determined. Real-wood veneers are in *italics*.

Estimated Price This is our estimate of the price you will pay for the instrument. For digitals sold online or through chain and warehouse outlets, this price is the Minimum Advertised Price (MAP) and is shown in *italics*. For digitals sold only through bricks-and-mortar piano dealers, the price shown is based on a profit margin that piano dealers typically aspire to when selling digitals, including an allowance for incoming freight and setup. Discounts from this price, if any, typically are small. For more information on MAP and other pricing issues, please read "**Buying a Digital Piano**," elsewhere in this issue.

MSRP Manufacturer's Suggested Retail Price, also known as "list" or "sticker" price. Not all manufacturers use them.

Voices The number of different musical voices the instrument can produce.

Key Off Indicates the presence of Key Off samples.

Sustain Samples Indicates the presence of samples with the sustain pedal depressed (allowing the strings to vibrate sympathetically).

String Resonance Indicates the presence of String Resonance.

Rhythms/Styles The number of rhythm patterns available.

Polyphony The maximum number of sounds the instrument can produce simultaneously.

Total Watts Total combined amplifier power.

Speakers The number of individual speakers.

Piano Pedals The number of piano pedals supplied with the model. A number in parentheses indicate the number of optional pedals.

A	Ash
AG	Amber Glow
Al	Alder
Bl	Blue
Bk	Black
C	Cherry
DB	Deep Brunette
E	Ebony
G	Gold
Iv	Ivory
M	Mahogany
MD	Mahogany Decor
O	Oak
Or	Orange
P	Polished (used with a wood or color designation)
R	Rosewood
Rd	Red
S	Satin (used with a wood or color designation)
Sr	Silver
VR	Velvette Rouge
W	Walnut
WG	Wood Grain (wood type not specified)
Wt	White

Half Pedal Indicates that the model supports half-pedaling. Many manufacturers do not specify this capability.

Action Indicates the type of action used, if specified.

Escapement Indicates the presence of escapement feel. Models using acoustic-piano actions with actual escapement are indicated by an underlined Y.

Wood Keys Indicates actions with wooden keys.

Ivory Texture Indicates actions with ivory-textured keytops.

Player Moving Keys Indicates that the keys move during playback of recordings.

Vocal Support The model supports some level of vocal performance. This support can vary from the piano simply having a microphone input, to its having the ability to produce the vocalist's voice in multi-part harmony, to pitch-correct the notes sung by the vocalist, or to alter the original voice.

Educational Features The model includes features that specifically support the learning experience. Note that while the ability to record and play back is an important learning tool, it is present on almost all models and so is not included in this definition.

External Memory Indicates the type of external memory accessible.

USB to Computer Indicates the model's ability to interface with a Mac or PC via USB cable.

Recording Tracks The number of recordable tracks.

Warranty (Parts/Labor) Indicates the manufacturer's warranty coverage period: the first number is the length of the parts coverage; the second number is the length of the labor coverage. Single digits indicate years; double digits indicate days.

Dimensions Width, Depth, and Height are rounded to the nearest inch. If space is particularly tight, refer to the manufacturer's specifications for the model's exact dimensions. Note that grand height measurements sometimes indicate the piano's height with its lid up.

Weight Weight of the model rounded to the nearest pound.

Brand & Model	Form	Ensemble	Finish	Estimated Price	MSRP	Voices	Key Off	Sustain Samples	String Resonance	Rhythms/Styles	Polyphony	Total Watts	Speakers	Piano Pedals	Half Pedal
Adagio															
KDP-88	V		C/O	500	1,995	8					64	60	4	1	
KDP-8826	V		EP/MP	1,000	2,995	128				99	64	60	4	3	
XD-400	V		R	800	2,995	128				99	64	60	4	3	
XD-500	V		Bk	800	2,995	128				99	64	60	4	3	
MGP1000	G	E	EP		4,995	137				114	64	120	4	2	
GDP8820	G	E	EP		5,995	138				100	64	120	2	3	
Behringer															
EG2180	V		WG-Bk	649	959	14					64	80		3	
EG2280USB	V		WG-Bk	699	1,029	14					64	80		3	
EG8180	G		EP/RdP	1,499	2,209	14					64	80		3	
EG8280USB	G		EP			14					64	80		3	
Blüthner															
e-Klavier 1	S		ES/WtS		4,765	25	Y	Y	Y		128	100	2	3	Y
e-Klavier 2	V		EP/WtP		6,511	25	Y	Y	Y		128	100	2	3	Y
Brodmann															
BDP 10	V		R	1,271	1,295	8						40	2	3	
BDP 15	V		R/ES	1,362	1,495	8						40	2	3	
BDP 20	V		R/ES	1,507	1,695	16						70	4	3	
BDP 100	V		R/ES/Mpl	1,453	1,895	8						40	4	3	
BDP 150	V		R/ES/Mpl	1,562	1,995	8						40	4	3	
BDP 500	V		EP	1,816	2,495	16						70	4	3	
BDP 500	V		WtP	1,907	2,495	16						70	4	3	
BDP 500	V		WP/EP-WtP	1,998	2,495	16						70	4	3	
Casio															
PX-3S	S		Bk	799	1,099	250			Y		128		-	1(3)	Y
PX-130BK	S		Bk	499	799	16			Y		128	16	2	1(3)	Y
PX-130CSSPW	S		Wht	599	999	16			Y		128	16	2	1(3)	Y
PX-330BK	S	E	Bk	699	999	250			Y	180	128	16	2	1(3)	Y
PX-830BK	V		ES	999	1,399	16			Y		128	40	2	3	Y
PX-830BP	V		EP	1,299	1,999	16			Y		128	40	2	3	Y
AP-220BN	V		W	799	1,199	16			Y		128	16	2	3	Y

Model	Action	Escapement	Wood Keys	Ivory Texture	Player Moving Keys	Vocal Support	Educational Features	External Memory	USB to Computer	Recording Tracks	Warranty (Parts/Labor)	Dimensions WxDxH (Inchees)	Weight (Pounds)
KDP-88										2	2/2	58x23x18	123
KDP-8826											2/2	52x21x35	131
XD-400											2/2		
XD-500											2/2		
MGP1000						Y		SD	Y	3	2/2		233
GDP8820						Y		SD	Y	3	2/2	47x54x35	258
EG2180										2	1/1	55x21x35	142
EG2280USB						Y	Y		Y	2	1/1		
EG8180										2	1/1	54x40x33	200
EG8280USB						Y	Y		Y	2	1/1		
e-Klavier 1	4-zone graded	Y		Y		Y	Y	USB	Y	1	1/90	57x22x35	187
e-Klavier 2	4-zone graded	Y	Y	Y		Y	Y	USB	Y	1	1/90	60x25x24	216
BDP 10									Y	2	1/1	52x11x5	25
BDP 15									Y	2	1/1	57x12x31	90
BDP 20									Y	2	1/1	54x19x34	117
BDP 100									Y	2	1/1	54x18x33	101
BDP 150									Y	2	1/1	52x11x5	25
BDP 500									Y	2	1/1	52x11x5	26
BDP 500									Y	2	1/1	52x11x5	26
BDP 500									Y	2	1/1	52x11x5	26
PX-3S	Tri-Sensor							SD	Y		3/3	52x11x5	24
PX-130BK	Tri-Sensor					Y			Y	2	3/3	52x11x5	25
PX-130CSSPW	Tri-Sensor					Y			Y	3	3/3	52x11x5	25
PX-330BK	Tri-Sensor					Y		SD	Y	16	3/3	52x11x5	26
PX-830BK	Tri-Sensor			Y		Y		SD	Y	2	3/3	54x14x35	74
PX-830BP	Tri-Sensor			Y		Y		SD	Y	2	3/3	54x14x35	74
AP-220BN	Tri-Sensor					Y			Y	2	3/3	55x17x33	83

Brand & Model	Form	Ensemble	Finish	Estimated Price	MSRP	Voices	Key Off	Sustain Samples	String Resonance	Rhythms/Styles	Polyphony	Total Watts	Speakers	Piano Pedals	Half Pedal
Casio (continued)															
AP-420BN	V		W	1,099	1,499	16			Y		128	40	4	3	Y
AP-620BK	V	E	ES	1,399	1,799	250			Y	180	128	60	4	3	Y
Galileo															
Milano II	S		R	2,995	3,995	138				100	64	20	2	1	
VP-91	V		WtP	2,495	3,495	11		Y	Y		128	44	2	1	
VP-111	V		R	2,695	3,695	11		Y	Y		128	44	4	3	
VP-121	V		R	3,295	4,295	20		Y	Y		128	100	4	3	
VP-121	V		EP	3,795	4,795	20		Y	Y		128	100	4	3	
Sonata	V		M	4,995	6,495	16					64	180	4	3	
Milano II	V		EP	5,495	6,495	138				100	64	40	4	3	
Milano II	V		R	4,995	5,995	138				100	64	40	4	3	
Milano IIG	G		EP	6,995	7,995	138				100	64	120	4	3	
Aria	G		EP	8,995	10,495	16		Y	Y		64	180	4	3	
Aria	G		MP	9,995	11,495	16		Y	Y		64	180	4	3	
Aria DigiPlay	G		EP	13,995	17,995	16		Y	Y		64	180	4	3	
Aria DigiPlay	G		MP	15,995	19,995	16		Y	Y		64	180	4	3	
Concerto	G		EP	11,995	13,995	16		Y	Y		64	180	4	3	
Concerto	G		MD	15,995	17,995	16		Y	Y		64	180	4	3	
Concerto DigiPlay	G		EP	17,995	21,995	16		Y	Y		64	180	4	3	
Concerto DigiPlay	G		MD	23,995	27,995	16		Y	Y		64	180	4	3	
Maestro II	G	E	EP	9,995	11,995	128		Y	Y	128	128	250	5	3	
Maestro II	G	E	WtP	10,495	12,495	128		Y	Y	128	128	250	5	3	
Maestro II	G	E	MP	11,995	13,995	128		Y	Y	128	128	250	5	3	
Maestro II	G	E	Rd	17,995	19,995	128		Y	Y	128	128	250	5	3	
Grande II	G	E	EP	13,995	15,995	128		Y	Y	128	128	250	5	3	
Kawai															
EP3	S			1,099	1,499	21		Y	Y	30	96	26	6	1	Y
MP6	S			1,499	1,799	256	Y	Y	Y		192	0	0	2	Y
MP10	S			2,499	2,999	27	Y	Y	Y		192	0	0	2	Y
ES6	S	E		1,699	2,195	32		Y	Y	100	192	26	6	1 (3)	Y
CL26	V		R	1,099	1,495	8		Y			93	30	2	1	Y
CE220	V		ES	1,899	2,199	22		Y	Y	100	192	40	2	3	Y
CN23	V		R	1,799	2,195	15		Y			96	40	2	3	Y
CN33	V		R	2,199	2,795	36		Y	Y		96	40	2	3	Y
CN33	V		M/ES	2,299	2,895	36		Y	Y		96	40	2	3	Y
CN43	V	E	R	2,749	3,395	323		Y	Y	100	192	100	4	3	Y

Model	Action	Escapement	Wood Keys	Ivory Texture	Player Moving Keys	Vocal Support	Educational Features	External Memory	USB to Computer	Recording Tracks	Warranty (Parts/Labor)	Dimensions WxDxH (Inchees)	Weight (Pounds)
AP-420BN	Tri-Sensor			Y			Y	SD	Y	2	3/3	55x17x33	88
AP-620BK	Tri-Sensor			Y			Y	SD	Y	17	3/3	55x19x35	126
Milano II	Graded Hammer									3	4/1	56x15x7	54
VP-91	Grand Response										4/1	54X14X6	48
VP-111	Grand Response										4/1	54X17X40	119
VP-121	Graded Hammer	Y								1	4/1	54X20x41	138
VP-121	Graded Hammer	Y								1	4/1	54X20x41	138
Sonata	Grand Touch Feeling	Y								2	4/1	54x22x39	234
Milano II	Graded Hammer									3	4/1	56x20x34	154
Milano II	Graded Hammer									3	4/1	56x20x34	154
Milano IIG	Graded Hammer									3	4/1	56x30x35	200
Aria	AGT Pro	Y	Y							2	4/1	54x38x56	315
Aria	AGT Pro	Y	Y						Y	2	4/1	54x38x56	315
Aria DigiPlay	AGT Pro	Y	Y		Y				Y	2	4/1	54x38x56	315+
Aria DigiPlay	AGT Pro	Y	Y		Y				Y	2	4/1	54x38x56	315+
Concerto	AGT Pro	Y	Y						Y	2	4/1	54x52x35	415
Concerto	AGT Pro	Y	Y						Y	2	4/1	54x52x35	415
Concerto DigiPlay	AGT Pro	Y	Y		Y				Y	2	4/1	54x52x35	415+
Concerto DigiPlay	AGT Pro	Y	Y		Y				Y	2	4/1	54x52x35	415+
Maestro II	AGT Pro	Y				Y	Y	USB	Y	5	4/1	54x39x35	345
Maestro II	AGT Pro	Y				Y	Y	USB	Y	5	4/1	54x39x35	345
Maestro II	AGT Pro	Y				Y	Y	USB	Y	5	4/1	54x39x35	345
Maestro II	AGT Pro	Y				Y	Y	USB	Y	5	4/1	54x39x35	345
Grande II	AGT Pro	Y				Y	Y	USB	Y	5	4/1	54X48X38	312
EP3	AHA IV-F								Y	2	3/3	55x14x6	46
MP6	RH	Y		Y				USB	Y	1	3/1	53x13x7	45
MP10	RM3	Y	Y	Y				USB	Y	1	3/1	58x18x8	77
ES6	AHA IV-F								Y	2	3/3	55x14x6	46
CL26	AHA IV										3/3	51x11x31	63
CE220	AWA PROII		Y					USB	Y	2	3/3	54x20x35	137
CN23	RH			Y			Y			1	5/5	55x16x34	93
CN33	RH	Y		Y			Y	USB	Y	2	5/5	55x19x35	119
CN33	RH	Y		Y			Y	USB	Y	2	5/5	55x19x35	119
CN43	RH	Y		Y			Y	USB	Y	16	5/5	55x19x35	125

Brand & Model	Form	Ensemble	Finish	Estimated Price	MSRP	Voices	Key Off	Sustain Samples	String Resonance	Rhythms/Styles	Polyphony	Total Watts	Speakers	Piano Pedals	Half Pedal
Kawai *(continued)*															
CN43	V	E	M/ES	2,849	3,495	323		Y	Y	100	192	100	4	3	Y
CA63	V		R	3,173	3,895	60	Y	Y	Y	100	192	100	4	3	Y
CA63	V		M	3,264	3,995	60	Y	Y	Y	100	192	100	4	3	Y
CA93	V		R	4,445	5,645	80	Y	Y	Y	100	192	135	6+SB	3	Y
CA93	V		ES	4,536	5,745	80	Y	Y	Y	100	192	135	6+SB	3	Y
CS3	V		EP	2,909	3,495	15		Y			96	40	4	3	Y
CS6	V		EP	4,545	5,695	60	Y	Y	Y	100	192	100	4	3	Y
CP119	V	E	R	3,445		700+	Y	Y	Y	183	96	100	2	3	Y
CP119	V	E	M	3,536		700+	Y	Y	Y	183	96	100	2	3	Y
CP139	V	E	*R*	4,991		900+	Y	Y	Y	306	192	100	4	3	Y
CP139	V	E	M/ES	5,082		900+	Y	Y	Y	306	192	100	4	3	Y
CP179	V	E	*CP*/EP	8,173		1000+	Y	Y	Y	390	192	100	6	3	Y
CP209	G	E	EP	15,890		1000+	Y	Y	Y	390	192	200	9	3	Y
CP209 CD	G	E	EP	22,950		1000+	Y	Y	Y	390	192	200	9	3	Y
CP209 IQ	G	E	EP	24,750		1000+	Y	Y	Y	390	192	200	9	3	Y
Ketron															
GP10	S		C&G/ Bk&Sr			16					64			1 (3)	
GP10A	S		C&G/ Bk&Sr			16					64	50	2	1 (3)	
DG20	V		R			8					64	50	2	2	
DG30	V		M/W/R			8					64	50	2	3	
DG90	V	E	EP			290				172	64	140	5	3	
DG100	G	E	EP/MP/ WtP			478				307	64	120	5	3	
Kingston															
K100	S		R/C		1,995	128				99	16	44	4	2	
K200	V	E	EP/MP		2,995	128				99	64	60	4	3	
KGP10	G		EP		5,995	12					64	80	4	3	
Kohler (Samick)															
KD26	V		R	1,595	1,595	30		Y			60	50	2	3	
KD30	V	E	EP	2,995	2,995	332		Y		128	64	80	4	3	
KD60	V	E	EP	4,995	4,995	332		Y		304	62	360	5	3	
KD7	G		EP/*MP*	7,907	8,499	30		Y			60	360	6	3	
KD150	G	E	EP	5,995	5,995	660		Y		304	62	360	5	3	
KD150	G	E	*MP*	6,498	6,995	660		Y		304	62	360	5	3	

Model	Action	Escapement	Wood Keys	Ivory Texture	Player Moving Keys	Vocal Support	Educational Features	External Memory	USB to Computer	Recording Tracks	Warranty (Parts/Labor)	Dimensions WxDxH (Inches)	Weight (Pounds)
CN43	RH	Y		Y			Y	USB	Y	16	5/5	55x19x35	125
CA63	RM3		Y	Y			Y	USB	Y	2	5/5	57x36x19	168
CA63	RM3		Y	Y			Y	USB	Y	2	5/5	57x36x19	168
CA93	RM3	Y	Y	Y			Y	USB	Y	2	5/5	58x36x19	192
CA93	RM3	Y	Y	Y			Y	USB	Y	2	5/5	58x36x19	192
CS3	RH	Y		Y			Y			1	5/5	55x16x35	121
CS6	RM3	Y	Y	Y			Y	USB	Y	2	5/5	57x19x37	176
CP119	RH			Y			Y	USB	Y	16	5/5	56x23x38	224
CP119	RH			Y			Y	USB	Y	16	5/5	56x23x38	224
CP139	RM3		Y	Y		Y	Y	USB	Y	16	5/5	56x23x38	248
CP139	RM3		Y	Y		Y	Y	USB	Y	16	5/5	56x23x38	248
CP179	RM3	Y	Y	Y		Y	Y	USB	Y	16	5/5	56x29x38	289
CP209	RM3	Y	Y	Y		Y	Y	USB	Y	16	5/5	59x63x39	430
CP209 CD	RM3	Y	Y	Y	Y	Y	Y	USB	Y	16	5/5	59x63x39	430
CP209 IQ	RM3	Y	Y	Y	Y	Y	Y	USB	Y	16	5/5	59x63x39	430
GP10										2		51x12x5	48
GP10A										2		51x15x6	55
DG20												53x20x33	116
DG30										2		53x20x33	116
DG90						Y		FD	Y			54x43x37	198
DG100						Y		FD	Y	16		54x43x37	198
K100											1/1		
K200											1/1		185
KGP10											1/1	49D	250
KD26											3/1	55x19x34	156
KD30	Fatar TP30					Y		FD		8	3/1	45x24x37	276
KD60						Y				16	3/1		376
KD7					Y			USB	Y	Opt	3/1	60D	530
KD150	Fatar TP30					Y				16	3/1	50D	404
KD150	Fatar TP30					Y				16	3/1	50D	404

Brand & Model	Form	Ensemble	Finish	Estimated Price	MSRP	Voices	Key Off	Sustain Samples	String Resonance	Rhythms/Styles	Polyphony	Total Watts	Speakers	Piano Pedals	Half Pedal
Kohler (*continued*)															
KD160	G	E	EP	6,495	6,495	660		Y		304	62	360	5	3	
KD160	G	E	*MP*	6,995	6,995	660		Y		304	62	360	5	3	
KD165	G	E	EP/ *MP*/IyP	8,495	8,495	660		Y		304	62	360	5	3	
KD165 French	G	E	*MP/CP*	9,495	9,495	660		Y		304	62	360	5	3	
Korg															
SP170/170s	S		Wt/Bk/ Rd	*500*	600	10					120	18	2	1	Y
SP250	S		Bk& WG	*699*	1,199	30					60	22	2	1	Y
SP250	S		Wt	*749*	1,199	30					60	22	2	1	Y
SV-1-88	S		Bk&?	*2,199*	3,000	36					80			1 (3)	Y
SV-1-88	S		Bk	*1,699*	3,000	36					80			1 (3)	Y
SV-1-88	S		Rd&Bk	*1,899*	3,000	36					80			1 (3)	Y
LP350	V		ES/Wt	*999*	1,499	30					60	22	2	3	Y
Kurzweil															
MP-10	V		EP	*1,799*	2,495	88		Y	Y	78	64	30	4	3	
MP-10	V		R	*1,499*	2,995	88		Y	Y	78	64	30	4	3	
CUP-2	V		EP	*4,299*	5,995	88		Y	Y	78	64	130	4	3	
Mark Pro ONEi F	V		R	1,816	2,695	64					64	30	2	3	
Mark Pro ONEi F	V		EP	1,998	2,695	64					64	30	2	3	
Mark Pro TWOi	V		R	2,362	3,295	64					64	60	4	3	
Mark Pro TWOi	V		EP	2,544	3,595	64					64	60	4	3	
Mark Pro 3i	V	E	R	3,398	4,495	256				32	64	60	4	3	
Mark Pro 3i	V	E	EP	3,798	4,995	256				32	64	60	4	3	
X-PRO UP	V		EP	*5,495*	7,995	999		Y	Y	128	128	140	4	3	
X-PRO MG	G		EP	*6,999*	9,995	999		Y	Y	128	128	140	4	3	
M-Audio															
ProKeys88	S		Bk	*600*	750	14					126			1	
ProKeys Sono 88	S		Bk	*450*	550	128					40			1	
Nord															
Nord Piano 2 HA88	S		Rd	*4,199*	4,599	1000+			Y		40–60			3	Y

Model	Action	Escapement	Wood Keys	Ivory Texture	Player Moving Keys	Vocal Support	Educational Features	External Memory	USB to Computer	Recording Tracks	Warranty (Parts/Labor)	Dimensions WxDxH (Inchees)	Weight (Pounds)
KD160	Fatar TP30					Y				16	3/1	58D	478
KD160	Fatar TP30					Y				16	3/1	58D	478
KD165	Fatar TP30				Y	Y				16	3/1		528
KD165 French	Fatar TP30				Y	Y				16	3/1		528
SP170/170s	NH										1/1	52x13x5	27
SP250	HA 3										1/1	51x15x6	42
SP250	HA 3										1/1	51x15x6	42
SV-1-88	RH3								Y		1/1	53x14x6	45
SV-1-88	RH3								Y		1/1	53x14x6	45
SV-1-88	RH3								Y		1/1	53x14x6	45
LP350	RH3										1/1	53x11x31	94
MP-10	LK								Y	2	2/3	56x19x35	115
MP-10	LK								Y	2	2/3	56x19x35	115
CUP-2	Fatar		Y						Y	2	2/3	56x17x42	214
Mark Pro ONEi F	Fatar								Y	1	2/3	54x17x32	112
Mark Pro ONEi F	Fatar								Y	1	2/3	54x17x32	112
Mark Pro TWOi	Fatar								Y	2	2/3	54x20x35	125
Mark Pro TWOi	Fatar								Y	2	2/3	54x20x35	125
Mark Pro 3i	Fatar								Y	4	2/3	54x20x35	120
Mark Pro 3i	Fatar								Y	4	2/3	54x20x35	120
X-PRO UP	Fatar							xD	Y	16	2/3	56x36x37	214
X-PRO MG	Fatar							xD	Y	16	2/3	56x36x37	225
ProKeys88									Y		1/1	57x13x6	48
ProKeys Sono 88						Y							
Nord Piano 2 HA88									Y		1/1	51x13x5	40

Brand & Model	Form	Ensemble	Finish	Estimated Price	MSRP	Voices	Key Off	Sustain Samples	String Resonance	Rhythms/Styles	Polyphony	Total Watts	Speakers	Piano Pedals	Half Pedal
Omega (Kaino)															
CR-202	V	E	M	1,609	2,360	96				96	64	40	2	3	
CR-301	V	E	M	2,027	3,050	128				100	64	40	2	3	
LX-502	V	E	M	2,355	3,590	128				100	64	80	4	3	
LX-505	V	E	M	2,718	4,190	128				200	64	80	4	3	
LX-505	V	E	EP	3,264	5,090	128				200	64	80	4	3	
LX-802	G	E	EP	5,690	7,790	128				200	64	80	4	3	
Princeton															
SP-88	S	E	Sr	1,495	1,995	350				130	64	20	4	1	
SP-88	V	E	R	1,995	2,495	350				130	64	20	4	1	
HP-310e	V	E	EP	2,995	3,995	142				100	64	100	4	3	
Roland															
RD-300GX	S		Bk	1,599	1,829	366	Y	Y	Y	200	128			1 (3)	Y
RD-300NX	S		Bk	1,699	1,999	366	Y	Y	Y	200	128			1 (3)	Y
RD-700GX	S		Bk	2,599	2,949	518	Y	Y	Y	200	128			1 (3)	Y
RD-700NX	S		Bk	2,599	2,999	518	Y	Y	Y	200	128			1 (3)	Y
V-Piano	S		Bk	5,995	6,999	24	Y	Y	Y		264			3	Y
FP-4	S	E	Bk/Wt	1,499	1,719	333	Y	Y	Y	80	128	14	2	1 (3)	Y
FP-4F	S	E	Bk	1,749	1,999	336	Y	Y	Y	80	128	24	2	1 (3)	Y
FP-4F	S	E	Wt	1,849	2,099	336	Y	Y	Y	80	128	24	2	1 (3)	Y
FP-7	S	E	Bk	1,999	2,289	339	Y	Y	Y	80	128	26	2	1 (3)	Y
FP-7F	S	E	Bk	1,899	2,199	339	Y	Y	Y	80	128	24	2	1 (3)	
FP-7F	S	E	Wt	1,999	2,299	339	Y	Y	Y	80	128	24	2	1 (3)	
F-110	V		ES/Wt	1,499	1,999	306	Y	Y	Y		128	24	2	3	Y
F-120	V		ES/Wt	1,299	1,799	30	Y	Y	Y		128	24	2	3	Y
RP-301	V		R/ES	1,699	2,199	30	Y	Y	Y		128	24	2	3	Y
RP-301R	V	E	R/ES	1,999	2,499	54	Y	Y	Y	60	128	24	2	3	Y
RP-201	V		R/ES	1,599	2,099	306	Y	Y	Y		128	24	2	3	Y
DP-990	V		C/ES	2,095	2,299	306	Y	Y	Y		128	24	2	3	Y
DP-990F	V		ES/C	2,299	2,699	337	Y	Y	Y		128	24	2	3	Y
DP-990R	V		EP	2,899	3,299	306	Y	Y	Y		128	24	2	3	Y
DP-990RF	V		EP	2,999	3,499	337	Y	Y	Y		128	24	2	3	Y
HP302	V		R/ES	2,499	2,999	337	Y	Y	Y		128	24	2	3	Y
HP305	V		R/ES	3,199	3,799	337	Y	Y	Y		128	60	4	3	*Y*

Model	Action	Escapement	Wood Keys	Ivory Texture	Player Moving Keys	Vocal Support	Educational Features	External Memory	USB to Computer	Recording Tracks	Warranty (Parts/Labor)	Dimensions WxDxH (Inchees)	Weight (Pounds)
CR-202	Graded Weighted						Y	USB		1	1/90		
CR-301	Fatar Graded						Y	USB		5	1/90		
LX-502	Fatar Graded						Y	USB	Y	7	1/90		
LX-505	Fatar Graded						Y	USB	Y	7	1/90		
LX-505	Fatar Graded						Y	USB	Y	7	1/90		
LX-802	Fatar Graded						Y	USB	Y	7	1/90		
SP-88	Acoustic Response									5	1/90	53x5x14	44
SP-88	Acoustic Response									5	1/90	53x14x31	75
HP-310e	Acoustic Response					Y				5	1/90	55x22x35	131
RD-300GX	PHA all							USB	Y		1/90	57x13x5	36
RD-300NX	PHA III	Y		Y				USB	Y		1/90	57x13x6	39
RD-700GX	PHA II	Y		Y				USB	Y		1/90	57x15x6	55
RD-700NX	PHA III	Y		Y				USB	Y		1/90	57x15x6	55
V-Piano	PHA III	Y		Y				USB	Y	1	3/1	56x21x7	84
FP-4	PHA all								Y	3	1/90	53x12x5	34
FP-4F	PHA III - G	Y		Y				USB	Y	1	1/90	53x12x5	36
FP-4F	PHA III - G	Y		Y				USB	Y	1	1/90	53x12x5	36
FP-7	PHA II							USB	Y	3	1/90	53x15x5	53
FP-7F	PHA III	Y		Y		Y		USB	Y	1	1/90	53x16x6	53
FP-7F	PHA III	Y		Y		Y		USB	Y	1	1/90	53x16x6	53
F-110	PHA all									3	5/1	54x12x31	78
F-120	Ivory Feel-G	Y		Y						1	5/1	54x12x31	75
RP-301	Ivory Feel-G	Y		Y						1	5/1	54x17x39	86
RP-301R	Ivory Feel-G	Y		Y				USB	Y	3	5/1	54x17x39	86
RP-201	PHA all									1	5/1	55x17x39	95
DP-990	PHA II	Y		Y				USB	Y	3	5/1	55x14x31	104
DP-990F	PHA II	Y						USB	Y	3	5/1	55x14x31	105
DP-990R	PHA II	Y		Y				USB	Y	3	5/1	55x14x31	106
DP-990RF	PHA II	Y		Y				USB	Y	3	5/1	55x14x31	107
HP302	PHA II	Y						USB	Y	3	5/1	55x17x41	117
HP305	PHA II	Y		Y				USB	Y	3	5/1	55x17x41	127

Brand & Model	Form	Ensemble	Finish	Estimated Price	MSRP	Voices	Key Off	Sustain Samples	String Resonance	Rhythms/Styles	Polyphony	Total Watts	Speakers	Piano Pedals	Half Pedal
Roland *(continued)*															
HP305	V		EP	3,799	4,599	337	Y	Y	Y		128	60	4	3	*Y*
HP307	V		R/ES	4,199	4,999	337	Y	Y	Y		128	120	4	3	*Y*
HP307	V		EP	4,799	5,899	337	Y	Y	Y		128	120	4	3	*Y*
HP503	V		R/ES	2,599	3,099	347	Y	Y	Y		128	24	2	3	*Y*
HP505	V		R/ES	2,999	3,599	347	Y	Y	Y		128	70	4	3	Y
HP505	V		EP	3,799	4,599	347	Y	Y	Y		128	70	4	3	Y
HP507	V		R/ES	3,999	4,700	347	Y	Y	Y		128	140	6	3	Y
HP507	V		EP	4,799	5,799	347	Y	Y	Y		128	140	6	3	Y
LX-10	V		ES	5,999	6,999	337	Y	Y	Y		128	120	6	3	Y
LX-10F	V		ES/PE	4,999	5,999	337	Y	Y	Y		128	120	6	3	Y
LX-15	V		EP	5,999	7,299	347	Y	Y	Y		128	160	6	3	Y
HPi-6s	V		ES	3,999	4,999	445	Y	Y	Y		128	60	4	3	Y
HPi-6F	V		R/ES	3,499	4,199	337	Y	Y	Y		128	60	4	3	Y
HPi-7s	V		M	6,199	7,199	596	Y	Y	Y		128	120	4	3	Y
HPi-7F	V	E	R/ES	4,499	5,999	337	Y	Y	Y		128	120	4	3	Y
FP-4C	V	E	ES	1,699	1,909	333	Y	Y	Y	80	128	14	2	1 (3)	Y
FP-7C	V	E	ES	2,199	2,449	339	Y	Y	Y	80	128	26	2	1 (3)	Y
FP-7FC	V	E	ES	2,099	2,499	339	Y	Y	Y	80	128	24	2	1 (3)	*Y*
FP-7FC	V	E	Wt	2,199	2,599	339	Y	Y	Y	80	128	24	2	1 (3)	Y
RM-700	V	E	ES/M	7,999	8,999	818	Y	Y	Y		128	120	4	3	Y
RG-1	G		ES	6,199	6,999	20	Y	Y	Y		128	80	4	3	Y
RG-1F	G		ES	6,999	8,399	337	Y	Y	Y		128	80	4	3	Y
RG-3	G		EP	9,999	10,999	20	Y	Y	Y		128	80	4	3	Y
RG-3F	G		EP	9,999	11,999	337	Y	Y	Y		128	120	4	3	Y
RG-3M	G		EP	10,999	12,999	20	Y	Y	Y		128	80	4	3	Y
RG-7-R	G		EP	16,999	19,999	20	Y	Y	Y		128	120	6	3	Y
KR-111	G	E	EP	7,995	8,799	400	Y	Y	Y	170	64	50	4	3	Y
KR-115	G	E	EP	12,999	13,999	780	Y	Y	Y	285	128	140	4	3	Y
KR-115M	G	E	EP	17,999	19,999	780	Y	Y	Y	285	128	140	4	3	Y
KR-117M	G	E	EP	24,999	27,999	780	Y	Y	Y	310	128	280	8	3	Y
V-Piano Grand	G		EP	19,950	22,999	30	Y	Y	Y		264	240	8	3	Y
Samick															
DCP-8	V		R	1,445	1,595	8					64		2	3	
DCP-12	V		R	1,627	1,795	16					64		2	3	
SSP-10 Stage	V		ES	1,264	1,295	16					64	30	2	1 (3)	
SSP-12 Stage	V		ES	1,627	1,795	480					64	10	2	1 (3)	
SSP-30 Stage Pro	V		ES	1,536	1,595	480					64	20	2	1 (3)	
SDP-10	V		R	1,718	1,795	9					64	40	2	3	

Model	Action	Escapement	Wood Keys	Ivory Texture	Player Moving Keys	Vocal Support	Educational Features	External Memory	USB to Computer	Recording Tracks	Warranty (Parts/Labor)	Dimensions WxDxH (Inchees)	Weight (Pounds)
HP305	PHA II	Y		Y				USB	Y	3	5/1	55x17x41	129
HP307	PHA III	Y		Y				USB	Y	3	5/1	56x21x43	173
HP307	PHA III	Y		Y				USB	Y	3	5/1	56x21x43	176
HP503	Ivory Feel-S	Y		Y				USB	Y	3	5/1	55x17x41	115
HP505	PHA III	Y		Y				USB	Y	3	5/1	55x17x42	122
HP505	PHA III	Y		Y				USB	Y	3	5/1	55x17x42	127
HP507	PHA III	Y		Y				USB	Y	3	5/1	55x20x45	178
HP507	PHA III	Y		Y				USB	Y	3	5/1	55x20x45	182
LX-10	PHA II	Y		Y				USB	Y	3	5/1	56x18x44	209
LX-10F	PHA III	Y		Y				USB	Y	3	5/1	56x18x45	209
LX-15	PHA III	Y		Y				USB	Y	3	5/1	55x19x42	201
HPi-6s	PHA II	Y				Y	Y	USB	Y	16	5/1	55x17x41	125
HPi-6F	PHA II	Y		Y			Y	USB	Y	4	5/1	56x17x41	128
HPi-7s	PHA II	Y		Y		Y	Y	USB	Y	16	5/1	56x21x43	176
HPi-7F	PHA III	Y		Y		Y	Y	USB	Y	16	5/1	56x21x44	176
FP-4C	PHA all								Y	3	1/90	53x13x37	59
FP-7C	PHA II							USB	Y	3	1/90	53x16x37	80
FP-7FC	PHA III	Y		Y		Y		USB	Y	1	1/90	53x16x37	81
FP-7FC	PHA III	Y		Y		Y		USB	Y	1	1/90	53x16x37	81
RM-700	PHA II	Y		Y		Y	Y	USB	Y	16	5/1	56x22x37	187
RG-1	PHA II	Y		Y				USB	Y	1	5/1	56x29x50	165
RG-1F	PHA III	Y		Y				USB	Y	1	5/1	56x29x50	165
RG-3	PHA II	Y		Y		Y		USB	Y	1	5/1	58x37x57	243
RG-3F	PHA III	Y		Y				USB	Y	1	5/1	58x37x57	242
RG-3M	PHA II	Y		Y	Y	Y		USB	Y	1	5/1	58x37x57	298
RG-7-R	PHA II	Y		Y	Y	Y		USB	Y	1	5/1	58x55x69	496
KR-111	PHA							FDD	Y	16	5/1	55x37x63	232
KR-115	PHA	Y		Y		Y	Y	USB	Y	16	5/1	58x37x57	254
KR-115M	PHA	Y		Y	Y	Y	Y	USB	Y	16	5/1	58x37x57	309
KR-117M	PHA	Y		Y	Y	Y	Y	USB	Y	16	5/1	59x62x69	529
V-Piano Grand	PHA III	Y		Y				USB	Y	1	5/1	59x59x61	375
DCP-8		Y							Y	2	3/1		
DCP-12		Y							Y	2	3/1		
SSP-10 Stage	Graded									2	3/1	54x14x33	64
SSP-12 Stage	Graded							USB	Y	16	3/1	52x13x32	57
SSP-30 Stage Pro	Graded							USB	Y	16	3/1	62x13x30	62
SDP-10									Y	2	3/1	54x18x35	148

Brand & Model	Form	Ensemble	Finish	Estimated Price	MSRP	Voices	Key Off	Sustain Samples	String Resonance	Rhythms/Styles	Polyphony	Total Watts	Speakers	Piano Pedals	Half Pedal
Samick (continued)															
SDP-31	V		R	1,809	2,095	385					64	120	6	3	
SDP-31	V		EP	1,991	2,295	385					64	120	6	3	
SSP-20 Stage	V	E	C	1,627	1,795	476				260	64	40	2	1 (3)	
SDP-45	V	E	R	1,991	2,295	476				260	64	40	2	3	
SDP-45	V	E	EP	2,173	2,495	476				260	64	40	2	3	
SG-210	G		EP	3,890	4,195	16					64	120	2	3	
SG-310	G		EP/WtP	4,290	4,595	385					64	120	6	3	
SG-450	G	E	EP/WtP	4,890	4,995	476				260	64	120	6	3	
Suzuki															
Home Digital Piano (HDP)	V		EP/R		995	16					64		2	3	
DP-1000	V	E	R		1,495	128				100	64		2	3	
DP-1000	V	E	EP		1,695	128				100	64		2	3	
HP-99	V	E	R		1,795	128				100	64	120	4	3	
HP-99	V	E	EP		1,895	128				100	64	120	4	3	
MDG-100	G	E	EP	*1,550*	2,995	128				100	64	120	4	3	
S-350	G	E	EP	*2,500*	2,995	128				100	64	120	6	3	
MG-350	G	E	EP		2,995	128				100	64	120	6	3	
Symphony															
DL-100	V	E	ES	1,247	1,295	138		Y	Y	100	64	40	2	3	
DL-200A	V	E	ES/R	1,257	1,495	150		Y	Y	118	64	60	2	3	
DL-600	V	E	ES/R	1,363	1,995	138		Y	Y	100	64	60	4	3	
DL-800	V	E	R	1,545	2,495	138		Y	Y	109	64	80	4	3	
DL-800A	V	E	C	1,545	2,495	138		Y	Y	109	64	80	4	3	
DL-900	V	E	R	1,620	2,795	138		Y	Y	100	64	80	4	3	
DL-900A	V	E	EP	1,802	2,995	138		Y	Y	100	64	80	4	3	
DL-1250	G	E	EP	3,480	3,495	138		Y	Y	109	64	100	4	3	
Viscount															
Sinfonia	V	E	ES	*3,995*	4,795	500+	Y	Y	Y	144	64	75	4	3	
Maestro	G	E	EP	*7,995*	9,995	500+	Y	Y	Y	144	64	150	4	3	
Maestro	G	E	WtP	*8,495*	10,495	500+	Y	Y	Y	144	64	150	4	3	
Maestro	G	E	MP/MS	*8,995*	10,995	500+	Y	Y	Y	144	64	150	4	3	
Maestro	G	E	MDP/MDS	*11,995*	13,995	500+	Y	Y	Y	144	64	150	4	3	

Model	Action	Escapement	Wood Keys	Ivory Texture	Player Moving Keys	Vocal Support	Educational Features	External Memory	USB to Computer	Recording Tracks	Warranty (Parts/Labor)	Dimensions WxDxH (Inchees)	Weight (Pounds)
SDP-31	Graded							USB			3/1	54x20x35	150
SDP-31	Graded							USB			3/1	54x20x35	150
SSP-20 Stage	Graded							USB	Y	16	3/1	53x13x30	62
SDP-45	Graded							USB	Y	16	3/1	54x20x36	150
SDP-45	Graded							USB	Y	16	3/1	54x20x36	150
SG-210	Graded									2	3/1	57x50x36	260
SG-310	Graded							USB		16	3/1	57x50x36	260
SG-450	Graded							USB	Y	16	3/1	57x50x36	260
Home Digital Piano (HDP)	Graded					Y			Y	1	1/1		
DP-1000	Graded					Y			Y	1	1/1		
DP-1000	Graded					Y			Y	1	1/1		
HP-99	Graded				Y			SD	Y	5	1/1	55x21x36	165
HP-99	Graded				Y			SD	Y	5	1/1	55x21x36	165
MDG-100	Graded				Y			SD	Y	3	1/1	55x29x36	165
S-350	Graded				Y			SD	Y	5	1/1	57x39x36	225
MG-350	Graded				Y			SD	Y	5	1/1	57x39x36	225
DL-100	TSHA							USB	Y	3	3/3	55x16x33	75
DL-200A	TSHA							USB	Y	6	3/3	54x22x34	85
DL-600	TSHA							USB	Y	6	3/3	54x21x34	95
DL-800	TSHA							USB	Y	6	3/3	55x21x35	110
DL-800A	TSHA							USB	Y	6	3/3	55x21x35	110
DL-900	TSHA							USB	Y	6	3/3	55x20x35	110
DL-900A	TSHA							USB	Y	6	3/3	55x20x35	110
DL-1250	TSHA							USB	Y	6	3/3	55x49x34	180
Sinfonia	Grand Response							FD			2/1		
Maestro	Grand Response							FD		16	2/1	54x38x35	310
Maestro	Grand Response							FD		16	2/1	54x38x35	310
Maestro	Grand Response							FD		16	2/1	54x38x35	310
Maestro	Grand Response							FD		16	2/1	54x38x35	310

Brand & Model	Form	Ensemble	Finish	Estimated Price	MSRP	Voices	Key Off	Sustain Samples	String Resonance	Rhythms/Styles	Polyphony	Total Watts	Speakers	Piano Pedals	Half Pedal
Williams															
Allegro	S		Bk	300	400	8					64			1	
Encore	S			500	700	30					32			1	
Overture	V		WG	600	900	15					64			3	
Serenade	V	E	WG	700	1,000	160				100			4	3	
Symphony	V		W	800	1,199	138				100	32	40	2	3	
Symphony Elite	V		W	900	1,300	138				100	64	40	2	3	
Digital Grand	G		EP	1,300	2,000	14					64			3	
Yamaha															
P85	S		Bk/Sr	629	899	10					64	12	2	1(3)	Y
P95	S		Bk/Sr	599	899	10					64	12	2	1(3)	Y
P155	S		BkM/SrC/BkEP	1,199	1,699	17	Y	Y			128	24	2	1	Y
CP33	S			1,299	1,700	28	Y	Y			64			2	Y
CP50	S			1,699	2,199	322	Y	Y	Y	100	128			1	Y
CP300	S			2,199	2,700	530	Y	Y	Y		128	60	2	3	Y
CP5	S			2,599	3,299	227	Y	Y	Y	100	128			1(2)	Y
CP1	S			4,999	5,999	17	Y	Y	Y		128			3	Y
YDPS31	V		Al	950	1,299	6					64	12	2	3	Y
YDP141	V		R	1,150	1,499	6					64	12	2	3	Y
YDP161	V		R/W	1,500	1,999	10					64	40	2	3	Y
YDP181	V		R	1,800	2,199	14					128	40	2	3	Y
YDPC71	V		EP	1,900	2,499	10					64	40	2	3	Y
CLP430	V		BW/M/R	2,533	2,999	14					128	60	2	3	Y
CLP430	V		EP	2,931	3,999	14					128	60	2	3	Y
CLP440	V		BW/M/R	3,164	3,899	28	Y	Y	Y		256	80	4	3	Y
CLP440	V		EP	3,705	4,699	28	Y	Y	Y		256	80	4	3	Y
CLP470	V		R	3,813	4,799	28	Y	Y	Y		256	80	4	3	Y
CLP470	V		EP	4,196	5,599	28	Y	Y	Y		256	80	4	3	Y
CLP480	V		R	5,364	6,999	532	Y	Y	Y		256	200	8	3	Y
CLP480	V		EP	6,164	7,899	532	Y	Y	Y		256	200	8	3	Y
CLPS406	V		W	3,364	4,499	28	Y	Y	Y		256	80	4	3	Y
CLPS408	V		EP	4,364	5,699	28	Y	Y	Y		256	80	4	3	Y
R01	V		Wt	4,899	7,199	1	Y	Y			128	24	2	3	Y
F01	V		EP/BlP/RdP/OrP	4,999	7,699	20	Y	Y			128	80	4	3	Y

Model	Action	Escapement	Wood Keys	Ivory Texture	Player Moving Keys	Vocal Support	Educational Features	External Memory	USB to Computer	Recording Tracks	Warranty (Parts/Labor)	Dimensions WxDxH (Inchees)	Weight (Pounds)
Allegro										2	1/1		
Encore										3	1/1	55x13x5	77
Overture									Y	2	1/1	54x20x34	132
Serenade									Y	2	1/1		
Symphony						Y			Y	3	1/1	54x20x34	154
Symphony Elite						Y			Y	3	1/1	54x20x34	165
Digital Grand										2	1/1	55x41x33	165
P85	GHS									1	1/1	52x12x6	29
P95	GHS									1	1/1	52x12x6	26
P155	GH							USB		2	1/1	53x6x14	41
CP33	GHE								Y		3/3	52x13x6	40
CP50	GH								Y		3/3	55x13x7	46
CP300	GHE								Y	16	3/3	54x18x7	72
CP5	NW-Stage		Y	Y		Y			Y		3/3	55x16x7	56
CP1	NW-Stage		Y	Y				USB	Y		3/3	55x17x7	60
YDPS31	GHS									1	3/3	55x12x31	80
YDP141	GHS									1	3/3	54x17x32	91
YDP161	GHE									1	3/3	54x17x32	95
YDP181	GHE								Y	2	3/3	54x34x20	110
YDPC71	GH									1	3/3	54x17x32	95
CLP430	GH3							USB	Y	2	5/5	56x20x36	146
CLP430	GH3							USB	Y	2	5/5	56x20x36	157
CLP440	GH3			Y				USB	Y	2	5/5	56x20x36	146
CLP440	GH3			Y				USB	Y	2	5/5	56x20x36	157
CLP470	NW-LGH		Y	Y				USB	Y	2	5/5	56x20x36	163
CLP470	NW-LGH		Y	Y				USB	Y	2	5/5	56x20x36	176
CLP480	NW-LGH		Y	Y				USB	Y	16	5/5	56x20x37	193
CLP480	NW-LGH		Y	Y				USB	Y	16	5/5	56x20x37	201
CLPS406	GH3			Y				USB	Y	2	5/5	57x17x38	153
CLPS408	NW-LGH		Y	Y				USB	Y	2	5/5	57x17x39	171
R01	NW		Y	Y								55x15x38	88
F01	NW		Y					USB	Y	1	5/5	56x16x39	168

Brand & Model	Form	Ensemble	Finish	Estimated Price	MSRP	Voices	Key Off	Sustain Samples	String Resonance	Rhythms/Styles	Polyphony	Total Watts	Speakers	Piano Pedals	Half Pedal
Yamaha (*continued*)															
F11	V		EP/ BIP/ RdP/ OrP	*7,499*	13,999	20	Y	Y			128	80	4	3	Y
N1	V		EP	8,180	9,999	5	Y	Y	Y		256	175	6	3	*Y*
N2	V		EP	12,362	14,999	5	Y	Y	Y		256	500	12	3	*Y*
DGX640	V	E	C/W	799	1,299	523				165	64	12	4	1(3)	(Y)
YDP-V240	V	E	R	2,000	2,699	491				161	64	40	2	3	*Y*
CVP501	V	E	R	3,820	4,799	776	Y	Y		191	128	40	2	3	*Y*
CVP501	V	E	EP	4,456	5,599	776	Y	Y		191	128	40	2	3	Y
CVP503	V	E	R	5,438	7,399	876	Y	Y		272	128	80	4	3	Y
CVP503	V	E	EP	6,149	8,299	876	Y	Y		272	128	80	4	3	Y
CVP505	V	E	R	6,798	9,499	1169	Y	Y	Y	362	128	80	4	3	Y
CVP505	V	E	EP	7,680	10,799	1169	Y	Y	Y	362	128	80	4	3	Y
CVP505	V	E	MP	7,823	11,099	1169	Y	Y	Y	362	128	80	4	3	Y
CVP509	V	E	R	8,873	12,699	1291	Y	Y	Y	442	256	195	8	3	Y
CVP509	V	E	EP	10,095	14,499	1291	Y	Y	Y	442	256	195	8	3	Y
CVP509	V	E	MP	10,284	14,799	1291	Y	Y	Y	442	256	195	8	3	Y
CLP265GP	G		EP	5,706	6,399	14					64	80	4	3	Y
CLP295GP	G		EP	9,316	10,799	518	Y	Y	Y		128	160	8	3	Y
CLP465GP	G		EP	5,500	5,999	14					128	60	2	3	Y
H01	G		AG/ VR/ DB	*7,499*	13,199	10	Y	Y			64	80	4	3	Y
H11	G		AG/ VR/ DB	*9,999*	20,799	10	Y	Y			64	80	4	3	*Y*
N3	G		EP	17,000	19,999	5	Y	Y	Y		256	500	12	3	Y
CGP1000	G	E	EP	21,100	28,999	1070	Y	Y	Y	408	256	240	10	3	Y

Model	Action	Escapement	Wood Keys	Ivory Texture	Player Moving Keys	Vocal Support	Educational Features	External Memory	USB to Computer	Recording Tracks	Warranty (Parts/Labor)	Dimensions WxDxH (Inchees)	Weight (Pounds)
F11	NW		Y		Y			USB	Y	1	5/5	56x16x39	198
N1	Grand	Y	Y					USB		1	5/5	58x24x39	266
N2	Grand	Y	Y	Y				USB	Y	1	5/5	58x21x40	313
DGX640	GHS						Y	USB	Y	6	1/90	55x18x30	61
YDP-V240	GHS						Y	USB	Y	6	3/3	54x20x34	108
CVP501	GH						Y	USB	Y	16	5/5	54x24x35	156
CVP501	GH						Y	USB	Y	16	5/5	54x24x35	156
CVP503	GH3			Y		Y	Y	USB	Y	16	5/5	54x24x35	160
CVP503	GH3			Y		Y	Y	USB	Y	16	5/5	54x24x35	160
CVP505	GH3			Y		Y	Y	USB	Y	16	5/5	56x24x34	167
CVP505	GH3			Y		Y	Y	USB	Y	16	5/5	56x24x34	171
CVP505	GH3			Y		Y	Y	USB	Y	16	5/5	56x24x34	171
CVP509	NW		Y	Y		Y	Y	USB	Y	16	5/5	56x24x34	180
CVP509	NW		Y	Y		Y	Y	USB	Y	16	5/5	56x24x34	185
CVP509	NW		Y	Y		Y	Y	USB	Y	16	5/5	56x24x34	185
CLP265GP	GH3									2	5/5	57x45x37	214
CLP295GP	NW		Y	Y				USB	Y	16	5/5	57x45x37	238
CLP465GP	GH3							USB	Y	2	5/5	56x45x37	216
H01	NW		Y					USB			5/5	58x30x30	181
H11	NW		Y		Y			USB			5/5	58x30x30	216
N3	Grand	Y	Y	Y				USB		1	5/5	58x47x40	439
CGP1000	NW		Y	Y		Y	Y	USB	Y	16	5/5	58x60x39	412

ADVERTISER INDEX

PHOTO CREDITS

Cover: Grand, Bösendorfer Klimt; Vertical, Sauter Vitrea 2; Slab, Kawai MP10

Page 4: header, www.art-design.si; Grand, Knabe WKG58M

Page 5: header, www.baileyworld.com; Slab, Yamaha P155S

Page 7: Mark Duffy

Page 13: Samick Music Corp.

Page 16: Douglas Gilbert

Page 18: Douglas Gilbert

Page 35: www.nasa.gov

Page 53: header, Young Chang; Cristofori, Metropolitan Museum of Art; Sq. Grand, www.liveauctioneers.com

Pages 69–81: Martha Taylor

Page 83: Faust Harrison Pianos

Page 89: © Galina Stepanova

Page 97: Yamaha

Page 105: header, © Tatiana Popova; Tuning, © Brent Bossom; Regulating, © Brent Bossom

Page 106: Samick Music Corp.

Page 110: © Ryan Lane

Page 115: Yamaha

Page 121: Roland

Page 128: Yamaha

Page 138: © Carl Keyes

Page 141: Yamaha

Page 146: PianoDisc

Page 147: © Martina Nehls-Sahabandu

Place your ad in the next issue of **PIANO BUYER**

The Consumer Reference to Buying a Piano